It Came from Horrorwood

OTHER INTERVIEW BOOKS BY TOM WEAVER
AND FROM MCFARLAND

*Science Fiction Stars and Fantasy Film Flashbacks:
Conversations with 24 Actors, Writers, Producers
and Directors from the Golden Age* (2004)

*Double Feature Creature Attack: A Monster Merger of
Two More Volumes of Classic Interviews* (2003)
(A combined edition of the two earlier Weaver titles
Attack of the Monster Movie Makers and
They Fought in the Creature Features)

*Eye on Science Fiction: 20 Interviews with Classic
SF and Horror Filmmakers* (2003)

*Science Fiction Confidential: Interviews with
23 Monster Stars and Filmmakers* (2002)

*I Was a Monster Movie Maker: Conversations
with 22 SF and Horror Filmmakers* (2001)

*Return of the B Science Fiction and Horror Heroes:
The Mutant Melding of Two Volumes
of Classic Interviews* (2000)
(A combined edition of the two earlier Weaver titles
Interviews with B Science Fiction and Horror Movie Makers
and *Science Fiction Stars and Horror Heroes*)

OTHER MCFARLAND BOOKS BY TOM WEAVER

*Poverty Row HORRORS! Monogram, PRC and
Republic Horror Films of the Forties* (1993)

John Carradine: The Films (1999)

BY TOM WEAVER WITH MICHAEL BRUNAS AND JOHN BRUNAS

*Universal Horrors: The Studio's Classic
Films, 1931–1946* (McFarland, 1990)

It Came from Horrorwood

Interviews with Moviemakers in the SF and Horror Tradition

by Tom Weaver

PREVIOUSLY PUBLISHED UNDER THE TITLE
It Came from Weaver Five

McFarland & Company, Inc., Publishers
Jefferson, North Carolina, and London

The present work is a reprint of the library bound edition previously published as It Came from Weaver Five: Interviews with 20 Zany, Glib and Earnest Moviemakers in the SF and Horror Traditions of the Thirties, Forties, Fifties and Sixties, first published in 1996 by McFarland.

NEW LIBRARY OF CONGRESS CATALOGUING-IN-PUBLICATION DATA ARE AVAILABLE

FOLLOWING DATA SUPPLIED BY PUBLISHER

Weaver, Tom
    [It came from Weaver five]
    It came from Horrorwood : interviews with moviemakers in the SF and horror tradition / by Tom Weaver.
    p.   cm.
    Work originally published: It came from Weaver five. Jefferson, N.C.: McFarland, ©1996
    Includes index.

    ISBN 0-7864-2069-3 (softcover binding: 50# alk. paper) ∞

    1. Science fiction films — History and criticism. 2. Horror films — History and criticism. 3. Motion picture actors and actresses — United States — Interviews. 4. Motion picture producers and directors — United States — Interviews. I. Weaver, Tom, 1958- It came from Weaver five. II. Title.
PN1995.9.S26W45   2004
791.43'615 — dc20   96-18033

British Library cataloguing data are available

©1996 Tom Weaver. All rights reserved

No part of this book may be reproduced or transmitted in any form or by any means, electronic or mechanical, including photocopying or recording, or by any information storage and retrieval system, without permission in writing from the publisher.

On the cover: Cast of *The Black Sleep* (1956); *cover design by Kerry Gammill (www.monsterkid.com)*

Manufactured in the United States of America

McFarland & Company, Inc., Publishers
  Box 611, Jefferson, North Carolina 28640
  www.mcfarlandpub.com

To all the magazine editors who initially publish
my interviews — the great guys who make
all this possible — among them:
Buddy Barnett, Ted Bohus, Jim Clatterbaugh,
Dave Everitt, Joe Kane, Bob King, Tim Lucas,
Dave McDonnell, and Tony Timpone.

Acknowledgments

Abridged versions of the interviews featured in this book originally appeared in the following magazines:

Charlotte Austin: "Gorillas in Her Midst." *Fangoria* #137, October, 1994.

Les Baxter: "Classic Com-Poe-ser." *Fangoria* #146, September, 1995.

Frank Coghlan, Jr.: "The Power of Billy Batson." *Comics Scene* #41, April, 1994.

John Clifford: "Souls Survivor." *The Phantom of the Movies' Videoscope* #16, Fall, 1995.

Mara Corday: "Mara Corday." *Movie Club* #5, Winter, 1995.

Kathleen Crowley: "Target Earthwoman." *Starlog* #201, April, 1994.

Michael Fox: "Man of the Lost Planet." *Starlog* #198, January, 1994.

Dolores Fuller: "Fuller Brushes with Fame." *Fangoria* #138, November, 1994, and "I Was a Woman for Ed Wood Jr.!", *The Phantom of the Movies' Videoscope* #17, Winter, 1996.

Anne Gwynne: "Universal Appeal." *Fangoria* #115, August, 1992.

Linda Harrison: "Woman of the Apes." *Starlog* #213, April, 1995.

Tom Hennesy: "The Other Creature." *Starlog* #206, September, 1994.

Michael Pate: "The Vampire Down Under." *Fangoria* #113, June, 1992.

Gil Perkins: "Kong Conversations." *Starlog* #194, September, 1993, and "Legend of the Falls." *Starlog Science-Fiction Explorer* #9, October, 1995.

Walter Reed: "Serial Hero." *Comics Scene* #51, July, 1995.

Joseph F. Robertson: "Good at Being Bad." *Fangoria* #136, September, 1994.

Aubrey Schenck: "Classic Creatures Revisited." *Fangoria* #147, October, 1995.

Sam Sherman: "The Mogul, the Man, the Fan ... Sam Sherman." *Filmfax* #27, June/July, 1991, and *Filmfax* #28, August/September, 1991.

Gloria Stuart: "Dark Houses and Invisible Men." *Bloody Best of Fangoria* #13, 1994.
Gregory Walcott: "The Reluctant Star of *Plan 9*." *Fangoria* #135, August, 1994.
Robert Wise: "Years After Stillness." *Starlog* #211, February, 1995.
A Salute to Ed Wood: "Man with the Plan (9)." *Starlog* #208, November, 1994.

Table of Contents

Acknowledgments   vii
Introduction   1
Charlotte Austin   5
Les Baxter   25
John Clifford   39
Frank Coghlan, Jr.   49
Mara Corday   65
Kathleen Crowley   87
Michael Fox   101
Dolores Fuller   123
Anne Gwynne   147
Linda Harrison   161
Tom Hennesy   175
Michael Pate   187
Gil Perkins   209
Walter Reed   235
Joseph F. Robertson   255
Aubrey Schenck   269
Sam Sherman   287
Gloria Stuart   313
Gregory Walcott   327
Robert Wise   341
A Salute to Edward D. Wood, Jr.   353
Index   369

Introduction

"A specialist is one who knows everything about something and nothing about anything else."
— Ambrose Bierce, American Writer

"Ambrose *who*??"
— Tom Weaver,
Science Fiction Movie Specialist

* * * *

    Everyone has in their mind an image of what it's like to interview a veteran of the motion picture industry. These lively chats are conducted in the moviemaker's den, surrounded by photos and books and other souvenirs of Hollywood's "Golden Age." Or in their garden, amidst the soothing twitter of birds. Or in a studio editing room, among the tools of the trade. The interviewees are garrulous and funny, and never at a loss to answer a question, no matter how arcane. That's the way you always see them conducted on television, so that's the way it *is*—right?
    Once in a while, I'm happy to say, yes. But the "game" of conducting these interviews has no hard and fast rules, particularly when the movies are on the level of *Cat-Women of the Moon*, *The Ghost in the Invisible Bikini* and *Creature from the Black Lagoon*—and when the only households in which many of these "celebrities" are household words are their *own*. Their present circumstances, their attitude about their movies, their opinion of you-the-interviewer — all of these are variables which make each encounter an adventure.
    For the last 15 years, I've made a hobby out of researching and writing about the behind-the-scenes activity which resulted in the science fiction and horror movies (1930s, 1940s, 1950s, 1960s) which I grew up with in the 1960s and 1970s. Prior to the start of my writing "career," I had to be content with the interviews and information found in the pages of *Castle of Frankenstein*,

Fangoria, Famous Monsters and similar magazines, along with the occasional book. Finally in 1981 I decided that once — just *once* — I'd like to take a stab at an interview myself. A friend who was writing a book on the Three Stooges told me that his experience of interviewing Edward Bernds, director of some of the Stooges' two-reelers and features, had been an exceptional one. To my friend's mind, Bernds' name conjured up memories of Stooge shorts (*Dopey Dicks, Punchy Cowpunchers,* etc.), but it was visions of his *Queen of Outer Space* and *Space Master X-7* which danced in *my* head. Bernds gladly talked to me about all five of his SF movies — pulling out scripts and production breakdowns, unearthing rare stills, supplying juicy gossip and quoting from the detailed *diaries* in which he had kept a day-by-day record of his adventures in picture-making! I was hooked.

That was about 180 interviews ago, but almost no one else has been as well-equipped, knowledgeable *and* affable as Ed. This is not meant to imply that the others were ever less than cordial and cooperative. But, often, I found myself talking with someone who couldn't remember which flick was which, and mixed up all the stories for me to unravel. Or someone who didn't remember a particular movie *at all.* (I've interviewed the director and three of the stars of *The Colossus of New York,* none of whom had the tiniest recollection of *anything* that went on.) It's always uncomfortable talking to someone who thinks that a worse-than-awful movie of theirs is a work of art. And it's sad when a movie commonly thought of as a gem is remembered with dejection or embarrassment by the people who made it.

It's reaching the point where I could conceivably be interviewed about my interviews;* there are lots of great memories and special moments. Composer Albert Glasser, warm, wacky and enthusiastic, excitedly talking with his hands, and accidentally knocking my tape recorder across the room — three times! John Ashley (then the producer of television's *The A-Team*) ignoring repeated requests to attend a meeting of network executives that couldn't start without him, because he was enjoying speaking to *me*(!). Director Richard Cunha sending me a video cassette of himself talking about his movies (and, as a surprise, recruiting their producer Arthur A. Jacobs to join him). Gene Fowler, Jr., an 80-ish film editor-turned-director, leaping onto the floor and wrestling with his German shepherd when I asked to take his picture ("How's *this* for a picture?!"). Great friendships with John Agar, Robert Clarke, Reginald LeBorg, Yvette Vickers, Susan Cabot, Susan Hart, William Alland and others.

Even the "flip" side has never been all that bad; the hardest part sometimes is just keeping a straight face. Jerry Warren told me all about a

---

* To tell the truth, I don't think I'd *like* being interviewed. I don't think I'd like it a *bit*!

movie in which he acted in 1944 — then, realizing just how long ago that was, tried to convince me that *it wasn't him*. In the stuffy den of one of my duller interviewees, the conversation stopped and we *both* looked over at a friend I had brought along — peacefully "sawing wood." Actor Richard Anderson sat under a heavy hanging plant, and hit his head every time he got up (and when he went to sit back down!). There's not enough room here to describe the time my brother and I nearly cost Sam Arkoff his life. Silly stories, I've got a million of 'em.

These are just some of the "perils of the trade." The easiest place to hit a snag is the initial phone call, where the occasional reprobate tells you you're a jerk for being interested in these movies, and hangs up on you. *Much* worse are the folks who agree to an interview — inspire you to prepare with several days of research — and then on the *second* call, call you a jerk, and hang up on you.

Enough with the negatives; here, at the risk of sounding immodest, are some of the plusses. What you get out of work like this is the thrill of rewatching these "pet" science fiction movies (and others) with the knowledge that some of the black-and-white figures flickering through them are now your three-dimensional, full-color, real-life acquaintances, and in some cases *friends*. And by bringing their colorful stories out into the open, you get the feeling that you've made this hobby of ours a little more entertaining not just for yourself, but also for some others. And it all began, in *my* case, because of the Three Stooges.

The last things I write for each of these books are obituaries for the folks who have died since the publication of the *last* volume. We've lost six this time around: John Howard, Robert Hutton, Charles Bennett, Cameron Mitchell, Virgil Vogel and Les Baxter.

Mitchell's death I was prepared for: The supermarket tabloid *The National Enquirer* (which I don't read, of course) featured a grim-sounding article on the 75-year-old actor's hospitalization ("*High Chaparral* star Cameron Mitchell battling cancer"), and then a second article ("Cameron Mitchell calls in psychic healer in his battle with deadly cancer") which ended up running a few days *after* Mitchell died (on June 29, 1994) in his Pacific Palisades home. Mitchell acted in some fine films in the late 1940s and early '50s before his career hit the skids and he ended up in trash like *The Toolbox Murders* and *Frankenstein Island*, but I couldn't wring a self-pitying comment out of him; "The way things have turned out," he told me, "I did get a chance to experiment, and as an actor, a pure actor, I could do and try many things which you couldn't do in a major film. I have been lucky in many ways." (See *Attack of the Monster Movie Makers*.)

I want to go the way John Howard did: The octogenarian actor was in his Santa Rosa, California, home, casually talking with his wife Eva, when he died, instantly and quietly, right in mid-conversation; Mrs. Howard didn't even know he *had* died until she realized he had stopped responding to her. (Eva Howard: "I never knew death could be so kind.") It was a February 19, 1995, heart attack that painlessly "switched off" the life of 82-year-old Howard, who acted in support in classics like *Lost Horizon* and *The Philadelphia Story* in the days before B-movie and television stardom. Friendly and self-effacing and highly articulate, he was the sort of actor that it was a joy to interview (twice—the first time over the phone, the second time in person at his L.A. home, with the Brothers Brunas contributing). A World War II hero (he was awarded the Navy Cross and the Croix de Guerre for Valor), he changed the subject whenever you tried to ask him about it. Put John Howard down as one of my favorite people. (See *Science Fiction Stars and Horror Heroes*. The Howard filmography which follows the interview is missing the following shorts: *Hedda Hopper's Hollywood* [Paramount, 1942], *Hollywood War Efforts* [RKO, 1942], *Screen Snapshots, No. 1. Series 23* [*Hollywood in Uniform*] [Columbia, 1943], *Hollywood Mothers* [Columbia, 1955] and *Hollywood Plays Golf* [Columbia, 1955].)

Talking with someone like Charles Bennett was one of my stranger experiences as an interviewer. Not that *he* was strange; in fact, he couldn't have been nicer. It was just the fact that I'm not used to speaking with someone born in the last century, or getting firsthand anecdotes about people like Arthur Conan Doyle. Bennett, 95 when he died on June 15, 1995, wrote plays in his native England in the mid–1920s before he veered off into screenwriting, penning movies like *The 39 Steps* and *The Man Who Knew Too Much* for director Alfred Hitchcock, *The Lost World* and *Voyage to the Bottom of the Sea* for Irwin Allen and *Curse of the Demon* for himself. (Jacques Tourneur, not Bennett, ended up directing *Demon*; see *Attack of the Monster Movie Makers* for the details.) "If I couldn't write, I wouldn't want to live," Bennett told me; and he had projects (including a remake of his old Hitchcock film *Blackmail*) going right up to the time of his death.

Robert Hutton was in his Kingston, New York, home one snowy night, watching the end of one of his own movies (*Destination Tokyo*) on television, when he stood up, felt dizzy, blacked out and hit the floor. Hours later, he was discovered by a friend and rushed by ambulance to Kingston Hospital, where doctors determined that he had sustained a badly broken back and internal injuries. Hutton subsequently spent the last years of his life in hospitals and in a nursing-care facility in Kingston, but with the help of friends (and the Bible) he refused to dwell on his pain and his problems; instead he organized movie nights at the nursing home, convinced other residents to sponsor an orphan and wrote a book (as yet unpublished) about his Hollywood experiences. "You know, the Lord has blessed me," Hutton told Andrew "Ace" Collins in *Plus* magazine. "I lived a fantasy in Hollywood. I met and worked with so many people now considered legends. And then, just when I wondered why I was even alive, I broke my back, and the Lord opened up a whole new world of opportunity for me." The star of *The Man Without a Body* was 73 when he died on August 7, 1994. (See *Science Fiction Stars and Horror Heroes*.)

Some people mentioned to me that they thought my interview with Virgil W. Vogel (in *Science Fiction Stars and Horror Heroes*) ended somewhat abruptly. They were right: Vogel told me as we began our telephone tête-à-tête that he was relaxing with a few drinks, and about an hour later, somewhere between *The Land Unknown* and *Invasion of the Animal People* in our conversation, that fact started to become painfully obvious. But, tipsy or not, he told great stories about the making of those movies (and *The Mole People*), and he invited me to visit and watch him work the next time he was in Boston directing an episode of television's *Spenser: For Hire* (which was cancelled before I could take him up on his offer). The editor of such well-remembered movies as *A Double Life* (1947), *This Island Earth* (1955) and *Touch of Evil* (1958) directed the forementioned science fiction flicks, TV movies a-plenty and also episodes of TV's *Wagon Train, Bonanza, M Squad, The Six Million Dollar Man, Mission: Impossible, Quantum Leap* ad infinitum. Even though his science fiction movies have bum raps, I've got soft spots in my head for all three of 'em. Vogel was 76 when he died January 7, 1996, of cancer.

When composer Les Baxter used to visit the home of American International honcho James H. Nicholson, Nicholson's actress-wife Susan Hart found him to be quiet, serious, almost professorial, but always with a smile and just a *hint* of a playful personality beneath. That sly, "fun" side of Les Baxter was much more in evidence when Mike Brunas and I met him for lunch and interviewed him for *Fangoria* years later; he displayed a touch of bitterness over the fact that there was little or no work for him in the "new Hollywood," but otherwise he was impish and chatty and (like many composers—and most writers!) very much in love with his own work. Unfortunately, he moved before our *Fangoria* interview appeared and I wasn't able to find him again, so he presumably never saw the article and he certainly never saw this book (see pages 25–37). The 1950s pioneer of orchestral lounge music died January 15, 1996, of a massive heart attack due to kidney failure, and every obit I subsequently read was filled with career tidbits that were new to me, including the fact that his credits included the whistling theme for *Lassie*(!). AIP's "house composer" was 73.

All the "usual suspects" helped in all the usual ways to make this book possible. Special thanks go to Dave McDonnell and the rest of the gang at *Starlog,* Tony Timpone and Mike Gingold of *Fangoria,* research consultants Mike and John Brunas and filmography co-compilers John Cocchi and Jack Dukesbery. Mike Fitzgerald co-compiled the questions for the Anne Gwynne interview, then conducted and transcribed it; that one is much more his than mine. Drew Friedman gave me permission to run some of his Ed Wood trading cards in my chapter on Wood; many thanks to Drew and to Kitchen Sink Press, his publisher. Mark Martucci came through with videotapes, John Antosiewicz, Buddy Barnett and Eric Caidin came through with stills and the rest of these people came though in general: Dan Scapperotti, Paul Parla, Fred Olen Ray, Joe and Jeff Indusi, Herman Cohen, Phil Chamberlin, Alex Lugones, Glenn Damato, Ruth Brunas, Rich Scrivani, Jon and Julie Weaver, Erin Ray Fresco, Bandit and Tigger, Howard W. Koch, Mark Carducci, Joe Kane, all the nice people at McFarland (———, ———, ———, ———, et al.) who invariably delete themselves from my thank-you lists, Lucy Chase Williams, Joe Dante, William K. Everson, John Foster, Ray Nielsen, Maurice Terenzio, Michael Weldon, Greg Luce, Tom Johnson, Merry Anders, Steve Swires and Herk Harvey.

Tom Weaver
North Tarrytown, New York

These [horror movies] were shot in twelve days, fourteen days, and there was no time to even think. We'd work till maybe midnight and have to be back at six o'clock the next morning. I'll never forget one director who told us, "Go home and sleep fast!"

———— *Charlotte Austin* ————

WHAT CHARLOTTE AUSTIN WANTED TO DO for several of the years that she worked in the movie industry was to get *out* of the movie industry. Another thing she wanted to do on film was sing, which no one permitted. Among the things she *didn't* want to do were to be dunked into a cold bathtub by *The Man Who Turned to Stone*, risk falling down a castle staircase in *Frankenstein 1970*, or be the love object of an amorous ape in *The Bride and the Beast*.

Named for her birthplace (Charlotte, North Carolina), she was the daughter of Gene Austin, a top crooner of the twenties and thirties and the composer of numerous popular songs. Dramatic training and a screen test led to a contract at 20th Century–Fox in the early fifties, when she had parts in the studio's *How to Marry a Millionaire*, *Desirée* and *Daddy Long Legs*, and costarred (on loanout to Columbia) in the musical *Rainbow 'Round My Shoulder*. Freelancing after the mid–1950s, she moved from musicals to monsters, perhaps most notoriously tackling half of the title role in the Ed Wood–scripted *Bride and the Beast*. Now a dealer in antiques, and with her "other life" (the movie years) comfortably far behind her, Charlotte Austin is free to reminisce about her horror movies with many laughs, few apologies, and no illusions about their quality.

How did you find yourself working in the movie business?

When I was nine, somebody shoved me into a *Herald Examiner* Better Babies contest. My father accompanied me on piano and he drowned me out, he played so loud [*laughs*]! I was singing this *awful* song called "Murder, He Says" and my father was *pounding* the piano, and I was trying to sing *over* that. Anyway, *somehow* I won the contest, and I was sent to Republic for a screen test. That didn't lead anywhere, but it was so typical, somebody was always *pushing* me into some kind of a contest or whatever. When I took piano lessons later, the partner of my piano teacher was [movie producer] Arthur Freed's brother, an agent, Clarence Freed. *He* decided he was going to be my agent! I kept saying, "I just want to finish school!" Later, I was a bridesmaid at the wedding of a girlfriend—my friend was marrying into [musical conductor] Alfred Newman's family. The groom's uncle was an agent, and he said, "I'm making an appointment *tomorrow*, I'm taking you to 20th Century–Fox." I remember being awake all night and saying to my mother, "I *don't* want to go, I *really* don't want to *do* this!" But I went, and they worked with me for maybe three or four weeks. I did a screen test—I had to sing, dance, play the piano, do *every*thing [*laughs*]! And then I was put under contract, and I was under contract for five years at Fox.

Previous page: Austin looks back in angora at the "vile wardrobe" she had to wear in the Ed Wood–scripted *The Bride and the Beast.*

Did you enjoy that experience?

That was a nice life. We worked hard, but it was lovely, and the people were just wonderful there. I finished my schooling in the little schoolroom at Fox; my teacher Frances Klamt had been Shirley Temple's tutor for years. In that classroom were Debra Paget, Merry Anders, Jean Moorhead, Gloria Gordon and a little guy named Billy Gray. Gloria and I used to take Billy shopping with us. We'd go to Saks every day, and this poor little kid was saying, "Do I have to go *with* you girls?" [*Laughs.*]

Was it tough, starting out that young on an acting career?

In some ways, yes. I was so young, and a very ... *sensitive* soul. It was difficult, because as an actress you're torn in so many directions. I always felt that everyone wanted a little piece of me, and I used to think, "Why would anyone want to act and *be* somebody other than who they are? *Be* all these different personalities, when it's hard enough to just be who *you* are!" As you grow older and mature, you become stronger, and it's much easier to do, but as a youngster, it was very demanding. We worked *very* hard. We worked then six days a week, Saturdays included, and we had a tutor always on the set and we had to have time for school. When we graduated from high school, the graduation ceremony was held while Merry Anders and I were doing a graduation scene in a *movie, The Farmer Takes a Wife* [1953], and we missed our own graduation! Our parents went to graduation but we were *working*— they sat there and we didn't show up [*laughs*]! But that's the way it was then. I also appeared in tests for the CinemaScope process: I acted in *many* scenes of *How to Marry a Millionaire* with Lauren Bacall, Betty Grable and David Wayne. I played the nearsighted girl, Loco, who was later played in the *real* movie by Marilyn Monroe. It was wonderful fun, and I *thought* I did good work. The scenes we did were designed as tests for the CinemaScope process, to show all the distributors, all over the world. (I did have a tiny part in the actual movie, as a model.) Also, I would test with all these wonderful people who were testing for things. I supported Anne Bancroft, David Wayne, Eli Wallach — really marvelous actors — in tests for certain roles that they did or didn't get. It was very interesting, a learning experience.

And, of course, dramatic lessons.

Marilyn Monroe had Natasha Lytess [as a coach], we had Helena Sorell. (We were all little girls with petticoats and waist-cinchers, and when Marilyn would walk around the studio, we'd all hiss and say, "Look at that girl! She's not even wearing a *bra*!" We were so upset with her, because she was

Gorilla at Large. George Barrows can't decide whether Anne Bancroft or Austin is the gorilla his dreams (SIC).

the total opposite of all of us.) Helena Sorell was very dramatic — I remember she had beaded eyelashes! And once I remember her saying to *me* [*in an affected, flamboyant voice*], "My *darling*, you have a voice like a tin can being dragged behind a car!" It *crushed* me, I thought I could never speak again! You know how low Merry Anders' voice is now? *That's* probably one of the reasons, because Sorell just drummed that into us! But what it did to *me* was just shut me up — I was afraid to speak! Then I worked with a drama coach named Joe Graham and we had wonderful classes. *Everybody,* all the kids in Hollywood, were in those classes. In those classes, the only thing I ever felt that I really did well was one scene which everybody in the world had done from *The Girl on the Via Flaminia.* I hit it right that one time, and I felt, "Gee, maybe I *am* good." But I always felt with everything, whether it was singing, acting, dancing — I did not want to do it unless I could do it *well.* So I felt that the horror movies were just ... *awful.* The dialogue! I watched *The Bride and the Beast* this morning because I needed to refresh my memory, I looked at myself and said, "Oh, you poor thing, having to say some of these lines!" I did the best I could do with what I had to work with, which was pretty awful.

When the dialogue was too awful on the B horror movies, would you suggest that it be changed?
   Occasionally, but I'll tell you something: These things were shot in twelve days, fourteen days, and there was no time to even *think*. We'd work till maybe midnight and have to be back at six o'clock the next morning. I'll never forget one director who told us, "Go home and sleep fast!" [*Laughs.*] So all you could do was learn words, you couldn't get into the character, because there was no time. It was a matter of learning words and spitting the words out and going on to the next scene, which was dreadful!

What recollections of Fox's 3-D Gorilla at Large?
   I felt at the time that some of the best actors in film were in that picture: Anne Bancroft, Lee J. Cobb, Cam Mitchell, Lee Marvin, Raymond Burr. I wondered at the time why we were all doing this [*laughs*]! The only thing I can remember is staying up for forty-eight hours — we all had to go on location to Long Beach, the pier, and that was kind of grueling. I remember poor Anne Bancroft being carried up and down the roller coaster by the gorilla, which was *very* hard on her, it really was. All of us were exhausted and bumping into each other coming and going — we'd sit down to eat and we couldn't remember whether to order breakfast, lunch or dinner [*laughs*]. We got all mixed up because we had been up so many hours. And I remember talking long hours to Raymond Burr, who was slim (*fairly* slim) then, and who talked about the shows he did in Korea, for the soldiers. He wanted me to go on tour with him. He was a very sweet, nice man; he struck me as a very vulnerable, sensitive man. Later I did a *Perry Mason* with him and he had changed a little bit. He was more powerful, he was in charge of the production; the vulnerable person had become very powerful. But he was still the nice person that he was.

Did you leave Fox, or did they drop you?
   I had been there five years and I didn't care whether they picked my contract up or not. So they *didn't* [*laughs*]. I wanted out.

Once you left Fox, who was "pushing" you to stick with acting then?
   No one, but that's all I was trained for at that point. Thank goodness

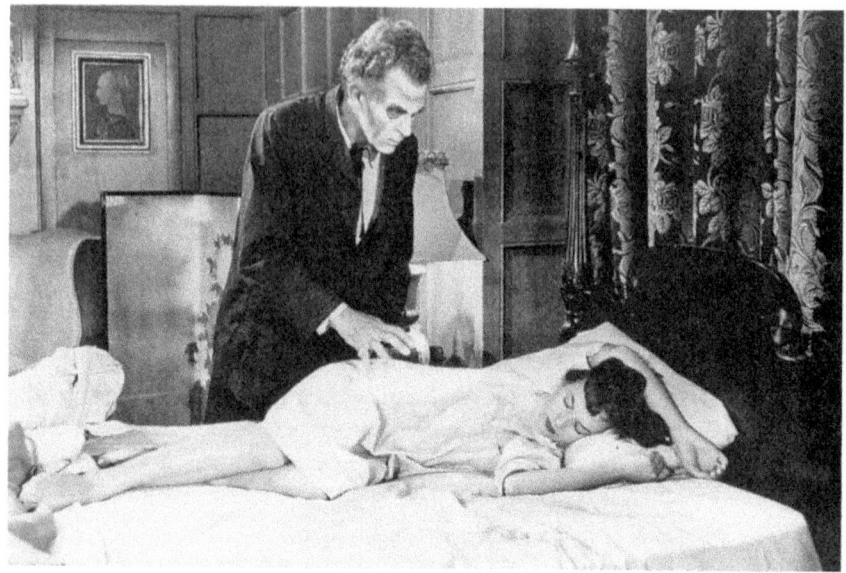

Why real-life nobleman/sportsman/big game hunter Friedrich Ledebur agreed to play *The Man Who Turned to Stone,* Austin doesn't know.

there were laws designed to protect minors. A certain percentage of one's salary had to be put aside and banked weekly; that started, I think, with Jackie Coogan. That was wonderful, because that's how I bought my house. I was twenty-one when I bought it and I'm still living in it. The little house I bought for nothing is worth a lot of money today.

Okay, fun's over. Time to talk about the horror movies.
    Oh, God!

Do you remember how you got into The Man Who Turned to Stone?
    No, but it was for Sam Katzman — whose name was kind of a joke [in Hollywood], so I knew it was going to be a really bad movie. But, again, there were some good people in that. Ann Doran was a wonderful actress. We were rehearsing something and she said, "Charlotte, I don't understand it. You can be *brilliant*, and then you can be just mediocre. What's the *matter* with you?!" [*Laughs.*] The reason was that it was very hard to say those words! I loved one line in particular: Some poor girl at the reformatory hangs herself and my character, the prison psychiatrist, says, "She didn't seem *that* depressed!" [*Laughs.*] Always, these [B movie] directors would tell you, "Play everything down. Be quiet. Be still." It was like you were never supposed to *show* or *feel* anything. *That* was very

hard for me, because I felt restricted, held in check. I felt that way most of the time.

The title monster was played by Friedrich Ledebur, who was a real-life count, sportsman and big game hunter.
    That's right. He was a very nice man and he had a grace about him. You could sense his background — he wasn't ordinary, he was a very well-bred man. He played the title role and he never had a word to say in it.

Why would somebody like that play the monster in a movie called The Man Who Turned to Stone?
    I don't know why. I think acting is a *disease* and that once people catch it, they just won't let go. And they can't take a pill to get rid of it.

Did you think the makeup was effective?
    I thought the makeup was *horrendous*. When I was watching the movie and he began to change, I fell on the floor laughing — I cannot believe how awful that was. And another thing that struck me about that movie was the lighting. When it was nighttime, we were *squinting*, we couldn't see, because they had bright reflectors in our eyes. And when it was daytime, it was pitch black! Everything was opposite! I'll never forget the scene where poor William Hudson was sitting outside at "night," using a flashlight to try to read a book, and yet you could see that it was bright sunlight [*laughs*]! Today if a movie like that were done, a mood would be created. What *we* did was sit in a stark white room, discussing how we were going to kill somebody — it was laughable!

Any anecdote about the big fire scene at the end of the movie?
    No, but I do remember that we all went out to dinner that night to a restaurant called the Smoke House, which was right around the corner from the studio — Jean Willes, Bill Hudson, myself, a *bunch* of us. We all had a margarita or a martini or something, and we were all late getting back to do the fire scene. And the director [Leslie Kardos] was mad at us — he was in a *fury*. But we had worked hours and hours and deserved a break.

Next came The Bride and the Beast *for producers Louis and Adrian Weiss.*
    When we made that, it was called *Queen of the Gorillas*. Being in that kind of brought me back to the days when I was a kid and I used to *love* to go down to the Los Angeles River and pretend I was Sheena, Queen of the Jungle [*laughs*]! I'd go through all the vines and leaves and crawdads and turtles, and I would fantasize that I was going to save everybody's life! *Bride*

and the Beast was "wonderful," it was every stock shot that was ever shot in Hollywood, spliced together. I don't remember how I got involved, but I *do* remember that when I read the script, I got physically sick to my stomach. I thought, "Oh, my God, *who* wrote this thing?" The dialogue was terrible, the whole premise, the whole idea — awful! And the Weiss family — what a family! *Ohhhhh!* [Producer-director] Adrian Weiss had an office on Fairfax and I met them there. They were going to use jungle stock shots and write a movie *around* them somehow.

Anyway, I agreed to do it; I said to myself, "If I want to make my house payments (and my house *was* very important to me!), I'll *try* this thing." Adrian Weiss said, "Now, we're going to design a wardrobe for you, and you get to keep the wardrobe at the end of the film. And everything you wear must have a little bit of fur on it, you know." They designed this god-awful navy blue and yellow striped angora sweater — I had never seen anything before and I have never seen anything since that looked like that! I'd have to go on fittings and I would just think, "Oh, God, *please* help me!" Thank goodness the movie wasn't in color! I also had a marabou bed jacket and I couldn't talk because the feathers kept going up my nose. Every single thing had a piece of fur on it. The angora, it's in your mouth, your nose, your eyes, everything, because it sheds like crazy.

Did you get to keep the sweater?

Oh, yes. All this vile wardrobe — I mean, it was the *worst*. The only thing I didn't get to keep was, I wore Grace Kelly's clothes from *Mogambo* [1953] and *those* had to go back to MGM. When I looked at the movie this morning, I thought, "Why was I so dressed up?" — I was walking through the jungle with this beautiful hat, with chiffon draping down the back. I think I gave that angora sweater to a friend, and eventually the Goodwill got it. I couldn't look at this thing, I didn't want it in my closet, it was so hideous. I looked like a giant bumblebee!

Then they used a bunch of stock shots from a Sabu movie [*Man-Eater of Kumaon*, 1948]. I was supposedly being chased by a tiger through the jungle — they had stock shots for that, shots of a tiger chasing a woman. So they had to match my clothes to that stock shot. I wore a navy blue jacket, like a soldier's jacket — like a French foreign legion jacket, with gold buttons [*laughs*]! I had that on, and some sort of paisley silk scarf wrapped around my head. I thought, "What an incongruous outfit!" but I had to match the stock shots! I got to the edge of a cliff and, oh my God, they poked this stuffed tiger head on a stick at me, and that's when I had to fall over the cliff. Most of the time in that movie was spent biting our lips to keep from laughing. It was so unbelievable, I can't even tell you.

Did you meet the writer, Ed Wood?
   I don't remember meeting him at all.

What do you think of the fact that a guy who could write a movie like Bride and the Beast *has a devoted following today?*
   The human mind is a strange thing. Very, *very* strange.

What else can you recall about the Weisses?
   Oh, *please*! I'm going to make a movie about this someday, a movie about the making of *The Bride and the Beast*. Louis [the production supervisor] was the father and Adrian was the son; another one [Adolph] was the wardrobe man and another one [Samuel] edited. The whole family was involved! And I had never met a family like this in my life, I can tell you that — it was really a hoot. One scene we shot was a bedroom scene and Lance Fuller was so deathly sick (he had the flu) and couldn't talk. So Adrian Weiss said, "That's all right, just mouth the words, we'll dub it in later!" Unbelievable! So Lance was moving his mouth and making no sound and I was responding to this! That picture was the *pièce de résistance*, I think. It was a *classic*, it was so *awful*. The whole premise was so awful.

Half the reviewers found it funny and atrocious and the other half found it scandalous *and atrocious.*
   They did a "European version" of one scene — which caught me by surprise. We shot the scene [of the gorilla acting lovestruck] and then Adrian Weiss said, "Now we're gonna do the European." I said, "What does that mean?" He said, "Well, it has to look like you don't have *any*thing on." I thought, "*What* is going *on* here??" I had to improvise and tie a bandanna around the front of me and stand with my back to the camera so it looked like I had *nothing* on. I was so humiliated, I thought, "This is disgusting, it really is."

The Catholic Church rated the movie "objectionable," because of its theme and also your "suggestive costuming."
   What they didn't like was the fact that the movie advanced the theory of reincarnation. As for the costuming, there was nothing suggestive, I had nightgowns with big puffed sleeves — oh, how silly! And Lance Fuller and I spent our wedding night [in the movie] in twin beds! We've come a long way in movies [*laughs*]. In another scene, Lance and I are supposed to be riding across the great veldt of Africa, bouncing along in a truck. We're on a sound stage in this stationary truck and I happened to glance out the window and here is this huge, six foot tall barrel with twigs and leaves and

branches nailed to it and the thing is spinning around and around, to make it look like the truck is moving. I glanced down and I saw two little feet at the bottom of this barrel, *running running running running* like crazy. There was one of Adrian Weiss' relatives inside this barrel, on a treadmill, running like a gerbil on a treadmill to turn this silly thing around! That's how cheap this movie was! Well, I burst out laughing, I got totally hysterical, *Lance* got hysterical, we couldn't shoot this scene at all. That was *it*, like for an hour — it was terrible. We'd just look at each other and crack up.

What was Lance Fuller like?

He was a darling, sweet guy from the South — I just loved him. He had a funny sense of humor and he was very naive, kind of, and vulnerable. We went out a couple of times, as friends.

And your leading man, the Beast?

Oh, he [Steve Calvert] was a nice guy. *Gorilla at Large* had a [gorilla actor] named George Barrows and he was a lovely man, too. They were both big, very gentle people; on *Gorilla at Large* I remember George dancing one day with Anne Bancroft and me. We did a little minuet, the three of us [*laughs*]! They were both very considerate people and I felt sorry for them, sweating it out in these gorilla costumes.

Which costume was better?

I thought George Barrows' was much better, much more realistic. Let's face it, neither one of them really looked like a gorilla, but George Barrows' face was wonderful. This'll sound strange, but I was in the St. Louis Zoo once when I was about sixteen, with my dad, and I remember standing a long, long time, absolutely mesmerized by one big huge gorilla that walked up to the bars and looked *right through* my soul. I have never had any human or animal look through me like that, it was unbelievable. I never forgot that; I thought, "This animal knows everything, everything there *is* to know."

Did you bring that little bit of "life experience" to your role when your Beast was being tender?

Consciously, no, but that experience was in my subconscious and it probably did come through. By the way, I was just heartbroken that that [zoo] gorilla was where he was; I don't believe in zoos anyway. The thought of this massive strength stuck behind bars — it hurt so much, it was terrible.

Newlywed Lance Fuller can't help wondering why his *Bride* (Austin) is more interested in the *Beast* (Steve Calvert) than she is in him.

Where was Bride and the Beast *shot?*

We were at Bronson Canyon at the end, when I ended up "marrying" a gorilla or whatever I did. It was freezing, freezing cold and I was wearing only a nightgown. I had a trailer with no lights, no electricity, and finally they got electricity hooked up just in my trailer. It was unbelievable, trying to get dressed and made-up under those conditions, freezing to death. This was at night and it was icy cold — January! The rest was shot at some little sound stage, I can't tell you which one. We shot for what felt like thousands of hours — this film, I think, was shot in twelve or fourteen days. We were shooting one night until all hours — this was probably the night that we were falling on the floor laughing. Finally, about eleven o'clock, someone yelled, "*Din-ner*! It's time for *din-ner*!" — we hadn't eaten for hours [*laughs*]. Louis Weiss stood with a clipboard next to a table and everyone had to stand in line, and as your turn came up, he would say, "Pastrami or corned beef?" And when you answered, he'd check you off—"Okay. One only!" [*Laughs.*] Oh, it was unbelievable! At Fox, things were so lovely, and I was so spoiled, coming out of there.

After the movie was finished, it didn't come out for a year and a half. Are you surprised by that?

I'm not surprised at all — who in the world would *want* to release it? And I wonder how long it played? Probably eight days somewhere!

Did you see Bride and the Beast *when it was released?*

Oh, we had a "theater party"! A friend of mine, Svea Grunfeld, had appeared in a movie called *The Beast of Budapest* [1958] and Allied Artists paired that in a double-bill with *Bride and the Beast*. So we really had fun — she and I and all our friends from our respective acting classes went to see these two movies and we rolled on the floor laughing!

Was The Beast of Budapest *any good?*

[*Groans.*] No, but it was better than mine, I'll tell you that — at least it made more sense. It was about the Hungarian revolution.

What did you never get the chance to do in movies, that you would have like to?

I never got a chance to sing, the thing that I *really* did, and did well, and the thing that my father wanted me to do. He begged me for years, he wanted me to go on the road with him and sing with him. I did do a couple of recordings with him that were not released.

Don't you sing in Rainbow 'Round My Shoulder?

My *dear*, they dubbed my voice, they never gave me a chance. I kept saying, "But, please, I *sing*...!" and they said, "Never mind! Never mind! We'll just dub your voice!" One day Frankie Laine and I were doing a number and I was singing *with* the dub, and he whispered in my ear, "Hey, you're a helluva singer." And I wanted to die, because I really *did* sing. They dubbed my voice, and the same girl [Jo Ann Greer] that dubbed my voice also dubbed for Rita Hayworth. And then they played the Rita Hayworth film [*Affair in Trinidad*, 1952] and *Rainbow 'Round My Shoulder* on the same bill together — I can't believe that! Out of Rita Hayworth's mouth comes this voice, and then out of a nineteen-year-old girl in the next picture comes the same voice! Unbelievable! I'll also tell you about the role I most wanted to play: My great-great-great-grandmother, according to my father, was Sacajawea, who led the Lewis and Clark expedition, so when Paramount did a movie about Lewis and Clark [*The Far Horizons*, 1955], I was desperate to do this part. And do you know who played Sacajawea? [*Sighs.*] Donna Reed! I wanted to *shoot* myself! I kept saying, "But ... but ... but ... but..." and nobody listened to me!

After Bride and the Beast, *you did* Frankenstein 1970 *for director Howard W. Koch.*

Howard Koch was wonderful. We called him "The Velvet Whip" —

that was our nickname for him. In fact, at the end of the movie, I got a riding crop and I covered it with black velvet. It was lovely, and that was our gift to him [*laughs*]! He was a nice, nice man, a *dear* man.

Maybe he was too "velvet." He agreed with me that Boris Karloff wasn't very good in Frankenstein 1970, *but he said he was in awe of Karloff and afraid to criticize him.*

That's the way Howard Koch was. And Boris Karloff, by the way, was lovely, the "last of the gentlemen" that there were, really. Like Fred Astaire, *there* was another man who was wonderful and a gentleman and who had background and wit and intelligence. Boris Karloff did, too, he was just a lovely human being.

Did you get to talk much with him?

He was a very quiet, very private person. He really *didn't* talk much with anyone; I never saw him sitting down, having a conversation. He would do his work and then sit quietly, or go back to his dressing room. I think he was just doing a job and wanting to go home. A very quiet, gentle person that you didn't trespass upon; you didn't try to step within his boundaries. I felt *sorry* for him having to be in a movie like *Frankenstein 1970*—it was degrading. But that's a drive which I never had. Actors who love their craft and love acting will act no matter where it is, what time it is, how big the part, how small the part. *I* never felt that way. I felt, toward the end of all of this, that I was not a product or a piece of meat at a meat counter, I was a human being and I wanted to be respected as a human being and not as a product. And I felt actors too easily just gave themselves away and said, "Here I am, I'm the product, sell me." I could never understand that.

What did you think of Karloff's acting in Frankenstein 1970?

[*Sighs.*] Truthfully? It was theatrical, it was overdone. I hate to say that, because he was such a gracious man. But when you're given this kind of dialogue, what can you do with it? Nothing. When you are given words that are so nonsensical, it's very difficult to do anything with them. He did the best he could do, I think.

Frankenstein 1970 *was shot at Warner Bros., correct?*

Right. When I was about nine years old, my family moved into a house on California Street, and the back lot of Warner Bros. was right across the street—they had a victory garden and everything while I was growing up.

So it was interesting to be working in the studio that I grew up wandering around. We were doing a scene for *Frankenstein 1970* out on the Warners lot one night, by the little pond, and there, less than a block away, was my mother's house! There was an actor in the cast I liked very much, a darling little old man named Norbert Schiller who played Boris Karloff's servant. And I asked my mother, "Can he *please* spend the night at your house?" He was a lovely man, too, very delicate — and a *very* good actor, just marvelous. So we *both* spent the night at my mother's house so we could be a minute away from work in the morning, and my mother cooked breakfast for both of us!

That scene where the monster chases the girl into the pond was the best scene — the only *good scene!— in the movie.*

Oh, that poor girl [Jana Lund]! That was again freezing, it was the middle of winter. He chased her into the water; they'd drag her out, throw a blanket around her, give her brandy; send her back *in* again, drag her out, throw a blanket...! I thought, "This girl is going to die!"— her whole body was absolutely shaking, head to toe. They used to put actors into a lot of grueling situations. The same thing in *The Man Who Turned to Stone*: I sat in that *stupid* bathtub for twelve hours, I think. I was a prune, it was awful. And it was *cold* water — not warm water, cold water! And me with a gag in my mouth — I couldn't even *talk*!

Any memories of the fellow who played Frankenstein's monster?

The guy that was wrapped in bandages? I remember him being a young, good-looking Italian, and that poor man had to carry me up a steep flight of stairs, and he started to lose me. Wrapped up in bandages, he was "slick," there was nothing to hang onto — he couldn't grab or hold me. I was slipping, slipping, slipping, and thinking, "This is how I'm going to die! I'm going to roll all the way down the staircase and die!" [*laughs*] — because he could not get a grip on me. *That* was kind of scary, it really was. [The scene ended up being cut.]

Frankenstein 1970 has the weirdest cast — Karloff, cowboy actor "Red" Barry, some L.A. television personalities —

Oh, what a funny cast that was! Tom Duggan [the hero] *wasn't* an actor, he was a talk show host, a very *controversial* talk show host — kind of a rabble-rouser. He was an interesting guy. He was quite natural even though he had never done this before. In fact, the night of the "wrap," "Red" Barry and I and another friend of mine all had dinner and we crashed Duggan's television show [*laughs*] — we were booing and razzing him from

Charlotte Austin acted in so many cheap horror flicks, she could just scream.

the audience and everything! He looked to see who it was and it was us. He made us come up on stage and we did a very funny, off-the-wall interview. It was great fun.

It was a different sort of role for you in Frankenstein 1970, *as Barry's caustic, wisecracking ex-wife.*

The only thing I enjoyed, if I can say I enjoyed *any*thing, was one little scene I had where the monster knocks on my door. I was able to "let go," no restrictions. I didn't have to be so uptight and held-back. That was kind of fun. The rest of the movie was silly — wisecracking, silly stuff. And being ground up in the garbage disposal was not fun — Karloff dropping one eyeball at a time in, and those terrible sound effects [*laughs*]! Oh, my God, that was corny!

Can you remember how you landed that part?

I *don't* remember, really; my agent probably just had me interview for that. The details of those things, I can never remember. This was a whole new world for me, to have to *read*, to compete for something, because at Fox, you didn't do this. They just said, "This is what you're going to do," and you did it. But to go out on your own and have to actually compete and read for things, that was very different. I remember meeting Elia Kazan one afternoon; someone had told him to call me, he was casting *Cat on a Hot Tin Roof* [1958]. I had just come back from the dentist and my face was all swollen [*laughs*]. We talked and talked, and he said, "I don't understand. There are girls *begging* for this part on their knees. I just spent two days listening to Julie Adams, *pleading*. And you're not interested? You don't even want to *read* for it?" And I said, "No, I don't think I really want to act." And this was for the *lead*, the part Elizabeth Taylor eventually played. What a dumbbell I was! But that was toward the end, when I *really* did not want to be doing this anymore.

To tell you the truth, I don't think any of your three horror movies are really very good.
    [*Laughs.*] They're so *bad*, they're good.

What horror movies have you liked?
    Here's the sort of film I go for: *The Innocents* with Deborah Kerr. *That* to me is a horror film. *The Haunting*, that's another one — that was one of the most terrifying things I had ever seen. And one of my all-time favorites was *The Uninvited* — I l-o-v-e-d it when I was little, and still today. To me, it's one of the most interesting films I've seen. I loved *that* sort of movie, the supernatural — I'm a Scorpio and I'm absolutely fascinated with those things. But science fiction I cannot bear. And monster-type movies, they're ridiculous, too silly.

You dropped out of acting around 1960.
    I really didn't want to do it anymore, I wanted to find myself and "who I was" and put myself together, and not be so fragmented. Jumping from one interview to another, being interviewed by people that I would not socialize in public with...! The last interview I went on, I remember sitting out in the waiting room for hours and hours, and when I finally walked in, here was this fat little man with his feet up on the desk. I thought, "*That's* it! It's over! I don't need this!" I wouldn't even talk to this person on a social level, so why was I there?

Now you're running your own antique shop in Pasadena.
    Yes, and I'm very proud of my shop; it's considered one of the most beautiful antique stores in California. I've had people tell me it's the most beautiful one they've seen *anywhere*. I started out making Victorian pillows and giving them as gifts to friends, and my mother said, "This is ridiculous,

you should be selling them, not just giving them away." So she took them to a couple of interior decorators and they bought them instantly. Then a friend said, "Why don't you put together some of your things and rent a little space in Pasadena?" So we sort of pooled all our resources, my mother and I, and opened the shop; I transformed it into a very Victorian parlor. I was there two years, then I went from there with three partners to another location. Eventually my partners, one by one, dropped out, and now I own the shop solely. It's like a home — I have an upstairs and downstairs, like a living room, dining room and bedroom. I concentrate mainly on Victorian, European, French, *some* American furniture. Very fine furnishings, silver, glass and porcelain. And I had started out just making those pillows.

What closing comments about your acting days? Any desire to try it again?

There were times, when my daughter was growing up [in the seventies and eighties], when I thought, "You know, *now* I would like to do it, *now* I'm *ready* to do it." I was "older and wiser" and more mature, and had a much greater understanding of myself, and I thought it would be interesting and a cinch to do. If that sounds arrogant, I don't mean it that way. So, yes, I've thought about it, because I see people doing things now that I would love to do. But then I think about that first day of shooting and the nerves — you can't help it, you *do* get stage fright. But, I'll tell you something, I think I'd like to be on the *other* side, in the production end of it. I have always been good at getting the right people together and putting things together and getting people energized. *Will* it ever happen? No, probably not. At heart, I'd rather be in Italy, growing vegetables and collecting great art, listening to great music, doing great cooking, *with* a restaurant, in the mountains, with a grape arbor [*laughs*]—! There are so many things in life!

CHARLOTTE AUSTIN FILMOGRAPHY

Belles on Their Toes (20th Century–Fox, 1952)
Rainbow 'Round My Shoulder (Columbia, 1952)
Les Misérables (20th Century–Fox, 1952)
Monkey Business (20th Century–Fox, 1952)
The Farmer Takes a Wife (20th Century–Fox, 1953)
How to Marry a Millionaire (20th Century–Fox, 1953)
Gorilla at Large (20th Century–Fox, 1954)
Desirée (20th Century–Fox, 1954)
There's No Business Like Show Business (20th Century–Fox, 1954)
Daddy Long Legs (20th Century–Fox, 1955)
How to Be Very, Very Popular (20th Century–Fox, 1955)
Pawnee (Republic, 1957)
The Man Who Turned to Stone (Columbia, 1957)

The Bride and the Beast (Allied Artists, 1958)
Frankenstein 1970 (Allied Artists, 1958)

   Scenes of Austin in *The Bride and the Beast* are seen in *It Came from Hollywood* (Paramount, 1982).

*I can't believe that I did all this thirty years ago —
some of it fifty years ago. Does that make me eighty?*

Les Baxter

IT IS EASY TO sometimes forget how far a musical score can go in adding to the atmosphere of a horror movie. While writer Richard Matheson, photographer Floyd Crosby, set designer Dan Haller and others have been widely lauded for working in concert on the Corman/Poe series, too often neglected is the American International staff composer whose aural contributions pervaded the movies, affecting the mood from first frame to last. During a harmonious association with AIP, Texas-born Les Baxter composed and conducted some of the best Poe scores as well as a plethora of other AIP movies — in addition to his prior (1950s) work on such non–AIPs as *The Black Sleep*, *The Bride and the Beast*, *Macabre* and the electronic tones of *The Invisible Boy*. From pop music to Poe music, "The Master of Things Musically Unusual" offers a few notes on his AIP career and reveals the key to writing unorthodox horror scores.

After all that you've accomplished in your long career, your scores for the early AIP/Poe movies are some of the main things you'll be remembered for.

I did *so* many Poe films for AIP, and I didn't want to do "stock" horror scores. As a matter of fact, I *never* did "stock" scores. When I did a Western, I think I was the first to introduce South American rhythms to this country — I *know* that I was. Westerns usually had "galloping" music and so forth. *I* put a Brazilian rhythm section under a period horse chase — to do a Brazilian rhythm section under a period horse chase was a little bit unusual! It was very daring. But I *was* very daring. And I had carte blanche there at AIP, which was marvelous. I had a theory that the audiences would accept *any*thing, and perhaps *wanted* something different. (This was before all the aberrations that are going on now.) I also used electronic instruments first; I introduced the theremin, which was the first electronic instrument, in an album called *Music Out of the Moon*. Then I went on to other electronic instruments as they came out. *Now* when I do an interview for a twenty-two-year-old producer, and he asks, "Do you know synthesizers? Do you know electronic instruments?" I take in a twenty-year-old composer who looks like Fonzie and I say, "No, *he* does all of that." And they believe it [*laughs*]!

I felt very privileged, by the way, to do the Poe films, because they were not "C"-horror movies, they were classic pieces of literature. *The Raven*, *House of Usher*, *Pit and the Pendulum* and so on. So I'm very pleased to have those among my credits. I did so many of these films for James Nicholson, who was with American International. It's too bad he had an

Previous page: Les Baxter in a recent pose.

early demise, because he would have been doing the *Star Wars* and *Raiders of the Lost Ark* and so forth. It was really a shame.

It was Nicholson who gave you carte blanche?

He chose me to write the music and gave me *absolute* carte blanche. I don't like to make egotistical comments, so please edit this out or put this in the way I'm saying it, because I'm embarrassed to word it this way. I basically hope to be a modest person — whether I am or not. Nicholson would give me a few ideas of what he wanted, and I would listen to them and give him everything he wanted. But most people don't realize that a composer has infinitely more technique at his command than the few suggestions that are given, and he can embellish those greatly. It's no problem to give a producer what he wants; I'm sure that some of the temperamental composers fight that and say, "No, I don't wanna be told what to do," or, "I wanna do just what *I* wanna do." It's also a simple matter to give the producer what he wants *and much more*. In Nicholson's case, I did one horror film, as a matter of fact, in six to eight, which is kind of based on the voodoo rhythm, with just strings and percussion. This was in *Cry of the Banshee*—I *think*. (I can *sing* these better than I can talk them!) It was a very daring and different thing. I used piano, strings and percussion. Bartok did that on one of his concert pieces, and this was somewhat Bartokian, I guess. We got in the dubbing room and Nicholson was sitting behind me, and he tapped me on the shoulder and he said, "Les ... you *didn't* do what I wanted. It was *better*." So I was *very* happy. And that's why I knew I could take chances, and *did* have complete freedom in any direction.

The first Poe film, House of Usher, *featured one of your best scores.*

Well, what more could a composer ask for — an old castle, and Vincent Price with a strange disease where he hears things from the dungeon and is sensitive beyond belief to touch and sound. Which was an actual illness, I understand. (I mean, Vincent didn't *have* it — the *character* had it!) A castle and Price and the castle finally burning and sinking into the mud — again, what more could I ask for? It was a composer's dream.

As I said before, I developed a theory — and, understand, this was before people were doing daring things — that you could do almost anything. I would try more and more different, unusual things, and when I would go into a theater to see it, I would think, "Now, is the audience going to be shocked?" They were *not* shocked. Some of these audiences were un-shockable; they would just sit there and watch it and be pleased with it and accept anything you give 'em. Which is the key to why we have such terrible music in television now. Today there are composers — they're not even one-note composers, they're one-finger composers. He sets the synthesizer and he pushes one note and it plays for the whole scene [*laughs*]! I see in films now where they score a whole scene with a note holding. Like a mystery scene, and the score is *mmmmmmmmm*. For two minutes, two and a half minutes, without changing tempo, without changing anything. There's no knowledge of counterpoint, no knowledge of excitement or whatever. Their minds, I think, run in a one-note track. I think I'm getting cruel now.

Don't worry about it, we're cruel all the time.
 Well, it's true, one note goes a long way these days. One of my favorite scores that I did was *Master of the World*. I think *Master of the World* has some good melodies and some lovely orchestration in it. Again, I had carte blanche—here I had Jules Verne and Vincent Price and airships going around the world, so we managed a lot of interesting orchestration. Pre–John Williams work. I have been said to have influenced all of these guys in their work. Unfortunately, "influenced" is a *kind* word. There's an awful lot of copying that goes on that makes me a little bit unhappy. I hate to hear my stuff quoted directly on the screen.

Do you agree that House of Usher *was one of your best?*
 I think *Usher* was one of the most sensual scores. It was very sensitive for a horror film. In this particular one, horror had a great deal to do with senses—Vincent Price's sensitive skin, his relationship with his sister who was buried alive and scratching on her coffin. The music was very much on the sensual side—in *some* scenes, almost to the point of passionate, the string writing. Unfortunately, it's under dialogue and sound effects, but it still can be heard.

You got away with a lot in your scores when the Poe pictures started to occasionally veer toward comedy.
 I introduced humor to horror scores. After doing so many, after a while, you're looking for different things to do in horror films. It was in *The Raven* that I first started doing this. Vincent Price did a little quick-step around the telescope, so I put in a little tap-dance motif. Most composers would be frightened. One way in which I was lucky was that I had carte blanche and I knew that I would be allowed to experiment. I did practically anything that I felt like doing, without fear. I used a lot of humor in that score. They liked it so well that they did a picture after that called *The Comedy of Terrors*, just because of the [humor in the music]. I used a lot of old themes in *The Raven*; for example, Vincent Price levitates himself

Between *House of Usher*'s castle setting, its fiery climax and Vincent Price's performance, "What more could I ask for?" ponders Baxter.

and I played *The Daring Young Man on the Flying Trapeze* in a symphonic style, more or less. Then there was a little flash somewhere and I played *Shine, Little Glow Worm*. That kind of thing.

How much time did AIP give you to knock out one of these scores?
   On the average, about two weeks. The actual recording of each score was done in four to six hours. Some of my friends would take all day just to do a main title, but I would finish the entire score in half that time! Believe me, when I had to, I could work *very* fast. Plus the fact that I was working with small orchestras that could perform miracles.

Were you on the sets of the Poe pictures a lot?

Not a *lot*, but Vinnie Price and I became friends, and whenever he used to see me, he kissed me on my bald head [*laughs*]—as nearly *everyone* does! Vinnie is a remarkable actor, very skilled. I was hired to do a television special [*An Evening of Edgar Allan Poe*] with Price doing a solo [recital] of four Poe stories. After it was over, the director, Ken Johnson, said, "Vinnie, this was an extraordinary amount of memorization to do"—to memorize an hour of four Poe stories, with no help from any other actors. A solo performance. Johnson said, "I don't know how in the world you got through it." Vincent said, "I don't know either. Somehow, when you get rolling, it just pours out from sheer energy, and the words all seem to be there when they're needed." But it was remarkable to be able to shoot the whole thing *live* and have all the words come out!

I watched the first of the four and I actually did not recognize Vincent Price. I knew that it was he, but I got so lost in it, and his character was so clear, I was not seeing Vincent Price at all. I had to remind myself that it was he. I was stunned. And he was different in each story—it was quite a remarkable performance. So he's a fantastic actor. He doesn't have the *voice* that Karloff or Rathbone had—Vinnie's voice is pitched rather high, which makes it less ominous (to *me*). But he has such a clear enunciation that it gets across.

Were you happy with the music you did for Evening of Edgar Allan Poe?

The music was good in that, that's a double string quartet. Very modern. The first one was completely atonal, with double string quartet, with the most remarkable orchestra sight-reading this extremely difficult music.

Didn't AIP take some of your music and slip it into others of their movies?

They're not supposed to do that, but they do. Just recently I was listening to a picture on television and I heard part of a score of mine, the one for *Goliath and the Barbarians*. That was really a very varied score—there were perhaps four or five violent chases, barbarians attacking people, trampling them on horseback, doing wonderful things like that. And each chase was vastly different, very heavy, it would have played as modern symphonic music. So I immediately recognized it—in a Western film!

Namely?

I shouldn't say.

Namely?

Well, all right, *Grayeagle* [1978]. I heard some very long cues. And it was interesting hearing it on a Western — the Indians were chasing on horseback. You could use almost any music anywhere. *Goliath and the Barbarians* had a strongly Oriental influence, period Oriental, but it worked over Indians, because Indians have a little ancient background in their culture. So it wasn't too bad, except occasionally.

Why did a cost-conscious company like AIP even bother to have you compose new scores for foreign films, Black Sunday, *for instance, that already had music?*

Because Jim Nicholson thought the Italian scores were awful. And the ones that I heard, I too thought they were terrible.

How did you happen to make music your life's work?

My family moved when I was a very early age from Texas to Detroit, Michigan — my mother went ahead to Detroit and the rest of us followed in a Model T. Great car. (Of course, we had to push it up hills, my father, my brother and myself, if they were too steep!) We got to Detroit and drove up behind the apartment building where we were going to live, and the car just settled down and died right there. It never moved again. I went to the Detroit Conservatory of Music — at seven years old. I had been playing piano for awhile; I was studying at the Conservatory on a concert piano. I also took up clarinet, because I liked it for some reason. I got myself on a bus and went across town and enrolled in the Youth Symphony, and played in the Youth Symphony.

I hear about parents having to *push* their kids now to get into school and study things. I didn't *tell* my parents these things — I'd pick up the clarinet and go over and play in the Youth Symphony and come back home! They worked in the daytime — they'd leave in the morning when it was still dark and then come home again in the dark and there I'd be, sitting there, practicing my clarinet or whatever. The same thing happened when I went to college. I got tired of high school. When you get into about eleventh or eleventh-and-a-half grade, wherever you are, if you have enough credits (which I did have), you can leave. So I left without ever graduating from high school and went over to [Pepperdine College] and got myself a scholarship, and enrolled myself, and then came back and told my parents I was in college! It was so different from now, when you have to *push* kids.

And then, early on, you played with dance bands.

Right. I played with Freddie Slack, who was the king of boogie-woogie years ago, at the time of Goodman and Dorsey and James and all that stuff. You know, I miss vaudeville. This was when they would screen movies, the

Master of the World, involving "Jules Verne and Vincent Price and airships going around the world," features one of Baxter's favorite scores.

movie would finish and then the band would come up playing. It was kind of a wonderful period.

Any comment on Roger Corman?
    [*Makes a groaning sound*] Can you put *that* into print?

[*Laughs*] *Yes, it's spelled g-r-o-a-n!*
    I never saw Roger at the recording sessions of the music — I guess his work finished after the picture finished shooting. But I watched Roger work on the set, and he was remarkable for getting a lot of work done very quickly. And if someone goofed lines, it didn't matter. Which is the way *I*

am with music, too. I think, as long as the end result is there, it's fine. So he would let things slip through. Roger is known for shooting a picture in one day, also. They used to say about him that, if there was an accident on the corner, he'd shoot a film real fast [*laughs*].

AIP gave you opportunities to score all sorts of movies.

Yes, but you couldn't ask for more than carte blanche on a horror film. Because you can write modern music, abstract music, and do anything you want. I've always said that it would be very difficult for me to write a Doris Day–Rock Hudson film. I don't know how I would do Doris Day giggling, or people waiting for a stoplight.

Did you do all the composing in your own home?

Yes. And, contrary to popular belief, I was a lone wolf. Therefore, no one knew what kind of a composer I was. I was trained, even pre-teens, at the Detroit Conservatory of Music — no one had any idea that I was that well-trained in music, in orchestration, in composition, in melody writing, *and* counterpoint. I was also able to work *away* from the piano. I once scored a film [*The Sacred Idol*, 1959] in Mexico City, in a hotel room looking out a window. I was at a desk with no piano, and I scored the whole film there.

You sometimes shared credit with "music coordinator" Al Simms.

He was the man who was in charge of the music at AIP. He would sit in the booth and try not to get in the way.

What about Boris Karloff— did you have any contact with him?

Karloff was absolutely wonderful, a marvelously interesting, humorous man. And he was a wonderful actor — a *superb* actor — who got *sidetracked* into horror. But a lot of people get typecast in films, as composers do, and whatever their success was, they continue doing that. Karloff could have been a great Shakespearean actor, or *whatever*.

How about Peter Lorre and Basil Rathbone?

Peter Lorre was a wonderfully delightful person, and quite *comic*. They could have used his comic talent very much more than they did. He was used in horror films, I guess, because he looked a little strange, and had a strange way of pronouncing his speeches, but he had a very pixie sense of humor that went along with it. He was somewhat amusing in *The Raven*, although not as much as he could have been, and in *Comedy of Terrors* he was good. I think it's one of the classic scenes of all films, the wine-drinking scene between Lorre and Vinnie in *Tales of Terror*. That was a gem, that should go down in history for acting students. They were superb in that, and I was very amused by it. The *funniest* thing that Peter Lorre did, I think, was to be turned into a little spot of raspberry jam on the floor by Boris Karloff [in *The Raven*].

And Rathbone?

Rathbone was the most polished actor imaginable, and that was miscasting, also, to put him in horror films. I was very lucky to do [*The Comedy of Terrors*] that had Vincent Price, Boris Karloff, Peter Lorre and Basil Rathbone — the four top guys. To watch them all perform together was marvelous.

Panic in Year Zero! had a very jazzy score, and a lot of people don't like it.

I don't care [*laughs*]! I felt that's what I wanted to do for that. I did other things people didn't like: I played a thing that sounded like *The Tennessee Waltz* when they were in that little woodsy scene, which was out of context.

Did any directors ever try to provide input on your scores?

No, they really didn't. Funnily enough, when I got the score, it usually was *after* the director had gone back to wherever he came from. I don't ever recall being given any instructions. I did one film that was produced and directed by one man, who knew absolutely zero about *anything* in *any* field. And he had *enormous* input, all of which I received and digested and nodded to, then I did his score for him. The ones who didn't know did the most talking.

One of my favorites is X — The Man with the X-Ray Eyes, *which is a science fiction story with "ghostly" music.*

It was just an attempt to get away from what I had done before, probably. Each piece of music that a person writes is the victim of the piece that preceded it. One would write the piece they had just written.

Any comment on Black Sabbath?

Black Sunday and *Black Sabbath* get terribly intermixed, and there was a very unfortunate happening: My publisher sent the tape of *Black Sabbath* to a gentleman who was putting out an album of *Black Sunday*. (Or was it the other way around?) And the album got put out with the wrong movie title on it. He was very upset with me and I think he withdrew it from the market, but I didn't have anything to do with hearing the music, sending the tape or putting the album out.

How about the Beach Party *pictures?*

They were tremendous fun. The Beach Party pictures were embarrassing to me at first, but I did them because I was doing all of the films for Nicholson and Arkoff at the time. I liked the opportunity of doing the Beach films, they were the first successful rock 'n' roll films. No one has since hired me to do a rock 'n' roll film, and yet I did the only ones that made any money. The reason I like them today is that, of all the films that I've ever done (and I've done films for Nicholas Ray, Ingmar Bergman and other famous directors), the Beach Party films pay the most performance money through ASCAP of any films, possibly, in the world. They just keep playing, continually!

The Dunwich Horror?

I like that *very* much. It's been ripped off a lot: It's a Bach-ish theme, it's like a Bach fugue, and I thought Bach fugues went with Lovecraft's style of writing. *And* there's some electronic music in it. I'm very happy with that score.

What was the story on Frogs?

Frogs I wrote and played at the synthesizer. It was a one-man score before they were *doing* one-man scores; I think it's probably the first one at the synthesizer. I composed, arranged and played it at the synthesizer with assistance from *no* one. I used a lot of spider sounds and actual frog "voices," slowed down. This was a year in which [the Academy] was trying to give credit to the co-composers, or the men who were *really* writing the scores for some of the guys who were *not* writing their own scores. It was very fortunate that, that year, I did all of those scores myself, and that particular film *was* a one-man job; there wasn't even an orchestra. There was no one who could share credit with me on that — unless you wish to credit the frogs who "sang" on the score!

Why did you leave AIP?

I was in New York in a hotel with Jim Nicholson. We were sharing a two bedroom hotel room. It was fairly late, ten o'clock at night, and Nicholson came in the room and collapsed. Then he stood up and said, "I don't know what happened. I've never done that before." There was no explanation for it. Several years later, he had a brain tumor. I was invited to his house — one of the last nights, I suppose, with a friend or two — just to say good-bye.

And Arkoff didn't keep you around?

I would like to have continued working but, again, this is a very strange business.

You mentioned before that Master of the World *was one of your favorites at AIP. What others?*

I liked the first long cue in *Cry of the Banshee*; *Pit and the Pendulum*, [part of which] was atonal music. People are doing today what I did on the main title of *Pit and the Pendulum* and they think they're doing something new and daring, but I did it on that picture thirty-odd years ago! Also *House of Usher*, which I mentioned already. You're testing a memory that has to go back thirty years to do this. (I can't believe that I did all this thirty years ago — some of it *fifty* years ago. Does that make me eighty?)

After the AIP era, you spent a few years at Universal.

The head of music hired me and I did two or three shows for him. The reaction to those scores from the producers, the other composers and the orchestra was *phenomenal*; I got a standing ovation from the orchestra, which they told me was the first time it had happened. I got a call from the producer from the dubbing booth, and the producer said, "There are eleven people here with cold chills and tears over your music, and the mixer said it's the first time it's ever happened here. I had to call you and tell you that." So I got a marvelous reaction. Then the head of music had a heart attack and retired — and *then* was killed in an automobile accident. And that ended my career at Universal! I didn't work then, for several years.

There are a lot of fine composers in Hollywood. There are also a lot of *poor* composers who were in the right place at the right time; they meet a producer at a party, "Oh, why don't you score my next film?" and they do, and they're buddies forever. And there are other fine composers around town — many, *many* fine composers. I'm not placing myself particularly in that category, I'm just saying that there *are* numbers of fine composers who are not working. So it's not unusual to have these long runs as I've had, and then have a long slump after your producer died, which mine did. I had rather poor luck with producers; perhaps they're avoiding me because they don't want to be hit by a car or get a brain tumor or have a heart attack or whatever. I seem to lose them frequently.

Another recent score was for The Beast Within.

This was Harvey Bernhard's follow-up to the *Omen* films. He was crazy about the music and gave me a letter, the likes of which I had never seen. He said, "I have worked with all of the major composers in films during my twenty-five years in films, and musically you have no peer." He was crazy about it, and should be, because that was a very heavy score. There were about fourteen people in the recording booth, and after each cue, a cheer would go up in the booth. The mixer would turn on the microphone to the studio so the orchestra could hear it. It was so unusual. And the orchestra, in the spirit of things, stood and applauded for me also. So I had some very good luck with the last few scores that I did — so much luck that I didn't work anymore [*laughs*], for some strange reason. One never knows, does one?

Reporters have asked me, "How come Carnival of Souls *is playing in theaters thirty years after it was made, when so many hundreds of other low-budget, black-and-white films are long forgotten?" From the* writer's *angle, I think a little of it had to do with the fact that I had no need to worry about Hollywood formats.*

John Clifford

IT WOULD BE DIFFICULT to name a horror movie more deserving of the adjective "sleeper" than *Carnival of Souls*. Made in Lawrence, Kansas, in 1961, the low-budget ($30,000) Herk Harvey production fell into the hands of a shyster distributor (Herts-Lion) who cut some key scenes, played it at drive-ins and other lowly venues, and ran off with the proceeds. But, rather than sinking into the vast sea of forgotten films, *Carnival* tenaciously clung to life in the minds of horror fans who caught its initial run or, years later, its television late-show reincarnations. Recently restored to its original running time, it enjoyed a 1989 theatrical (revival and art house) re-release, raking in $1,200,000 with showings in 47 cities, reinforcing the cult status of the movie's star Candace Hilligoss and particularly its producer/director/co-star Herk Harvey, who has been subsequently honored at film festivals in the U.S. and throughout the rest of the world.

John Clifford, who wrote the subtle, atmospheric chiller, has often been passed over in discussions of the film (an occupational hazard for writers!) even though the eerie plot sprang from his fertile imagination, cued only by Herk Harvey's proposal of a movie featuring "creatures coming out of [a lake] and dancing...." A *Souls* survivor, Clifford takes pride in the wide recognition that his movie has finally received—30 years late—and reminisces here about the experience of writing *Carnival of Souls*.

I was born in Springfield, Illinois, and when my parents died, I moved to Chicago and lived with relatives. This was back during the Depression, and I was trying to find something to do for a living. Since I didn't want to work in warehouses [*laughs*], why, I realized that if I could become a writer, that would be ideal. But I didn't think I could write anything longer than a joke—so I learned how to write *jokes*! I got interviews with Bob Hope and Milton Berle when they came to Chicago, I'd contact 'em and see 'em in person, but I wasn't very good, I was just learning.

Who did you make your first sales to?

To Ken Murray, a big radio comedian at the time—I sold him a bunch of jokes and material for awhile. And then I went to Hollywood and I got a contract with a literary agent who was going to get me a job as a junior writer in one of the film studios. I had several things that he submitted around. But at that time, World War II was imminent and my draft number was up, and he said I'd better go in and get my year over with, because he couldn't place me. So I went in the Army and World War II started, and I got out *five* years later [*laughs*]!

Later, on the G.I. Bill, I went to a Hollywood school for writers for

---

Previous page: "Hell, *every*body wants to make a movie," says John Clifford, writer of *Carnival of Souls*. "I'd have done it for nothing, to be honest with you." (Photo courtesy of Val Paulsen.)

awhile and studied, and then I came back to the Midwest and went to college. I had various writing jobs, and eventually I ended up with Centron Films here in Lawrence. At Centron we made industrial films and we had a large educational film department. Herk Harvey was a director and I was a script writer. We had at one time about fifty-some people employed there, and I think we were probably one of the two or three *quality* film companies in the country at that time, in that field.

Why did Herk Harvey come to you when he had the idea to do a horror film?
I had just published a Western novel [*The Shooting of Storey James*]—that was back in 1961—and for that and other reasons, Herk approached me one day with this idea of writing a feature. (Herk had also read some other things of mine; in fact, he had read an article of mine that inspired *him* to write a screenplay once.) He came to me one day after he'd just come back from out West, and he described to me this strange outdoor ballroom he had seen on the shores of the Great Salt Lake. It was kind of a rotting old ballroom, and he said that when he was there, he thought what a creepy place it was, and he told me he'd like to make a film about some creatures coming out of the lake there and dancing in this pavilion. Other than that, he pretty much gave me carte blanche. I wrote it in the evenings, on my own time. I don't remember how long [the writing] took, maybe three weeks or so.

Did you think, going into it, that writing a horror picture was something you'd be able to do well?
Yeah, I had a lot of confidence. I'd always wanted to write films, which is really why I came to work at Centron. Even though I had come there first as an advertising executive [*laughs*], I knew I was going to get over onto the film side, and I thought this would help me.

Were you much of a fan of horror movies? Were there any that inspired you?
No. I mean, I *liked* horror movies—I liked *all* kinds of movies, and always have. But, no, I didn't have an example, really. Frankly, what Herk told me was that we wouldn't have much of a budget and we couldn't indulge ourselves in expensive effects. For example, he thought it would be very expensive to have *too* much sound and dialogue out on the streets, so I wrote a script that really had very little dialogue in it. Thinking about Mary Henry [Candace Hilligoss], the main character in the story, I was trying to think where we could go to get some major effects without spending a lot of money, and I remembered the Reuter Organ Company here in town. They had this big room where they tested their organs and it was very

impressive, because the pipes were all there, exposed. I thought, "Well, that would make a nice location," and then *that* gave me the idea of making the heroine an organist. And *that* suggested *other* ideas. Once I established the lead character and the mood, really, it flowed kind of easy. I had one of those writers' experiences where a film story just sort of "unreels" in your mind, and night after night, it's there on the mental screen, like a serial. It wasn't really a difficult thing for me to write. I had no great, high, "artistic" ideas for it. Herk maybe had some, but I was just into the material. That was really the first full-length film I ever wrote. I wrote it fast and we had a little time for revision.

Who came up with the title?

Herk and I kicked around titles and one of us, or *both* of us, came up with it. I remember having the discussion with him, but I couldn't tell you which one of us suggested it.

Initially you were thinking about having a man *as the central character.*

Well, when Herk was ad-libbing ideas, he suggested that. But I thought a girl would be more vulnerable.

You know, I've heard reviewers say that the film's ending was inevitable or obvious, but *I* don't think it was obvious back then. The truth is, I created the story in sequence, from beginning to end. When I had Mary Henry [Hilligoss] emerge from the river in the beginning, I really had no idea how I was going to explain it. I just created that sort of supernatural event to get the *mood* I wanted. Then, I don't know, maybe about a third or halfway through, it just occurred to me that it "goes around" [the story goes full circle]. I know it's been compared to *An Occurrence at Owl Creek Bridge,* but actually I hadn't read that at the time.

There's also a Twilight Zone *episode that's a lot like* Carnival of Souls. *Inger Stevens has a near-death experience while driving cross-country, then keeps seeing the same spooky-looking hitchhiker.*

Oh, is that so? Well, that's coincidence—or maybe I saw it and subconsciously stole it [*laughs*]! But I *know* that the "spooky hitchhiker" idea is an old one.

You talked a minute ago about the mood you were trying to create. What mood was that?

It was an eerie, "fright" mood—the kind of mood that makes you uneasy. Reporters have asked me, "How come *Carnival of Souls* is playing in theaters thirty years after it was made, when so many hundreds of other low-budget, black-and-white films are long forgotten?" From the *writer's* angle, I think a little of it had to do with the fact that I had no need to worry about Hollywood formats. That made *Carnival of Souls* maybe just a little bit different. I didn't need to conform (I probably didn't know *how* to conform), and I knew who the producer/director would be and that he'd be open to whatever I'd propose. For instance, it's one of the few films from that period, or even today, that has no love story or romance, even as a subplot. Considering the miniscule budget, there're some good things in *Carnival* as far as the directing and cinematography and all that. And Herk deserves full credit for all that.

But it's interesting to me that, after all the people who have written about *Carnival of Souls*, there's one thing I put in there that nobody's *ever* noticed — and I think it's one of the reasons why it stays in the minds of some people. I decided early on to give the heroine *no* real sympathy or understanding from *any* other character. So, for the viewer, there's no relief from her dilemma. There's no catharsis, even, except what the viewer creates for himself. Hardly anybody seems to tumble to that.

Candace Hilligoss told me she wanted the character to be more *sympathetic. She thought it'd be scarier that way.*

Yeah, I know. Somebody who wrote about the film suggested I should have made the neighbor [Sidney Berger] more of a romantic person. But to me, that kind of lets you emotionally off the hook. I wanted her to have nobody to turn to. The doctor [Stan Levitt] *tries* to give her a little sympathy, but he really just lectures her. I think if I had it to do over, I'd leave that [the lectures] *out* [*laughs*], but I thought then that I had to explain something. I realize now that it probably wasn't necessary.

Do you remember any scenes, or any ideas, that were in your script, that didn't make it to the screen?

No, pretty much all of it was there. As Herk went along, a couple of times he added little things that I hadn't thought of. But, no, it's all there; if you read the script, you'd see most of the film. It interests me that so many reviewers seem to think that writers only write the scenes that have *dialogue*. Have you noticed that [*laughs*]? The only time they mention *me* is when they say the dialogue is lousy! Well, the dialogue *is* kind of bad in some places, and a couple of the actors weren't any help.

Herk Harvey told me that when Hilligoss first showed up, she wasn't what he had envisioned. Was she what you *envisioned? Do you think she did a good job?*

She was close enough for me, and I thought she did a good job, yes. I

Part of the reason for the popularity of *Carnival of Souls,* according to Clifford, is the fact that he gave the heroine (Candace Hilligoss) no real sympathy or understanding from any other character.

had written a rather passive character — deliberately. Unlike most lead characters, things happen to *her* that she can't explain. That's not quite a popular way to do it, but I did that, and by and large that's the kind of performance Herk got out of her. I was working full-time and I only saw a little bit of the shooting, and I only talked to Candace two or three times. I never really got into a deep discussion with her about it.

And Hilligoss personally?
   Oh, she was a nice, friendly young woman. I had dinner with 'em a couple of times, and I drove her to the scene a couple of times. I have nothing but good things to say about her, or anybody else in the cast.

Would you like to rate some of the other performances? I realize these people are still your friends and neighbors.
   Yeah, they are. Maybe we shouldn't get into that [*laughs*]!

What scenes in the picture are you particularly happy with?

The scene that comes to mind is the scene when she's taking a bath and gets up and goes in the hall and looks over the banister, and the Man [Harvey] is in her house. And I think it was an interesting *idea* to do the scenes where she "fades out" of the world and nobody can see her. The scene in the department store, for instance. I remember that Herk just walked into that department store and asked if they could shoot there [*laughs*] — that's all he had to do! He only had three or four [production] people with him the whole time.

Which scenes don't *you like? Which scenes would you like to have seen done differently?*

Scenes with the minister [Art Ellison] kind of irritate me a little bit [*laughs*]. There are a couple of minor things like that; well, actually, there're all *kinds* of things Herk and I would probably do again. Although, as *Herk* says, some of the amateurishness of it is maybe part of its appeal.

How much of the film were you able to watch being shot?

Just a few scenes. I didn't go with 'em to Salt Lake, where they shot most of it, 'cause I was working. I watched Herk shoot the scene of Mary Henry driving at night — that was shot at the studio [Centron], and I was there that night, helping. The doctor's office scene was shot at the studio, too, and I was there for part of that. The first night they shot in the "boarding house," I was there when they started shooting. But they shot all night that first night and I didn't stay, I had to go to work the next day. It was real interesting, though, to be engaged in that kind of a production as opposed to "workaday work." After it was shot, Herk would get rough cuts and we'd be there looking at it projected — we had an old 35mm projector. We'd be projecting it there at Centron at three o'clock in the morning [*laughs*]! But there was just something fascinating about it, and we both got caught up in it — we wanted to go ahead and do a dozen of 'em.

Herk Harvey was on "vacation" from Centron while doing this?

Yes, he took a leave of absence to make the film.

The "danse macabre" at the end — did that live up to your expectations?

Yeah. That was really something that Herk wanted in there, and I think he got what he wanted. I didn't describe that in detail [in the script]; I knew he wanted that, and I set it up for him.

Are you in the picture?

No. I don't know why; everyone seems to *think* I was, and I *should* have been [*laughs*]. I should have been in the bridge scene, or *some*thing; I'm in dozens of other Centron films, because we always used each other in the background somewhere. There were a couple of Centron employees in the film; [editor] Bill De Jarnette worked at Centron and *he* had a small part in it, as an auto mechanic, and then Dan Palmquist played the service station attendant who gives Candace directions. Dan was our senior editor at Centron. One of the bodies that comes up out of the water was Peter Schnitzler, who worked at Centron then; he's the grandson of Arthur Schnitzler, the Viennese playwright. I remember those; I don't remember who else might have been in it.

Were you one of the investors?
No. I was one of the stock participants; several of us took a share of stock. I *needed* the script, because I wanted to show people at Centron that I could write films. It must have worked, 'cause I wrote films for the next twenty-five years.

Were you at the premiere?
Yes, and it was interesting. We had the "world premiere" here at Lawrence and it was a typical Midwest audience — well, *not* "typical," 'cause there were a certain number of university people there, too. And I don't think they "got" it. I mean, we're talking about 1962, and as I told Herk, if we had made a recognizable, class–C, Hollywood-type movie — a straight plot, one where they recognized everything — I think they would have appreciated it a lot more. They'd have thought, "Boy, these guys can make movies!" But nobody gives local people credit for doing something *that* original; at the time, people weren't that sophisticated about it.

Were you discouraged by that audience's reaction?
No. But we *were* a little bit discouraged by the fact that, when Herk took it to Hollywood, nobody would look at it. We felt a little responsible for that, [on behalf of] the investors — even though I think they only had about $17,000 invested, something like that. So it was kind of a relief, maybe too *much* of a relief, when Herts-Lion showed an interest.

The loyal following that Carnival *has attracted — are you surprised by that?*
Well, I wasn't *too* surprised, because every once in a while, Herk or I would get a letter, usually from *kids*. Junior high kids, especially, it seemed to be. They saw it on late-night television — this was when it was totally obscure — and they'd write to us. But I never expected it to get the play it did when it "came back." I've done, oh, I don't know, 100, 200 other short

films and things since then, and I've got a play called *Jack Be Quick* in rehearsal at the local theater right now. And yet *Carnival of Souls* is what gave us our fifteen minutes of fame. A couple years ago we had a showing and a nice big reception at a theater here [in Lawrence], when they raised money for the film activities locally. I think it was like $25 for the evening, and the house was packed — Candace came back for it and all of us got up on the stage and talked about it. A Topeka television station made a half-hour film called *The Movie That Wouldn't Die*; clips from *Carnival of Souls* were on *Entertainment Tonight* and *Siskel and Ebert* and all of that.

It's a long way back for me and I feel I've done better work, and maybe more *worthy* work, in films that raised money for good causes and things like that. I don't think *Carnival of Souls* is the best thing I ever did [*laughs*]! But as so often happens, you get most of your credit for about the first thing you ever did. But I have absolutely no regrets, and we've even made a little money out of it now — not *much*, but we got a *little* return on it. But, hell, everybody wants to make a movie. I'd have done it for *nothing*, to be honest with you.

> Herk Harvey, star/producer/director/co-writer of *Carnival of Souls*, died of pancreatic cancer in his Lawrence, Kansas, home in April 1996, while this book was in the final stage of production.

[Adventures of Captain Marvel] *had so much class ...
I think we had a damn fine product when we got through with it.*

Frank Coghlan, Jr.

IT WAS ONE of those career decisions which either immortalizes an actor or permanently pigeonholes him (depending on the actor's outlook). In 1940, Frank Coghlan, Jr., took the role of Billy Batson in Republic's 12-episode *Adventures of Captain Marvel*, where the mystical cry "Shazam!" transformed him into the two-fisted, nails-tough flying superhero (played by Tom Tyler). In the more than 50 years since, his participation in this superlative serial (widely considered *the* best ever) has become Coghlan's major claim to fame, eclipsing the big studio films in which the former child actor appeared opposite some of the screen's great stars. But Coghlan looks back on his "superhero" days with far more pride than prejudice, and recently wrote glowingly about the experience in his 1993 autobiography *They Still Call Me Junior*.

The son of a railroad clerk/pro-boxer, Coghlan was born in Connecticut and soon after moved with his family to California, where all three did extra work in silent pictures. Freckle-faced Coghlan was soon one of the era's most popular child actors, but with the advent of sound (and the onslaught of adolescence), he was reduced to smaller parts. After starring (opposite Louise Currie and Billy Benedict) in *Captain Marvel*, Coghlan was a naval aviator in World War II. He later headed the Navy's motion picture cooperation program (and other similar programs), acting as liaison between the Navy and the Hollywood studios. When his 23-year active duty stint ended in 1965, he returned to acting in movies and on television (where he had a supporting role in the pilot of the *Captain Marvel*-esque comedy series *Mr. Terrific*). He wrote his autobiography "because my kids just kept bugging me to do it," does the occasional television commercial, and is a popular figure at movie conventions where, to the ongoing amazement of the 80-ish "Junior," fans still line up to meet *Captain Marvel*'s alter ego.

Why were you not able to hang onto stardom, once you got a little older and talkies came in?

If you recall, until Mickey Rooney as Andy Hardy made adolescents popular [in the late thirties], *all* kids dropped out of the business. We got pimples and buck teeth, lost our freckles, our voices got high and didn't record well — there were all kinds of reasons the studios wanted to get rid of you [*laughs*]! Adolescence was the kiss of death for kid actors. At least, it *was* until some smart apples made Rooney into Andy Hardy. (That's the most humorous age a kid goes through.) But before Andy Hardy and Henry Aldrich and [movie series] like that, you got to be thirteen and you were out of work!

How unhappy were you when your career started to slump, and you began playing bit parts?

Previous page: More than a half-century after playing Billy Batson, "*Captain Marvel* is still getting me invited to film festivals," says Frank Coghlan, Jr.

Coghlan has played hundreds of screen and television roles, but "if people want to recognize me for [*Captain Marvel*], be my guest." (Pictured: Stanley Price, Coghlan.)

It didn't break my heart. Maybe I didn't have starring roles anymore but, golly, I've made 125 movies, so I was still workin'! Maybe I was only delivering a telegram in a movie [*laughs*], but I was still around!

Talk about how you became involved on Adventures of Captain Marvel.

I was working in *Men of Boys Town* [1941] at MGM, and during my last week on it, my agent called to ask if I could get a few hours off—he wanted me to go for an interview over at Republic. They were about to make a serial called *Captain Marvel* and they were considering me for [the role of] Billy Batson. One of the assistant directors there at MGM told me I wouldn't be needed for the next few hours, so I drove to Republic. (By the way, I had no idea who Captain Marvel or Billy Batson were.) At Republic, I was interviewed in the office of a producer named Hiram Brown and I met Bill Witney and Jack English, who were going to be directing *Captain Marvel*. After the interview, on the way back to MGM, I stopped by one of the big drug stores and found the Whiz comics, I bought the *Captain Marvel* comic and I read it with interest back at MGM on the set of *Men of Boys Town*, and then also at home. I thought to myself, "Hey, I *do* kind of look like that kid." And then it was a couple of days later that I was told I had the job.

What made Republic think of you?
 I think because I looked like Billy Batson — I was the right age, I was available, and I didn't demand a fortune in money (which Republic wouldn't spend anyway!) [Serial authority] William C. Cline wrote that my casting was just a stroke of genius, as far as looking like the kid. Other writers have said that I was too old, and they objected to my voice, but what the heck, I'm sure the kid Billy Batson had a high voice, too! It was just considered good casting.

How quickly was Captain Marvel *shot?*
 It was made in December [1940] and January [1941] and we had a twenty-eight-day shooting schedule. There were a lot of exterior scenes, and if there was inclement weather on a given day, there was always an interior cover set where we could go and shoot a different scene instead. Unfortunately, we just had more bad weather than we could cover, and we went four days over schedule. But thirty-two days, that's not bad for twelve episodes!

Did you feel that you were being rushed?
 Toward the end, when we were falling behind, we were working both directors, and we'd hop from one director to the other. We were really frantic toward the end — a couple of days over is a big, big blow to the budget. Louis Germonprez, the production manager, was sensational — what a great organizational mind he had. He had in his office the largest breakdown board I'd ever seen. The thing ran the whole length of the room and across the top it was divided into the twenty-eight days of production. Lou knew where we were supposed to be every minute of every day! But when the weather got bad and we couldn't cover shots, then he was in trouble; that's why we had to work two shifts. He was an organizational genius, and he doesn't even get screen credit — isn't that amazing?

As you were making Captain Marvel, *what was the general attitude about it? That it was "for kids only"?*
 Well, the serials *were* aimed mainly at the kids. When I was a kid, ten or twelve, I went to the serials faithfully, but in later years I didn't. And, after all, it *did* spring from a comic book. So I kind of think that we had to regard it [as a kids' picture]. But ours had so much class to

Coghlan gauges reactions as the "Scorpion suspects" (George Pembroke, Robert Strange, George Lynn, John Davidson, Harry Worth) inspect a new clue.

it — Republic put a lot of marvelous stock shots into it, to give it quality, and I think we had a damn fine product when we got through with it. Leonard Maltin has had me on *Entertainment Tonight* three times, and he's said publicly that *Adventures of Captain Marvel* is the finest action serial ever made.

How did working at a small studio like Republic compare to working for one of the majors?
    In the big studios, you could relax a little bit more, take a longer lunch, things like that. At Republic, they cracked the whip every minute.

Louise Currie, who was also in Citizen Kane, *said that she found the long waits on* Kane *boring — that she preferred rush-rush places like Republic.*
    Well, she's right, one of the most boring things in the movie business is when you're actually not working, when you're sitting there watchin' and waitin'. And you can't even wander off, walk around the lot, unless they say you can have an hour off or whatever. But in a Republic production, you were working all the time!

What can you remember about Tom Tyler (Captain Marvel)?

Well, my good friend Tom and I were never in a scene together — we *could* not be, because he was my alter ego. But we were on the set together all the time, because we'd have to shift roles. I knew Tom from years before: When he was making Westerns with Frankie Darro in the 1920s, his director was Robert de Lacy, and de Lacy's wife Leona was my mother's best friend. My mom used to have the de Lacys over for dinner several times a year, and they'd bring this big, handsome, bashful bachelor with 'em. That was Tom Tyler — he was a guest at our house a number of times over those years in the twenties. Then, all of sudden, here I was on the set of *Captain Marvel* with him in 1940-41. But I hadn't seen much of him in the interim. And after *Captain Marvel* I went in the Navy, so I didn't see much of him in later years either. The poor guy had a sad demise — he had this terrible auto accident, I hear, that caused him a lot of facial change, and then arthritis crippled him up before he died. He was a very pleasant, business-like man — he just sat there all day long, patiently. Just a real nice person.

Billy Benedict? Louise Currie?

Prior to *Captain Marvel*, I had never really known Bill, but today we're best friends. Louise was lovely on the set, very nice — business-like, too, but attractive and friendly. We never became socially friendly because she had different interests — she was an interior decorator married to a wealthy importer, living in this mansion in Beverly Hills. They're a very nice couple. We've been to two film festivals together. Two years ago, I was able to delight Leonard Maltin: When Leonard put on Cinecon 24 at the Hollywood Roosevelt Hotel in L.A., I was able to put together a panel of Bill Witney, Louise Currie, Bill Benedict and me — the first time ever that all four of us had been on a panel. We filled that auditorium, and Leonard just drooled!

Any memories of the supporting players in Captain Marvel?

In support, we had people like Jack Mulhall, who had once been a *star*; John Davidson, an excellent actor; Bryant Washburn; Nigel De Brulier, who played Shazam, played Cardinal Richelieu opposite Douglas Fairbanks twice. And Carleton Young — when I was later head of the Navy office in Hollywood, I was very pleasantly surprised and pleased to see that he was an Army colonel, a full *bird colonel*. I got billing over him [in *Captain Marvel*], but here he outranked me! Harry Worth played one of the archeologists, and in the end it turned out to be Harry who was the evil Scorpion. Well, a year or so after we did Captain Marvel, I was in Bullock's Wilshire, our classiest department store at the time, and I saw Harry selling neckties in the haberdashery. And he was so embarrassed! He was workin', what's wrong with that? But he was so embarrassed for me to see him there—I guess he considered it degrading. There's nothing wrong with selling neckties! (And they were *expensive* neckties [*laughs*]!)

When we see the Scorpion in Captain Marvel, *is it always Worth underneath the hood and robes?*
  No, I'm almost sure that they kept switchin' people so that you would not know.

Describe how Captain Marvel's *flying scenes were done.*
  That was the work of the Lydecker brothers [Howard and Theodore], who were the special effects men at Republic. They had a seven-foot papier-mâché dummy of Captain Marvel — it was beautifully proportioned. It was seven feet from head to toe, then the arms were extended out farther. They stretched out a wire until there was tremendous tension, then they put the dummy on it — and the effect was beautiful. I saw them slide it 200 yards down Mulholland Drive, and that wire didn't sag an inch. The Lydeckers were so clever! In one episode, Captain Marvel leaps from the street up to the sixth floor roof of the Biltmore Hotel, and they used that dummy there again. Actually, that time they slid the dummy down backwards, and then reversed the film. It makes sense when you talk about it, but who would have thought of it? Well, the *Lydeckers* did [*laughs*]!

What real-life injuries do you recall, amidst all Captain Marvel's *action?*
  The main stuntman was Dave Sharpe. He was so beautifully coordinated that he was rarely injured. He was a smaller guy than Tom Tyler, but their builds were enough alike that he could get away with doubling for Tyler. Dave did some death-defying stunts — he used a small trampoline to help him make those unbelievable leaps, and he'd be caught by a bunch of guys with a small fireman's net. I did see him fall short on one of his trampoline jumps, and I know he hit his coccyx bone on the rim of that fireman's net. He never let us know it, but he had to have hurt himself — he fell right on it with his tailbone. And that back flip he did in Chapter One! Two natives were coming at him and he did a back flip, catching each native under the chin with his foot as he went over, knocking them out. I thought that was a work of art!
  Speaking of Dave, I got $175 a week [on *Captain Marvel*]; Bill Benedict got $150; Tom Tyler got $250; and Dave Sharpe got $250. A stuntman of his quality, on a flat salary...! Today, he'd make more than that on a single stunt! I went to see Dave at the Motion Picture Country Home toward

Only after 12 slambang episodes did Coghlan come face-to-hood with the sinister Scorpion.

the end of his life, when he had Lou Gehrig's disease. He couldn't even talk, he'd just flash his eyes to show you that he recognized you.

Over the course of making Captain Marvel, *were you ever asked to do something that you would have preferred that a stuntman do?*

Not that I recall. And I wasn't doubled very often, either. William Witney was at a festival where he was asked that question, and he told the person, "No, Frankie was a pretty handy guy." And I was — I was twenty-three years old and I was in great physical condition from running, playing football, things like that. But if there was anything that was really going to hurt me, of course they had people stand in for me. The funny situation I remember was when I was swimming with Louise Currie's double on the final day. We were out at Lake Malibu and I was supposedly saving her life, towing her to shore after she'd been knocked out in the shipwreck. I had a tweed suit on, and when it got wet, that thing weighed about fifty pounds! Then with one arm around the girl, I didn't have much to keep me afloat! After a couple of tries, I asked Bill Witney if I could at least take off my trousers and my shoes — and I did!

Also, in Chapter One, there's a scene where the natives attack the archeologists' compound and set it afire — that was shot up near the Iverson Ranch. And once the fire got going, we realized that we were surrounded by burning barrels of oil. The wind shifted on us, and we felt the heat. I don't think we were in tremendous danger but, hey, you never can tell — it *was* hot, and we could have gotten French-fried! Then there were the scenes where I said "Shazam!" and turned into Captain Marvel. Every time we did that, they ignited flash powder which was in a trough in front of me. And if the wind was unkind, I'd get the powder flash in my face and lose some eyebrows.

Now, I was in a serial called *The Last of the Mohicans* [1932] where I *did* object to a few of the things that this jerk Wyndham Gittens asked me to do. Gittens was a writer who wrote many serials — he evidently was a very clever writer — but he was a pompous ass. He was asked to take over directing one day, after [director] "Breezy" Eason was fired for coming in with a hangover. And Gittens just didn't know how to direct. He was one of those guys that got in there and he acted it, and then wanted *you* to do what *he* did. And that's how I got even with him. For one of the cliffhanger endings, I was supposed to fall backwards off a cliff; there were going to be two crew members on a ledge below who'd use a net to catch me. This jerk Gittens picked a very high, steep cliff with only a very narrow ledge below, and I knew that there was no way these guys could catch me — my weight would throw them off-balance and we'd *all* fall a hundred feet to our deaths. So I said to him, "Okay, Mr. Gittens, you show me how you want me to make this fall and I'll do it the same way you do." He looked down the cliff and immediately decided to shoot the scene in a safer place!

Do you remember where you saw Captain Marvel *for the first time?*
    The first time I saw any part of *Adventures of Captain Marvel* was when

I had just gotten married. I was a brand-new ensign at Pensacola, Florida, and my little bride had never seen me in a movie. *Captain Marvel* was playing in Pensacola at a segregated theater. We went down there and I walked up to the ticket office, where a little black girl was working. I said, "I would like to come in and see this movie. I worked in it." And she said, "Oh, no, sir, we can't let you in; this is a *black* theater." I asked, "Is the manager here?" He came out; he was a white man, and he recognized me immediately. So they let us in, but they made us sit in the very back row!

[Laughs.] Reverse discrimination?

No, no — it was the fact that they didn't want the kids who were there to see me. They thought there'd be a riot! And when the lights came up and the kids started walking out, there was a lot of, "Ooh, there's Captain Marvel!" And when I went through my flight training, most of the stewards in the Navy — the kitchen help — were black. And, boy, when I went through that chow line, there it was again — "Ooh, there's Captain Marvel!" And, *wham,* I'd get another pork chop and a bigger scoop of potatoes — really! I was well recognized through my flight training!

Would you have done more serials for Republic if they asked you?

Oh, of course. I did *The Great Circus Mystery* [1925] as a kid; then *The Last of the Mohicans, Scouts to the Rescue* [1938] with Jackie Cooper, and *Captain Marvel.* And I do believe that if I hadn't gone away [into the Navy], Republic would have had me back for others.

So you enjoyed the experience of Captain Marvel?

Bill Benedict and I had a ball. Toward the end of production, he and I decided to buy a present for everyone in the crew and for the few actors who were still working. We put forty bucks together — that was big dough in 1940, '41 — and we went down to the five-and-dime store on Hollywood Boulevard and bought forty gag presents on a budget of a dollar a gift. For instance, we gave Tom Tyler a jockstrap — that wasn't disrespectful, but with his tight Captain Marvel outfit, we thought it would *help* him [*laughs*]. And we gave Davey Sharpe this little toy man with a parachute, and he had a ball with that — he went all over the set blowing that thing up into the air and letting it come down. That's how Bill and I felt, we liked this crew so much. And I think it was reciprocated.

Why do the lives of so many kid actors go sour?

I don't think I can truthfully answer that. I've read the books of Baby Peggy and Jackie Cooper and Mickey Rooney and Dickie Moore, and they all bemoan that they never had a childhood. I *loved* my childhood! Golly, going to sea with William Boyd for six weeks [*The Yankee Clipper*, 1927], being on the field with the New York Yankees [*Slide, Kelly, Slide*, 1927] — man, I have *great* memories! Also, I had a marvelous mother, and I think she kept my feet on the ground. I never made the big money that a lot of the guys did, like [Jackie] Coogan and Baby Peggy, but we enjoyed life. So, I just don't know. So many [former] kid actors are actually bitter now, like Jackie Searl — he won't answer his mail or talk to people. I can't understand why they're so bitter.

When you read or hear their reasons, do they make sense to you?
 I don't think so — not comparative to my feelings. Dickie Moore goes on, page after page, of how his folks forced him into this "undesirable occupation." That's baloney. It made them wealthy, made them recognized and famous, and I don't know why they feel bitter about it.

And you think a big part of the reason you kept your head screwed on straight was your mother's influence.
 Oh, I think so — she was a wonderful woman. I was not permitted to go to professional schools, I went to public schools, I played sports, and I think that has a lot to do with it. I think a lot of these kids that went to the professional schools kind of buttered up each others' egos [*laughs*].

By "professional schools," do you mean the studio schoolhouses?
 No, we all had to do that while we were working. But there was a school here in Hollywood called Mrs. Lawler's Professional School and all of the kids, Rooney and Garland and most of 'em, went there. It was three hours a day, it was a private school, and I guess you almost *had* to be in the movies to be admitted to it. But that was like livin' in the studio all day long! I got away from it, and I think that was good.

After all the major pictures in which you've had good roles, is the fact that Captain Marvel *is your claim to fame a bitter pill?*
 Oh, hell, no — why should I be bitter? I'm not that kind of a guy. Look, if people want to recognize me for that film, be my guest. Also, I did have a tiny, tiny role in *Gone with the Wind* [1939], and at festivals there are people that drool over me because I was in *that* picture.

Let's put it this way: Years from now, only one of your movies still exists. Should it be Captain Marvel, *or something else?*
 Well, I would think it should be *Captain Marvel*. But then I was in other movies like *The Yankee Clipper* with Bill Boyd, a fabulous seagoing

movie. And then another one that Bill and I did together, *The Last Frontier* [1926]—if that's ever found, I think it will compare very favorably with *The Covered Wagon*. (And we "discovered" Monument Valley, I think, long before [John] Ford did.) But, shucks, if people want to remember me for *Captain Marvel*, that's fine; just to be *remembered* is fine! I mean, it's been fifty-two years, and *Captain Marvel* is still getting me invited to film festivals. So it's a recognized fact: Superman and Captain Marvel, they were the best!

Kirk Alyn and I were guests at a film festival in Atlanta, along with little Johnny Duncan, who played Robin [in *Batman and Robin*, 1949], and Frankie Thomas, who played *Tom Corbett, Space Cadet* and Tim Tyler [in *Tim Tyler's Luck*, 1937]. At the big banquet, I walked over behind Kirk and I said, "You know, I think Billy Batson was a much sharper guy than Clark Kent. And he didn't need a phone booth to change clothes in!" *It brought down the house.* So I just said "Shazam!" and sat down!

FRANK COGHLAN, JR., FILMOGRAPHY

Mid Channel (Garson Studios/Equity Pictures Corporation, 1920)
To Please One Woman (Paramount, 1920)
The Suitor (Vitagraph short, 1920)
Rookies (Universal short, 1921)
The Poverty of Riches (Goldwyn, 1921)
Bobbed Hair (Paramount, 1922)
Bow Wow (Mack Sennett–First National, 1922)
Giants vs. Yanks (Pathé short, 1923)
Our Alley (Arrow Film Corp., 1923)
The Fourth Musketeer (R.C. Pictures–FBO, 1923)
Little Old New York (Goldwyn/Cosmopolitan, 1923)
The Spanish Dancer (Paramount, 1923)
The Darling of New York (Universal, 1923)
A Woman of Paris (United Artists, 1923)
Cause for Divorce (Selznick Distributing Corp., 1923)
The Law of the Lawless (Famous Players–Lasky, 1923)
Garrison's Finish (Jack Pickford Productions/Allied Producers and Distributors, 1923)
Winning His Way (Universal short, 1924)
The Great Circus Mystery (Universal serial, 1925)
The Great Love (MGM, 1925)
The Road to Yesterday (Producers Distributing Corp., 1925)
Whispering Smith (Metropolitan, 1925)
Her Man o' War (Producers Distributing Corp., 1926)
Mike (MGM, 1926)
The Skyrocket (Associated Exhibitors, 1926)
The Last Frontier (Producers Distributing Corp., 1926)
Rubber Tires (Producers Distributing Corp., 1927)

The Yankee Clipper (Producers Distributing Corp., 1927)
The Country Doctor (Producers Distributing Corp., 1927)
Slide, Kelly, Slide (MGM, 1927)
A Harp in Hock (Pathé Exchange, 1927)
Marked Money (Pathé Exchange, 1928)
Let 'Er Go Gallegher (Pathé Exchange, 1928)
Square Shoulders (Pathé Exchange, 1929)
The Girl Said No (MGM, 1930)
River's End (Warners, 1930)
Penrod and Sam (Warners, 1931)
The Public Enemy (Warners, 1931)
It Pays to Advertise (Paramount, 1931)
Hell's House (Capital Films Exchange, 1932)
Union Depot (Gentleman for a Day) (Warners, 1932)
Man Wanted (Warners, 1932)
The Last of the Mohicans (Mascot serial, 1932)
Fireman Save My Child (Warners, 1932)
Racetrack (World Wide, 1933)
Merrily Yours (Educational short, 1933)
This Day and Age (Paramount, 1933)
What's to Do? (Educational short, 1933)
Drum Taps (World Wide, 1933)
In the Money (Chesterfield, 1933)
Pardon My Pups (Educational short, 1934)
Managed Money (Educational short, 1934)
Stranded (Warners, 1935)
Kentucky Blue Streak (Puritan Pictures, 1935)
It Never Rains (Educational short, 1935)
Happiness C.O.D. (Chesterfield, 1935)
Alibi Ike (Warners, 1935)
The Little Red Schoolhouse (Chesterfield, 1936)
Melody in May (RKO short, 1936)
The New Average Man (RKO short, 1936)
Make Way for a Lady (RKO, 1936)
Charlie Chan at the Race Track (20th Century–Fox, 1936)
Let Them Live! (The Stones Cry Out) (Universal, 1937)
Saturday's Heroes (RKO, 1937)
Red Lights Ahead (Chesterfield, 1937)
Blazing Barriers (Monogram, 1937)
His Exciting Night (Adam's Evening) (Universal, 1938)
Service de Luxe (Universal, 1938)
Brother Rat (Warners, 1938)
Love Finds Andy Hardy (MGM, 1938)
Angels with Dirty Faces (Warners, 1938)
The Flying Irishman (RKO, 1939)
Scouts to the Rescue (Universal serial, 1939)
Second Fiddle (20th Century–Fox, 1939)
The Angels Wash Their Faces (Warners, 1939)
Off the Record (Warners, 1939)
Meet Dr. Christian (RKO, 1939)
It's a Wonderful World (MGM, 1939)

Dust Be My Destiny (Warners, 1939)
Two Bright Boys (Universal, 1939)
Ex-Champ (Universal, 1939)
Chicken Feed (RKO short, 1939)
Here I Am a Stranger (20th Century–Fox, 1939)
Andy Hardy Gets Spring Fever (MGM, 1939)
East Side of Heaven (Universal, 1939)
Boys' Reformatory (Monogram, 1939)
Day-Time Wife (20th Century–Fox, 1939)
Lucky Night (MGM, 1939)
Gone with the Wind (MGM, 1939)
Remedy for Riches (RKO, 1940)
Love Thy Neighbor (Paramount, 1940)
Yesterday's Heroes (20th Century–Fox, 1940)
Double Alibi (Universal, 1940)
The Fighting 69th (Warners, 1940)
Murder Over New York (20th Century–Fox, 1940)
Knute Rockne — All American (Warners, 1940)
Free, Blonde and 21 (20th Century–Fox, 1940)
Star Dust (20th Century–Fox, 1940)
Golden Gloves (Paramount, 1940)
Those Were the Days (Good Old Schooldays; At Good Old Siwash) (Paramount, 1940)
Men of Boys Town (MGM, 1941)
Adventures of Captain Marvel (Return of Captain Marvel) (Republic serial, 1941)
The Man Who Came to Dinner (Warners, 1941)
Glamour Boy (Paramount, 1941)
Henry Aldrich for President (Paramount, 1941)
Unfinished Business (Universal, 1941)
Out of the Fog (Warners, 1941)
To the Shores of Tripoli (20th Century–Fox, 1942)
Pardon My Stripes (Republic, 1942)
Footlight Serenade (20th Century–Fox, 1942)
Andy Hardy's Double Life (MGM, 1942)
The Court Martial (Army training film, 1942)
The Rear Gunner (Army training film, 1942)
Personal Placement in the Army (Army training film, 1942)
Lady in a Jam (Universal, 1942)
Wings for the Eagle (Warners, 1942)
Rings on Her Fingers (20th Century–Fox, 1942)
The Courtship of Andy Hardy (MGM, 1942)
Girl Trouble (20th Century–Fox, 1942)
Youth on Parade (Republic, 1942)
This Is the Army (Warners, 1943)
Follow the Band (Trombone from Heaven) (Universal, 1943)
Presenting Lily Mars (MGM, 1943)
Corvette K-225 (Universal, 1943)
One More Tomorrow (Warners, 1946)
The Sand Pebbles (20th Century–Fox, 1966)
Valley of the Dolls (20th Century–Fox, 1967)
The Love-Ins (Columbia, 1967)
Fitzwilly (United Artists, 1967)

The Shakiest Gun in the West (Universal, 1968)
The Love God? (Universal, 1969)

Coghlan is in a 1921 Universal short whose working title was *The Sin Buster* (the release title is unknown). He also appeared in industrial films and in a 1931 instructional golf short with amateur great Bobby Jones. A photo of Coghlan is seen in *White Gold* (Producers Distributing Corp., 1927).

*In [a science fiction] film, what's there to do?...
You're at the mercy of the "fright," the "horror," or whatever.
You're at the mercy of the special effects people,
'cause if they don't do a good job, then the
whole picture goes in the toilet.*

Mara Corday

IN THE EARLY to mid–1950s, Universal's bustling stable of stock players had starlets for every type of role, but few played the *variety* of roles tackled by Mara Corday: One might find her in a movie as an Indian squaw (*Raw Edge*) or a Middle Eastern maiden (*Yankee Pasha*), a flirty French gal (*So This Is Paris*) or a Western leading lady (*The Man from Bitter Ridge*).

The actress who looked right at home in the studio's back lot palaces *and* saloons — and who helped save the world from the mighty *Tarantula*— was born Marilyn Watts in Santa Monica 17 years before she put her foot on the bottom step of the show biz ladder, dancing in the back row of the chorus in "Earl Carroll's Revue" at the famed showman's theater-restaurant in Hollywood. Modeling for photographers led to wider exposure and ultimately to television roles and bit parts in low-budget movies. She was in every type of B picture that Universal made during her stint at that studio, then (as a freelancer) saved the world again, not only from *The Black Scorpion* but also from *The Giant Claw*. She gave up acting to concentrate on marriage and motherhood during her 17 tumultuous years as the wife of actor Richard Long (*77 Sunset Strip, The Big Valley*); since his 1974 death, she's been playing supporting roles in her friend Clint Eastwood's movies, just as *he* had played a tiny role in one of *hers* (*Tarantula*).

How early on did you know that you wanted to be in show business?

I think I've *always* wanted to be in show business, from the time when I was a child. My mother and I used to go to the beach, and in those days people would be playing ukuleles and dancing around and doing the hula; my mother tells me that when I was about three, I waddled up there and started doing the hula with everyone else! They all thought that was very cute. So my mother thought, "Oh, my God, this child has so much talent! I'm gonna get her in the Meglin Kiddies!" So she got me into [tryouts for] the Meglin Kiddies, which was a group of little kids dancing. I couldn't do back bends or anything like that, and I sort of rebelled against the conformity of it all. I went about three times and I wasn't getting it right, and my mother threw her hands up in disgust, she just gave up.

But I always *dreamed* of performing in some way, and I kept talking about it. Finally, when I was about fifteen, my girlfriend's mother was a wardrobe woman for the Shrine Auditorium [stage shows]. Her oldest girl, who was seventeen, and her other daughter, fifteen, who was *my* friend, they were going to go audition and try to be in the chorus. I said, "Well, I guess I'll go along, too." So we all tried, and of course I couldn't dance worth a damn. But they were *so-o-o* desperate for dancers — the film musicals were using all the good dancers. They had me do turns, and I didn't know how to "spot" in those days; and then they tried me on the toes, and I

Previous page: **Fifties starlet extraordinaire: The incomparable Mara Corday.**

thought my toes were gonna break. Finally, after everyone was picked, the director said, "Well, we can always make you a *statue*." [*Laughs.*] I was getting the same money, and all I did was stand over in a corner with Jan Peerce singing "Bluebird of Happiness" to me! And I *did* get into two numbers which were not that difficult. But the big numbers, I couldn't make it. (The resentment, you could cut it with a knife!) But that was my first deal, and they had guest stars every week — Red Skelton, Frank Sinatra, Jack Benny, Danny Kaye, all these big people.

My mother kept hearing me talk about, "I don't have to go to school because I'm gonna be a big star" and dah-dah-dah-dah. She finally saw this little article in the newspaper that said that Earl Carroll was looking for New Faces, and she said, "All right — you've got a face that might be new." [*Laughs.*] She told me, "You go over there and see what you can do, or you're going back to school and study stenography and learn typing, and stop this wishful thinking." So she and I *both* went over and we watched the first show, and then during intermission I went backstage and I got into this little skimpy outfit. Mr. Carroll came in with the dance director, he took one look and said, "You're in." I said, "*What?*" I couldn't believe it! I was seventeen, but to get the job I had to be eighteen. When they asked me for proof of my age, I told my mother, "My God, I'm not going to make it, Mother, because I'm only seventeen. What am I gonna do?" So *she* forged my birth certificate, made it one year older for me. (Oh, *my* mother used to be a bootlegger, *she* knows how to get through this life [*laughs*]!) So that's how I got in the show, and I was there two and a half years. I graduated from the production line of just the girls to being up front with the principal dancers. And I gradually got into doing the skits with the star, who was Pinky Lee. That was *real* fun 'cause then I had lines and did little shtick with him on stage. That's where I really got my thirst to continue.

And when did Marilyn Watts become Mara Corday?

When I went into Earl Carroll's. I thought "Marilyn Watts" did not suit an Earl Carroll girl — it was too plain. In those days the actresses had names like Lamarr and Lamour and DeCarlo, so I thought, "I'm gonna be something exotic." So I named myself Mara Corday, because when I had been an usher at a legitimate theater — the Mayan Theater — they had a show there called "A Night in Havana" starring the Lecuona Cuban Boys. I would be going backstage to deliver messages from time to time, and the bongo player used to call me Marita. Marita means "pretty little Mara" — I don't know where he picked up that name, Mara, but I thought, "*That's* an interesting name, it's different. I'm gonna name myself Mara." Corday I got from a perfume bottle.

Corday recoils from the hundred-foot-high co-star of one of her most popular pictures, Universal's *Tarantula*.

You also did lots of modeling early on, which helped your career get going.
    In the Earl Carroll days, I did *all* this publicity for the theater, and consequently I met tons of photographers. And they in turn told *other* photographers, and the next thing I knew, completely *away* from the theater, I was doing modeling for these photographers on my own. All these magazine covers started coming out, and articles about me, and I began getting a following, even in 1949 — that's when it started, from forty-seven to forty-nine, all this publicity.

How did you break into pictures?

A lot of the [Earl Carroll] girls moonlighted — they did the show, and then they did extra work in the daytime. Two of them did quite a bit of it, and they kept talking about being an extra. And I thought, "Gee, I think *I'll* try to get to be an extra." But before that happened, I got into this play on Highland, in a theater right across from Hollywood High School. The theater was called Charm Unlimited and they put on little plays and charged $8 to get in. The play was *The Time of Your Life* by William Saroyan, and Walter Kohner was in it as a *joke*—his older brother was Paul Kohner, who was one of the top agents out here, he had all the Hollywood *crème de la crème*. Paul Kohner came to see the show, to see his brother, and there I was — I played the part of Mary L. He came backstage and he said, "Would you be interested in signing with our agency?" And I was just *shocked*! I said, "My God, of *course!*" So I went over and I read something for him, and he said, "Okay, sign here." And then he began to represent me and I started doing television — little schlocky things like *Kit Carson* and *Craig Kennedy, Criminologist* and *Jeffrey Jones, Private Eye*. I don't know *who* today would remember any of them, they were like the worst of the worst.

What made them bad?

Oh, God, the acting — the people they hired were terrible. Well, for instance, *me* [*laughs*]! The star of one of 'em was Donald Woods, and he was right in the middle of a nervous breakdown. They had to cart him out one day and that killed the show, he wound up in a mental hospital somewhere!

Then one of my magazine pictures got seen by Hal Wallis, and he called my agent. I read for Hal Wallis a scene from *Gilda*, the Rita Hayworth picture, and *he* signed me to a contract. I was there only six months and all I did was a small part in *Money from Home* [1953] as a waitress, which they cut out. The movie was overlong and it was a silly scene with Jerry Lewis that meant nothing to the plot, so they just cut it out. Then before I could do anything else, Hal Wallis dissolved the company for tax reasons and he let [all his actors] go. He said, "I'm re-structuring, so hold tight," but my agent took that test I did from *Gilda* to Universal-International. I was a *little* hesitant [to sign with Universal] because I had the loyalty of being with Hal Wallis and I thought about the caliber of pictures he was hopefully going to do. But Universal could offer me that enormous program they had — you'd learn how to ride a horse, get diction lessons, get singing lessons, dance lessons, *all* that was there. And for the same amount of money. So I said, "I think we'll go for Universal."

Before Universal, in addition to your television work, you also worked in the occasional "small" movie.

Yes, like *Problem Girls* [1953], which I just saw again. It was done in a big mansion called the Brunswick Mansion on Adams Boulevard in L.A. Usually when you do a film, you go to a "pick-up" spot—there's a designated location, and a car comes by and picks everyone up and takes you to the actual location where you're going to shoot. That's for insurance reasons. To show you how skimpy the budget was on this thing, in *this* picture, everyone had to drive their own car, which is unheard of. No one does that, because of the insurance problem—and the Guild frowns on that, too. Unless you're the *star*, the Guild didn't allow that in those days. So I drove my own car there. It was the most horrible sound system and the lighting was just *atrocious*, because we were in a house, not in a real studio. And it was directed by a man [E.A. Dupont] who was like ninety years old. He had done a classic German picture called *Variety* [1925], he could *barely* speak English, and he was just hanging by a thread [*laughs*]! Helen Walker, the star of that film, had just gotten arrested for hit-and-run and it literally destroyed her career, because she *was* guilty, she was drunk—and she was drinking all through the picture, too. The director would yell up, "Quiet!", and she'd yell down, "*F* you!" [*Laughs.*] Oh, she hated him!

Then there's the scene they put on the poster, the shot of you strung up in the shower.

They did two versions of that, one with the bra on and another version that they *say* went to Europe. In that one, you don't see anything, but I had my bare back to the camera. I do not believe in frontal nudity, that's just the way I am. If you show that, what's left, what do you do for an encore? So my back was to the camera and I was in this little shower, and there was only enough room for the cameraman, the guy with the boom and another guy. They strung me up, and then this one girl came in and took my bra off. That was the European version.

And another pre–Universal credit, Tarzan and the She-Devil.

They were looking for a girl to play *Sheena, Queen of the Jungle* on television, and my agent had the ridiculous idea that I should apply for that role. I said, "I am not Sheena, Queen of the Jungle. She's an Amazon, she's a huge girl—*I'm* not that build." He said, "Mara, you're gonna go for it." So I went over and the producer said, "Look, why don't we try her out in a small role in *Tarzan and the She-Devil*? We can see how she photographs." So there I was, running through the jungle as this dumb little native. The only good thing that came out of that was that I fell in love with Lex Barker

[Tarzan] during that time and we went out twice. I thought, "This is magic," and then the next thing I knew, he dumped me. I couldn't go to some party with him because I was sick that night, so he took Susan Morrow (who, by the way, was in *Problem Girls*). Well, I'm so glad I wasn't there because — how humiliating for poor Susan! — Lex spotted Lana Turner, and that was the end of anyone else. I didn't see him again until I was under contract to Universal and they put me in *The Man from Bitter Ridge* [1955], and they said, "Your leading man will be Lex Barker." I went, "Oh, my God!" [*laughs*] — and we resumed our romance during that film.

Did you like the "buildup" you got at Universal?
    Well, it wasn't like a progression from bit parts to leads. One of the first things I did was *Drums Across the River* [1954] where I played the girlfriend of Lyle Bettger — he was the main heavy and I was a heavy, too. That starred Audie Murphy. I thought, "Oh, wow, this is good. I'm going right in, I'm not doing bits." Then they'd hand me something like *Yankee Pasha* [1954] where I have half a line: "It is said in the halls of the Caliph's palace..." and I whispered the rest into some girl's ear. That was it [*laughs*] — good God! I didn't think I was *that* bad in *Drums Across the River*! And then I did this dumb thing in *Francis Joins the Wacs* [1954] where I had two lines, then another *good* part — it went up and down until *Foxfire* [1955], which was sort of the breakthrough. But that was a nightmare because the director [Joseph Pevney] did *not* want me, he did not want *any* contract player, he wanted Linda Christian. There was a big article in the newspaper that she was going to play this role, so I didn't think I had a prayer of getting it. Also, Allison Hayes, my dear, dear friend, was up for it. But I got it — the studio picked *me* to groom, for some reason. Actually, *I* think the reason was all these magazine covers — it all kicked in. My God, I was getting more publicity than anyone under contract! So I think that helped, I think they said, "Okay, let's push this kid here."

I wanted to ask you about Allison Hayes, and also about two other Universal contract players that have passed on, Mari Blanchard and Susan Cabot.
    Oh, I adored Allison, she and I were very dear friends. I didn't make many friends over there, but Allison did become a friend for some reason, I don't know why. I guess because she was so *genuine*, she had not a jealous bone in her body. She was a giving person. But she wasn't used nearly enough by Universal, she was one of the ones they cast aside, they never really pushed her over there. Very statuesque, beautiful face — but they didn't push her. She didn't get any real credit until after she *left* Universal.

We lost touch because I got married, but we'd run into each other at different places and throw our arms around each other and all that. But once I got married, I just sort of put blinders on and concentrated on my children; that was the most important thing in my life, my family.

Mari Blanchard, oh, my God, I loved Mari. I always thought Mari had the greatest walk—she'd swing those hips back and forth...! She didn't get too friendly with people, but I'm happy to say that I got to see her just before she died. She'd married a fellow named Vince, and my husband and I ran into them at an Italian restaurant—they weren't seated yet, so we told them to come and join us. She told me that she had bought an apartment building, and to come down and see her one day. I never did; and then she got very ill with cancer and died at the Motion Picture Home. She was a very sweet girl.

Susan Cabot? Well, Susan was very *weird*, a strange little girl. She had this enormous head and then this little tiny body, and she was *paranoid*. I remember, I was going to go to lunch with her in the commissary, and she fussed and fussed and *fussed* over the tiniest little thing: At that particular time, women were wearing scarves around the neck, like a cowboy would wear, and she was fussing about one of those damn things! I said, "Look, lunch hour's gonna be over before we get there!" and finally I just left her fussing around with the scarf, I just *left*! She finally joined me later. Interestingly enough, Tony Curtis came up to me after that and he said, "You know, Mara, you'd really do yourself a favor if you wouldn't hang out with the other contract players. *That* lumps you in with *them*." That was a very good clue that he gave me, he said, "Make yourself a loner, at least during the lunch hour. You'll find that it'll be much more beneficial to your career." Maybe that helped, I don't know, but I took his advice, and never hung out with the rest of the contract players at lunch.

What was the best picture you did at Universal?
So This Is Paris [1954]—I thought I looked extremely well in that one, and I thought I was a pretty authentic-sounding French girl. Universal liked it so much that they sent me on tour, which is *really* the big push. You get the mink coats—*loaned* [laughs]—and a nice wardrobe, and you go to all these different cities and do all these different things. Then when I came back, then, lo and behold, I got the lead opposite Lex Barker in *The Man from Bitter Ridge*. That was my first leading lady role.

In my opinion, your best movie was A Day of Fury *[1956].*
Oh, I *hated* me in that, I thought I was so wooden.

I meant from a standpoint of being a sizable, challenging role.

I don't think it was as challenging as *Girls on the Loose* [1958] — I had more range there, playing sweet, then angry. I *don't* smoke, and that also was a challenge [*laughs*]. Paul Henreid, the director on *Girls on the Loose*, was *obsessed* with cigarettes. It gave such an impact to that one scene he had with Bette Davis in *Now, Voyager* [1942] where he put the two cigarettes in his mouth; he said, "Mara, it'll enhance *everything* if you do what I tell you. Just pick up a cigarette, put the cigarette out — it just gives it *so much more!*" So that's what I had to do, I had to fake holding it in my mouth 'cause I *can't* inhale — oh, I'd die if I had to inhale! So that was *another* challenge for me in that picture.

How did you get involved with Tarantula?

Well, they'd just *tell* you — "Look, your next picture is going to be *Tarantula*." And I said, "That's fine with me," because it was Jack Arnold again [Arnold directed *The Man from Bitter Ridge*] and I got along great with Jack. He was a prankster, and I happen to like a very fun set, I like to tell jokes and kid around and that's what he did. It was fine, except I didn't like the wardrobe, I thought it was *really* conservative. I thought maybe I could at least wear a negligee for the ending — the whole last part of that show was me running away from this tarantula in a night outfit. But they said, "Oh, no, not on your life" — I had to wear pajamas, and even a light cover over *that*! So there was no sex appeal there [*laughs*]!

In what way was Jack Arnold a prankster?

Oh, he would tell dirty jokes, and then all of a sudden he'd break into a little dance. He used to be a chorus boy in New York, a little dancer, so he'd do steps. He'd fix your chair so that when you sat on it, you'd almost fall, things like that.

Was he a good director?

He was not the kind of director that gives you a lot, but then, in this kind of a film, what's there to do? There's not much plot. You're at the mercy of the "fright," the "horror," or whatever. You're at the mercy of the special effects people [*laughs*], 'cause if they don't do a good job, then the whole picture goes in the toilet. For instance, *The Giant Claw!*

Where were the different places you shot Tarantula?

The desert scenes were shot in Apple Valley. I had a space between two of my front teeth for many years, like Lauren Hutton has, although mine

Corday and Jeff Morrow were even *more* horrified when they saw *The Giant Claw*'s completed special effects.

wasn't *that* big. But it was enough that I was concerned about it. Up to that point, the studio didn't even know about it 'cause I wore a little veneer that a dentist had made for me, that I stuck up there. The studio finally realized it and took me to an orthodontist, and he said, "I can bring your teeth together in six months, as long as you don't keep putting that damn veneer up there"—the veneer kept the space open. He gave me a retainer to wear when I wasn't working, and when I did work, he gave me some wax to melt down and stick in the space. So that's what I did and it worked great—*until* we hit Apple Valley, which was 120 degrees! I would be standing there talking and then my teeth would melt [*laughs*]! We could barely get any of these shots, especially the ones where John Agar and I are standing by the rocks. That's when it fell out, and I had to keep getting my little Sterno going to melt more wax! One hundred twenty degrees, it was awful — when I wasn't working, I was in a bathing suit.

Was that a one-day location trek, those desert scenes?

No, we were there like four days. We stayed at a lovely lodge there, and swam in the pool at night. It was wonderful. The house in the movie [known at Universal as "the Dabney Home"] is way up on a hill on the Universal back lot; it was used originally in *Tap Roots* [1948], which Richard Long was in. They built it for that and they used it for a lot of things. The interiors were shot on sound stages. The desert town was on the back lot, too.

Them! *was a big hit the year before. Did everybody feel as they were making* Tarantula, *"We're doing this because* Them! *was a big hit"?*

I can't speak for anyone else, but I wouldn't be at all surprised if that was the general attitude. Instead of *many* monsters [the ants], they just singled out *one* [the tarantula].

What was your attitude about appearing in a science fiction movie?

I had no opinion at all. Actually, I was hoping that I could get something that had some real depth to it, like an intimate story, a love story, a human interest story — even a murder mystery would have been nice. But Universal just wasn't doing that kind of thing.

Especially not down on the B-budget level where you were working.

That's right. And when Universal did do something of merit, they got a big star like Jane Wyman (who did *Magnificent Obsession*), not people like me, and not even people who had been there longer than I had. Like Barbara Rush and Julie Adams weren't really given that many good roles.

By the way, I remember all the hubbub around the studio, how *surprised* they were that Julie Adams had a gorgeous figure, when she did *Creature from the Black Lagoon*. I couldn't *believe* it — all you had to do was look at her to know *that!* But they had her covered up so much of the time [in movies]. So this time she got to show her figure and it was just terrific. That's another example of what I was saying before, that they really didn't know what the hell to do with most of their people. They completely wasted Clint Eastwood and David Janssen and Allison Hayes.

What memories of John Agar?

Poor John, he was just coming out of ... a *slump*. He was like a brother to me, he was very quiet, very respectful, but he couldn't drink, you could *not* give this man a drink of alcohol. He'd *turn* into ... something else. Luckily, I did not see that (except, maybe once), because he was straight-arrow on that set, he did a fine little job for us and we got along great.

The "maybe once" you mentioned didn't *happen on* Tarantula?

That's right. By the way, the one scene I thought was disgusting in *Tarantula* was when John climbs the hill and sees a pool of "residue" that the insect left behind, and he dips his finger in and *tastes* it [*laughs*]! When I saw it with an audience, they all went *eeeewwww*!

Leo G. Carroll?

Very dignified little Englishman — I had lunch with him once. He had a terrible time with that makeup; he had to have everything sipped through a straw 'cause it was like a mask that he had to wear. It took forever to get it on, so you don't take that off for lunch [*laughs*]! It was sort of like what Roddy McDowall told me he had to do during *Planet of the Apes*. I thought Leo G. Carroll's makeup was effective — although I don't know what "acromegalia" really *looks* like [*laughs*]! Thank God I don't, I don't *want* to know!

Did you ever "meet" the spider?

They had the big spider leg [prop], covered with hair, which came down after me when the tarantula attacked the house. And then I did see the cameramen working with various tarantulas, filming them climb over little balls of cotton. They climbed over the cotton and then the special effects people could integrate that footage into the movie so that it looked like the spider was climbing a hill. They said, "Oh, you wanna touch one?" I said, "Not on your *life*!" [*Laughs.*] Also, there's a lab scene in the picture, and in a "hand insert," they wanted me to pick up a mouse or a rat or something. I couldn't do it, my stand-in did that.

Did you like the producer, William Alland?

William Alland was very dear. And it was not until *years* later, when I saw *Citizen Kane* [1941], in which he acted, that I realized that *that* was the same William Alland! I didn't *know* that, I would have had much more respect for him, because I thought he was very good in *Citizen Kane* — even though you didn't really see him, he was always like a silhouette. He was very dear to me, he wanted my autographed picture — it was a big 11×14 that he had in his office, a picture of me in a negligee by a waterfall. I was very flattered that he wanted that.

What about Clint Eastwood, who was just starting in pictures then?
Well, Clint is my "brother," I adore Clint Eastwood. Next to Roddy McDowall, I think he's the most loyal human being in this business. He's just a love and he's got this lovely, sardonic, wry humor. I love him as a director — he's so easy, it's like *play*, it's not like work at all.

Did you think your "undressing-in-front-of-the-spider" scene was effective?
I thought so, yeah! I thought the *picture* was very good, for what it was — very, very good — and I'm very proud to be in it, to tell you the truth. Shortly after it was released, I ran into my agent and he said, "My God, Mara, it's number one in France"—I couldn't believe it, I was *thrilled*.

Using cheesecake as a springboard — any regrets, looking back at that?
Oh, no — that was probably the launching pad for me. But Universal certainly didn't utilize any of that at all; in fact, in the films that they put me in, I was all covered up. They even had like a little netting over my cleavage in *Day of Fury*, which I thought was ridiculous. They always brushed out [of photographs] this mole I have between my cleavage, 'cause it would draw attention. Ridiculous! I did do a lot of cheesecake there, anyway [in photo sessions], but they never let me *portray* anything sexy in their movies. I was an Indian or a scientist or a Western girl; they gave all the sexy roles to Mamie Van Doren, she was a little *vamp*.

When and why did you leave Universal?
It all started with *The Incredible Shrinking Man*. They wanted me to play the wife, and by that point I was fed up to my eyeballs with screaming and Indians. I thought, "When is my break going to happen? When am I going to be offered something with some more substance?" The title was *The Incredible Shrinking **Man*** and it was all Grant Williams, all the way through it. The role of the wife was a thankless role. I told my agent, "There is no way I am going to do this. I don't care if they suspend me or *what* the hell happens." So [producer] Al Zugsmith approached me—he took it *very* personally. He said, "One day you are going to get down on your knees and wish to *God* that you had done this film. This is going to be an enormous breakthrough." I said, "Sure, sure." Well, maybe he was right [*laughs*]—it would have been nice to have been associated with it, because it *was* another classic.

But you were right about it not doing anything career-wise for the girl who played the wife.

No, it did nothing for Randy [Stuart], nothing at all. Then after that, they gave me *The Deadly Mantis*—which is *Tarantula*, only it's in New York, it's in the Holland Tunnel. I had nine changes [of wardrobe]. I liked *that* part of it, I got *that* done. Then I went across the street to a bar with my best friend, who was David Janssen, and I said, "David, what am I doing? I cannot do this movie. This is ridiculous!" So I sat there and I took the script and I started tearing out the pages. And we started making little airplanes of them, and we were flying the pages all over the bar. And it got back to the studio that Mara was over there, getting drunk, with David Janssen, and she's making paper airplanes out of the script of *The Deadly Mantis* [*laughs*]! They were just horrified! Then they sent me to Palm Springs to do a layout with George Nader, 'cause we were supposed to be an "item." (Of course, we *all* were supposed to be "items" with George, but he was actually homosexual with Rock!) Anyway, we were there at the racquet club, and I'd cut my hair (as another show of defiance). We came back and my agent said, "Guess what? They have just informed me that they are dropping you, and I think it's because of your behavior about this *Deadly Mantis*." But they just wanted me to feel guilty—I *later* found out that they were dumping *every*one. The whole policy had changed, the development program was all over with and they were only going to keep Audie Murphy, Rock Hudson and maybe Tony [Curtis]. MCA was in the process of buying the thing and everyone was *out*, even Ed Muhl, the guy who ran the studio. So I didn't feel too bad, 'cause I went out with everyone. That was that. And I didn't do *Deadly Mantis* [*laughs*]!

That's fine—except you did *do* The Black Scorpion!

I didn't think *that* was that bad—did *you* think that it was?

It's so-o-o long and dragged out.

It *is* anticlimactic—once they get rid of the scorpions in the cave, you think, "Well, that's the end of the film." And then I'll be damned if they don't come *back*! It was ridiculous!

Was that your first movie after leaving Universal?

No, the very first one after Universal was a *horrible* thing called *The Naked Gun* [1956]. I knew it was going to be atrocious when the producer said to me, "Do you wanna be the ingenue or the heavy?" Then I *knew* I was in trouble! I felt like saying, "Why don't you offer me the leading man, too?" Good Lord [*laughs*]! *The Naked Gun* was made in five days—swear to God!—and it had three different titles. It started out as *The Saracen Treasure*—that's the script I got. Then as we're shooting it, like the third day, it became *The Hanging Judge* and the whole focus of the movie became the judge. And by the time it finished, it turned out to be *The Naked Gun*. Incredible!

As for *The Black Scorpion*, I think my agent just called me and told me to go on this interview, and I went. I was going with Richard Long at that time, and we'd sort of talked it out and thought it would be great if he could play the lead in it and I could be the girl, and we could have a wonderful time in Mexico. So I mentioned it when I went in to read, I told 'em, "I think Richard Long would be great for this role." And they said, "Oh, no, he's way too young-looking." I couldn't believe it, it made *me* feel like I was an old bag *then*. So they got Richard Denning, who of course was older than Richard Long. And I remember marveling at Denning at the makeup table. This guy did his own makeup, and by the time he got through, he looked *gorgeous*.

But I'll tell you one thing that I was *horrified* about, and quite miffed: There was an interview with Richard Denning in a magazine called *Starlog*, and he had the nerve to say that I was *coming on to him* during the filming of that film. Well, anyone that knows me and knows the way I am will know that that was not my style even if I was attracted to him, which I was *not*, in that way. I had only great respect for him *and* his wife [Evelyn Ankers] who finally did come down there—*gorgeous* woman. In fact, Richard Long came down and he proposed to me there—that was when we became engaged. We were all at dinner one night [Corday, Long and the Dennings] and I told them that we were engaged, and I even remember saying, "I just hope to God that our marriage is as beautiful as yours." And now I read that this guy [Denning] says that I was coming on to him, even though my boyfriend was there! The whole thing is so outlandish, it makes no sense—how could that be even *thought*? I can't quite understand what his motive was there!

His Starlog *comments aside, what did you think of Denning?*

I *adored* him, I thought he was a fun guy, wonderful and professional and easy to work with. I have no hint why he said what he did. I think we had one love scene, and even then it was just a little quick kiss.

Where did you stay in Mexico?

We stayed in a beautiful place—which reminds me that, in that interview, Denning said that the accommodations were horrible and that he got sick. Well, he *did* get sick, because he wouldn't listen. My stand-in said, "Don't eat anything unless you put lemon on it"—you had to squeeze lemon over everything and you could not drink the water. Well, I don't think he listened, and I think that's how he got so sick. We stayed at the most beautiful hotel, a very intimate place called the Bamer in Mexico City. Also there were Anthony Quinn and Ray Milland and Debra Paget, who were also doing a film in Mexico [*The River's Edge*, 1957]. That was fun—we'd all be at the elevators in the morning, waiting for our different cars.

Denning complained about the primitive conditions that the movie was shot under.
There were maybe two or three days that we had to shoot near the volcano, and they had this outhouse kind of a thing. I made sure that I never did any serious numbers in *that* thing [*laughs*]—are you kidding? I'd rather go in the *volcano*! But *Denning* was in there, so that's probably what he meant by "primitive."

The hacienda in the movie—was that a sound stage, or somebody's hacienda?
My God, that was the actual, gorgeous home of Cortés, the man who conquered Mexico—that's where he stayed, that's how *old* that thing was! They showed me his bathtub; the swimming pool had these gorgeous gargoyles—it was very ornate, early, early, *early* Mexican, or Aztec, or whatever the hell it was. The only problem was, it was so cold, and there was no hot water. So every morning I had to shower in cold water. I had to bite my lip and jump in! That was the worst part of it.

What about the Black Scorpion *director, Edward Ludwig?*
He was from the old school of screaming, so the Mexican people did not like him at all. They sabotaged some of the equipment and we had a little bit of tough times there. And I didn't get along with him too well, either. I can't stand people who make it tough on the set. *I* like to joke and make it loose. We're not doing *Gone with the Wind*—I mean, if we can't have a few laughs...! He got mad at me because I would not go right to my dressing room after the scene, like the old stars did. He said, "You go right to your dressing room. You don't stand around and crack jokes with the cameramen and the grips. You're the star, you go to your dressing room!" I said, "Please don't tell me how I'm going to behave. I'm not going to do that. *That's* none of your business. Once you say *cut*, that's it!" I didn't like that one bit.

The producers, Jack Dietz and Frank Melford?
There was a *rumor* around that one of them might have something to do with "the boys" [the mob]. I don't know if it was true or not, but that's what everyone was saying.

You were down there in Mexico over the holidays.
We were there *nine weeks*. And it was possibly the most wonderful New Year's I'd ever had in my life. We formed a chain in the restaurant and we all did the conga, *al-l-l* over, up and down the steps and all around. It was incredible, just the most fun! Our cameraman, by the way, was Lionel Lindon, who won an Academy Award later for *Around the World in 80 Days* [1956]; he was there with his wife.

He went back and forth between top pictures and "nothing" pictures.
And then television! We caught him on the downslide, he wasn't doing well at all. He was a *very quiet* man, barely opened his mouth. He had about three expressions and that was it. He was a very troubled man, I think.

Was Black Scorpion *as good as* Tarantula?
No, not really. It did go too long. But I think [the special effects team] did a good job on the scorpions.

Some of the newspapers reported that you married Richard Long in Mexico around Christmas of 1956, others said it was in Las Vegas in January '57.
January 27, 1957, in Las Vegas. Mexico was where he proposed to me.

Without wishing to open any old wounds, what can you tell me about The Giant Claw?
When I went in to meet Mr. [Sam] Katzman, who was the producer, he was *raving* on and on about the wonderful special effects people in Mexico that he had hired. "Boy, this is gonna be something! I'm spending most of the budget on the special effects!" So when we made the movie and we were supposedly looking at the giant bird, I was envisioning something really horrifying. And when I saw the movie, I couldn't believe it! It was incredible!

I was pregnant during the film with my first child. They didn't know that, and I didn't *want* 'em to know. If they knew, they might not want me in the film [for insurance purposes]. The first day, they asked Jeff Morrow and me to fall in one scene — it was a scene where the plane explodes, and they threw all this fiery debris at us. I protected my stomach as best I could, and interestingly enough, the first assistant on that picture Lenny Katzman (Sam's nephew) came up to me and said, "Are you pregnant?" I said [*defensively*], "*Why* are you saying that? Do I look pregnant?" "No, but you favor your stomach a lot." He had figured it out!

Was that first meeting with Sam Katzman your only encounter with him?

No, I saw him again the first day at Griffith Park, the day when we did that falling scene. He came out and I was getting a cup of coffee, and he said, "You look like hell. Don't you go to bed at night?" I apologized; I felt horrible, because my *dear* husband had given a party the night before, when I was trying to learn these lines. And so I had to go to my mother's house with my tape recorder to learn the lines. Every time I did work, Richard saw to it that I would not be able to do my best. He did some kind of sabotage to me, every time. So when I did come back from my mother's, the party was in full swing and they kept me up the whole night with the loud noise. It was a nightmare.

He did all this to be "funny" or to be mean?

No, he did it to ruin me. He didn't want me working. He made that very obvious.

Fred F. Sears, the director of Giant Claw?

Fred was a very nervous man, I felt, a man without any sense of humor whatsoever. Just very *frightened*—not loose at all. Uptight. Of course, Jeff Morrow was very uptight, too. He treated that film like we were doing Shakespeare or something. He was a very serious man. *The Giant Claw* was all done at one studio—it was called the Columbia Annex, a little studio right near where Monogram used to be. I think it was made in about nine days.

Where did you see the movie for the first time?

Seems to me I saw it in a theater with Richard, and I slunk down in the seat. I said, "Oh, my God, isn't this dreadful!" Then I started to think, "Maybe Richard's right, I'd *better* get out of the business, if *this* is what I'm gonna be doing!" He thought it was dreadful, too.

After you stopped making fifties movies, you stayed with television?

Yes, I did quite a few things: I did *Wanted: Dead or Alive* with Steve [McQueen] and I did a thing called *Restless Gun* starring John Payne. I did *Laramie* with Bob Fuller and John Smith, *Peter Gunn* (my third time working with Jack Arnold), [*Tales of*] *Wells Fargo* with Dale Robertson again, *SurfSide 6* with Lee Patterson, and a thing called *Man from Blackhawk* that was a blink — it lasted maybe six segments. *Adventures in Paradise* was the last thing I did.

So to keep peace in the family, or as much peace as you could keep in that particular family, you just gave up on the acting?

I did, because it was just getting too much. I will say this, that during the filming of *SurfSide 6*, I knew Richard was miserable with me working. At the end of the filming, we were all going to go to the Smoke House to have a drink because it was "in the can," it was over. The director was Michael O'Herlihy and it was his first directing [job] — he's the brother of Dan O'Herlihy. He and the cutter and the cameraman and I were going to go to the Smoke House. Richard came on the set — he was under contract at that time to Warner Bros., so he could come and go wherever he wanted. We were not really speaking too much, because he didn't even want me to do the show. But, in a weak moment, I said, "Well, Richard, why don't you join us?" He said okay.

We went over, we all ordered martinis, and we were naturally talking about the film and what had transpired, and laughing. Meanwhile, Richard had already had three drinks to our *one*. We had been there about thirty-five, forty minutes when he stood up after belting these drinks down and he announced that he's drunk and he's going home and am I coming with him? I said, no, I'm not going right now, I'm still sipping on my drink and I'm enjoying the time, and if he wanted to go, go ahead, I'd see him at the house.

That humiliated him, so when I finally did show up, two hours later, I was greeted by this madman who grabbed my throat, threw me on the couch, and was strangling me. A cowboy bandleader named Spade Cooley had just killed his wife by strangling her, and that's all I could envision: That I would be dead. So I brought my knees up and kicked him right in the crotch ... grabbed my keys ... and ran out. Went to my mother and father's house, about fifteen minutes from my house. They weren't home, so I fell asleep in the car. Anyway, to make a long story short, I tried to get back in the house and he wouldn't let me, so I called the police and had him arrested. The police asked him, "Did you try to kill your wife?" and he said, "*Yes* and I'd do it again, the dirty *bitch*." So the handcuffs behind the back and off he went to jail. And it got in the papers and it was a terrible thing, but I was glad I did it because, I'm telling you, if you don't get them arrested, you could be dead. (I'm thinking of O.J. now, you know.) And he never struck me again after that.

And then he passed away in the mid-seventies.

He died December 21, 1974, at Tarzana Hospital, at twenty minutes of two. Just before the bars closed.

Were things better toward the end between the two of you?
Oh, yeah. I was retired and I just let him do what he wanted to do. He was dying, and there was nothing I could do about it. You can't say much when a man is dying. If he doesn't want to come home at night ... well, that's that.

After that, you started acting again in Clint Eastwood's movies.
I did a *Joe Forrester*, which was a television show with Lloyd Bridges — that was the very first thing I did when I was trying to make some kind of a comeback. I couldn't get an agent — they didn't want to know me, I guess. I did *Joe Forrester* only because of friends. Then the next thing I knew, Clint called me out of the blue to play in *The Outlaw Josey Wales* [1976]. But when I went in to see him, he said he'd had a change of heart; he said, "No, I don't think you're right for it." It was a blowsy old whore and I said, "*Thank* you, Clint! [*Laughs.*] I haven't reached that point yet!" Later he called me in to do *The Gauntlet* [1977]. He wanted me to play the waitress and I said sure, but I added, "You know what, Clint? I envision that this waitress should be a real *character*. Somebody like Carole Cook. Or somebody with a Jewish accent. Nita Talbot would be great." He said, "Why don't *you* do that?" I said, "I just can't, I'm not really up to that kind of a thing. But I'll *take* it." He said okay. So I drove home, and by the time I walked in the door the phone was ringing and Clint said, "Mara, I'm taking your advice. I agree with you. It *should* be more of a way-out character." I said, "I'm gonna keep my mouth shut [from now on]!" He said, "Don't worry, there's something else here for you. You'll have the same amount of days, four days in Vegas, and you're the matron of the jail." I said, "I'm not sayin' a word!" [*laughs*], and that was it. And he's been keeping me busy enough: *The Gauntlet*, *Sudden Impact* [1983], *Pink Cadillac* [1989] and *The Rookie* [1990], where I'm all in shadow in a dream sequence with Charlie Sheen.

Are you aware that you have a lot of fans?
Well, I'm beginning to realize that.

Do you want to work more than you do?
Oh, yeah. I enjoy acting, but it's not like it used to be. I sort of enjoy being semi-retired and just maybe working *behind* the camera now, because I've gotten myself involved with my oldest son — he's trying to put together a *Big Valley* reunion show. He wrote a treatment and I've helped him with

that, and it looks like there's going to be interest with Brandon Tartikoff at NBC. I spoke to Linda Evans and she's all gung ho to do it, and Lee Majors, also. I'm sort of involved in that, and I've also written a story about Richard and his first wife, which is a bittersweet love story. Her name was Suzan Ball, and she was Lucille Ball's first cousin.

I've done the other [acting], and now I think producing and writing would be interesting for me. And maybe I could also act in these pictures — and maybe not just a few lines here and there!

MARA CORDAY FILMOGRAPHY

Two Tickets to Braodway (RKO, 1951)
Sea Tiger (Monogram, 1952)
Toughest Man in Arizona (Republic, 1952)
Son of Ali Baba (Universal, 1952)
Problem Girls (Columbia, 1953)
The Lady Wants Mink (Republic, 1953)
Tarzan and the She-Devil (RKO, 1953)
Sweethearts on Parade (Republic, 1953)
Drums Across the River (Universal, 1954)
Yankee Pasha (Universal, 1954)
Playgirl (Universal, 1954)
Francis Joins the WACs (Universal, 1954)
Dawn at Socorro (Universal, 1954)
So This Is Paris (Universal, 1954)
Man Without a Star (Universal, 1955)
The Man from Bitter Ridge (Universal, 1955)
Foxfire (Universal, 1955)
Tarantula (Universal, 1955)
A Day of Fury (Universal, 1956)
Raw Edge (Universal, 1956)
The Naked Gun (Associated Film Releasing Corp., 1956)
The Black Scorpion (Warners, 1957)
The Quiet Gun (20th Century–Fox, 1957)
The Giant Claw (Columbia, 1957)
Undersea Girl (Allied Artists, 1957)
Girls on the Loose (Universal, 1958)
The Gauntlet (Warner Bros., 1977)
Sudden Impact (Warner Bros., 1983)
Pink Cadillac (Warner Bros., 1989)
The Rookie (Warner Bros., 1990)

Corday's scene was cut out of *Money from Home* (Paramount, 1953). Some sources erroneously credit her with an appearance in *The Caddy* (Paramount, 1953).

I think that the people who write these [science fiction] movies were more talented than some people would like to admit. ...I didn't get to do many of them, but I sort of wish now that I had done more.

Kathleen Crowley

THERE ARE OTHER LEADING LADIES from the 1950s who have longer lists of science fiction and horror credits, but few with the sort of acting credentials which Kathleen Crowley brought to her movies — and still fewer with the added distinction of having been a Miss America finalist. She represented her home state of New Jersey in the Atlantic City pageant, placed sixth and, with the scholarship money she won, enrolled at the American Academy of Dramatic Art in New York. Crowley played the plum title roles in well-publicized television of *A Star Is Born* and *Jane Eyre*, caught the eye of Hollywood, and became a 20th Century–Fox contractee in 1952. A freelancer after leaving the studio, she was in the forefront of the fight against outer space menaces in *Target Earth* and *The Flame Barrier*, and risked her neck in a different sort of way in the vampire Western *Curse of the Undead*. In her acting heyday she was known for the "unusual intensity" with which she "lived" every part (including the science fiction and horror roles), and she remembers them today with equal seriousness — and fondness.

How early on did you know you wanted to be an actress?
I think from the time I was ten years old, it was going around in my head. I grew up with a good family in a good home, but never would my father have thought of allowing me to leave to do anything like that! I was the only little girl in the neighborhood and I didn't have dolls, I climbed trees and walked in the woods and did things like that — I had a lot of time to *imagine* things. I had quite an imagination because of being a bit of a loner as a child.

I was in the Miss America pageant, and there had never ever been a pageant with a South Jersey girl entering. I got involved [in beauty contests] because Bess Myerson had won a $5000 scholarship when she became Miss America in 1945. I had listened to that on the radio, and said to myself, "Maybe *that's* my way out of here — being in a pageant and winning a scholarship." That way I could go away and study acting. When they finally got a little local pageant together, my father would not allow me to enter; no daughter of *his* was ever going to parade up and down in a convention hall in a bathing suit. (He had to be *tricked* into allowing me to enter!) It happened and I won and I went on to the state contest, and I was the first South Jersey girl ever to win. Then I went into the Miss America pageant, only having to travel 26 miles [to Atlantic City]. I was a finalist and I won my scholarship. I went to New York and studied at the American Academy of Dramatic Art, and that very year I went to Kennebunkport, Maine, to

Previous page: "At first, I wanted to stay away from [science fiction movies] like the plague — isn't that awful?" (Kathleen Crowley portrait from *Curse of the Undead*.)

Fledgling producer Herman Cohen poses with Crowley between takes on *Target Earth*.

do my first year of stock. At night, I was their ingenue, and in the daytime I was scrubbing toilets [*laughs*]!

That fall, I went back to New York and Robert Montgomery was looking for a lead (he'd been looking for about six months) for his production of *A Star Is Born* [on television's *Robert Montgomery Presents*, 2/13/51]. I was interviewed by him and they chose me to play the lead, Esther Blodgett. It was live, shot with three cameras, out at NBC, Studio 8H, the same studio where Toscanini used to direct all of his symphonies. I was on the cover of *Cue* magazine and there was a spread on me in *Life*—it was a great beginning. These were the days of live television from New York; there was *Kraft Television Theatre* where I did *Jane Eyre* [2/28/51] with John Baragrey as Rochester, all very important things. So I never even went back to the Academy to get my diploma [*laughs*]! I started to work with Lee Strasberg at the Actors Studio, and somehow my work was being noticed by Hollywood— they have their scouts. I was offered movie contracts by Universal, Warners and Fox, and I just didn't want to go. My dream was to be a stage actress, and I wanted to join the Abbey Players in Ireland. I talked with Lee Strasberg about it and he said it would be tough. I wrote to a couple of playwrights there and they gave me some very discouraging replies—"If you don't know Gaelic, stay the hell out of our country!" [*Laughs.*] But I really wanted to do it, I wasn't out for the money. These Hollywood contracts kept coming to me, and my father had a stroke, and I decided that, instead of eating bouillon cubes and being so idealistic, I would go to Hollywood. I remember Lee said, "You won't get lost because you know how to think and you know how to work."

What was your first movie?
    I left in May of 1952 and went under contract at 20th Century–Fox and they put me in a movie immediately, *The Farmer Takes a Wife* [1953] with Dale Robertson and Betty Grable—just a little tiny part. Then they put me with Robert Wagner and Dale and Rory Calhoun in *The Silver Whip* [1953]—that was my first lead. *Photoplay* magazine called me one of the most promising newcomers of the year, fifty-three or fifty-four, something like that. The other one to receive that award was Merv Griffin [*laughs*]! Then CinemaScope came in, and Fox let everyone go that year. One Friday afternoon, they started giving out pink slips—people who'd been there eighteen and twenty years got them. I had just been put under contract, and now here they were closing down! My timing couldn't have been worse; after about a year there, I got my walking papers. So I started to freelance. It was a decision for me to stay there [in Hollywood] and learn my craft as a screen actor.

And that's when you started doing the occasional science fiction movie, beginning with Target Earth.
    At first, I wanted to stay away from those things like the plague—isn't that awful? I tried to stay away from the B movies. I didn't want to be the B queen, because I'd started out on such a high plain. I didn't *have* to do

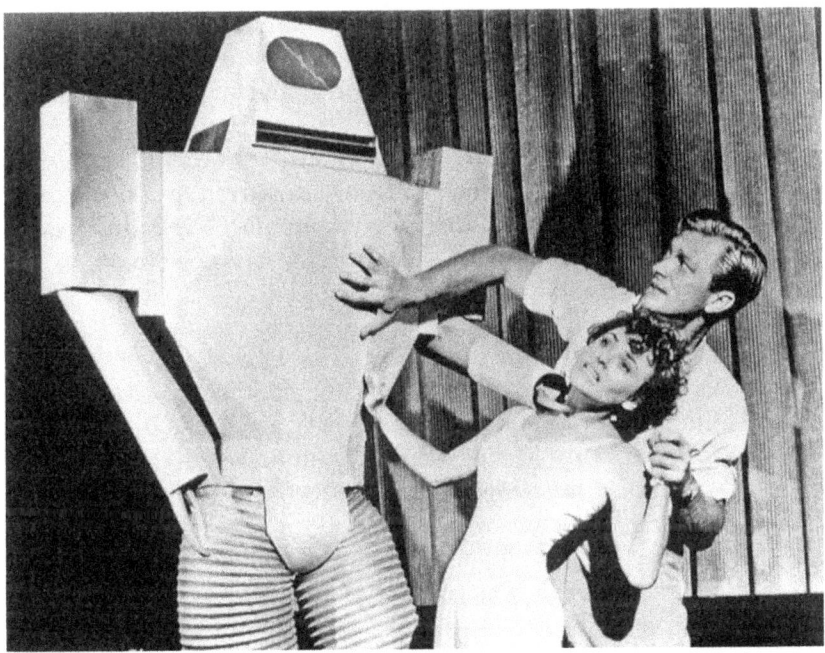

"The more I think about [*Target Earth*], the more I love it!" Crowley insists. (Pictured: Steve Calvert [robot], Crowley, Richard Denning.)

them. From my 20th Century–Fox contract, I went into this little series with Preston Foster called *Waterfront*, and so I was *always* doing top things and I never was hungry enough to go after [B movies]. I tried so hard not to do them, but it was very tempting at times. *But*, when *Target Earth* came up, I was *so* happy to do it. I read the script and I knew I'd be with old-timers, good people — Richard Denning had a good career, and Virginia Grey was a good actress with a *wonderful* background. So I felt I'd be in good company; and when you're with good company, you know there's going to be care taken, then you should do it.

How did they happen to think of you for Target Earth*?*
It would have been through my wonderful agent, Dick Clayton. I had never met the producer, Herman Cohen, so Dick probably sold me to Herman. But once I was involved, I was thrilled, because my character was the lead. And the more I think back on Herman Cohen, the more I respect and admire him. He was so young, and he must have done that film with two dimes rubbed together — I'm more impressed with him now than I was even then! He was such a nice gentleman, I remember that, and a very

hard-working man. And a *decent* person. He worked hard to make a good film on what must have been *such* a low, low budget. I remember that all of the actors were together, and there was an actress there that some guy, one of the actors maybe, was trying to move in on. Herman stepped right up and said, "Look, none of this. Not on *this* set. We have a difficult show to do here and we don't want any problems." I could see then that he was really a serious producer, and I just loved that in him. The budget was so small, one of the sets started to fall one time! That happened to me on live television, on *Jane Eyre*, which was horrible.

So Target Earth *was rush-rush compared to working at Fox.*
    Oh, yes, because the things I'd done at 20th Century–Fox had that big studio behind them, with full crews. I guess Herman had a full crew, too, I don't mean to imply that he didn't, but a big studio had all their locations on the lot — whatever they wanted, they had. On *Target Earth*, Herman had to scout locations. We worked on Sundays in those days — this was before Mr. Ronald Reagan decided that he was going to fight for the actors and see that they got Saturdays and Sundays off. To get some scenes of empty streets in a busy Los Angeles district, we went out there and shot that one Sunday morning, about six in the morning, just as the sun was coming up. At a big studio, you could shoot that on the back lot anytime you wanted to. So Herman had that pressure of shooting on location in lower Los Angeles, when it was just desolate.

What do you recall about the robot?
    Just that we loved it! That was really fascinating to me, because that was before robots were "fashionable" — that one was really ahead of its time. That robot was big, and I think the fellow that was inside it [Steve Calvert] had an awful time. And I also remember what a hot day that was.

It must have been even hotter for the robot!
    [*Laughs.*] Oh, it must have been, but he was a robot, he didn't mind! By the way, I recently dug out my script of *Target Earth*, and one day after work, I had written in it, "A *robot*? Is this what our leading men are going to look like in forty years?" And here we are, exactly forty years hence right now, and robots *still* haven't taken over! You know, the more I think about that movie, the more I love it! Richard Denning was a gentleman, a *very* nice man. At the time, I thought of him as "old," but when I look back on it now, he wasn't old at *all*! (At that age, in your twenties, you think that someone seven years older is old!) He was an actor who I respected as an experienced leading man — and a very handsome one. I was thrilled to death to be on a par with him, billing-wise and

A knee injury and an "ungentle manly" co-star were Crowley's lot in *The Flame Barrier* with Arthur Franz and Robert Brown.

everything. I'm so happy that I had a chance to do something like *Target Earth*, because it was a *wild* film. We all worked very hard in it.

You worked with John Carradine in a minor mystery called Female Jungle *[1956]. Any anecdotes about knowing him?*
  Oh, I'd worked with him on stage in Kennebunkport, Maine — he was

wild. *Wild!* I was really young, doing stock, and he was shipped in as the star. He asked me to rehearse with him at night, and I was so young and innocent, I said, "Oh, yes, Mr. Carradine!" And one of the older actors found out and told me, "*Don't* you go to his room!" [*Laughs.*] He had his little kids running around the stage — his boys, who are now such well-known stars. I also remember him fighting with his wife [actress Sonia Sorel], and he was *such* a drinker...! He was in *Female Jungle*, too — oh, Lord, that was terrible, a very bad experience. Jayne Mansfield had a small role in it also, and it was such a bad movie that they couldn't release it until after she made her splash. [*Female Jungle* was shot in 1954.]

Did you enjoy doing The Flame Barrier *as much as you had* Target Earth?

It was very, very hard work, and the only reason I did it was — not the story, particularly [*laughs*] — but the fact that the producers, Levy-Gardner-Laven, had a good track record. I worked darn hard in that (although I don't know how happy *they* were with *me*!). That was a strange picture, a *wild* picture. When you get into these outer space–type things, like *Flame Barrier* and *Target Earth*, or when you're doing a crazy scene like the one in *Flame Barrier* where I find my dead husband engulfed inside that blob, you just have to have an *imagination*. I think that the people who write these movies were more talented than some people would like to admit. They have great imaginations, and there really *is* a place for those movies — you *have* to respect them. I didn't get to do many of them, but I sort of wish now that I had done more. But when you approach them, you have to believe in the given circumstances of the script. I'm fascinated by some of those stories. I mean, to put a Dracula-type thing in a Western background [*Curse of the Undead*] — that took some imagination, didn't it [*laughs*]? I wanted to believe that it was all true, and I did. You have to have an actor's faith, and a *real* actor finds a way of eliminating the doubt. *Then* you can bring a good performance to your public and *they* will believe it.

Why do you think the Flame Barrier *people were unhappy with you?*

They said they had cast me because they thought I had so much emotion, they thought I was such a warm, emotional actress. And I guess they thought it wasn't coming through, because they talked to me after they saw me in dailies. I was thrown by that, I was hurt, because I knew what I was doing; I didn't want to let it all out in the first scene and I knew where I was going with the role. Late in the movie, I was supposed to warm up to Arthur Franz, so I didn't want to be warm to him in the very beginning — if I had, there'd have been no place to go! But they came on the set and I had to tell 'em I knew what I was doing!

Then something else happened, and it wasn't pleasant. There's a scene where I go into the jungle and sit down on a log, and a snake comes up behind me. Off-camera, someone said, very seriously, "Don't move." That was the line of dialogue I was expecting, so I didn't even think about it. Then the voice said, "Don't *really* move. Don't move, Kathleen. *Don't move.*" What had happened was, the snake had come loose of his wire — the trainer had anesthetized it, but it had worn off. Suddenly all hell broke loose. People shot right by me, and I didn't know whether the snake was striking out at me or *what*. I lunged toward the camera to get away from it, and I came down hard on my knee on concrete — and cracked my knee cap. We still had some shooting to do and, oh, it was terrible. And by the time we finished on the twentieth of December [1957], I had to be *carried* home and put in bed. I was there all through Christmas. That was the end of *The Flame Barrier*, all because of that snake — which I think they shot.

Even though Flame Barrier is supposed to be a science fiction movie, there's too much jungle and animal hijinks.

There's another scene where I'm in a tent and the two men [Arthur Franz and Robert Brown] are giving me the business. An iguana was in the tent with me and it had to go over my legs. I love animals, but I was scared to death of him — I didn't enjoy that at *all*. I also had to undress in that scene, which was quite daring way back then, and I didn't like it — I didn't like being like that in front of a crew.

By the way, my leading man was not that easy to work with. Arthur Franz had a star complex that never shone in the sky, and I think maybe there was something wrong there. Here I was, this young, single actress, and I was putting all my money into my home — I'd bought the Hopalong Cassidy estate, up in the hills in Hollywood, in 1957. I bought it because I love a home and I loved the beauty and serenity up there — that's the type of person I was. (It kept me off the psychiatrist's couch!) Before we started to shoot *The Flame Barrier*, the director Paul Landres asked if we could meet on a Sunday afternoon, before the first day's shooting. We met at my home, Mr. Landres and Arthur Franz and myself, and we were going to go over the script. Franz walked around my deck and, not being gentlemanly at all, he almost indicated, "Well, who are *you* sleeping with? How did you get *this*?" After that, I didn't know how I was going to work with him; that was the day before we started shooting! It was an insult to me. I don't know what women *he* knew, and I guess it's common in Hollywood for women to be "kept," but I certainly wasn't; I was taking care of my mother and paying off that house. And he *wasn't* that easy to work with — he was just not that friendly. But I have to say that I respected him highly as an actor.

What roles did you most enjoy playing?

I just wanted to do good, dramatic things. When you're young, you're either very dramatic in your thoughts *or* you're the opposite, you're a comic. I never was a stand-up comic and I never did variety things, I was a very serious actress who'd done serious things in New York. The one thing I wanted to do—that I'm sure I wasn't right for physically—was *The Diary of Anne Frank* [1959]. Here I was, a little Irish girl, and Anne Frank wasn't exactly Irish [*laughs*], but I wanted to do it. My agent was absolutely adamant that I *not* do it—I couldn't believe it, I *cried*. So I left his office and went to a hair dresser, had my hair dyed black, went to a photographer that same afternoon, spent quite a bit of money having the photos blown up, and sent them to the director, George Stevens. But he'd already selected his Anne Frank [Millie Perkins].

You also starred in Curse of the Undead, *the vampire Western.*

That was with Eric Fleming, Clint Eastwood's sidekick from *Rawhide*. Eric happened to be my neighbor, but [prior to *Curse*] we never met. While I was still living in the Hopalong Cassidy estate, I wanted to plant geraniums and ivy on the side of the mountain, and so what I'd do was tie a rope around an iron rail and use the rope to walk myself down this *very* steep hill and plant geraniums and trees. Eric was renting a little room on the other side of the hill, and when he was doing *Rawhide*, he would go into makeup and say, "There's a mountain goat living over on the next hill! There are no cameras around, nobody's around but her, so I *know* it's not a publicity gig. I just wonder who in the *hell* she is!" Then all of a sudden, on *Curse of the Undead*, I walked in and he found out who I was, and he almost fell out of the makeup chair! So that's how we met, although we were practically neighbors. He was a very sweet person and, of course, *very* involved with *Rawhide*, and when you're doing a series like that, you have no other life. Eric never even had a chance to enjoy his money; he drowned several years later, while making a movie in Peru.

And what about the vampire, Michael Pate?

I think he was very romantic and exciting [*laughs*], just like my old co-worker Richard Boone. People didn't think Richard was romantic and exciting, they said he had a pock-marked face and he wasn't handsome at all. Well, I *liked* working with someone like that, because you don't want just some pretty-faced Lothario talking lines to you from six in the morning until midnight, you want someone who's really going to *work* with you in a scene. Richard Boone was an exciting actor, and when you did live things

Vampire (Michael Pate) and victim (Crowley) seem to get along fine when the *Curse of the Undead* cameras aren't rolling.

with him, you knew that you'd *worked*. I loved character actors, much more (I think) than the pretty boys. Michael Pate was one of those men. I always will remember being in bed in *Curse of the Undead* and Michael taking the blood from my neck [*laughs*]—that was so exciting. He was very nice and I enjoyed working with him.

Your director, Edward Dein, is usually remembered as being an agreeable sort of... oddball.

Oh, wonderful Edward Dein! He knew how to "get inside" of people—*very* unorthodox, but an excellent director and a very truthful person. I enjoyed working with him, I think he brought out some good work in me in that. He and his wife Mildred invited me to his house, which was tucked away in Laurel Canyon—it seemed rather bohemian! It was a *strange* house, with a *drawbridge*, and *cats* all over the place! It was almost like the Addams Family [*laughs*]! But they were both very nice to me, and Mildred was very involved with Edward's work.

Thinking back now, I can't recall *why* I was invited; I didn't really fraternize with people with whom I worked. When I'm working with someone, I won't even have lunch with them usually. I'd be the character I was playing, I wouldn't be Kathleen Crowley. I would have to concentrate on my character; this is the way I learned to work, and I was very *remote* with people when I worked with them, till it was all over.

You also did mountains of television in the early sixties.

Television was wonderful if you were willing to just try anything, and if they knew you were a good responsible actor, you could *work*. When I look back and see all I did, I cannot believe that this one actress did so much, and still didn't get burned out.

Every actor wanted to get in a series, but I didn't; I *refused* series. I had a chance to do *Hazel* [as the wife] and I didn't want to do it; there was money in it, but it was a nothing part. They also called me in for *Mr. Ed* and they offered me the role—not the horse, but the wife [*laughs*]! I remember George Burns sitting on the floor with a cap on, interviewing me, and I said, "If I could talk to the horse, I'd do it. But she doesn't know anything about the horse—she's stuck in the kitchen, with an apron on!" I wanted to do *adventuresome* things.

Do you have any memory of being on television's Thriller?

Was that with the Democrat, Robert Vaughn? He and Arthur Franz should get together, they would appreciate each other [*laughs*]! I know he's a good actor, but he was not that easy. We had a scene in a bell tower where he went mad; we were up there in the tower and the bells were going back and forth, and he was strangling me. He got ahold of my neck and he just wouldn't let go. I don't think he's a Method actor, so he must have snapped! And they had an awful time the next day, covering the red mark on my neck—and I wasn't too happy about him not being in control, either. You can forgive someone if it's an accident and you can forgive someone if they're really an endearing person — but *he* wasn't that endearing! The other thing I remember is that there's a quick scene with a young girl with "bell" earrings. Who do you think that was? It was Marlo Thomas — that was her debut, I think. Her father wanted to get some film on her.

And what about Batman, *with Burgess Meredith?*
  Wasn't he marvelous? I just loved him. The thing about that which I remember was sort of sad, but this is how studios worked. There's a wedding scene where I'm about to marry the Penguin [Meredith] in a hotel room, but in order to get away he flips a switch or something and water starts coming down from the ceiling. Well, all the extras in the scene wore their own clothes and they had to *pay* for their clothes. I had a wedding gown on, furnished to me by the studio. And whose gown do you think it was? It was *the* gown that they made for Julie Andrews in *The Sound of Music* [1965]. I was so thrilled to wear it, and I was being extra careful of it. But when the water came down, I heard all the people around me screaming for real — there was dye in the water and it ruined their clothes. I looked down at this beautiful gown, and it was just *ruined* with dye. I felt so sad, because she was so exquisite in it, and it had such a wonderful life.

I think you were a good enough actress that you should have gone a lot further than you did.
  The one thing that I *didn't* do, that maybe I should have done, was publicity — I didn't particularly care for it. I realize now that that's part of being an actor. I was so serious about my work that I told myself, "Oh, well, my work will carry me." I thought it was what happened at eight o'clock in the morning when the director says *action*, it's not who you're with at a nightclub the night before.

After The Lawyer *[1970], you married and dropped out of the industry.*
  I did, I felt that raising my son Matthew and always being there for him should take precedence over my career. That's something that never would have been believed by those who knew me during my days of making films and building a career, that I would have walked away like that. But I was *not* young when I married, I was *not* young when I had Matthew, and I think I was very lucky. Also, to be honest with you, I didn't like the direction the cinema was going.
  Older is what we get, I guess. I'm still very vigorous. I'm not treated like a celebrity here [in New Jersey], but I'll do what I can with what's left of my life, and I'm still trying to grow. I love my little place here, but recently my son Matthew is encouraging me to return to Hollywood to

make films. I said, "You're crazy!" It's something I somehow doubt that I'll do, due to the fact that, at this point in time, I think everybody I knew in the old days has passed on [*laughs*]! And, actually, I think it was really wonderful to have left the way I left. Poor Inger Stevens slit her wrists, and there's Marilyn, and we could go right down the line. I live right on the river, I'm from a seagoing family, I love the outdoors and I so love this little community — it's like a little emerald here. I'm here and I'm healthy and I love my informal, low-profile life.

KATHLEEN CROWLEY FILMOGRAPHY

The Farmer Takes a Wife (20th Century–Fox, 1953)
The Silver Whip (20th Century–Fox, 1953)
Sabre Jet (United Artists, 1953)
Target Earth (Allied Artists, 1954)
Seven Cities of Gold (20th Century–Fox, 1955)
Ten Wanted Men (Columbia, 1955)
City of Shadows (Republic, 1955)
Female Jungle (American Releasing [AIP], 1956)
Westward Ho the Wagons! (Buena Vista, 1956)
The Phantom Stagecoach (Columbia, 1957)
The Quiet Gun (20th Century–Fox, 1957)
The Flame Barrier (United Artists, 1958)
The Rebel Set (Beatsville) (Allied Artists, 1959)
Curse of the Undead (Universal, 1959)
Showdown (Universal, 1963)
FBI Code 98 (Warners, 1964)
Downhill Racer (Paramount, 1969)
The Lawyer (Paramount, 1970)

*Generally on low-budget pictures,
it is rare that a director will be able to tell an actor
more than, "Okay, play it tough," or whatever,
and that's the direction.*

Michael Fox

HE IS, OF COURSE, yet another one of those long-time character players whose face is well known even if the name might not immediately spring to mind. An actor since the 1940s, Michael Fox cropped up regularly in Science Fiction fare in the early 1950s, from the juvenile outer space serial *The Lost Planet* to the "adult," realistic Ivan Tors thrillers *The Magnetic Monster, Riders to the Stars* and *Gog* (on these, he not only worked as an actor, but also dialogue-directed and helped to cast). Still busy in television (as a regular in the daytime drama *The Bold and the Beautiful*), Fox affectionately recalls the days of playing serial baddies, frozen-alive physicists, mad scientists and two-headed aliens.

Fox first "trod the boards" in grade school plays in his hometown of Yonkers, New York. After toying with the idea of becoming a history teacher, Fox did "something as foreign to my nature as one could think of," becoming a "boomer" (a migratory railroad worker) and taking jobs as a brakeman with various lines. His interest in acting was rekindled in the mid–forties and he appeared in several "little theater" plays in Los Angeles. An acting/directing stint in a Players Ring production of *Home of the Brave* caught the eye of Harry Sauber, an associate of exploitation mogul "Jungle Sam" Katzman, and Fox landed his first film role (*A Yank in Indo-China*, 1952) in a movie career which has included *The Beast from 20,000 Fathoms, Conquest of Space, The Dunwich Horror, Young Frankenstein* and many more.

How did you break into the acting profession?

Around 1945, I started to get active looking around the theaters in Los Angeles. I saw an ad in *Variety* that a theater group was looking for actors for a play called *The Dybbuk*, which was Ansky's great Yiddish-language play. I don't speak Yiddish, but they were doing it in English. So I went to the theater and met Lou Smuckler, who was Lee J. Cobb's father-in-law — he was running this little theater on Melrose Avenue. (I believe it's now a liquor warehouse. I don't know if that's progress or not [*laughs*]!) I auditioned for him and he hired me, and I played *The Dybbuk* for several months. I first met my wife Hannah there, in fact; she was an actress when I met her. After that play closed, I saw an audition notice at Equity—they were doing a play called *The Story of Mary Surratt* with Dorothy Gish and Kent Smith, which was about the plotters of the assassination of Lincoln. I went and auditioned and met the playwright John Patrick, who was also directing it. He wanted me to read David Herold — Herold was the man who escorted [John Wilkes] Booth out of Washington, and was with Booth when Booth was killed. Mr. Patrick and I became rather friendly, and when

Previous page: Film and television perennial Michael Fox also enjoys working on the stage, where he considers curtain calls and applause "part of my paycheck — a rather large part."

he found out that Lincoln was my love and my major field in history, I wrote the souvenir program for the show [*laughs*]! We opened in Santa Barbara at the Lobero Theater; then we went to San Francisco; then back to Los Angeles, where we played the Biltmore. The last day of the show was a Saturday: We played the matinee, I borrowed Dorothy Gish's car (a 1939 Buick convertible sedan), Hannah and I drove to a judge, got married, came back, did the evening performance, and the show left for Broadway that night. Unfortunately, we only lasted a week on Broadway, although we got fairly decent reviews.

I struggled in New York and got really no place; I did a couple of radio shows, which in those days paid enough for you to brush your teeth. I came back to California and worked in the haberdashery business while I auditioned. There was a theatrical group out here called the Players Ring, which had a little theater on Santa Monica Boulevard, and they were going to do *Home of the Brave*. I played the psychiatrist and I also directed the play, which was quite successful. In those days, the Players Ring was very well covered by Hollywood producers. A gentleman came backstage to see me, and he said, "I like your work, and I'll use you in a film the first chance I get." His name was Harry Sauber, and he worked with Sam Katzman at Columbia. (In fact, Sauber's son Larry Stewart was in the cast of *Home of the Brave*. I cast Larry, but I didn't know who his father was.) I thought, "Oh, the same old shit," but three days later, Mr. Sauber phoned and said, "Do you have an S.A.G. card?" I said, "No, I've got an Equity card." He said, "Well, I've got a little shtick here in a movie called *A Yank in Indo-China*. It'll pay for your S.A.G. card." So I did *A Yank in Indo-China* and I had one line, and to this day I remember it: I played a Communist courier and I drove up to an airplane, got out of the car, gave something to the pilot and said, "See that this gets to General Wang!" You don't forget a line like that!

Who was your big booster in the Sam Katzman organization, the one who got you all those early parts?

Harry was my strongest supporter. Harry introduced me to Sam, and I did an *awful* lot of stuff for Katzman in fifty-one, fifty-two, fifty-three. A week or two after we'd done *Yank*, Harry called me and said, "Mike, I've got a job for you. It's in a serial." It was called *Blackhawk*, starring Kirk Alyn. I played the "heavy"; I *always* did the heavy. Every serial had a "brains heavy" and a "physical heavy." The "physical heavy" was always a stuntman, Davey Sharpe or somebody like that, who did all the dirty work and all the fighting. I was the "brains heavy," the boss, the one that did all the dialogue. I did the heavy in *Blackhawk*, and it was an interesting role because I played three different people: At first I was posing as a "good guy," a fellow named Mr. Case who wore a hearing aid; then Mr. Case disguised himself as a Spaniard, and I played that with a dialect; and then at the end I also turned out to be the "brains heavy," the leader of *all* the bad guys.

Where were the serial interiors shot? At Columbia?

No, at Lyman Place, which was a studio right near the corner of Sunset and Hollywood Boulevard. It's now a Ralph's Market, I believe. It was owned by Columbia, and Katzman leased it. The interiors were shot there, and the exteriors at the Columbia Ranch.

Talk about how making a serial was different from making a feature.

The serials were, frankly, terribly hard work. You shot fifteen episodes — that's thirty reels of cut film — in seventeen days. Say six reels is average for a film, so that's the equivalent of five features in seventeen days. Mine were all directed by a wonderful gentleman named Spencer Gordon Bennet; he died [in 1987] at age ninety-three. In those days, you had a twelve-hour day and a six-day week. I would start at six A.M. on Monday and shoot through to six P.M. on Saturday — seventy-two hours a week for that entire stretch of seventeen days.

When we were doing *Blackhawk*, I wasn't yet very familiar with film. It was a Saturday, and we were going to shoot at Signal Hill in Long Beach, at the oil fields. I woke up and it was pouring rain, and I thought, "Oh, Christ, we're not gonna go down there!" But there was no phone call, so I got in my car and drove over to the Lyman Place lot, and there was the limo and everything else. They said, "Sure we'll shoot," and I said, "My God, how can you shoot in this rain?" This was second unit, and Freddie Sears was directing. Fred said, "If we don't back-light it, you won't see the rain" — which was *true*! However, I was wearing a white suit. So when I looked at the scene in the dailies, I could see spots appearing on my white suit. You didn't see the downpour, but you saw these discolorations [*laughs*]!

What other memories do you have of Blackhawk *and* The Lost Planet, *your other science fiction serial?*

These were written by a chap named George Plympton. It got to be a game between us: He tried to write lines *I couldn't say*. In *The Lost Planet* I played the evil Dr. Grood and I was in my mountain laboratory, looking into a periscope, and I had a line: "It worked! The atom propulse set up a radiation wall which cut off the neutron detonator impulse!" Now that's a tongue-twister, and of course, George had written it accordingly. So we rehearsed it *once*, as you always did with Spencer [*laughs*], and then I went for a take. I dashed over to the periscope and I looked into it, and one of the prop men had lowered into the periscope a slide, a crotch shot — a young lady with no clothing on and her legs spread. I looked — but I didn't break up! And I said, "It worked! The atom propulse set up a radiation wall which cut off the neutron detonator impulse!" I turned (congratulating myself mentally), and I had forgotten that Jack George, who played my assistant, had a line; his line was, "For every weapon, there is a *counter*-weapon." And when he said that, I went *right* through the roof [*laughs*]! I just broke up, and it took me nine takes before I could get the goddamned line out again!

What was Spencer Bennet like?

Spencer was very funny. Spencer was then in his sixties and used to always come out wearing a short-sleeved silk polo shirt and a light gray turned-down-brim Stetson hat, with a thin band. When we were doing *Riding with Buffalo Bill* [1954], there was some stunt that had to be done — one of the cowboys had to vault over a fence. And the cowboy was complaining, moaning that he didn't know how he was going to do it. And Spence went, "Oh, it's easy, go like this." He walked over, put his hand on the fence, vaulted over it, came back again and said, "That's all you have to do." [*Laughs.*] And he was in his sixties at the time! But that was Spencer.

Also, he really had no sense of humor — which made him *so* funny. Every time I raised an objection to a line, he would say, "Oh, it doesn't work?" — it would never have occurred to him. You'd say, "No, Spencer, it doesn't," and he'd tell you to change it! Spencer had *no concept* about acting or the script or anything else. But what Spencer *could* do was shoot action stuff.

You were usually the best actor in each of your serials. For instance, Judd Holdren seemed very wooden in The Lost Planet.

Judd was. Well, frankly, in *The Lost Planet*, the only decent part *was* the heavy, my character, Dr. Grood. I could eat the scenery to my heart's content! Generally in a serial, the writing for the hero is not very outstanding. *Blackhawk* was a little better, simply because the characters that they took out of the comic strip *had* to have some development to them, so Kirk Alyn [Blackhawk] and Johnny Crawford [Chuck] had that advantage.

Apart from the paychecks, are there any rewards for actors in playing parts like Mr. Case and Dr. Grood?

Yes, there *are* rewards. About *Blackhawk*—I suppose I shouldn't say this, but I'm really very proud of it. Because I think there *is* a difference between each of the three characters that I play. That's a great feeling for an actor. Another reward for actors is to work on stage. By God, when you come down for that curtain call and you hear that applause—there's no substitute for it. I consider it *part* of my paycheck—a rather large part. It's just an enormous amount of satisfaction. Just as when I do a film that I consider one of the *worst* ever made, I walk around kicking myself about *that*, too!

I did *The Girl in the Kremlin* [1957], which certainly has got to be on any Ten Worst list ever made. It *starred*, and I'm using that word in its loosest sense, Zsa Zsa Gabor and Lex Barker, and it was produced by Albert Zugsmith. I was the head of the OGPU, the Russian secret police. We saw it in a projection room—Barker was then married to Lana Turner, who was there, too. Hannah and I went and Hannah was sitting next to Turner, and the picture was god-awful. And I am *dying*. At the end of the film, there's a fight in a wine cellar and I kill Jeffrey Stone, who played Barker's sidekick. Then *I'm* killed in the fight. Zsa Zsa runs over to Jeff's body and she looks down, and her line was, "Oh, he's dead." And Barker's line was, "What a lousy break." I swear to God! And Hannah started to laugh—and started getting dirty looks from Turner. And I am trying to die—drop down through the floor—or *something*!

You were also in a pair of Jungle Jim *films for Katzman,* Voodoo Tiger *and* Killer Ape.

I played a Gestapo colonel in *Voodoo Tiger*, and there's a scene where I commandeer an airplane full of dancers. The line that was written for me was, "Sit tight, and nobody's gonna get hurt." Again, Spencer Bennet was directing. I said to him, "Spencer—forgive me, but a Gestapo colonel is *not* going to say, 'Sit tight, and nobody's gonna get hurt.'" Particularly not with a German dialect—it *vouldn't vurk* [*laughs*]! So I changed it, I said, "Don't anybody move."

*What was Johnny Weissmuller (*Jungle Jim*) like?*

I liked Johnny very much. I guess he had a deal with Katzman: He shot two *Jungle Jims* a year, they were shot in nine days each, and he shot them virtually back-to-back. My understanding was that he got fifty grand a piece for them, plus a "piece." That was his income. And that was all he worked! I think Johnny was living in Mexico at the time; he would come out here to Hollywood for a month to do the two pictures back-to-back, and there would be a break of maybe two days between. Of course, on the list of great actors, I don't think you'd find Johnny's name much before the number 4000 [*laughs*], but he was a very nice man, and most enjoyable. We used to lunch together.

Did you ever have to contend with real animals on the set of a Jungle Jim, *or was it all stock footage?*

No, there was a lion there on *Voodoo Tiger*. It was pathetic. It *looked* great, but it was so old, it could hardly stand up. And when you *got* him to stand up, *youhadtoshoothimquick*. Of course, we had two lions, we had a lion who moved around, and then this one, who was more photogenic, but he was so old, poor fellow. Johnny was very good with him. By the way, the reason that the *Jungle Jim*s were shown in sepia in theaters was because none of that stock footage matched. I once said to Spencer, "My God, some of these cuts, how are they gonna work?" And Spencer said, "It's all right, we do the whole thing in sepia, so you don't notice." And, of course, you *didn't* notice!

Certainly you weren't looking forward to spending your whole career as a Katzman regular. What sort of slot did you have in mind for yourself in pictures?

My god as an actor was Walter Huston—I'd always regarded him as one of the best I'd ever seen, I still *do*. My dream was to get a chance to play some of the roles that Huston was playing. I didn't think I was good-looking enough, I *certainly* wasn't going to be a matinee idol, but I *did* think I was a good character actor, and I wanted to play that kind of role. Another actor I had *enormous* regard for was [Paul] Muni, and I also wanted to do the kind of things that Muni did. I worked on my dialects; they came very naturally to me, but I also worked on them because of the work I'd seen Muni do.

Did you get to know Sam Katzman well at all?

[*Laughs.*] His nickname, of course, was "Jungle Sam," because he did the *Jungle Jim*s. He used to walk around carrying a riding crop—I don't know if that was to goose the girls, or whatever. And he was a rather unpretentious looking man—he wasn't *small*, but he had no chin. On one of the *Jungle Jim*s that we did, we were on the back lot at Columbia with Peggy the chimpanzee, who was really wonderful, and certainly much brighter than Sam. Peggy sat next to Sam, and Johnny Weissmuller said, "Look! They're carrying on a conversation!" [*Laughs.*] Me, I got along splendidly with Sam, although I think for some reason he regarded me as an intellectual. (I think anybody who had gone past the sixth grade was an intellectual to Sam!) Harry Sauber sort of was the "class side" of Katzman's operation. When stars would come to do a Katzman movie, it was always Harry who handled everything. He was a gentleman.

You also did three science fiction films for Ivan Tors in the early fifties.
   While I was doing *Home of the Brave*, Ivan Tors also had come to see the play. Ivan came to see me backstage, and during somewhere in this era, I heard from Ivan. He was doing a picture called *The Glass Wall* [1953] with Vittorio Gassman, and I played an immigration officer for him in that. Ivan and I became very good friends; Ivan was then wooing [actress] Constance Dowling, later they married, and Constance and [her actress-sister] Doris and I all became extremely good friends. (Constance and Ivan have both since passed away.) I appeared on *Science Fiction Theatre* for Ivan, I did several of those, and of course his science fiction movies — *The Magnetic Monster*, *Riders to the Stars* and *Gog*.

These were low budget, too, like the Katzmans?
   That's right, Ivan didn't have a lot of money to spend on these pictures. The first science fiction film I did for him was *The Magnetic Monster*, and that was shot for $96,000 cash and $20,000 deferred. You couldn't make a trailer for that today [*laughs*]! Curt Siodmak wrote it and we put that together — I was the casting director, the dialogue director, and I also acted in it. Ivan had gotten hold of some footage from a German film called *Gold* [1934] — an Ufa film with a wonderful German actor named Hans Albers. All the scenes of the giant cyclotron that you see at the end of *The Magnetic Monster* were taken from that film — *we* didn't build that stuff. Curt wrote the script around that scene so that we could include that footage, and that's how the picture was shot for that kind of money.

What was Tors like as a filmmaker?
   Oh, Ivan was very good. He was an old-fashioned moviemaker, despite the fact that he came in at the end of that era. *Ivan knew how to make a movie.* And one of the reasons was, Ivan was a real nut on preparation. The only way we could have *done* those pictures for the kind of money we did them for was by really planning. Ivan had, of course, enormous help from Curt Siodmak and also from a wonderful editor, Herb Strock. Ivan had a lot of imagination — obviously!— and conversation with him was quite *intriguing*. I didn't feel that was reflected in some of the other people who did science fiction movies.

How much of Magnetic Monster *did Curt Siodmak direct?*

Curt Siodmak directed the picture. But because we used film from Ufa and so on, putting that film together in the editing room took an absolute artist. And although the Directors Guild says the director has first cut, everyone who worked on that picture knew that it was Herb Strock who [put everything together]; at least eighty percent of the success of that film goes to Strock. No question in my mind about that. As an *actor*, I looked to my director, and that was Curt Siodmak. And Curt was *extremely* helpful to the actors. It was one of those films (and I don't think there are many) where I could not say that one man did more work than the other; it ended up being a mutual effort.

Strock told me that Siodmak started directing the picture, but two or three days into it, Ivan Tors bumped him and Strock directed everything else.

That is possible. I don't remember clearly, so I can't speak on it authoritatively. I *do* know that Curt and Ivan disagreed constantly, there's no question about that. And Curt's knowledge of directing was, in my opinion, not particularly great. Curt's brother Robert was an extremely successful director, and I think Curt — who certainly ranks very highly among screenwriters — always was somewhat envious of Robert. But Curt and I had a wonderful affinity for one another and we kept it up all these years.

Did you think Strock was a good director when you worked for him later on?

He was certainly very satisfactory. But actors have affinities for certain directors. What makes a director like Ford or Aldrich so popular with actors is that they have that ability to communicate with the actor very well. One of the reasons that I as an actor don't usually like an editor who becomes a director is because he's attached to the *mechanics* of the business, and not to the *acting* of it. Most actors like writers and actors who are directors.

How did you get the job of dialogue director, through Tors?

Yeah. Ivan had seen my directing at the Players Ring — in fact, the first time we met on *Home of the Brave*, he said, "I like you as an actor and I like you as a director." In pictures, a dialogue director works with the actors prior to shooting. He can be as valuable as the director wants him to be. It can be just making sure that the actors learn their lines; it can *also* be suggesting to them, if you feel the reading is not right, how to alter that reading, so that it becomes more directorial. It depends on the director. Curt relied on me totally.

Where was Magnetic Monster *shot?*

The old Hal Roach lot. That's where Ivan shot the bulk of his stuff.

How did you like Richard Carlson?

I suppose our egos clashed. Richard was a *Phi Beta Kappa*. I happen to have some collegiate honors as well. And somehow, he knew that I was ambitious as a director. He was used to being the intellectual limelight on a set. He did not like to share it with someone who was, in his opinion, lesser than he.

Was Carlson financially involved with these pictures?

He had a piece of 'em. Ivan couldn't pay his salary—Richard's salary was higher than what Ivan could pay, so he took a piece. So he *was* financially involved.

Did he have his drinking problem then?

Not to my knowledge. And when I worked with Herbert Marshall, I must say that, if he'd *had* one, it was over by that time. (Somebody had told me that he did, but I had no difficulty with him at all.) In fact, the man who put up the money for those pictures with Marshall [*Riders to the Stars* and *Gog*] said that I should "ride herd" on Bart—be with him at lunchtime and so on. But I found him to be an absolutely gracious gentleman, and I had a wonderful time.

A lot of science fiction fans find these Tors pictures too talky, too crammed with science-fact.

That was Ivan, Ivan was *nuts* about that scientific stuff. My wife was going to college at that time—Hannah became a mathematician—and Hannah got very involved with computers. She in fact helped us with some of the stuff for the pictures. When we would go over to Ivan's house on Sundays, Ivan would talk to her for *hours* about all of the computer techniques. SWAK was the big item at that point, the big computer at UCLA. (Those were the days of the *enormous* computers.) When Hannah was at UCLA, I went out and looked at SWAK one day and, my God, the damn thing took up all sides of a room! *Now*, you can get a PC that does all the work SWAK did *plus*, and it sits on your desk!

But to get back to your question, years ago John Ford said, "We used to make moving pictures. Then we learned how to talk, and we stopped making moving pictures and we made *talking* pictures." Although Mr. Ford was not the most pleasant of men, there's no question of his genius, and he was absolutely right. Ivan's problem was that he overused language. Needless to say, it *is* much cheaper to describe something than it is to present something.

What did you think of the films that resulted from this passion for science that Ivan Tors had?

Well, this'll sound crazy: I'm not a science fiction fan. Far from it. But I thought that *Gog* and *Riders* were extremely well done. They're *talky*, but they *all* have some kind of basis in fact, whereas most of the other science fiction all called for somebody to come from outer space, or whatever. I keep hearing about life on different worlds, and my answer always is this: Light travels at the rate of 186,000 miles per second. To reach us from Arcturus, it takes light forty years — and Arcturus is a close star. So somebody who leaves Arcturus *today* to come to us — even if he's traveling at the speed of *light*—will be out there *forty years*. How in the hell does that make sense? Now, of course, if you get into the Einstein theory of relativity, you can understand how *some* of that could happen — but I don't know that much about it! [*Laughs.*]

You had another small part in Riders to the Stars, *as the psychiatrist who evaluates the scientists.*

That's one of my favorite roles. I think Ivan liked me very much in it, and I enjoyed doing it. That was a pleasure. I was the dialogue director on that one, also [uncredited], and it too was shot at Hal Roach.

Richard Carlson directed Riders. *What kind of director was he?*

Interestingly enough, we got along fine. As a dialogue director, I interfered in *his* case extremely little. Curt and Herb Strock, who directed *Gog*— they regarded me as a confrere. With Richard, I purposely sidestepped it.

Talking about Riders, *Herb Strock said that Carlson was in over his head as a director— he was acting, trying to rewrite, trying to direct...*

I would say that Herb's absolutely right. That was part of Richard's problem, I think: Richard envisioned himself as a writer/director/actor/producer. There's a wonderful old Albert Einstein story that it reminded me of. When Einstein fled the Nazis and came to America, someone said that twenty-four German scientists had written an article disproving the theory of relativity. A reporter said to Einstein, "Twenty-four scientists said you're wrong." And Einstein said, "If I was really wrong, *one* would have been enough!" [*Laughs.*] And that really was Richard Carlson's problem in reverse. It was sad, because he was a good-looking man, he was bright, he was quite well read in many areas, but the moment he thought that somebody else was in authority, he would tell you how to do the job. He'd tell Herb Strock how to *cut*. For Christ's sake, Herb's one of the greatest editors this business has known in my time, and you don't *do* that. It was like the terrible experience I had one day when I was working on *Let's Make Love* [1960] and I happened to be walking out behind George Cukor and [playwright] Arthur Miller, who was married to Marilyn Monroe. And Miller said to Cukor, "You know, what you could do is, you cut from *this* shot of Marilyn to..." Well, I couldn't bear to listen, I *stopped* to let them get ahead of me [*laughs*]! I would not tell George Cukor how to direct—and I knew more about directing than that!

And you said that you enjoyed working with Herbert Marshall in Riders *and* Gog.

Herbert Marshall was a real gentleman. Bart came from the old school, he was a delight, and we got along famously. Early on, however, the producers weren't sure that Bart would pass the physical—Bart had blood pressure problems. So Ivan approached another actor who at that time I guess had a bigger name. That was Dean Jagger. I was not high on Jagger—I didn't like him as well by *any* means. We kicked it around in the office for three, four hours. A friend of mine had once said to me about Marshall, "He won't sell any tickets, but Herbert Marshall's name is always *class*." He only did class movies, so the exhibitors would always look to buy a Marshall picture. I *remembered* that, and Ivan and I discussed it on that level. Thank heaven, Bart passed the physical and we had no further problem [*laughs*]!

Would Jagger have been more expensive?

The deal we made with Bart was, for the two pictures, $25,000—$10,000 for one and $15,000 for the other. He worked a week in one and eight days in the other, something like that. For Jagger to have done 'em, I think the figure that Ivan gave me was *double*, or almost—it was somewhere between $40,000 and $50,000.

The future caught up with these Ivan Tors pictures pretty quickly. Looking back at these gadgets that we're supposed to be amazed by, the amazing part is how primitive and bulky all this junk is!

Oh, absolutely! That was the thing that intrigued Ivan many years later. When we were making these pictures, Hannah told Ivan, "One day, all of this is going to be miniaturized," and that intrigued Ivan—he wanted to do a picture about that later.

William Lundigan, the star of Riders to the Stars—*was he really the pain in the ass he's generally described as?*

[*Laughs.*] Wel-l-l, he was not what I would have called an actor. *I* had

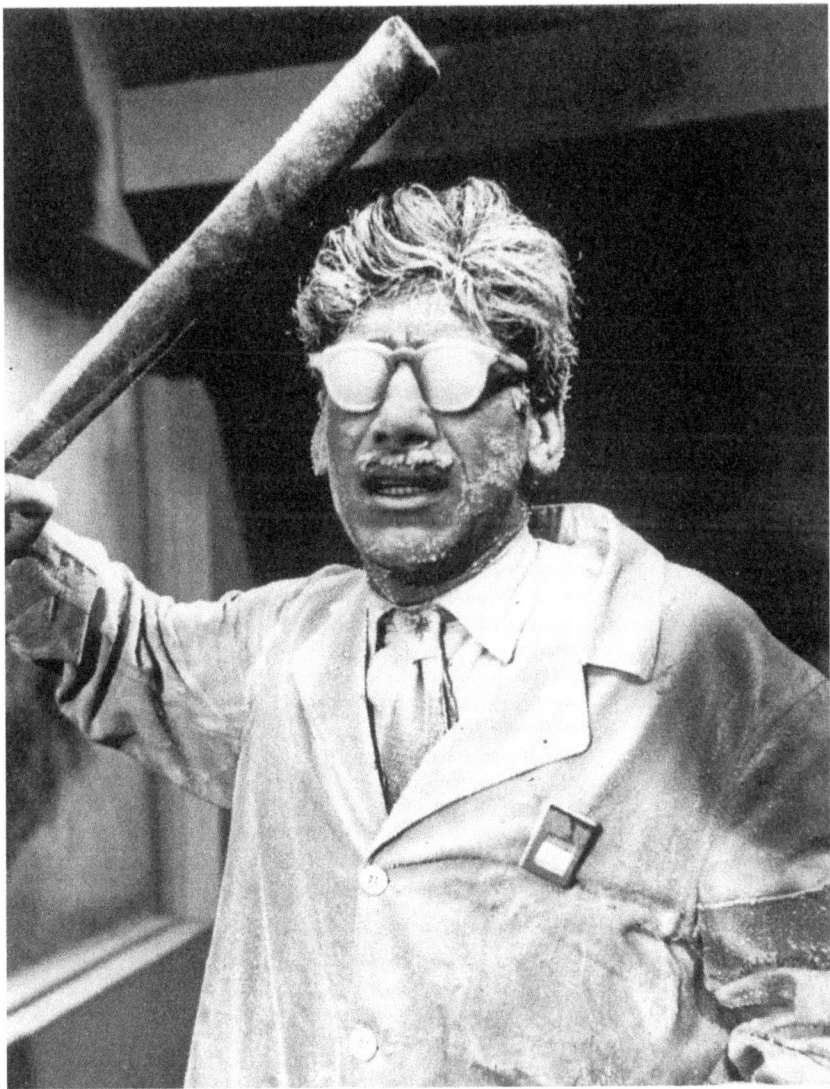

A victim of cold chamber chicanery, Fox suffered a frozen-alive fate in Ivan Tors' *Gog*.

already been in a picture with him, a Katzman thing called *Serpent of the Nile* [1953], so by the time I worked with him for Ivan, he knew me. We didn't become *friends*, we didn't socialize together — he drank far more than I was able to do, and I was pretty good in those days [*laughs*]! But I think I know why people would say he was a pain in the ass: He sloughed everything he did. In other words, at no point was he really serious. He would not learn the lines, he would not come in prepared. He did a little more with me because, as I said, we had met on that other film.

What memories do you have of Gog?

That was done in 3-D, which I hated. That was one time I disagreed with Ivan strongly, I said, "Three-D is going to last six and a half days," but Ivan didn't quite agree with me. My one scene in that film was at the beginning, I was trapped in a cold chamber and I froze to death. And they wanted to make the frost on my face come out *on camera*. Well, the way to do that, they figured, was to take powdered alum, dissolve it in acetone, and then spray me with it; and as the acetone evaporates very quickly, the alum turns out white. And that's what we used. Then eventually they sprayed me with liquid wax, to make the *extreme* white, and I did a back-fall out of camera and you heard the body break up.

That was a great scene.

Yeah, that really was. And it was extremely well worked out: Ivan was concerned that I wouldn't be injured or anything like that. I *did* get a slight burn on the edge of one eye, from the wax.

What was the star, Richard Egan, like?

Dick was a very nice man. I worked with him later when he had his series *Empire*, which was shot in New Mexico — I went out and did two of 'em. I got along with Dick, but — he was prone to swagger a little bit, rather like Lundigan. I think it was a *disease* with 20th Century–Fox actors [laughs] — they all had kind of a swagger to them, all those young leading men from 20th. Because they were all in the shadow of Tyrone Power. Egan was a much better actor than Bill Lundigan, *I* thought.

Do you recall the scenes with the robots, Gog and Magog?

We used midgets for those. One of them was Billy Curtis. Billy was rather an interesting individual, because Billy was a perfectly formed human, only he was very small, and he was quite good-looking. And he always had women around him who were bigger than *I* am, and I'm 5'11½"! And I think he married some of them at various times — I don't think *simultaneously*, but at various times [laughs]! You talk about pains in the ass — *Billy* was a pain in the ass! But his job *was* difficult — it's hot, any time you get into that kind of a rig. We had made arrangements: I told Ivan they could only be in the robot outfits for fifteen minutes at a time, which was correct, and that was what we did. But Billy — have you ever heard the word *kvetch*? Billy was a *kvetch.* I must say I liked him in spite of it. He used to swagger around that set and he always smoked cigars — and the cigar was about half as big as he was! He liked those big Panetelas. He was a character! There was another midget there too, but Billy did the bulk of the work.

All the scientific equipment you see in these movies — how much of it was real?
Maxwell Smith would come up with half of the this stuff—find it and so on, and quite a bit *was* real. It was not necessarily meant for the purpose *we* were using it for, though [*laughs*]!

Maxwell Smith was "scientific consultant" for all three of those Tors movies.
That's right. I also remember that, around that time, he had an explosion at his home. He had a very lovely house up off of Sunset, near the beach, up in one of those canyons, and he had a workshop there in the back of the house. And I remember somebody called me and told me that there had been an explosion and Maxwell lost an arm. He was a charming man, and very adept at this kind of crap. He was wonderful.

You acted in and dialogue-directed The Beast from 20,000 Fathoms.
That was for a producer named Hal E. Chester. Hal was a character, as anyone who has ever worked for him will tell you. He was a former actor, one of the Dead End Kids, and he was like he was in the movies! If you were to make a movie of a Hollywood producer of the thirties, Hal would have been perfect! He's a little bigger than Billy Curtis [*laughs*], and he talked like a Dead End Kid. The hair on his head was an eighth of an inch long, and he always ran his hands over his head. He was one of the stranger producers [*laughs*]! Jack Dietz was another producer who was in on the picture — I liked Jack. Chester was very volatile, and after he talked to you for ten minutes, you would need an interpreter. So I would look up Dietz to find out what *really* was meant! We shot the film at the Motion Picture Center.

What can you remember about working with Cecil Kellaway, who played the absent-minded professor?
Cecil Kellaway was wonderful. That reminds me of another story about that picture, about the scene in the diving bell. They had not written anything to cover that long descent into the ocean, there were just a few lines. Kellaway talked to me about it one night, that there was no provision for cutaway, and he was *right*. So I started that night, after the talk with Kellaway, to write some stuff, "fill" dialogue, just gibberish, a series of bromides between the two men in the bell. I wrote about three pages of dialogue.

Did you get to meet Ray Harryhausen on Beast?

Yes, I did. He did the special effects—designed the Beast and all that. Harryhausen was a wonderful guy and he did an awful lot of that stuff for a *lot* of films. I dialogue-directed and Eugene Lourie directed it. Eugene was an art director, and *Beast* was his first directorial job. He was a charming man, but not *thoroughly* knowledgeable as a director—which I think is why Hal wanted a dialogue director on the set.

How much directing of actors does a B or serial director generally do?

Generally, virtually none. Ivan Tors and Hal Chester tried to cover that by having a dialogue director. As I said before, a dialogue director is as effective as the director wants him to be. But generally on low-budget pictures, it is rare that a director will be able to tell an actor more than, "Okay, play it tough," or whatever, and *that's* the direction.

Then how does an actor feel when he gives a good performance in a B movie, and in reviews the performance is credited to the director?

Bitter. The fact that the performance has been complimented makes the actor feel better, but you do feel that it's not recognized by the reviewer the way it should have been. I can't speak for every actor, but I would say that most actors work very hard to make what we do *believable*. When a director knows that and helps you, that's wonderful. When a director gets in your way, you've got a problem. On a low-budget picture, when you're on a tight schedule, the actors are on their own. When I was working for Ivan, or when I was working for Hal, if I was casting I tried very hard to make sure I had the kind of actor who could handle that. For example, the diving bell scene in *Beast from 20,000 Fathoms* and the actor [Richard Norris] that I hired to play the sailor who descends with Kellaway. I had seen him in a couple of things on stage at little theaters in Hollywood and I knew he could handle an emergency situation. And he *did*, very well.

When *Beast from 20,000 Fathoms* was finished, it had cost more than they had expected. I think the only one who thought it was going to make money was Ray Harryhausen. Chester was nervous as hell about it; somehow *every*body got very uncertain. But Ray was convinced it would be a hit—we were having a drink about a week after the picture was finished and he said, "This picture's gonna make money. If Hal Chester hangs on, it's gonna make money." Eventually Hal sold it outright to Jack Warner, and Warner put a lot of money into publicity and it did *very* well. Hal didn't have a piece of it later.

What can you remember about some of your genre television appearances— Science Fiction Theatre, Superman *and* The Twilight Zone?

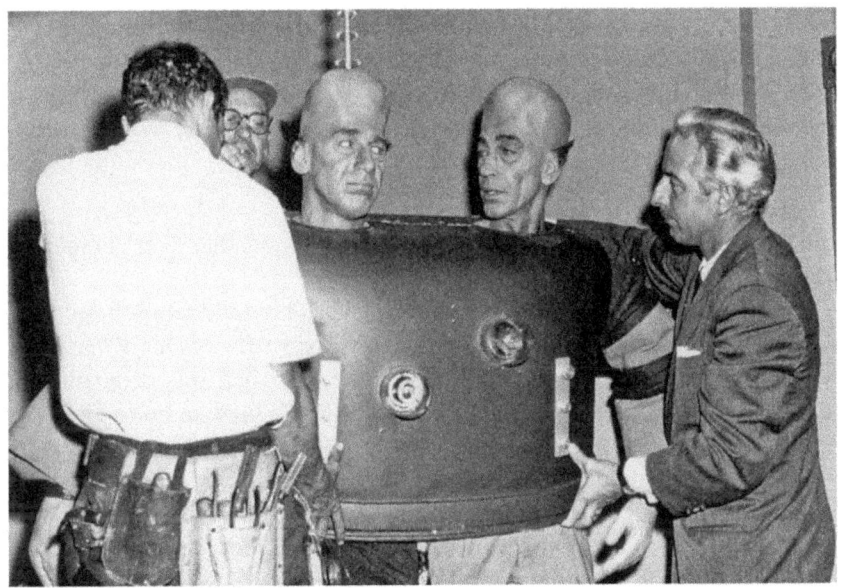

Fox and Douglas Spencer are outfitted in Martian mufti; for the *Twilight Zone* episode "Mr. Dingle, the Strong."

I did six or eight *Science Fiction Theatre*s, including one called "The Brain of John Emerson." It was about a brain transplant operation — really, it was sort of a takeoff on *Donovan's Brain*. I did that with an actor I liked immensely, John Howard, and that was one of my all-time favorite roles. I liked working with Howard, and the script I loved — I played the psychiatrist in it. (I've played so many psychiatrists, I could hang out a shingle!) My feeling about *Superman* was that they shot them for around $11 — it was *very* cheaply produced. But I liked George Reeves.

And Twilight Zone?

Oh, the *Twilight Zone*s I loved — I did a few of those. The one that I'm remembered for was the one where I played half of a two-headed monster ["Mr. Dingle, the Strong"] and that was delightful. I got to know Serling fairly well — he was a charming and most talented man, and one of the few writers who really understood an actor's problems, I thought.

What can you tell us about George Pal's Conquest of Space?

That was, in my opinion, a beautifully made film and [director] Byron Haskin was a delight, a most pleasant man to work with. That was fine company. I met [actor] Walter Brooke on that, and Walter and I became very good friends afterwards. I only had that one scene; I walked onto that set at Paramount and, having worked for Ivan, I thought, "My God, they're spending as much money on this scene as we spent on a movie!" It was a very lavish production, and the amount of money available was considerably more than Ivan had when we did *his* movies.

You were in several Robert Aldrich films, starting with What Ever Happened to Baby Jane?

Well, you're talking about my all-time favorite individual, Bob Aldrich. I'd met Bob when he was directing some television stuff—*Mayor of the Town* with Tommy Mitchell. I did several of those, and Bob was originally an assistant director on there and then a director. We became quite friendly, and I did *Baby Jane, The Legend of Lylah Clare* [1968] and *The Longest Yard* [1974] for him. I made more money on *The Longest Yard*, but my favorite was *Lylah Clare*; I thought that was an underrated movie. (Now it has become some kind of cult film.) He had wonderful people in it, wonderful character actors, and I come in at the end and do interviews with these people who knew Lylah Clare [Kim Novak]. Bob said to me, "Mike, make him as loathsome as [he mentioned some guy who did a local late-night television show here] and as smug as [somebody else]." And I *think* I accomplished it. That's something I'm very proud of.

You also worked on a number of occasions with Roger Corman.

Roger was delightful, a lot of fun — nice man! I enjoyed working for him. The biggest picture I did for him was *Bloody Mama* [1970] — we shot that in Arkansas one summer. Shelley Winters was in it and Shelley brought her daughter with her, and I brought my wife and two children. That was a big-budget picture for Corman. Another one I did for him was a science fiction, *War of the Satellites*. Corman had an actor he used all the time, Dick Miller — he couldn't act, but he was a nice little fellow! I was playing an Indian member of the U.N. and I had to deliver a speech, and Dick Miller was a scientist who spoke after I finished. He walked up to the podium, and I almost broke up. He walked with a rather colloquial walk; his speech was kind of colloquial; and he was wearing tassel loafers. And I had a great deal of trouble keeping a straight face, that this was the United Nations and Dick Miller was a scientist representing the United States [*laughs*]!

It was the same sort of experience when we did *Serpent of the Nile*: I got out of a chariot, and there was this Katzman relative who had one line. He was playing a Roman soldier and he was supposed to say to me, "Cassius awaits you in the tent." I got out of the chariot and he said, "Cassius

Fox (in Mr. Hyde makeup) posed with George Sanders in publicity shots for the latter's *Mystery Theater* television series.

wanna see ya inna tent." I said, "No shit!" got back in the chariot, went back around and brought the army up again [*laughs*]!

Any anecdote about your role in Young Frankenstein?
 I play the father of the little girl. When I got the script, the mother's first line was, "Papa, where is Helga? There's a monster loose in the woods!" Mel Brooks said, "That's not funny." There were some laths lying on the floor of the stage, and he said, "Why don't you nail the window closed?" I pick up this lath and I'm nailing the window closed, and the line he gave

me was [*with a dialect*], "Ven monsters is loose, boards must be tight!" It made no sense, but it played very funny [*laughs*]! Mel is crazy as hell — and he's wonderful. I enjoyed working with him very much.

Any closing comments?

I suppose I would like to say that I've been lucky. I've worked on the stage, in films, in television, in radio; I hold a Directors Guild card, I've made a lot of documentaries; I've worked as a writer. So I've done pretty much in this industry what I had wanted. I say *industry*, which always bothers me, because I like to think of what I do as an *art*. I've *enjoyed* it, I've had a ball. When things were lousy, I knew that I was going to be successful somewhere along the line, at no matter what it would be. And I turned my hand to almost everything. Now I'm doing a soap opera, *The Bold and the Beautiful* — I've been doing it for over four years, and I'm enjoying it. The wonderful thing people forget about a soap is that the character goes *on*, and you can develop him along very different lines. I've been fortunate, the producers and writers have given me great leeway and I've been able to make Saul a character that (I *hope*) has more than one side.

I give talks on acting, and someone once asked me, "How many *rules* are there?" I said, "There's one, and it's two words: *Think* and *listen*." If you listen, you react to a stimulus, and that reaction causes another reaction, and then another stimulus is introduced. So acting is *reacting*. To do that naturally, the way an actor the stature of a Muni or an Olivier or a Huston would do it — *that's* what an actor has to do. And the other thing is, *never stop learning*. I'll be seventy-two soon, and I don't think I've ever stopped.

MICHAEL FOX FILMOGRAPHY

A Yank in Indo-China (Columbia, 1952)
Blackhawk (Columbia serial, 1952)
Last Train from Bombay (Columbia, 1952)
Voodoo Tiger (Columbia, 1952)
Run for the Hills (Realart, 1953)
Jack McCall, Desperado (Columbia, 1953)
The Lost Planet (Columbia serial, 1953)
Killer Ape (Columbia, 1953)
Siren of Bagdad (Columbia, 1953)
The Glass Wall (Columbia, 1953)
The Beast from 20,000 Fathoms (Warners, 1953) also Dialogue Director
The Magnetic Monster (United Artists, 1953) also Dialogue Director
Serpent of the Nile (Columbia, 1953)
Sky Commando (Columbia, 1953)

Naked Alibi (Universal, 1954)
Rogue Cop (MGM, 1954)
Masterson of Kansas (Columbia, 1954)
Riding with Buffalo Bill (Columbia serial, 1954)
Riders to the Stars (United Artists, 1954) also Diaglogue Director
Down Three Dark Streets (United Artists, 1954)
Gog (United Artists, 1954) also Dialogue Director
Crashout (Filmakers, 1955) also Dialogue Director
The Scarlet Coat (MGM, 1955)
Conquest of Space (Paramount, 1955)
Adventures of Captain Africa (Columbia serial, 1955)
Running Wild (Universal, 1955)
My Sister Eileen (Columbia, 1955)
The Big Knife (United Artists, 1955)
Kiss Them for Me (20th Century–Fox, 1957)
The Girl in the Kremlin (Universal, 1957)
Top Secret Affair (Warners, 1957)
The Tijuana Story (Columbia, 1957)
Plunder Road (20th Century–Fox, 1957)
Machine-Gun Kelly (AIP, 1958)
War of the Satellites (Allied Artists, 1958)
Let's Make Love (20th Century–Fox, 1960)
What Ever Happened to Baby Jane? (Warners, 1962)
The Interns (Columbia, 1962)
The Misadventures of Merlin Jones (Buena Vista, 1964)
A Tiger Walks (Buena Vista, 1964)
The New Interns (Columbia, 1964)
Billie (United Artists, 1965)
The Legend of Lylah Clare (MGM, 1968)
Bloody Mama (AIP, 1970)
The Dunwich Horror (AIP, 1970)
Young Frankenstein (20th Century–Fox, 1974)
The Longest Yard (Paramount, 1974)

Michael Fox died of pneumonia on June 1, 1996, while this book was in the final stages of production.

*I cared for [Ed Wood] a great deal, probably loved him,
but just not enough to make my life with him.
I think it was possibly the drinking.*

Dolores Fuller

FOR THE PAST DOZEN YEARS, Ed Wood has been *the* most celebrated of all the directors of bad horror movies — perhaps, even, of horror movies in general. And yet still under-reported is the importance of Dolores Fuller in his life and to his films. Part of the reason rests with Fuller, who for decades quietly distanced herself from Wood and from the movies they made; busy (starting in the late 1950s) with songwriting and with her own record company, she had put behind her the days when she supported Wood financially, "probably loved him," and shared with him not only her angora sweater but also the experience of cobbling together the now-notorious *Glen or Glenda*, *Jail Bait* and *Bride of the Monster*. After their split, Wood would sob (to people like makeup man Harry Thomas) that she was "the only woman [he] ever loved," and now, as Sarah Jessica Parker immortalizes Dolores Fuller on film in the Tim Burton movie *Ed Wood*, the real McCoy steps out into the spotlight to accept full credit (responsibility?) for her contributions to the cockeyed canon of Edward D. Wood.

When did you make your first film appearance?

When I was a kid. My parents had to get me out of the cold weather of back east — Chicago — so we drove west and we were staying at a motel in El Monte, about ten miles east of downtown Los Angeles. We were looking into buying a house there. The picture *It Happened One Night* [1934] with Clark Gable and Claudette Colbert, directed by Frank Capra, was shooting, and Capra chose as a location this little motel on the Camino Real. You may remember the famous motel sequence where Gable and Colbert were separated by a sheet when Claudette had to sleep in the same room with Clark. Well, Capra saw me playing around with some other children and put me in his movie as part of the background. I was ten years old. So that was my first picture — you can see me, very briefly, in the scene that they shot at that motel. And I got so interested in the shooting — the way that Colbert and Gable were put in a scene, and the way they "made rain." I was so intrigued with the behind-the-scenes of how a picture is made, I think it had a great influence on me [*laughs*], because from then on, I wanted to be part of that.

Did you do any acting in school?

Oh, yes, I did the lead in the senior play, *Stage Door*. I tried out for a minor part and they gave me the lead! And when I was about sixteen, seventeen, I started modeling. Then I got out of high school one week and

Previous page: After distancing herself for years from Ed Wood's movies, his lover/collaborator Dolores has recently started giving fans a Fuller picture of the man and his art.

[*laughs*] got married the next, at seventeen years old! It was the *stupidest* thing to do! I was working as a model for Westwood Knitting Mills and, while I was still in high school, they sponsored me along with the El Monte Chamber of Commerce and the American Legion Auxiliary in the Miss America contest. I got as far as Long Beach as a contestant — it was staged in the Long Beach Park. And my boyfriend saw me walking across the stage in a little two-piece leopard skin bikini I made for myself — my 36½-22-36 figure at 5'5½" and 114 lbs. stuffed into the bikini, which was sort of ahead of its time [*laughs*]! He took my hand as I was walking across the stage and walked me right off the stage, down the steps, and said, "We're getting in the car right now, and we're getting married!"

He didn't like to see you appearing in public like that.
Yes. He didn't want me appearing anywhere at all, especially showing off my figure like that! And all during our marriage, if I tried to write songs, he'd blast the radio and say, "You can't write! You can't sing!" He never got behind me or any of my talents, and that was the reason that I couldn't continue the marriage after ten years. I felt squelched. I raised my two boys, but after that, I had to have some self-expression.

You worked a lot in television, including as a regular on Queen for a Day.
One day I went into Hollywood, to the *Queen for a Day* show, at NBC on Vine Street, just to take in the show. They gave the women a card: "If you're chosen Queen, what is your uppermost wish?" So I put down on the card, "I want to be on the show." [*Laughs.*] And they chose me as Queen! I thought it'd be a one-time thing, but I ended up with a regular job on the show with Jack Bailey. Gustinette was a sponsor of *Queen for a Day* and I was the Gustinette Girl. An array of beautiful marabou slippers in different rainbow colors — hot pink, yellow, green, blue — was mounted on a big round palette that I would carry. I put on mesh hose and a very short artist's smock (to show my legs) and a tam, and I held a big paintbrush like I was painting these slippers. They kept me as a steady on the show — I worked that show quite a few years, five days a week. I was holding down another job modeling and bookkeeping: I asked for fifteen minutes more on my lunch hour; I'd eat my lunch driving in the car *to* the show; jump into my costume, and do my modeling bit on television. It was a steady income.

So you had a couple of different jobs when you first met Ed Wood.
I was doing movie parts when I could get them, and working as a model, and holding down *another* job. I was also working steadily as Dinah Shore's double on her television show. That was a three-day-a-week job: During

Fuller (bottom) didn't make bad movies for Wood exclusively; she also acted with Mona (*Plan 9 from Outer Space*) McKinnon, middle, and unidentified actress, top, in the dreadful *Mesa of Lost Women*.

the hours of lighting the set, while she was in her dressing room resting or getting ready, I got to do whatever *she* did on the show that evening. Then in the evening, I'd get to do a little speaking part, whatever they could fit me into. So I made pretty good money before I met Ed.

At the time, I was living with an actress named Mona McKinnon;

Mona's the one that got to [star in] *Plan 9 from Outer Space* for Eddie after I left him. She was my best girlfriend all through my marriage ... at least since 1941 or '42. She lived in a beautiful big house in Monterey Park, she was going through a divorce and so was I, so we lived together. One day we saw a *Variety* squib, a casting call, and went to the call. At the time Mona didn't have a Screen Actors Guild card but she had done her own radio show in Pomona, a *Sesame Street*-type thing that she wrote and then did all the different voices for. (I thought she was very creative and clever and I loved her dearly. She died much too young. We were friends until the end.) When I got to the casting call and first laid eyes on the young Edward [Wood], I just thought he was extremely handsome, and his personality was bubbly and fun. Then when I found out he was also a director and writer as well as a producer and actor, I was *very* impressed ... even though I didn't recognize the titles of any of the films he told me he had done. I knew immediately that he liked me, too. As the interview went on, he told me he was going to make me a star. It's a tired old line [*laughs*], but I fell for it hook, line and sinker. When Mona and I went back home, we just couldn't stop talking about the handsome young Eddie Wood and how talented he was, and that maybe [knowing him] would give us a break in the movies.

What was Wood doing for a living at this point?

He was writing and trying to sell his stories. And of course whatever money he would make would go into the movie work. I moved in with him because Mona's husband was coming from San Francisco and intended to win her back. Mona said, "Don't leave me alone with him, please! He'll talk me into it, then *I'll* never have a career!" Her husband did the same thing as mine, he tried to squelch her and keep her from doing her own thing, instead of getting behind her and helping her. But I did move out when her husband came back; I didn't want to interfere. She begged me not to leave, but I said, "No, you two have to work this out." So then I briefly moved into Ed's little place with him, and very soon after that, we moved out of there and got a nice big apartment on Doheny off of Sunset. I was the breadwinner for the two of us.

Was Glen or Glenda *in production by this time?*

No, not yet. By the way, some of these things I'm telling you now are things that I kept secret all these forty years. I wouldn't tell anybody I was ever associated with Ed. For years, the only thing I ever said about my relationship with Wood (I never mentioned *his* name) was that, "Oh, I starred in a couple of low-budget pictures." I never told *any*body, nobody knew.

But now that this Tim Burton movie is coming out, a $22 million movie, and I'm in sixty pages of the script, it's hard for me to hide it anymore — what can I *do*?

I didn't know Eddie was a transvestite when we first got together — even the first *year*, I didn't know. My first clue was when he was writing one evening and we were having a glass of wine together, and he said he'd like to borrow my white angora sweater. It had a V-neck and a collar, it wasn't *that* feminine — it *almost* looked like a man's sweater. I said, "Why do you want to borrow it?" and he said, "Well, it *helps* me write, I feel so much more comfortable. I *hate* men's hard clothes, I like soft, cuddly things. It makes my 'creative juices' flow!" Well, we were all alone and I saw no harm in it — I'm pretty broad-minded [*laughs*] — so I said okay. And that was kind of the start of it, that was my first inkling that maybe he had a fetish. But I didn't realize it went any further.

How much time elapsed between that first meeting with Wood — that casting call — and the making of Glen or Glenda?

I'm awfully bad on dates, but I'd say I met him in the latter part of fifty-two and the movie was made in fifty-three. [Producer] George Weiss had a script that he was planning to do, a movie about [Christine] Jorgensen, about the sex change, but he couldn't get the rights from Jorgensen to do it. So when Eddie found that out, he went to Weiss and pleaded with him, he said, "I'm the best one to rewrite this because I know the *feelings*." It was the first time he came out of the closet and told George Weiss about his transvestism. Before that, no one in Hollywood knew about it. When he was writing the script, usually he would bounce ideas off me and we'd act out little things, what did I think of this or that. I had a good story sense, and I would throw out ideas, and I'm sure it helped Ed a little, having me around.

And you knew, while all this was going on, that you were going to play the girlfriend in it.

Yeah, he always promised to make me a star. But I didn't see the part of the script where he actually dressed *all* up like a woman. I was really kind of shocked when I saw the part with him with a wig on, and dressed totally like a woman, 'cause I wasn't allowed on the set during those scenes.

So the first you knew about it was when the movie was all finished.

Yes! Oh my gosh, I wanted to crawl under the seat [*laughs*]!

Had you spent enough time working on television and in real movies to know that Glen or Glenda *really wasn't the way that movies are supposed to be made?*

Of course. Of *course!* And that's the reason I never talked about them later on. But I was getting a knowledge of what to do, from the script-writing, to the looking-for-the-sets, to ... *every*thing! Tracking down the sets was quite a challenge. We knew we had to save money on every end. For *Jail Bait* [1954], we went right up to a police station and told 'em about the movie, and could we use the outside of the building, and could we use the desk? The desk captain was very cooperative, and he even threw in some policemen for atmosphere. Then we went to the fire department and I flirted with the firemen and got them to furnish us a fire truck! Then we went to many, many nightclubs around Monterey Park to find one with a twenty-foot–high ceiling—we needed to get the crew up into the rafters. Luckily, we got in touch with the owner of a place called the Hunters' Inn and we convinced him that we were going to make his nightclub "famous"! And we kept our end of the bargain, we showed the marquee in *Jail Bait* as the two stars were walking up to the club — it was publicity for his place, and I'm sure it helped. That's the way we had to promote *every*thing! And all the people I modeled for—like Westwood Knitting Mills, a very high-class company that made dresses and sweaters—I got them to give us clothes to use in the films. The girls in beautiful lingerie in *Jail Bait*—one negligee covered with rhinestones cost $700 retail. All these lovely clothes, *any*thing that's worn by a woman in Eddie's first three features was furnished by the people I modeled for, through *me*. These were *some* of the things that I helped Eddie with, things that I pulled together for him. We didn't have Edith Head to design clothes for us, but our costumes would have been a credit to a much more expensive movie.

By the way, the terrible thing about that scene at the Hunters' Inn was that we shot all night, all through the wee hours of the morning; we came in when the customers left, and then we had to be out by two the next afternoon. By shooting all night, I lost track of time and I got fired from my steady job with Dinah Shore, as her double.

Because you were a no-show.

Yes! And that was very good pay. Don Sharp, the man that had hired me to be Dinah Shore's double, said, "Oh, you're just impressed because you're doing a starring part in a movie." I was in tears, I said, "Oh, no, I just completely lost track of what time, what *day* it was!" But he fired me.

If you had gotten an on-screen credit for helping Wood behind-the-scenes as much as you did, what would it have been?

I never asked for one, but I guess it should have been associate producer.

These were all non-union movies?

If he could get away with it [*laughs*]! But we had agreements with the "talent" — I think Bela got $1000 a day, I got $350 or whatever [the amount] was that was scale. But a lot of people just wanted to be *in* the movies, and would work for free.

What was Wood like when he was directing?

He really knew what he was doing when he was on the set. It was as if he had a storyboard in his mind. When he was on a set, he amazed me, I really had a appreciation and an admiration for him. The way he could *know* where (maybe) ten, fifteen people were and what they were supposed to be doing at any one time, it was remarkable. He would yell out his commands, and when he was directing, no doubt about it, he was in complete charge.

Were you on the set the day that Lugosi worked in Glen or Glenda?

Yes. In fact, Bela Lugosi came over to our apartment on Doheny a great deal — I would cook his favorite dish, which was Hungarian goulash. See, I'm of Hungarian descent — my grandmother was an opera singer in Budapest. So we always talked about that kinship.

So he liked you.

Oh! He *loved* me! In fact, Mona told me that one of the last things Bela said to Eddie, just before Bela died (he had his arm around Eddie), was [*Fuller imitates Lugosi's voice and accent*], "Ed-die, take good care of Do-lor-es."

But by that time, 1956, you and Wood had already split.

Right. Bela, I guess, didn't know that.

Would Lugosi come over to your house alone?

Yes. I'm not sure if he was married then or not, because he never brought his wife. My younger son Darrel was there quite a bit. He was about seven years old and he'd sit on Bela's lap and Bela would tell him stories. This was a gentle, sweet man — I *loved* him! And there was continual talk between Bela and Ed, talking about Bela's old movie days. That's all Ed ever lived and breathed for, movies and their history.

Now, I had the unfortunate experience of seeing Bela "shoot up" one time at our apartment. He was in a great deal of pain and he took a little

Rapping with Bela Lugosi at the *Bride of the Monster* wrap party, Fuller neglected to mention that she and Ed Wood were splitsville.

pot and started boiling water, sterilizing a needle. I was *sympathetic* but I *had* to ask, "How did you get started on this, Bela?" He said, "I was going on stage in Europe, and I was in such agonizing pain, I couldn't go on. And so they called the doctor and the doctor gave me morphine." I'd never seen anyone do anything like that before; very quickly, he managed to tie up his arm and give himself an injection. And then the rest of the evening, he was all smiles and congenial and everything. But he was in terrible pain before he gave the injection to himself.

The Ed Wood biography says that Lugosi knew all about Wood's cross-dressing, but Alex Gordon says that if Lugosi had known, he'd have dropped Wood instantly.

Well, I'm inclined to believe Alex Gordon. Bela and Eddie and I were always very close, and Bela *did not know* about Eddie's cross-dressing any more than I did *at that time*. During those days, Eddie never let on. He wanted to marry me, and I don't think a day went by when he didn't ask me to marry him. I just tittered it off and said, "Hey, I just got out of a marriage, I'm not ready yet." Of course Eddie was supportive of me (which my first husband wasn't), I cared for him a great deal, probably loved him, but just not enough to make my *life* with him. I think it was possibly the drinking. (Later on, I bought a home in Burbank, right off of Magnolia Street, and nearby there was a corner bar where Eddie would go quite a bit.) But still, he was healthier then than he was at any other time because I cooked a nice healthy meal every night, with fresh veggies, and made sure that he had a good balanced diet. And so he looked real good, as his photographs show; he didn't fall apart till later.

I've always been a health nut, with vitamins, *long* before they were popular. I taught a class called "Body Beautiful" to a bunch of women when I was about eighteen years old. And I tried to talk a producer, Nat Perrin, into doing an exercise show on television — this was *way* before Jane Fonda did it! I had a script written and I wanted to have beautiful women on the show and teach my exercise class on television and get people more interested in taking care of themselves. In order to get Nat Perrin to read the script, I got on a plane and sat next to him! I did things like this all my life, to try and get something accomplished!

Why does Wood act as "Daniel Davis" in Glen or Glenda?

Probably because he didn't want people to know he was a transvestite.

There were a lot of cross-dressing "actors" in the movie. Were these real-life cross-dressers?

Yes. George Weiss and Eddie got them together. They wanted realism, but they *should* have got good actors, they would have been a lot better.

"Tommy" Haynes — did you meet him, or her, or it, or whatever it was?

Yeah, yeah. (I never cared for those people...!) Oh, Eddie would have

Fuller and Ed Wood never tied the knot in real life, just in Wood's surreal *Glen or Glenda*.

been *so* much better off if he'd have got good actors and let them play the parts! Now, Lyle Talbot was in *Glen or Glenda*, too, playing a detective, and *he* spent a lot of time with Eddie and me. He was having some drinking problems at the time (and, of course, Eddie loved drinking buddies). Once in a while, Lyle and his wife would have problems: He'd be out drinking and she'd lock him out! So he'd come back to our house and sleep on the couch [*laughs*]! And then I remember going to court with [the Talbots]: They were in the primary proceedings of the divorce and they were sitting next to each other and the judge was talking to them. (I guess he was talking to 'em about Lyle's drinking habit.) Well, all of a sudden, Lyle put his hand in his wife's hand, and squeezed her hand, and there was a look of love on both their faces, and he promised not to drink anymore. And they got back together!

What did your boys think of Wood?

Oh, Donald and Darrel liked him — except one time he threw Darrel in the swimming pool and *made* him learn to swim! *That* was resented [*laughs*], but most of the time, they liked him. Eddie being very creative, he went to the dime store with Darrel and bought plastic toy soldiers and he weighted the bottoms down with little chips. He made chessmen and painted them with Darrel. That was one project they did together. We played a *lot* of chess; Darrel became a very good chess player. And Dudley Manlove was like a chess *master, so* good. He and I and Eddie played chess a great deal.

What do you make of Glen or Glenda *today?*
I wish that I'd had more experience and a little more direction. (And, of course, my hairstyle is not so hot!) I always thought I could do better. By the way, later on I went to New York and studied three years with Stella Adler's acting academy. I was determined to do better. In my class were Rita Gam and Warren Beatty.

What can you recall about Wood's unmade The Ghoul Goes West?
I was supposed to be cast as the star! And I looked forward to that one, that was my real "cup of tea." I always felt that Eddie never developed my potential — for instance, he never let me wear sexy clothes because the parts never called for it. I *could* have been developed into a lasting ... commodity [*laughs*], had he taken advantage of what he had.

If he hadn't had the drinking problem, would Ed Wood have had enough talent to pass muster as a legitimate moviemaker?
Oh, *certainly.* He had creativity and the ability to make *something* out of nothing. If he'd had decent budgets *and been dependable,* I think he might have contributed a great deal to our industry. But once he started drinking, people wouldn't give him a chance. I'm afraid his drinking just ruined his life.

You've read the Tim Burton movie's script. What do you think of the way they've written your character?
Well, the language that Sarah Jessica Parker uses is not what we would have used in those days — the four-letter words. But I respect Tim Burton highly. I never met him but I know his work, I've seen all his pictures and I certainly think a great deal of his creativity.

Your last movie for Wood was Bride of the Monster.
He wrote that picture for me to star in. Here I was, supporting him in every way...

It's the other way around in the Tim Burton movie.
Yes, in that script, I'm portrayed as a conniving young actress who would do anything to get a part with him. It doesn't show that I was behind

him 100 percent, working with him — they don't show that at all. I was "carrying" him most of the time during our relationship.

Anyway, while we were trying to put *Bride of the Monster* together, some of Ed's friends told us that there was a girl [Loretta King] who'd inherited some money — "old family money" — and she was interested in financing a picture. We met her in the Valley, on Ventura Boulevard, at the Tail o' the Cock [restaurant], and she was sitting in the bar area with nothing in front of her — no water, no Coca-Cola, nothing to drink. Eddie and I ordered drinks and asked her what she wanted. Loretta King said she never drank liquids. Here I am, this health nut who has to have eight glasses of water a day, and I told her, "That's very bad for your skin, it'll dry up, it'll wrinkle." She was worried that it'd put weight on her, or something like that. So we didn't hit it off too well [*laughs*] because here I was, suggesting that she'll dry up like a prune!

We sat down at a table and ordered some food, and she started thumbing through the script. She found my part and said, "Oh, this is a part I'd like to play!" (I probably turned all colors!) Of course, we're thinking she's gonna put up at least $60,000 — that was the amount she was supposed to put up.

Now, that's a lot more money than had gone into Glen *or* Glenda *or* Jail Bait.

Right. But that amount was what *Bride of the Monster* really needed. It was *still* a little amount by [the usual standards of] picturemaking, but Eddie could *do* it. Well, Eddie must have met with her other times without me along, because she got the part and then the picture started shooting.

Did Wood ever "step out" on you?

For the most part, during our relationship, I would say that Eddie never did. He was always home in the evening with me. There's a lot of talk going on about how much he liked girls and all that; well, he never had time for "another woman." And he *loved* me. Maybe all that talk [of Wood's womanizing] means after I left, because I would swear that he never stepped out on me, that we had a one-on-one relationship.

Anyway, on *Bride of the Monster*, the man that owned the studio they were working in wanted his money. So Eddie went over to Loretta and asked her for the rest of the money (I think she'd given him about $350 or so to get started). And she said, "*What* money?" He said, "Well, the money we *contracted* for." She said, "*I* don't have any money!" Well, I was just livid, because that was my part and I *earned* it! So I began asking myself, "What the heck is this relationship [Fuller-Wood] *leading* to?? I gotta go on to better things, this is not what I want to do with my life!"

So that was what tore it for you and Wood?
  Well, the drinking, too. I think if I'd have kept working with Eddie, I might have got him to stop drinking.

Loretta King says it was a misunderstanding, that she never said she could put up the money. Did she really represent herself as having the money?
  She *told us* that she was going to give $60,000 and that she wanted my part. To get the part, Eddie told her, she *had* to put up the money to finance the picture.

You couldn't have dropped Wood completely when he gave Loretta King your part, because you're in the movie and you attended the premiere.
  Well, I usually finish what I start [*laughs*]!

Outside of your small part, were you on the set of Bride of the Monster *much?*
  No, I wasn't. I was busy, I was always working, or *looking* for work. I think I did a good job in that bit part; I showed a little antagonism toward Loretta King, which was okay.

[Laughs.] Which was probably easy! Did you get to meet Tor Johnson at all?
  Oh, yes, he was over at the house quite a bit. He would sit on the toilet seats and break 'em [*laughs*]! Sweet as could be, like a little lamb. Didn't speak very good English.

Alex Gordon says that the Bride of the Monster *prop octopus was rented, that Wood didn't sneak into Republic and steal it.*
  He *sure did*. I wasn't there, but I *know* it happened.

So, between Wood's drinking and his giving your part to Loretta King, you'd had enough at that point.
  That's right. I changed the locks on my Burbank house and said, "This is it. This is enough." This was right after Loretta King took my part, and Eddie was drinking too much. It was about dusk, and Eddie was *drunk*. He stood outside of the house and he *cried*—"Dolores, let me *in*, let me *in*. I *love* you, I *love* you! Please let me in!" I *didn't* hear him say, "I'll never *drink* again!" [*laughs*]—all I heard was how much he loved me. Well, I refused to let him in—it was too late. (It was a very sad scene. The whole neighborhood heard him.) His loyalty was to his picture and *how* he could get it done—*whatever way* he could get that picture done. And *I* thought he should've been loyal to *me*, and we'd have got it done somehow, some other way, without giving Loretta King my part.

How long was it before he stopped "serenading" you like that?

Well, he never stopped "serenading" me, I finally left town — I went to New York. I got a chance for a job at $50 a day, modeling shoes for a big company. I was picked up at the airport by Stanley Kramer and shown the George Washington Bridge and Times Square, and my eyes popped out of my head! My God, I thought New York was impressive! So I decided to move there. And I went to Hunter College and to Stella Adler's acting academy because I wanted to better myself.

How did you get into songwriting?

I had worked with [producer] Hal Wallis and was a friend of his while I was in Hollywood. He came into New York and took me to dinner and took me to a movie, and I started telling him about the songs I'd been writing. (Everything I had written, by the way, I'd sold to a publisher. I'd go in and get a couple hundred dollars in advance every time I wrote a song! So this also supplied me with a nice little income.) Hal Wallis was very interested in hearing them. I had a lot of good stereo equipment in my apartment and he was quite impressed; after hearing a few demos, he said to me, "Dolores, if you can write like this, why do you want to be an actress?" (Hal's *Blue Hawaii* [1961] was coming up, and I was up for the part of the schoolteacher.) I said, "Come on, Hal! I want to go to Hawaii with Elvis and be in the picture." But Hal insisted that writing songs was a much more rewarding career: "Tomorrow morning, I want to introduce you to [music publisher] Freddy Bienstock. I want you to write for this picture." Apparently he felt I was a better songwriter than an actress [*laughs*]. Well, I appreciate what he did for me, because the first song I wrote for him was "Rock-a-Hula Baby," co-written with Ben Weisman. We got in on the twist craze, and when the picture premiered, Hal Wallis had a big banner that went across the whole theater: SEE ELVIS DO THE ROCK-A-HULA TWIST. And *that* really launched the song. It was on the charts for six months. When the song was released [as a record], the other side was a smash hit, too, a much more lasting song than mine, "Can't Help Falling in Love." On the charts, "Can't Help Falling in Love" was number one for six months and mine was number three. In Japan, they liked *mine* better; *it* was number one and "Can't Help Falling in Love" was number three!

Who are some of the other singers you've written for over the years?

About the time I began writing for the Elvis movies, a song I had been working on, "Someone to Tell It To," was recorded by Nat "King" Cole. My friend, the great Jimmy Van Heusen, wrote the music. Sammy Cahn wrote an introductory verse which appears on the sheet music but Nat never recorded the verse, my lyrics are the only ones he sings. Peggy Lee recorded one of my songs, "Losers Weepers"; and a fun little ditty that I wrote with Sammy Fain, "How Can Anyone Keep from Singing," made it into the *Mary Poppins* album.

After I had a few hit records with the Elvis movie songs, I got my own record company, Dee Dee Records, which was financed by Desilu and my dear friend Martin Leeds. I took an unknown Johnny Rivers to Nashville and recorded his first four songs, using Ricky Nelson's band on my own label, and launched Johnny's career. Starting in the mid-1960s, I put together music groups, booked them and got them record contracts. When Tanya Tucker was only thirteen years old, living in a trailer in Henderson, Nevada, her father brought her to me. I took her to Billy Sherrill in Nashville, we picked her song "Delta Dawn," got her a Columbia Records contract and within six months, she was a star. I was her first personal manager, but her father completely dominated her and finally made her switch to him as her personal manager. She was too young to understand the ethics of what was going on, not to mention the legalities of contract violation. I've never been litigation-minded but I was sorry to see her go after all the time and money I put into getting her career in gear. The loss of Tanya actually made me quite ill.

When you came back West to California, did you ever see or hear from Wood again?

I came back in sixty-four and I wish now that I had contacted him, but I didn't. I heard from Mona McKinnon that he was married and that he was making porno pictures. That was enough to make me stay away. I didn't want any part of it. I moved back and bought a beautiful house at 8115 Mulholland Terrace in the Hollywood Hills and I used to give a lot of wonderful parties. If I could have been sure that Eddie wouldn't drink too much, I could have invited him. I often had producers and show people and politicians at the house. I had two and a half acres of grounds on top of Mulholland and it was beautiful — it was a party house! But I had put Eddie behind me.

When did you find out that he had passed away?

Years after he died. It was Rudy Grey [Wood's biographer] who told me.

And what do you think of the fact that Ed Wood and his movies and his entire circle of friends have acquired this very strange cult following?

It surprises me. He influenced our lives. His high energy level, his effervescence and what he did with nothing, you gotta give him credit for that. At least he brought each picture to an end *somehow*, he'd always finish 'em, against all odds. I've looked at the movies again lately, and there *are* parts of 'em that are interesting. Eddie let me have an insight into what picturemaking was all about, from start to finish. And even though his pictures weren't the best, it was fun doing 'em.

[The foregoing interview was conducted in 1994, before the release of *Ed Wood*. The following "update" interview took place a year later, after *Ed Wood*'s critical success, box office failure and Martin Landau's Best Supporting Actor Oscar win.]

When did you first become aware that Tim Burton wanted to make a movie about Ed Wood?

I first heard that Burton was making *Ed Wood* during an interview by an Italian journalist who was doing a story for the independent film journal *Anteprima*. I could hardly believe it! It sounded very exciting, and I tried to find out more about it. I got ahold of the script, and originally the part of Dolores Fuller was in about sixty pages.

Were you approached at any point by the Burton people for permission, for input, for anything?

No, I wasn't, I didn't get to speak to the young writers [Scott Alexander and Larry Karaszewski] until the premiere of the movie. I said, "My God, I know more about Eddie than anyone alive. Why didn't you contact me?" They said, "We didn't want to contact you. We were *afraid*." They told me that Burton wanted to film the script he'd seen exactly as it was, so there was no point in doing any further research or rewrites. I think they were afraid the project might be contaminated by too much reality and Burton might back off if changes were made. Why-fix-it-if-it-ain't-broke? sort of thinking.

Where and when did you see the movie for the first time?

My husband Philip Chamberlin and I knew it was going to be premiered, so we came into Hollywood at Disney's invitation and saw it at the Hollywood Galaxy Theatre. Disney sent a limo for us where we were staying. Their publicity people and Howard Green, especially, were wonderful to me. There were photographers, interviewers and everything — it was an exciting night! Then there was a party afterwards at Musso and Frank's. I loved the movie, I was just thrilled. It was wonderful entertainment and it captured the fifties days of making low-budget movies, it captured the feeling of having fun with a group of friends who know and respect each other and just love working together. The part of Ed Wood was captured beautifully by Johnny Depp, the *effervescence*. Now, [the real] Ed Wood wasn't *always* "up," he got — well, not depressed, but *discouraged* once in a while. The movie played it more like Andy Hardy.

You come off as one of the closest-to-normal people in the movie.

Yes, but the movie didn't show how Eddie and I worked together and how close we were and how much in love we were. We did just *everything* together. Sarah Jessica Parker didn't have an understanding of the part of Dolores Fuller at all — she didn't get the depth of our relationship, Eddie's and mine. (By the way, a lot of her work landed on the cutting room floor — she was in much more of the picture originally.) She never bothered to *call* me, she didn't do any research. Patricia Arquette got together with Kathy Wood, Lisa Marie took Vampira to dinner and so on, but I never even got a *phone call* from Sarah Jessica Parker. It was very unprofessional of her. But even more unprofessional was the way she trashed me on *David Letterman, Conan O'Brien, Good Morning America, Jay Leno* and all over national television. I think she was trying to explain to herself why her performance was so weak in the movie. At one point when some reviewer bemoaned the lack of appreciation for her by the press, she actually said, "What do you expect? I was playing the part of the worst actress ever in the history of film." It's as if the lack of attention for her work was my fault! I think it hurt the film's box office. Who wants to see a movie about a bad actress? The more she went around, supposedly on behalf of the film, the shorter the run.

Did you mind the fact that the movie made a lot of fun of your acting ability?

Well, I *was* uncomfortable when I played the part in *Glen or Glenda*. Eddie wrote the script in four days and shot it in five, and I didn't *want* our life to be put on the screen; in fact, I was the one that got him to change his name in the credits [to Daniel Davis], hoping that nobody would realize that it was taken from our own lives. That's the *only* research that Sarah Jessica Parker did, looking at that one movie of mine, where I was kind of embarrassed to even be doing it. Eddie just told me to play the part as myself, and that it was going to be a documentary.

But were you offended by the fact that, throughout Ed Wood, *Dolores Fuller is depicted as a bad actress?*

Yeah, I didn't feel good about it, because I had done some much bigger movies. I was a well-established actress — I was a regular on *Queen for a Day* and *Dinah Shore*. Also, I was on Bob Hope's show often and Danny Thomas's,

Dolores Fuller

I was on *Superman* and often on the old Johnny Carson show and others. I was in demand as an actress and a model. I was most proud of being featured in a Barbara Stanwyck/Fred MacMurray movie, *The Moonlighter* [1953], before I met and began working with Eddie.

And began supporting Ed Wood.

Well, I contributed a lot to the support, but I didn't mind at all because we were working together and accomplishing what we wanted. We were accomplishing our *dreams*.

I still don't know what to call Ed Wood. *It's a "tribute" that makes everybody look worse than they were, it's a "biography" where everything's a lie—*

You're absolutely right, it doesn't fit into any category. It's very original, and of course that's Tim Burton's style.

Some of the real-life people came off very badly in the movie, like George Weiss, who's falsely depicted as a fat, vulgar slob. Who did you feel sorriest for, who was the most maligned?

I thought *I* was [*laughs*]! And I thought that Martin Landau was absolutely marvelous. He was *perfect* when he imitated Bela's speeches and extraordinary when he created his Bela Lugosi character getting out of the coffin, being so caustic and mean and using foul language. But it upset me because it just was not the real Bela Lugosi; it was the invention of the two kids who did the script [Alexander and Karaszewski] and, even more so, the inventive mind of Martin Landau. I think Landau certainly deserved the Academy Award and he was marvelous, but Bela never used foul language!

Is Bela Lugosi up in Heaven smiling about Ed Wood, *or is he rolling over in his grave?*

Bela would have mixed feelings. He was a true aristocrat in person, a real Old World gentleman. He'd come over to my house often for dinner with Eddie and me and I'd make him Hungarian goulash. (My grandmother was Hungarian and I had a good recipe.) And Bela would just be charming—he'd sit with my little six-year-old son Darrel Fuller on his knee and tell him stories! He wasn't like he is on screen [in *Ed Wood*]. And I hate to have people thinking that Bela was that mean, because he *wasn't*.

So much of the Lugosi material in Ed Wood *is fictionalized. Is their fabrication more interesting than his real life and his real personality?*

I don't think it would have hurt to show some of his aristocratic, Old World charm.

So what they did wasn't nice and wasn't necessary.

No, it wasn't necessary for him to be so *mean*. I think it would have been more interesting if Lugosi had been *himself*, if the Martin Landau character had been more like Lugosi in real life — suave, the twinkle in his eye, flirting. He was a lovable person. The way Landau recreated the [*Glen or Glenda*, *Bride of the Monster* and *Plan 9 from Outer Space*] scenes was incredible, just beautiful. It was only when the off-screen Bela Lugosi was being portrayed that the real Bela would feel a stake through his heart there in his coffin. But his character in *Ed Wood* was unique and those who know nothing about the real Bela will never care. What's on the screen may not be as interesting as the real thing in some ways and it may be more interesting in other ways, but it is more real in the long run because it is movie art. For me, the real Bela only pretended to die. He will live forever through his art. He may not be smiling about the way he was shown as a character in *Ed Wood*, but I'm sure he is looking down and smiling to think that a movie has been made about him and his friend Eddie. I certainly hope so, and I'm sure he's delighted with the phenomenal media coverage we three are getting these days!

And how about Ed Wood? What is he thinking in the Next World about Ed Wood*?*

Oh, he would be very happy about everything that's happened. He's looking down at me and thinking, "See! I *told* you I'd make you a star!"

What did you think of Ed Wood's *box office chances when you first saw it?*

I can't say; all I knew at that moment was how *thrilled* I was with it. A critic here in town [Las Vegas], a well-known movie critic named Carol Cling, voted it Number One in the Best Films of 1994. Number one! And I certainly agreed with her. But it was in wide release when it *should* have had special handling. The word-of-mouth was just wonderful — everyone that I talked to just raved about it, they all agreed that it was the best picture of the year. But before a lot of my friends could see it, it was *gone*! It could have built steadily over the months if it was just in one theater.

I have a book coming out soon, it's called *Eddie and Me: My Bizarre Life with Edward D. Wood, Jr.* It was something I had to do to correct a lot of things and tell the real story. I think it'll be about 100 pages — not a long book — and it'll have a lot of pictures. There were a lot of things Eddie and I did together that weren't in the *Ed Wood* script.

*The Rudolph Grey biography [*Nightmare of Ecstasy*] — what kind of marks would you give that for accuracy?*

It depends on how open each of Rudolph's interviewees were with him. At the time I talked to Rudolph, I never realized there was going to be a movie out or that I would have to do a tell-all type of thing. So I held back a lot. All my life, I never told people that I did these movies with Eddie. I felt they were low-budget and they would never be seen, so I would never talk about them. And I didn't talk too much to Rudolph Grey. In my book I'm just lettin' everything come out.

But in general, how accurate a picture of Ed Wood does the Rudolph Grey book paint?

Very accurate, as accurate as the people that Rudolph interviewed could recall. It's a *Citizen Kane* book in some ways, because different people had different perceptions, and some were not in agreement with my views. (These were usually people who didn't *know* Eddie very well.) Even Loretta King does not remember one point accurately. Eddie and I met her together at the Tail o' the Cock restaurant on Ventura Boulevard and we both heard her say that she didn't think that $60,000 was very much money for *Bride of the Monster*. In the context of the conversation, she led us to believe that she was going to put money into the film. But after seeing Loretta's interview in the new Brett Thompson documentary *The Haunted World of Edward D. Wood, Jr.*, I'm now thinking that we could have been interpreting what she said in a way she may not have intended. We needed money for that movie so desperately and we had been told that she had inherited a lot of money. But intentional or not, *that* was the reason that she got my part. That and an agent named Marge Usher, who handled Loretta and "Kelton the Cop" [Paul Marco] and others. Marge Usher found the money man, and so she sort of got her way about who was going to be in *Bride of the Monster*.

For you, what have been the repercussions of Ed Wood*?*

Well, my husband Philip and I just got back from Munich, where I was the guest of honor at the Film Festival. I was in such demand — I was doing five, six television shows every day, and the interviewers just kept coming! We didn't have time to go sightseeing — we didn't even have time to go to the *movies*, which is a little ridiculous at a film festival [*laughs*]! The press coverage there was phenomenal, and they showed *Glen or Glenda, Jail Bait, Bride of the Monster, Plan 9* and the Brett Thompson documentary, which I am principally featured in. I would get up and speak and take questions from the

"[This] still shows more about our relationship [Fuller and Ed Wood] than the whole *Ed Wood* movie does." Left to right, Wood, Fuller, Bud Osborne and Lyle Talbot in *Jail Bait*.

audience after each of the movies I was in. Not only that, I appeared and did a little skit with my marvelous host, Prof. Albert Johnson, following the German premiere of *Ed Wood*. It was like a dream come true.

Was Ed Wood *well-received at the Festival?*
    It was so crowded, you couldn't walk down the stairs — the seats were all full, and people were sitting on the stairs. And this was a 600-seat theater, not a small one! They also showed the restored *Crossroads at Laredo* [1948], Ed Wood's first little movie, which had never been seen before because it had never been finished. The sound was lost, so with all the recent attention on Eddie, the original producer [C.J. Thomas, who plays a part in *Crossroads*] got in touch with me and asked me to be the music director. I got my husband Philip involved and we got the restoration done. I wrote two songs for it, one with my longtime Elvis Presley collaborator and one with Philip. Finally, with Philip's help, we wrote and recorded a narration with my old friend, country Hall-of-Famer Cliffie Stone. We hope to get a record deal for the complete soundtrack, which features the voice of Elvis Presley, Jr. When people hear him, they are going to be amazed. What a voice and what feeling!

This "restoration" of Crossroads at Laredo *has all taken place in the last year or so, right?*

Yes, this year [1995]. It'll be released in theaters first, together with the Brett Thompson documentary as one program. There was an excellent review of both the documentary and *Crossroads at Laredo* in weekly *Variety* on August 7. They called *Crossroads at Laredo* "the dessert" [*laughs*]!

If you could change one thing in Ed Wood, *what would it be?*

It would be how Eddie and I worked together. We bounced ideas off each other and looked for locations and had to promote *everything*. I really don't think that those three movies [*Glen or Glenda, Jail Bait, Bride of the Monster*] would have been made without my help. For the last year I've been calling Sarah Jessica Parker, Sarah *Jurassic* Parker [*laughs*], because she reminds me of one of these cold, prehistoric animals! I was sexy and feminine and cuddly, and she didn't catch any of that, she didn't catch our deep love for each other. Now, she was good in *Striking Distance* [1993], where she played a macho cop — and where she was being pulled by a major star, Bruce Willis. But in her *Miami Rhapsody* [1995], where she had to carry it, it flopped!

I recently came across a production shot from *Jail Bait*, a shot of me working with Eddie on the set. That still shows more about our relationship than the whole *Ed Wood* movie does. When Eddie was directing, I just respected him and adored him and I looked at him with awe. In the photo, I'm looking at him very adoringly, because it's on the set when he's working. He knew where everybody should be and what they should be doing, and he was yelling out his commands on the megaphone. He was such a character and such fun to be with.

DOLORES FULLER FILMOGRAPHY

It Happened One Night (Columbia, 1934)
Outlaw Women (Lippert, 1952)
Glen or Glenda (I Changed My Sex; I Led Two Lives) (Screen Classics, 1953)
The Body Beautiful (Phoenix, 1953)
College Capers (Lippert short, 1953)
The Moonlighter (Warners, 1953)
Girls in the Night (Universal, 1953)
The Blue Gardenia (Warners, 1953)
Mesa of Lost Women (Lost Women) (Howco, 1953)
The Raid (20th Century–Fox, 1954)
Playgirl (Universal, 1954)

Jail Bait (The Hidden Face) (Howco, 1954)
This Is My Love (Night Music) (RKO, 1954)
Bride of the Monster (Bride of the Atom) (Banner Productions, 1955)

It Came from Hollywood (Paramount, 1982) features footage of Fuller in *Glen or Glenda*.

[Universal was] like a stock company. One time you got a good role, then you landed a small part in the next movie. That irked me about Universal. I felt that you should always advance, not take two steps backward for each step forward.

Anne Gwynne

NO MOTION PICTURE STUDIO ever had a gallery of ghastlies that could compare with Universal's, nor the selection of lovely starlets who would shriek and swoon in the clutches of their classic movie monsters. In the 1940s, the late Evelyn Ankers was Universal's preeminent scream queen, but ranking a close second was Anne Gwynne, the Texas-born beauty and former model who appeared in dozens of the studio's features and serials in the early 1940s. She was Boris Karloff's daughter in the brain-switching tale *Black Friday* and Dracula's (John Carradine) quarry in *House of Frankenstein*, not to mention the lead in other memorable B-grade entertainment like *Weird Woman*, *The Strange Case of Doctor Rx*, *Flash Gordon Conquers the Universe* and the 1941 *The Black Cat*. Long-retired (her last leading role was in 1958's *Teenage Monster*), she retains fond memories of "the good old days" and candid recollections of her encounters with Universal's great ghouls.

Your first film in the genre field was Black Friday.

Well, not exactly. Though released in 1940, *Flash Gordon Conquers the Universe* was actually shot in 1939. It featured all kinds of weird creatures, prehistoric monsters, ray guns, you name it.

Did you have any encounters with that serial's special effects people?

No, I wasn't in the same scenes with the monsters — I'd see them and scream, but they didn't have us in the same shot, so I didn't deal with the effects in that. A black background was used, with the film of various dinosaurs or whatever being matted together with great results. I liked Buster Crabbe [Flash Gordon] a lot; he was a very nice guy. Carol Hughes was also friendly, but it was Charles Middleton [Ming] and Don Rowan who were in most of my scenes. It was a hectic but fun experience. I saw it again only recently, and didn't realize that I did as much in it as I did. I don't recall being on it for all that long, but that was around the time I was doing thirteen pictures a year — sometimes two or three at a time. The memory tends to blur on such matters!

Any Black Friday *memories?*

Boris Karloff. What an actor; what a *man*! I had a key scene with Boris, the one where I'm urging him to take Stanley Ridges back home from New York. Well, we shot the entire scene with the camera on Boris. Arthur Lubin was the director, and for some reason I've always felt that he didn't like me. He said, "Wrap!" but Boris came to my rescue and said, "*Don't do this to*

Previous page: Anne Gwynne falls under the spell of Court Dracula in her final Universal horror, *House of Frankenstein.*

her. Give Anne a close-up." Which is exactly what Lubin had to do, and it's in the picture! Now that is a really terrific guy. Most actors wouldn't think of it, or do it if they *did* think of it, but Boris Karloff I'll always admire. He was not only a fine actor who could play just about anything, but a really terrific human being. He is sorely missed.

There was much press during Black Friday *concerning a hypnotist who supposedly put Bela Lugosi under his spell, making him believe he was about to suffocate, just before he shot his death scene in the film.*
    All hype. All for publicity. I didn't believe it — it was all a put-on for the camera and the press. The studios always did those sorts of things.

In the scene where Anne Nagel is being strangled, her scream sounds suspiciously like yours.
    You're right, they had me dub it in later. Originally, there was no scream — after all, when you are being strangled, you can't very well scream, now *can* you [*laughs*]? But someone decided, after the fact, that they needed a scream in that scene, so I came in to do it.

Did you do any other "after-the-fact" screaming in movies?
    Well, as a matter of fact, I did. Whenever a girl couldn't get it out, they always called on me. I never had any trouble handling them, so I was called upon many, many times. However, I don't know what pictures they were in. I just did the scream, then went back to whatever else I was doing at the time. It really was a busy, busy period in my life. I worked with the same people over and over again, so it is sometimes hard to remember all the details. Incidentally, some people used to confuse Anne Nagel with me. We worked in a few pictures together, and did a lot of publicity together, and I can see some similarities. I think she should have gone much further. Her coming to Universal was really a step down for her. She had leads at Warners [in the thirties], but after her husband Ross Alexander killed himself, it sort of did her in. She more or less started over, doing bits with me before working back up to leads in Bs. She died so very young of cancer. It's a shame.

Your next genre film was the mystery/comedy The Black Cat *with Broderick Crawford.*
    Now *that* is one of my all-time favorite pictures. The cast was terrific, and the director, Al Rogell, was a doll. Along with a few others, including *Ride 'Em Cowboy, Men of Texas* [both 1942], *We've Never Been Licked* [1943] and a couple more, it really is tops with me.

That was your second film with Lugosi, but your first chance to have any scenes with him.

Again, he was a very nice, pleasant fellow. But he was a foreigner who didn't speak English that well, so my relationship with him was just pleasantries, nothing much to speak of. He was very different in every picture. That was something I also tried to do—I tried to be a different character in each of my movies. My hairstyles would change; the hair color would change. Bela seemed to be able to carry that off better than Boris, although both were very good.

What about Crawford? You later worked with him quite often.

If you asked who my favorite leading men were, Broderick Crawford's name would come at the top of the list. He was a man's man, very helpful and supportive of me. He had a fabulous background—his father was Lester Crawford and his mother was the marvelous Helen Broderick, who made several pictures at Universal. We had lots of fun on all our pictures together. There were lots of pranks, but all done in fun. He was a heavy drinker—he'd go out with the boys for lunch and drink it, but what a guy. He liked to indulge in ad-libs, but if they were good, they could be left in the picture. I had absolutely no problem with him, although Lois Collier and I were having lunch together recently, and she mentioned that his pranks on her, during the filming of *Slave Girl* [1947], verged on being cruel. I was shocked because we got along famously. I got back at Brod one day: There's a scene in *Tight Shoes* [1941] where a free-for-all is taking place. He had to slap me, and that was something that was very hard for him to do. I told him to hit me, so we could get it over with. The next day, when my father was visiting the set, I went to makeup and had them put black-and-blue makeup on me, so that Brod would think I was all bruised up. I put a jawbreaker in my mouth, to add to the effect, and it really got to him. He was so upset that I got tickled, and nearly choked on that jawbreaker!

Brod and I were almost like a screen team, we did so many pictures together—*Black Cat, Tight Shoes, Sin Town* [1942] and *Broadway* [1942]. I wanted so very much to play Pearl, the murderess, in *Broadway*. That was about the only time I stood up for myself. I went into Dan Kelly's office; he was the casting director at Universal. When I asked him if I could play the part, he said, "No. You haven't lived yet." I was angry, and went and told Broderick. That really burned him up. He said that you don't have to go out and kill someone to play a murderer. He stormed into Kelly's office, and although I didn't know what went on behind those closed doors, I do know that I got the part!

Were you happy with the job you did in Broadway?

I was not pleased with the results. My boyfriend at the time, Gil Valle, who was a first assistant director at Universal, took me to some dives, to see how real chorus girls, "tarts," acted. One day, when I was simply in a background scene, the director, William Seiter, screamed at me, "You're overdoing it, Anne." I was so embarrassed, I've never gotten over it. He thought he was such a great director, but he was really awful. The best director I've worked with was Henry Koster. If I had had more directors like him, maybe I'd have been a bigger star. I played a flirt in *Spring Parade* [1940]. Not knowing what a flirt would do (I was so *green* in those days!), Henry Koster took me aside and told me to gently stroke my feather boa. Now *that's* what a director is for — to help the actors. Be supportive, not yell when they do something they don't like. That reminds me of another Arthur Lubin story. On *Ride 'Em Cowboy* with the marvelous Abbott and Costello, there's a scene where I have to wrestle with a Brahman bull, rope and tie it. Now, I'm from Texas, but not from a ranch! I was told to do the scene myself. I was too naive to tell him to use a double. I could have been killed! But the scene does play better, because you can definitely see that it's me with the bull! Incidentally, I did know enough to realize when the bull was getting angry, and it was time to stop fooling with it. I did speak up that time, thank goodness, or else I wouldn't be here with you now, telling you this story.

What about some of the other Black Cat *people, Alan Ladd, Gladys Cooper and Gale Sondergaard?*

Well, Gladys Cooper was a very highly regarded actress. It seemed as though she was slumming, working in this picture. But she was very good in it.

There's a scene where she is supposedly carrying you through secret passageways. Was that really you?

No, it was a stunt double — for *both* of us. I believe hers was a man, dressed in Gladys' evening gown. She never could have lifted me. She was too tiny, too fragile, but a great lady.

Did you think that Alan Ladd might be on the verge of stardom?

Absolutely not. That little insecure man, in person, didn't seem to have it. I don't believe anything surprised me more than his rocketing to stardom. He didn't impress me in the least; he was very quiet, very nothing. But he had what I didn't have — an agent with push and drive who helped him become the big star that he did. And, of course, he was *married* to her! Sue Carol [Mrs. Ladd], who had been in pictures years earlier, was a much better agent than she was an actress. If not for her, he wouldn't have gotten anywhere.

And Sondergaard?
All I remember was that she was a Commie and got herself blacklisted. Rather reserved, but striking — a real beauty. We certainly never warmed up to one another. I did see her again only a few years before her death: Richard Lamparski, who does those *Whatever Became of...* books, asked several of his favorites to sign our names in cement at his home in the hills near Universal. Gale was there, as was another Universal vet, Susanna Foster.

Al Rogell mentioned that Marlene Dietrich, who was then having a romance with Broderick Crawford, visited the set of Black Cat, *and doubled for Claire Dodd in some long shots.*
I don't recall this happening, but I'm sure it did. Brod and Marlene did have this thing together. I guess that's why Brod and I never went anywhere — we were always dating other people. I saw her around, of course, and she was even supposed to be in *Sin Town* with Brod and me, but that didn't happen. [Constance Bennett played the part.] As far as Dietrich doubling for Claire Dodd, I never actually saw this happen, but it is the type of thing that *would* happen on that set. A really enjoyable experience.

Your next horror film was The Strange Case of Doctor Rx. *What was that one like?*
Fun, fun, fun. I loved working with Patric Knowles. So very tall and handsome. A Britisher and very nice — but married. He and I also worked together in *Sin Town*.

Reportedly, much of Doctor Rx *was ad-libbed.*
Right, it was done off-the-cuff. I would go home at night and study my lines, only to arrive the next morning to learn that everything was thrown out! It didn't take me too many nights to know to just go home and relax — there was no telling what to expect the next day — but it was an anxious-to-get-to-the-studio feeling, that was for sure. Like in *The Black Cat*, the ad-libs were used, only much more so. Each of us would suggest things, and the director, William Nigh, would use them. That was just great, an experience I never had before or since. Of course, as a result, there are some plot loopholes in the finished product, but who cares? It was an hour of laughs and chills, a real crowd-pleaser.

Ad-libs and off-the-cuff rewriting was part of the fun of making *The Strange Case of Doctor Rx*, says Gwynne. (The gorilla is cowboy star Ray Corrigan.)

You also starred in another spooky comedy/mystery, Murder in the Blue Room.

Oh, I liked that one, too. I ran it for my grandson, Chris, when I was baby-sitting him one night. His father, my son-in-law, is Robert Pine, the sergeant on *CHiPs*, who was also in *Munster, Go Home!* and *Empire of the Ants*—he keeps a still of himself, being devoured by an ant, in his office, just to remind him of the low point in his career! My daughter is Gwynne Gilford, who starred in *Beware! The Blob* [*Son of Blob*] and *Fade to Black*. But back to *Murder in the Blue Room*. The ghost in the story turns out to be a real spook — they usually had some sort of explanation for the ghosts in those days, but not in this one—but I still liked it a lot. I am not always pleased with myself, but I did especially like my "singing" of the song in the opening party scene. Martha Tilton sang for me, but it really sounded and looked like I was doing it. It comes across on film when the cast is having a good time, and we certainly did on that one.

Talk about the Inner Sanctum mystery Weird Woman.

Another movie with pleasant memories. Evelyn Ankers and Lois Collier were in it, and we became lifelong friends. In fact, I was having lunch with Lois the day after Evelyn had passed away, and I told her about it. She hadn't heard yet.

What about your experiences with Lon Chaney, Jr.?

Well, now you've got me. I have nothing but glowing things to say about Boris Karloff, and only praise for Bela Lugosi, but Lon Chaney was something else, although we actually got along fine together. For some reason, I was considered the "virgin" on the lot. Those rowdy rascals wouldn't act that way around me. No one ever used profanity in my presence. Nothing off-color was brought up around me.

But, back to Lon Chaney. He would pull practical jokes on people—and they did become quite cruel. He never bothered me at all—it was Evelyn who incurred his wrath. They worked together more often, and yet they couldn't stand each other, sort of like the way Jon Hall and Maria Montez never got along. As far as Chaney was concerned, he was wrong for the role in *Weird Woman*—in the picture, both Evelyn Ankers and Lois Collier are mad about him, but he's my husband. I think of Lon as a character heavy, like he was in *Frontier Badmen* [1943], or as a monster. It seems strange that he would be in this type of part. I just didn't feel he was the leading-man type, and luckily I had no direct contact with his pranks.

However, when we did *Frontier Badmen* together, he really let Bob Paige have it. Seems Bob was afraid of horses, and it didn't take Lon long to find that out. Well, he made fun of Bob whenever he could. It really was funny, although Bob didn't think so—he complained about it until the day he died. (But Bob really *did* look funny in that huge cowboy hat, plopped down on his horse. It was a funny sight, and I didn't blame Lon for his wisecracks.) And incidentally, Lon was another of those heavy drinkers, like Brod Crawford. I'd say about seventy-five percent of my leading men either had a drinking problem or were full-fledged alcoholics. So many of those guys "drank" their lunch, but again, none were drunk or obnoxious around me. They always seemed to have held their liquor.

Voo-doo you trust? Gwynne and Lon Chaney, Jr., were besieged by evil forces in the Universal "Inner Sanctum" mystery *Weird Woman*.

You and Evelyn Ankers played enemies in Weird Woman.

[*Laughs.*] Yes, and Evelyn and I were really such very good friends — she was the matron of honor at my wedding, and I stood up for her when she got her citizenship papers. There was a scene in *Weird Woman* where she was flaring her nostrils at me. It all seemed so funny, because in real life we were so close. We broke down and laughed away. It took quite a while before we could compose ourselves.

Your last Universal film was House of Frankenstein, *and it's rumored that you got out of your Universal contract because of dissatisfaction with that movie.*

No, not at all! I mean, the part was nice, but not great. I had fun with it, but I'm only in the first twenty-five minutes and then zap, I'm off for the rest of the film! That's not good showmanship. Universal was like a little town, everybody knew everybody and generally liked one another, with some exceptions I've mentioned. But it was also like a stock company. One time you got a good role, then you landed a small part in the next movie. That irked me about Universal. I felt that you should always advance, not take two steps backward for each step forward.

Noah Beery, Jr., and I had done two pictures together, both reasonably big productions. From that, we were tossed into a Donald O'Connor picture, *Top Man* [1943]. And Susanna Foster, fresh from her *Phantom of the Opera* smash, was put opposite him — just because she was a teenager! She went back and forth between playing women in big-budget Technicolor pictures to playing opposite O'Connor in teenage films. It was a big waste of so much talent.

What else can you recall about House of Frankenstein?

John Carradine was a good choice for the role of Dracula; both Bela Lugosi and Lon Chaney were too heavy for the part. I felt that my scenes with Carradine were some of the best acting I ever did, and of course the picture plays often on television — I wish I had a piece of those Universal horror films! And I still see Peter Coe, who played my husband in the film, each year at the Universal reunion party. [Coe died in 1994.] He was married, briefly, to Kerry Vaughn, a girl under contract to Universal for a spell. I never paid married men any attention, even though later I was told — by *them* — that they had mad crushes on me. But it wouldn't have mattered if I *had* known it at the time. In those days, that marriage license meant hands off. And it still does.

What can you say about Karloff in House of Frankenstein?

I don't think he was too interested in doing that picture. He'd just starred on Broadway in *Arsenic and Old Lace*, and owed Universal some pictures. Like I said earlier, if they had you under contract, they'd stick you in *anything*, no matter how large or small the role. I don't think he was happy with his mad scientist part.

John Carradine only has eyes for Gwynne as she prepares for a take in *House of Frankenstein*.

Why did you leave Universal after House of Frankenstein?

One day, [actor] James Craig told me I should go with his agent, Harold Rose. I was led to believe — by both Rose and another agent — that they would really do big things for me, if only I would obtain my release from Universal. They said they would see that I went places. Well, I went places, all right — out the door to Poverty Row! I did some very well-received pictures, but they had no backing. I eventually just gave up, raised my two kids, and only took an occasional assignment.

Were you pleased with your freelance work in general?

Frankly, not as much as the critics were. I did a picture called *Fear* [1946] that looks sort of like a Universal, and it was populated by people who were veterans of Universal horror pictures — people like Warren William, who was with Evelyn in *The Wolf Man*. *Fear* was an eerie, *Crime and Punishment*–like tale, and the critics loved it. I felt it was rather slow. The director [Alfred Zeisler] was hung up on my legs, because it seemed like he was always shooting them from different angles.

What about The Ghost Goes Wild, *the ghost comedy you made at Republic?*

Yuck. I tried to sit through that one a few years ago, and just couldn't. It was embarrassing, although I did finally watch it again a year or so ago. Edward Everett Horton, such a fine actor, behaving so silly in that schlock. I couldn't believe it. James Ellison was so handsome, so pleasant, but so wasted in what was a dumb role for him. They really muffed it on that one — lots of good talent wasted. Jimmy Lydon and Jane Withers call Republic "Repulsive." That's a funny tag, but to a certain extent it was true.

You were united with Karloff a third time when you played Tess Trueheart in Dick Tracy Meets Gruesome.

I was excited to get to see Boris, but except for one tiny little scene where I'm pretending to be frozen — and, of course, the obligatory publicity stills — we didn't have anything to do together, and that was disappointing.

What is your opinion of Dick Tracy?

That one I really liked. I saw it again recently, when I noticed at the store it was available on tape. My picture was on the box, and on the poster that is also on the box. I had forgotten it was a comedy — very well done, with funny character names, something like Damon Runyon would have used. It was so cute; I really enjoyed it. It was probably one of the better jobs I had in the freelance field. Also, the still photographer at RKO was absolutely the tops. Those portraits he took of me are the best I've ever had done. I had long blond hair, and I looked my best.

Your last journey into the horror field was in 1958's Teenage Monster.

Oh, do you have to bring *that* up? It was absolutely the worst thing I ever did, the worst thing I ever *could* have done.

Then why did you do it?

Just for the exposure, just to say that I was still in the business. That was a very bad movie. The script was bad, *I* was bad, every*body* and every*thing* was bad, except, maybe, for Gloria Castillo. She somehow managed to rise above the material. I expected big things from her, but she didn't go anywhere. Stuart Wade was nice, and good-looking. He had been a big band singer in the forties, but his part in this was nothing. And to top it off, the producers turned around three years later and re-released it under the title *Meteor Monster*. It was still the same picture, the same bomb. I refuse to look at it.

Teenage Monster *was your last leading role.*

After how that turned out, I simply said, "No more." I refused to work for several years, but then came back and did a Head and Shoulders commercial, and I played Michael Douglas' mother in *Adam at 6 A.M.* [1970].

But I really shouldn't end on such a negative note. For the most part, I am proud of what I did. I like most of my pictures, and I liked most of the people I worked with. The good ol' boys like Dick Foran, Johnny Mack Brown, Jon Hall, Rod Cameron and so many of the others—I cannot say enough nice things about them. Those *were* the good ol' days, and I am so pleased that so many of the films I made are still enjoyed by fans, many of whom weren't even born when the films were made.

ANNE GWYNNE FILMOGRAPHY

Unexpected Father (Universal, 1939)
The Big Guy (Universal, 1939)
Charlie McCarthy, Detective (Universal, 1939)
Little Accident (Universal, 1939)
Oklahoma Frontier (Universal, 1939)
It's a Date (Universal, 1940)
The Green Hornet (Universal serial, 1940)
The Man from Montreal (Universal, 1940)
Black Friday (Universal, 1940)
Sandy Is a Lady (Universal, 1940)
Spring Parade (Universal, 1940)
Give Us Wings (Universal, 1940)
Flash Gordon Conquers the Universe (Universal serial, 1940)
Bad Man from Red Butte (Universal, 1940)
Framed (Universal, 1940)
Honeymoon Deferred (Universal, 1940)
The Black Cat (Universal, 1941)
Nice Girl? (Universal, 1941)
Tight Shoes (Universal, 1941)

Mob Town (Universal, 1941)
Washington Melodrama (MGM, 1941)
Melody Lane (Universal, 1941)
Road Agent (Universal, 1941)
Keeping Fit (Universal short, 1942)
Ride 'em Cowboy (Universal, 1942)
You're Telling Me (Universal, 1942)
The Strange Case of Doctor Rx (Universal, 1942)
Broadway (Universal, 1942)
Sin Town (Universal, 1942)
Jail House Blues (Universal, 1942)
Men of Texas (Universal, 1942)
Don't Get Personal (Universal, 1942)
We've Never Been Licked (Universal, 1943)
Frontier Badmen (Universal, 1943)
Top Man (Universal, 1943)
Ladies Courageous (Universal, 1944)
Weird Woman (Universal, 1944)
Moon Over Las Vegas (Universal, 1944)
Murder in the Blue Room (Universal, 1944)
South of Dixie (Universal, 1944)
Babes on Swing Street (Universal, 1944)
House of Frankenstein (Universal, 1944)
Fear (Monogram, 1946)
The Glass Alibi (Republic, 1946)
I Ring Doorbells (PRC, 1946)
Killer Dill (Screen Guild, 1947)
The Ghost Goes Wild (Republic, 1947)
Dick Tracy Meets Gruesome (RKO, 1947)
The Enchanted Valley (Eagle-Lion, 1948)
Panhandle (Allied Artists, 1948)
Arson, Inc. (Lippert, 1949)
Call of the Klondike (Monogram, 1950)
The Blazing Sun (Columbia, 1950)
King of the Bullwhip (Western Adventure/Realart, 1950)
Breakdown (Realart, 1952)
Teenage Monster (Meteor Monster) (Howco, 1958)
Adam at 6 A.M. (National General, 1970)

Gwynne additionally appeared in a promotional film in St. Louis (1936); a newsreel, *Swimming Under Water*; and an Edgar Bergen charity short. Three Gwynne *Ramar of the Jungle* television episodes were compiled together into the feature-length release *Phantom of the Jungle* (Lippert, 1955).

*Nova was a very good part for me,
I had kind of the quality for it. ...
Looking the way I looked, I got
these more sexy roles.*

Linda Harrison

NO DOUBT MOST of the reason that *Planet of the Apes* became one of *the* top-grossing science fiction movies was its array of special effects, its amazing "Ape City" and the superb, groundbreaking makeups which transformed some of Hollywood's great character actors into simian scene-stealers. And yet all it required to take every eye (every *male* eye, anyway!) away from the hard work of all of these talented effects and makeup artisans was a sun-tanned, skimpilyclad *homo sapien* beauty with a long mane of brunette hair and big brown, "deer-caught-in-headlights" eyes. The character for whom red-blooded audiences went ape was, of course, "Nova," and the specially "introduced" actress, former beauty queen Linda Harrison.

A native of Berlin, Maryland, Harrison was Miss Berlin at 16, then a model in New York's Garment Center. Homesickness brought her back to Maryland, where she entered and won the state beauty pageant. During the finals in the Miss International contest (held in Long Beach, California), she was "spotted" by then-talent scout Mike Medavoy and presented at 20th Century–Fox. Throughout her acting years at Fox, and amidst movie roles in *Planet* and its sequel *Beneath the Planet of the Apes*, she dated studio boss Richard Zanuck and married him in 1969. (Divorced in 1978, she's more recently been seen in Zanuck's *Cocoon* movies.) Once again a Marylander, and "probably the happiest [she's] ever been," Linda Harrison looks back with contagious cheerfulness on her show biz years — and the adventure of being the sole Beauty on a planet of Beasts.

While competing in these beauty pageants, did you have designs on becoming an actress?

Yes, *very* definitely. In fact, it was all "pre-planned" in my mind to enter the beauty contest and get to California and be *seen*. And it really turned out exactly the way I wanted it to.

Did you have to do a screen test at Fox?

They gave me a "personality test," which was very interesting. They set the camera in front of me and I'd talk to the camera — and then I turned to each side. They asked me what kind of man I would be attracted to, and *why*, and I just remember so clearly what I said: I just said I wanted a man that had a lot of interests in common with me, that we had to have a wonderful chemistry. I just went on talkin' like I'd done it all my life! They then signed me up for what is called a "sixty-day option" and I went and studied with Pamela Danova, the studio coach. At the time, Richard Zanuck was head of the studio and his father, Darryl Zanuck, was chairman of the board. Richard's assistant Harry Sokolov, a lawyer, was looking for a date for the premiere of *The Agony and the Ecstasy* [1965] starring Charlton

Previous page: According to Linda Harrison, she "didn't have the personality or the desire to be 'a star.'"

Heston. Well, I was very thrilled; I had never been to a premiere, I was all of twenty years old, and Heston was my *idol* as a little girl — you know, Ben-Hur! So they picked me because Harry was from Baltimore. That's when I first met Richard Zanuck, *that* evening. He became quite smitten, and that started a romance. It was during the sixty-day period that I started dating Richard, and then I was signed to a seven-year contract.

What was the first thing you were ever in?
It was a pilot called *Men Against Evil*, which turned into a television series called *The Felony Squad* with Dennis Cole. Then I did a *Batman*. Oh, God, *Batman*! You gotta remember, I'm now with Richard Zanuck, who was a big guy on campus, and he was then in the process of getting separated. (He was married to a Lili back then and then he married *me*, and now he's back to *another* girl named Lili. He likes the "L," I guess [*laughs*]!) Dick had become my mentor and teacher, and he said, "Just do what they tell you." So I started out *early* in the morning on *Batman*—it was a cheerleading scene. I was twenty and I had been a cheerleader in high school. And the dance teacher at 20th Century-Fox worked us so hard, by the time the shot came at five o'clock, the scene that they *kept* was me falling over, because I literally gave out! And the dance teacher came back and she said, "Linda Harrison gave me a hard time," complained about my "attitude." I just kept telling her, "You're going to use up all my energy, so when the shot comes, I won't *have* any."

What was it like, dating "the boss"?
Dick just fell madly in love, and so did I with him. And he did *not* like me going to the acting school I was attending, working with other actors like Ron Ely. So he *built* a talent school! It was famous, 'cause out of it came Tom Selleck, Sam Elliott, Cristina Ferrare, Jackie Bisset, Jim Brolin, myself — all these actors were just *thrilled* to be getting into this school. Well, *one* reason Dick had the school was so he would know where I *was* [*laughs*]. It was a wonderful experience, wonderful development for the actors. We had coaching, we had fencing, we had dancing — we went for eight hours and we really formed a bond. Of course, I wasn't there as much as the rest because I was flyin' off with Dick Zanuck, all over the world. So it was kind of neat, being his girl. Everybody else was shaking, *would* they get their contract, *would* they get in a film? *You* know what that business is all about — especially back then, when the heads of studios had a *lot* of power. So it was neat, it was just a wonderful time.

What was your first movie?
The first movie I did was *Way ... Way Out* [1966] with Jerry Lewis; it

was a nice cameo part, a wonderful scene between Jim Brolin and I. After that I did *A Guide for the Married Man* [1967]. And all during this period, Dick is telling me about this fabulous book called *Planet of the Apes* and that it was going to make a great movie. He said, "I want you to play the ape, Dr. Zira"—in fact, during the testing for the makeup, I had to go through the whole business with the mask and everything and I played Zira, the part that eventually went to Kim Hunter.

That was the part he wanted you to play in the movie?

No, I think they always had me in mind for Nova. But they needed someone to do the screen test, and you keep trying to employ your actors. So I did the screen test. The part that was hard for me was actually doing the mask, where they have to put all that plaster on your face and you have to lie there for a long time. You have to really be still. Fortunately, I was an acrobat growing up, and a very *good* one—I won a lot of contests—so I knew how to control my body and be "quiet." You *had* to do that, you had to be very still and lay there and be a "good patient." (A young actor will do *any*thing to get their mug on the screen!) [Director] Franklin Schaffner got involved on the movie and liked it, and [producer] Arthur Jacobs, and there was just a tremendous amount of enthusiasm for it. Arthur was a great showman and Dick was crazy about him. So the two of 'em just got together and there was lots of enthusiasm. It took a *lotta, lotta* work, especially in the makeup department. You know, it takes a certain kind of producer to do a film like that, with *apes* running around!

Did you ever read the book?

Yes.

You did?

Well, I might've read a few pages [*laughs*]. I really wasn't into reading those kinds of books!

Kim Hunter told me that there was a bit of trepidation — that people thought it would be a giant hit or a terrible embarrassment.

You know, from my experience on working on films that have kind of "stayed" and become classics, you almost sense it when you're doing it. There is a current, there is an energy that's going on. I sensed that. If you're going to analyze it *from the brain*, you'll say, "It could go one way or the other," but the *intuitive* feeling was that we had something unique. I'm an intuitive person, and I would say that that's what I was reading.

Did you enjoy all the location shooting?

It was wonderful. We went to Page, Arizona, *beautiful* country, and I just marveled at how they move an entire production, like a little mini-town, and set up. It was just beautiful working out there in the desert. That was where we shot the beginning, the spaceship crashing and the astronauts walking around. Schaffner was just fabulous. He was a very laconic man, he didn't *say* much, but he was *very* aware of everything he was doing. Every day, the complaints were that he "kept everything in his back pocket," what he was going to *do* during the day. But when you think about it from an artistic point of view, he was very smart because he didn't let anything else interfere with his focus. The elements were all there — the [behind-the-scenes] people; Leon Shamroy, who was an Academy Award cinematographer; the cast; *everything*. It was fabulous! Dick and I were like joined-at-the-hip but he didn't come out to Page — I had my sister Kay there. So at one point I told him, "You come *out* here!" He said, "Okay, how do I get out there?" I said, "Get your Lear jet and get *out* here." [*Laughs.*] And he did! It was very, very exciting, it was *moviemaking*.

Your Nova outfit was very reminiscent of what Raquel Welch wore in One Million Years B.C.

That's true. That's been the traditional costume for "cave girls."

Where did you shoot the apes' first scene, where they beat the bushes and hunt the humans?

That was done at the Malibu Ranch. We had built Ape City there. And it was *stinking* hot! *Whew*! The scenes of us in cages were also shot at Ape City.

It must have been worse for the ape actors than for you.

Oh, God! And they reported at three o'clock in the morning! But they were *fabulous* troupers, Roddy McDowall and Kim, and those were difficult, difficult roles. Maurice Evans was older and I don't know if his health was that good, and he had an even harder time. But actors have to endure all that sort of stuff, just like everybody else. We had good morale, good people.

How about the "ape" bit players and extras? Did they seem to be having any problems?

Well, the extras just had a mask that they'd pull on over their heads. The primary actors had the tough part. But, you know, I was so delighted and grateful to be in this picture that I probably never saw the *negative* side as much. I just *didn't*. I remember one piece of advice Dick gave me: He said, "You go to work on time and listen to your director and do your job.

And I don't want to hear any complaints about you!" I had to be *even more* careful, and *nice*, because I *was* his girlfriend.

The end of the movie was shot at Point Dume, on the California coast.

Right. That's where we shot the part where Heston and I ride off and find the Statue of Liberty. Actually, that was a matte. And that [special effect] took a lot of innovation and talent. You've got to remember that this film was made in sixty-seven, and a lot of new things were tried that were never done before. There were a lot of breakthroughs, in the makeup and shooting and everything. So it's really contributed a lot to the industry. By the way, it was *wonderful* there at Point Dume. We shot there at the very end of this long [production] and we were probably there a full month. We did a lot of beach stuff—Dr. Zira talking about what Man had done, *that* long speech, *all* that stuff.

Any "lighter" moments during the making of the movie, that you can remember?

I remember I turned twenty-two during production, and at lunchtime one day at Point Dume a big cake was brought out. I was sitting with Heston, who was kidding me about being "all of twenty-two." (He must have been in his forties.) And then I came back, with all my makeup on, to the studio, and Dick had a big party there, in the commissary. He made a wonderful speech about this girl who had come into his life, and how grateful he was. He had all of the executives he was very close with, and his friends. It was very exciting, it was a good time.

How did you like working with Heston?

Loved it—he was a wonderful actor to work with. He knew Dick very well, he knew it was my first [big] picture, he taught me how to "favor" the camera (I was kind of camera-shy). We spent a lot of time together, waiting for shots and everything, and he was just very, very pleasant, a very good person.

Did you watch rushes?

Sometimes. And it was just a fabulous experience, to be able to sit in on those. It was so beautifully shot and so different and so professional with Schaffner [running the show].

And what more can you remember about Arthur Jacobs?

Well, Arthur was just a fabulous promoter, and his wife was a very

Harrison concedes that Nova is her best-known role, bar none.

good friend of mine. What I remember most was just the enthusiasm of the people. The way Dick did things, he really *inspired* his people — he was always "up." (At the time, I think we had the logo "Think 20th.") Arthur was a great party-giver and promoter — everything "apes," you know! — and he was a perfect guy for this picture.

Did you ever meet Pierre Boulle or Rod Serling?

Not [Boulle], I don't think; they bought the book from him and then Rod Serling came on and did the screenplay. I met Rod, he came on the set.

Had you ever watched Twilight Zone? *Did you have any preconceived notions about Serling?*

I watched *Twilight Zone* a *little* bit, but, you know, I was never into television or film too much as a young person. You've got to remember, I was twenty-one, twenty-two years old and there were all these "new personalities" coming in my life.

If as a kid you were "never into television or film too much," how did you manage to decide to become an actress?

Well, it's funny — the people that are "movie buffs" aren't necessarily artistic people or people that are inclined to be actors. I just was more interested in *concentrating* and *focusing* my goal, rather than utilizing a lot of my time watching film. You gotta remember, I was eighteen, going to high school in Maryland, working in the summertime at a famous restaurant called Phillips Crab House. I was a normal kid, dating and falling in love, and there wasn't much time, really, to watch movies. I don't even watch a lot of films *today*.

When the movie came out, some of the Fox publicity materials called it a satire. Was that their way of hedging their bets, in case no one would take it seriously?

I'm not sure what was in their minds. I think they just did what they thought was the best presentation. *I* thought it was a serious science fiction picture — that's what it was. They knew what they had and they knew it was "different," and they must have felt it could go one way or the other. But you'll find a *lot* of the great pictures can go one way or the other.

Did you tour with the movie, or do any sort of promotional stuff?

Being Dick's girl, I was always on the "executive end" — I was behind the camera as well as in front of the camera. I think we took it to several different places to be previewed.

What kind of roles did you want *to play? Or would you play whatever they told* you *to play?*

Nova was a very good part for me, I had kind of the quality for it. Always, my career was never top priority, I was very interested in my relationship with Dick and eventually becoming his wife and having a family. I *enjoyed* working in front of the camera but *not* full-time. I didn't have the personality or the desire to be a "star" — put *star* in quotes. I didn't really *think* about it too much. But as an actress, when they offered you something, you were supposed to take it and you do the best you could. You *know* it's a tough business, and you're just grateful for any piece of film that you may be able to have. Looking the way I looked, I got these more sexy roles [*laughs*].

How long did it take for someone to figure out that a sequel to Planet of the Apes *would be a good idea?*

Oh, well, that was *immediate* — those were the years of the sequels!

Beneath the Planet of the Apes reportedly had half the budget of the first film. Did you feel the pinch at all?

No, I didn't. Of course, they "cashed in" on the first one [reused costumes, sets, etc.] and that, in a way, takes away from some of the artistic challenge that the first had. But that's how the producer saw fit to do it, and Ted Post was a wonderful television director. And *I* was really featured a lot, so as an actress, *that* sat well. It wasn't as *good* as the first [laughs], 'cause of course we had Franklin Schaffner on that one and he was one of the top, top directors.

Burt Reynolds was supposedly up for the James Franciscus role, and he didn't want it.

I don't recall that. I remember they thought that Jim would be good because he looked a lot like Heston. Jim was the kind of actor that did a lot of homework behind the camera, kind of a Method actor. He took it very seriously, he was very dedicated.

Surrounded by gorillas and mutants, etc. in these Apes *movies, did you fear that your character might get lost in the shuffle?*

No, the fact that I was the human, I kind of *stood out*.

You were on horseback in both movies. Were you a good horsewoman?

No, not particularly. And I had to *look* like I had never been on a horse, so try to do that *and* get the horse where he's supposed to go! But I do remember having a *lot* of fun in the second one; it was Ted Post and it was more relaxed. I remember running down this hill and getting up so much speed that one of these *fabulous* makeup men — big guy, burly chest — had to step in and stop me. Otherwise, I would have tumbled, God knows where! It was a very arduous picture, *physically*, with those horses and everything, but we just got in there and did our jobs! After *Beneath*, I was cast as one of the starlets in a new television series called *Bracken's World*, which was a series Dick for a long time had wanted to do, about a Hollywood studio. So I got that part and I had to finish *Beneath* and go right into the pilot — I didn't even get a day's rest. And I had to start remembering lines [laughs]!

Apart from Bracken's World, *did you do much acting while you were married to Richard Zanuck?*

No. I gave birth to two sons, Harrison Richard Zanuck on February 23, 1971, and Dean Francis Zanuck August 11, 1972. I *think* I did a couple of guest spots on television, and then *Airport 1975*.

"It was kind of neat, being [the boss'] girl," Linda Harrison recalls of her stint at Richard Zanuck's 20th Century-Fox.

When big decisions needed to be made at Fox, did he ever ask your opinion? Did you offer opinions? Were you the Hillary Clinton of 20th Century-Fox?

He did get my opinions. His partner was David Brown (a wonderful man), and David's wife was Helen Gurley Brown, editor of *Cosmopolitan*.

And we went all around the world together. So at all those dinners you would throw out ideas — we were constantly trying to figure out what worked and what didn't and what to go with. And you just kind of go by your gut. So I was always "into" those conversations. Dick is a *listener*, so you would throw out different things and he'd take it all in. But his decision to actually go with a certain picture or a certain actor or director was something *he* did himself. After hearing and gathering all of the information, he went by his own instinct.

That was around the time of X-rated Fox movies like Myra Breckinridge *and* Beyond the Valley of the Dolls.

It's such a hard business, running a studio and trying to figure out the hits. For some reason, Dick and David decided to go with films that were quite beneath them, that they hadn't done. But sometimes you've got to *do* something to get back on track. It was a series of things: The relationship with his father [Darryl F. Zanuck] was strained, because "the son was rising" — "the son also rises" — and Dick needed to spread *his* wings. And the father wasn't ready to let go. Pretty soon there was a wedge between the father and son, and there was a terrible change in their relationship. It was like a divorce, it was like any situation where two people come to a crossroad and things splinter. The father fired Dick, *and* David, and *myself* [*laughs*] — *I* was under contract, I was eight months pregnant. But something good comes out of bad; I'd always said [to Richard Zanuck], "You go on your own." He was, what, thirty-four years old, thirty-five, and he needed to show that *he's* also his own man, apart from his father. So Dick and David went and got a job at Warner Bros., and then from there formed Zanuck-Brown. That's *history*, what happened when they formed their own company! So something *good* came out of it, and I *always* told him, "Something good's gonna come out of this. You and David are the best team in Hollywood." And they turned out to be!

It's very interesting to "get in the heads" of these two men. Here are two men that ran a major corporation, Dick and David, and then they formed little Zanuck-Brown. They wanted to start humbly [*laughs*], and they got a screenplay called *SSSSSSS* by a makeup man [Dan Striepeke] they thought a lot of. You know, a lot of this business has to do with developing *friendships*; [a big factor] is the personality of the person you're working with, what they're like as a human being. A lot of times you'll take a script because you like the guy and it looks good and it fits well into *your* agenda at that particular time, so you'll give him a chance. That's actually how that movie *SSSSSS* came along. It was something they could shoot for under a million dollars, *very* inexpensive, so they did it. But then they got

James Franciscus and Harrison contemplate their new leash on life in *Beneath the Planet of the Apes.*

ahold of *The Sting* [1973], and you know the rest. I was with a famous team of producers, Dick and David, and they had such an extraordinary life, so colorful and so dramatic. Most people [in her hometown] think of me as, "She led this glamorous life, they were out there doin' drugs," or something like that [*laughs*]! It wasn't like that at *all*, I had a very stable husband. He had a *job*, he had to go to *work* every day. He was a fundamental *family* man. But we had so many great experiences. They should do a book just on *him*.

Why are you billed as "Augusta Summerland" in Airport 1975?

[*Laughs.*] Well-l-l, you know life can make its turns! I was married to Dick, and for one reason or the other, I got involved with a guru — which was kind of the "in" thing at the time. The guru claimed in his cult that you change from who you were born, and so as you make that change, you need a new name [Augusta Summerland]. Unfortunately, this guru wanted to make movies from *his* screenplays — you get these people on the fringe. And for whatever reason, he put a terrible wedge through my relationship with Dick. It ended that I left Dick and the guru turned out to be ... a con artist. It was a pretty rough period. I was analyzed a lot during that time; I think so much, at twenty years old, was thrown at me. I came from a small town of 2,000 and I think a lot of what was given to me there, the *values*, have put me in good stead. But I think that I got "lost" somewhere, my "identity." Or the women's lib made us think that we were supposed to be unfulfilled. Or *whatever* got into my "being" at the time — it was rough. I left Dick, and it was very hard.

How did you become involved on Cocoon?

I was going to an acting class, studying, and we did a showcase and I invited Dick and Lili, his present wife. About this time, *Cocoon* was in development stages. Dick said, "I think there's a part for you. In about six months, Ron Howard will be auditioning." So I just got myself psyched up for it, went in, read and *got* it. Ron was just a fabulous guy to work with, because he *really* works from your naturalness, *who you are*. He gives you a lot of range, a lot of space, to kind of bring out that naturalness, *not* do the usual shtick of an actor and close that down. And I loved doing that. And *Cocoon* was another picture where you sensed, intuitively, that it was a special picture. The elements were right, the people were right, and each day it was just a "high" to work on the film.

You have a much smaller part in Cocoon: The Return.

They had to cut *everybody's* part down — lots, lots got cut. We overshot. They didn't cut us because we weren't acting right or anything; [it was a case of] the movie not being the way they wanted it, so they started cutting to try to salvage it, to pull it together. Sometimes in the editing, they can pull off miracles. So that was the case with *Cocoon: The Return*, a lot of people got cut down.

You'll always be remembered as Nova. Is that okay?

Yes. And, you know, they're doing a remake. Oliver Stone!

Would you be tempted by the offer of a part in that?

Sure!

What else do you want your fans to know about Linda Harrison?

For me, for Linda Harrison, I feel extraordinarily lucky. I started here in Ocean City [Maryland], working at Phillips Crab House, and I dated their son Stephen Phillips, and he was the last man I dated before I went to California and met Dick. And then I came back here four years ago and now I'm back with *him*. So I feel very privileged, it's kind of neat being with somebody you've known a long time and were with when you were very young. I experienced twenty-five years in California where I married a wonderful man, had two wonderful children, and met so many wonderful people — a *full life* there. And now I have *another* full life! So it's almost two lives, two lifetimes already in this *one*.

I still look great and I *feel* good, but I really think the acting phase of my life is over with. I don't like to say that, because then you're closing that door, but there's another door opening which is probably going to bring me *more* happiness. And so, to me, that's very, very exciting. I *like* the name recognition that I got from my work, and I have two sons that will be in the work, and I *love* filmmaking — I think what they can do and who it reaches is a very exciting medium. Yeah, I'd like to get a part, but I'm *not* the kind that'll give up everything and go move and go to classes. It's going to have to be handed to me — which basically it was before. There *might* be a part in my future — and there might *not*. But right now I'm probably the happiest I've ever been, and that's important to me.

LINDA HARRISON FILMOGRAPHY

Way... Way Out (20th Century–Fox, 1966)
A Guide for the Married Man (20th Century–Fox, 1967)
Planet of the Apes (20th Century–Fox, 1968)
Beneath the Planet of the Apes (20th Century–Fox, 1970)
Cocoon (20th Century–Fox, 1985)
Cocoon: The Return (20th Century–Fox, 1988)

[T]he job had its moments, it was interesting, and you could kind of get into the "feel" of the thing and believe that you actually were a monster.

Tom Hennesy

HE WAS THE *unsung* Creature from the Black Lagoon: While Ricou Browning and Ben Chapman have become well known in fan circles for playing the Gill Man in the original *Creature*, less has been heard about Tom Hennesy, who tackled the title role in the 1955 sequel *Revenge of the Creature*. A bit actor and stuntman who made his film debut while in college in the early 1940s, Hennesy squeezed into the foam rubber costume for the movie's on-land Creature scenes — a break from the usual run of Westerns in which 6'5" Hennesy generally played. Still looking as though he could whip his weight in wildcats, Tom Hennesy dives headfirst into his *Revenge* reminiscences.

How did you break into the acting and stunt field?
While I was a student at USC [in the early forties] — a football player — we used to get calls in through the athletic department or the fraternity house for people to do part-time work in movies as an extra or bit player, often resulting in stunt activity. That sort of thing started, I guess, back in the days of John Wayne, who also was an SC student and a football player, and got his break while he was working in the studio part-time as a prop man. So that's how I first got started. After three years in the Navy during World War II, I worked two years as a police officer and forest ranger–game warden on Catalina Island. It was there that I first met John Wayne and John Ford — they spent a lot of time at the isthmus on Ford's yacht. I returned to college at UCLA where I again played football, and I continued doing some film work since I'd had a taste of it. After I graduated, my profession was teaching, but I got several opportunities to do stunt work and bit parts and so forth, so that's what I just drifted into. Over the years, I worked on quite a number of John Ford and John Wayne films, and the Wayne family became very good friends of mine. I was an especially good friend of Mike Wayne, the oldest son; I met him on a picture that we did up in San Rafael, California, called *Blood Alley* [1955]. Later on, I was a teacher for Patrick; I worked as a general secondary and elementary teacher in virtually all the Hollywood film and television studios. I taught a lot of film kids. A couple of 'em are dead now, like Natalie Wood and Sal Mineo; I worked with Tim Considine, Lauren Chapin, Molly Bee, Paul Anka, Tommy Rettig [who died in 1996], Annette Funicello and many others.

How did you land the Creature part?
I was called out to Universal for an interview with the producer, Bill

Previous page: Movie stuntman Tom Hennesy between takes on Universal's *Revenge of the Creature*. Hennesy's other "monster" credits include doubling Buddy Baer in Abbott and Costello's *Jack and the Beanstalk* (1952) and playing the Familiar in the *Thriller* television episode "The Return of Andrew Bentley" (1961).

Alland. I had a *couple* of interviews with him — I had to wear a swimsuit and so forth, so that he could determine how I would look in the Creature suit. I was hired on the basis of those interviews, apparently, and on the basis of my experience as a stuntman and actor. I then started to work [on the Creature costume] with the fellows in the makeup department, like Bud Westmore, who I knew very well. Bud and Jack Kevan and Tom Case and Bo Hickman were the ones who I worked with, mainly. And Wally Westmore also did some work on that project.

How many people are there playing the Gill Man in Revenge of the Creature?
Initially there was myself and another fellow, John Lamb. John was a "water man," and they had hired him to do part of the swimming — they figured that it was too much work for one person. They did makeup tests and built a suit for John; he spent quite a bit of time in the [makeup department] before he went to Florida [where *Revenge* was shot, at Marineland and other locations]. But he ended up doing very little. I guess they shot a couple of things with John as the Creature, and the director [Jack Arnold] became disenchanted with the way that John looked in the water; he said he looked like a man in a suit! So, unfortunately for John, they decided to terminate his employment [as the Creature] and they called Ricou Browning. Ricou had played the Creature in the water on the first picture, so they put him in the suit. I remember the sequence where Ricou played the Creature in a cargo net, being transported into the oceanarium at Marineland. They had an air hose in there for him so that he could get air when needed; they incorporated it into the scene in such a way that it looked like a line. John Lamb, myself and one or two underwater attendants [played the men who] introduced the Creature into the oceanarium. That was the last thing that John did; they sent him home, I guess, the next day.

Did you mind having to get into that oceanarium, with all the sharks and whatnot that were in there?
In that scene where I played one of the attendants? That *was* kind of a frightening experience, because not many people have been in a tank like that, with large sharks and sea turtles and barracudas and sawfish. There was no chance to prepare for that or anything, we just had to do it. Later on I went into the tank myself, at night, with just my trunks on, to try to get some photographs with these large sharks. I got the still man to take pictures of me through the window. (It's not often you get a chance to do anything like that!) But they liked to use Ricou Browning in the suit in the underwater oceanarium scenes because they wanted the sharks and eels and things to look extra large. Browning was a small person, probably no

more than 5'8" or 5'9", so it worked out well. He was an expert "hose breather"—he made his living at it at Weeki Wachee Springs and other places in Florida, swimming with the "mermaid girls" and so forth. He did most of the underwater stuff.

When they first brought the Creature into the small receiving tank, I did that part of it. I was in a small tank of water on the back of a truck and they hoisted me up in a stretcher hoist and lowered me down into the receiving tank. One thing I remember about that is that the operator of the hoist said that it was very ancient and rickety and noisy, and he said that he hoped that it worked better than it did the last time. When asked what he meant by that, he said that they had been hoisting a shark or a porpoise into the tank and the thing unwound and collapsed, and the fish was dropped onto the pavement below, and killed, evidently.

Did you encounter the same problems with the suit that Ricou Browning has talked about?

Oh, sure. It was terribly uncomfortable and very restrictive. You had to wear weights to stay submerged in the thing—it was made of foam rubber and it was buoyant. The vision was terrible. you had no peripheral vision, there were just little holes in the center of each [Creature] eye and you'd try to line up your own eyes. It was difficult to move, it was difficult even to *breathe*—you had to breathe through the mouth. And it was incredibly hot and humid down there. I probably weighed about 225 pounds when I went down to Florida, and about 200 when I came back to Hollywood. I also developed kidney stones later on, and I was told that more than likely the reason was that [while doing *Revenge of the Creature*] I was in the area of the highest incidence of kidney stones in the country; there's something about the minerals in the water. Plus, the *constriction*—you couldn't relieve yourself whenever nature called, they only took the suit off you once a day, at noon.

Getting in and out of it was a hassle?

There was *no way* of getting out of the thing except to have two or three people help you, and it took a considerable amount of time. (It took even longer to get *into* it!) Everything that you did in that thing was probably three times as difficult as it would be for someone else who wasn't restricted like that. All things considered, Ricou did a hell of a job—it was very difficult to move in it. Ricou was a nice guy, I liked him, and also Ginger Stanley, who was the stuntgirl who doubled Lori Nelson in all the water shots. They were very nice people. Later on, Ricou came out to California to see if he could get some work, and he stayed at my house one or two nights.

John Bromfield tries to prevent Hennesy's seaquarium escape.

Did you come up with any solutions of your own to the suit problems?

No, there *weren't* any solutions, you just had to grin and bear it and do the best you could. As I said, the original plan was to have John Lamb spell me, because there was just too much involved. Then when they sent him home, there was no one else to do it *but* myself! The underwater work [that Browning did] was *not* a great part of the picture; the scenes that he shot in the oceanarium were accomplished very quickly. Then there were a few other short sequences [with Browning as the Gill Man], like when the Creature was swimming below John Agar and Lori Nelson in the river. All the rest of it was me. It was me who escapes from the oceanarium — I climbed out and panicked the tourists. From then on, except for the one sequence where Ricou swam under John and Lori, it was all me. And it was a heck of a lot of work. It was very difficult, very exhausting — one of the toughest things that I've done.

Ben Chapman, who played the Gill Man in parts of the first movie, squeezed a little extra money out of Universal for his troubles.

They were very cheap with me, they didn't want to pay any stunt adjustments, they just wanted to pay the contract-agreed price, which is not normal practice for stunt work. The whole portrayal of the Creature was not just an acting job, it was a *stunt* job, a *difficult* stunt job. In order to be fair, they should have made adjustments for a number of things. I asked for some adjustments on various occasions and was refused, and they acted as though I'd be terminated if I asked again. (Although they'd have been *totally* out of luck if they fired me, because they didn't have anyone else to *do* it!)

Memories of Agar or Nelson?

Agar was a nice guy, too. I don't have any *particular* thoughts about him except that he was always pleasant and seemed to do an adequate job. I knew that he had had quite a bit of publicity and *notoriety* at one time, when he was married to Shirley Temple. Lori was very pleasant and professional, also. I don't know how old she was at the time, but if I'm remembering right, her *mother* was there constantly [*laughs*]! Then, of course, there was [second lead] John Bromfield; I liked him, he was a sort of rough and tumble guy. We all got along great, and we even had a big shrimp boil on the beach one night and everyone from the cast was there.

One of your "big scenes" was the fight with Bromfield in the receiving tank.

Not just Bromfield, but there were also the attendants who came down the ladder and jumped into the tank. So I was fighting at least three people there, Bromfield and two local Florida stuntmen. It was very difficult, and I had to fight to keep from being drowned. They weren't accomplished Hollywood stuntmen, *any* of 'em, so I had a hell of a fight with all three of them. I got frustrated, 'cause these guys were choking me, and if they had gotten me underwater, they would have held me down and drowned me! I could tell immediately that this was no game — maybe these guys thought I *was* a creature! Maybe they thought they were fighting for *their* lives, but I felt that I was fighting for *mine*. So I finally said *the heck with it*, it was do-or-die, so I did what I had to do, and it became a knock-down, drag-out brawl!

After escaping from the oceanarium, the Creature flipped over a car on his way to the beach.

They had a tow car up above, out of camera range, and they had cables running to this car which I was supposed to roll over, a Pontiac sedan. As I grabbed the sedan and pretended to be lifting it, the cables were pulling it up and over. It *was* a dangerous thing for people working around there, because if that cable had broken and whipped back, it could have killed *every*one!

Then there was the scene at the Lobster House, on the St. Johns River, which almost cost me *my* life. We were shooting at night; inside the Lobster House they had a large number of extras from around the Jacksonville area and they had a band, and Agar and Lori Nelson were dancing. I walked in as the Creature and grabbed Lori and carried her out the door. (From then on, Ginger Stanley stood in for Lori, in the same outfit.) Well, this river was a notorious river, it flowed in the opposite direction from a normal river and it had treacherous currents. I was told that they'd had several drownings at this location, and there were warning signs everywhere for people not to swim there. So there should have been more preparation and precautions taken for our scene in the water there; the only "lifeguard" or *any*thing of that nature was Ricou Browning, who was there that night, standing by.

The first thing Ginger and I had to do was dive off of the pier and into the water, and swim underwater to a buoy, some distance out from the pier. Ginger just had a light chiffon dress on, sort of like a slip or a nightgown, but I must have had at least thirty pounds of weights on, to keep submerged in that suit. We went off the pier and made it out to the buoy. Before we could do the next shot, there was a lot of changing of camera angles and working with equipment that had to be done. We were standing in a pickup boat — this was two or three o'clock in the morning, as I recall. Even though I could hardly see, I remember looking around, because you always like to see what to anticipate, what might happen. I noticed a hawser line hanging down behind the stern of this pickup boat, into the water. I called it to the attention of several people who were nearby, and Jack Arnold said, "You do *your* work and we'll do *ours*! We know what we're doing, we have men that are taking care of that." I said, "Well, I certainly hope so, because it's very, very important." "Well, you just do *your* job and we'll do ours!"

So we went ahead and did the next shot, and I stayed underwater as long as possible, and there was a considerable current — there was an undertow there. I was dragged down and came up some distance away from the buoy. I could hear yelling and screaming; Ginger Stanley had been swept away, too, and although she was a powerful swimmer, someone who made her *living* as a swimmer, she wasn't able to get back. Ricou Browning dove in and went after *her*, and had help from some other people, and they managed to get *her* back. But I was *gone*. I couldn't see anything — I'd come to the surface and it was pitch black, and all I could do was yell. Every time I'd come to the surface, I'd try to get some air before I went back down again. After what seemed like an eternity, I heard some voices when I came up, and I saw a skiff approaching me — a large skiff, with a couple of guys in it. So I grabbed ahold of the bow and held on. It happened that they were there on the banks of the river with a lot of spectators, and heard me yelling, so they came out to help me. When they showed up, I think I was about to go down for the last time. So I was really grateful — I was exhausted.

So where were Jack Arnold and the rest of the people who were all supposedly "doing their jobs"?

When I got back there, why, Jack Arnold was in partying with all of the local extra girls and people — they were eating and drinking and so forth! Well, one of the crew became incensed with Arnold — Arnold was totally responsible for what happened, he was in charge of the operation. So this person lit into him in no uncertain terms — he was a big, burly guy, I think he was a grip. He told Arnold that *he* should be thrown in the river — amongst other things! — and that it was unthinkable for them to do any more work that night, after damn near killing a man. He told Arnold that they weren't going to do any more work, that that was *it*. So they quit for the night, and I think I got back to the hotel about five o'clock in the morning. That's a night I'll never forget.

So you had no love for Arnold, obviously.

[*Laughs.*] You said it! He demanded a great deal and didn't have much consideration — no consideration for *me*, anyway, I don't know about the rest of the actors. I think that he was *in*considerate and insensitive. He was limited [by the fact that] he only had one person to use in those Creature scenes, and he wanted to get as much done as fast as he could. So he took advantage of the situation. I've worked with a lot of directors, and he wouldn't rate too highly, from a standpoint of being considerate, in my book.

Years ago, a story went around that Clint Eastwood was inside the Gill Man suit for some of the scenes in Revenge.

Clint Eastwood didn't do anything in that picture except that one brief scene in the beginning with Agar, where he played a laboratory assistant and had three or four lines. They had just signed him to a stock contract prior to this picture. I was in the casting office at Universal when I saw him for the first time. He came to the window — instead of coming through the main lobby and into casting, he came to the window — and he was complaining that the guards wouldn't let him drive his car onto the lot. He said he was a contract player and he thought he had that right and that

Playing good Samaritans to kidnapped cutie Lori Nelson is about to cost Brett Halsey and Robert Hoy their lives in *Revenge of the Creature*.

privilege, and he was very upset. I don't want to belittle him, but I thought to myself that he was new to the business, he was "green," and that he thought that he was more important than he was! And, as I recall, they *didn't* cater to him, they told him that he'd have to park outside [*laughs*]! So it's interesting to look back on that incident, after what's happened to his career.

You also worked as the Creature in some scenes on the back lot at Universal.

Yeah, like the scene where I attack the two college students [Robert Hoy and Brett Halsey] — we did that by the pond at Universal, a night shot. They used wires and a hoist of some kind to help me pick up Bobby Hoy. I lifted him and threw him, and from that point until he hit the tree, he was being suspended on those wires. The last scene, where I carry Lori Nelson into the water, was shot at Universal, too.

Were you asked to play the Gill Man in the second sequel, The Creature Walks Among Us?

No—that little run-in with the director may have had something to do with the fact that I wasn't used in the third picture. Although if they *had* asked me, I wouldn't have done it anyway!

What were some of the John Wayne and John Ford movies you worked in?

I worked in fourteen Wayne films and several for Ford—*The Alamo* [1960], *The Comancheros* [1961], *The Man Who Shot Liberty Valance* [1962], *Big Jake* [1971], *The Long Gray Line* [1955], etc.

Who are some of the actors you've stunt-doubled for in movies?

My first Western stunt double job was for Randolph Scott. I've doubled Charlton Heston, Rod Cameron, Robert Francis, Rock Hudson, Jeff Chandler, Clint Walker, Van Johnson and Walter Matthau — just to name a few. In the 1950s I worked as a contract player at Warner Bros., doing bit parts and stunts in numerous films and television shows. I spent ten years in studio teaching welfare work, twenty years in acting and stunts, ten years as an educator with the Los Angeles County Special Schools, Probation Section, teaching emotionally disturbed juvenile offenders, and ten years as an oil production company president, chairman and CEO. John Wayne's oldest son Mike Wayne, the president of Batjac Productions, was first vice-president and a director of the same oil company. I've been semi-retired since 1991.

What positive things can you say about playing the Gill Man? Or was it just an uncomfortable, dangerous job?

Well, the job had its moments, it was interesting, and you *could* kind of get into the "feel" of the thing and believe that you actually *were* a monster. They used my voice in the thing, rather than an animal's; they tried lions and gorillas and God only knows what-all, and didn't like the results. I made growling and roaring noises all through, which was an aid to me while I was creating this thing, and they liked it so well that they kept my voice in my picture. (I got so hoarse that I almost lost my voice completely, *several* times.) And then I was told that they dubbed my roars into the third picture [*The Creature Walks Among Us*] also. So I enjoyed the "feel" of the thing, but it was a very taxing, very difficult job. And there wasn't any glory in it, because the studio tried to maintain the feeling that this really *was* a monster, so they didn't give me any screen credit, no notoriety or mention at all.

Ben Chapman says that he actually takes pride in having played the Creature. Can you?

Yes, it's enjoyable, looking back upon it, particularly since it's now gained some more attention. It's a movie that comes up constantly. And it's a good trivia question — "Who played the title role in Clint Eastwood's first motion picture?" Well, since the movie is *Revenge of the Creature*, the answer is *me*!

I remember one critic who used to write for a magazine in New York who said that I played the most likable villains that he'd ever seen in the movies. Well, what may have accounted for it was the fact that I always played my villains as if I was the hero and all the others were the villains!

Michael Pate

THE ACTOR WHO PLAYED many a Western tough guy, Indian chief and European meanie in Hollywood A- and B-films from the 1950s and 1960s was actually born in Drummoyne, a suburb of Sydney, Australia, and got his career start as an interviewer on the government's radio network. Michael Pate also worked on the Australian stage and in Down Under movies before relocating to the U.S. in the early 1950s and establishing himself as a solid character actor specializing in villainous portrayals. The evil glint in those narrow eyes made him a natural for horror pics and Pate racked up an imposing list of fright film credits, from the Gothic adventures *The Strange Door* and *The Black Castle* (both with Boris Karloff) to *The Maze*, United Artists' *Tower of London* and *Beauty and the Beast* and — most notably — the horror/Western *Curse of the Undead*, in which he played the screen's first frontier vampire. That "evil glint," of course, is missing in between screen roles; relaxing on the sun deck of his Sydney home on a warm autumn March day, actor/screenwriter/producer/director/author Michael Pate is most affable as he reminisces about a bright career built on dark deeds.

I was born in Drummoyne, a riverside suburb of Sydney, Australia. I went to school at Drummoyne Primary and came out of there at eleven years of age, the middle one of three dux of the school — 886 marks out of a possible 1000 marks. On these marks, I was able to go to a very exclusive high school in another suburb of Sydney called Petersham, which was maybe five or six miles away from Drummoyne. Of course, when I got to this new high school, I found that instead of being one of the top boys at Fort Street scholastically, I was about 120th out of the 150 admitted to the school that year [*laughs*]! Fort Street was a very demanding school — standards were very high. I stayed there for about four years or more. I was a top sportsman at the school — I played two seasons of soccer, and we were undefeated both seasons. Nobody would play us after that. But scholastically, I was a somewhat tardy scholar in many ways. I was *really* quite clever and quite brilliant, but I was so wrapped up in sports and things like that that I never paid much attention to my lessons. *Except* for English and history; I somehow had an idea that I might go on to university and become a lecturer in both those subjects.

Did you go right from school into "show biz"?

No, I had a number of jobs in commerce, as a junior accountant, before I was given the opportunity by George Ivan Smith to become a writer and a broadcaster for what was then known as the Australian Broadcasting Commission — our official government radio network at that time. I started

Previous page: Actor/writer/producer/director Michael Pate's advice to any aspiring actor is to "Enjoy."

there doing young people's sessions such as "Youth Speaks," "Youth Forum," etc., during which we interviewed visiting personalities, often musicians such as Yehudi Menuhin and Dr. Malcolm Sargent. Also visiting scientists and other intellectuals of note; well-known authors when we could get them. H.G. Wells was one of the people that *I* personally interviewed. He was most impressed with my (you could call it) photographic memory, the ability to remember the details of the total of the interview without having to take any notes. These were half-hour radio shows. This was all before World War II.

That's how I began in radio *per se*. Then I was asked to do other radio shows, and shows in theater. Well, of course, I'd been in the theater as an amateur actor as a youngster, and I'd also sung in many eisteddfods; I'd even sung on one of the Australian Broadcasting Commission stations in a four-part boys' choir. I also was doing some writing for some of the smaller, more literary magazines such as *The Australasian* in Sydney. Short stories, 1500 words — I had about half a dozen published before the War in that magazine, and then in 1941 I had one published in the United States by *Harper's Bazaar*. I was already in the Australian Army by that time, and on active service. After the war, of course, I did more writing; I adapted for radio, and then later, in America, I did write two screenplays with my brother-in-law Phillip Rock, and also some stuff for [television's] *Rawhide*.

So there was no ambition, at the time you were leaving school, to become an actor?

No. If anything, I was thinking of *trying* to be a writer; or, if I had the luck to be able to go to the university, to be a lawyer. That appealed to me. (Well, maybe that was part actor as well!) Anyway, out of the blue, I had the opportunity to write and broadcast on radio. I also noticed that they were paying very handsome fees for doing this, so *that* was encouraging. I obviously had a talent for radio acting — I had a very pleasant voice. Subsequently I became very well known around Sydney (first in radio and then in the theater) as a young professional actor of some talent.

It was about the end of thirty-nine, beginning of 1940 that I did a number of legitimate plays at the Minerva Theater. I was a member of the company there, and naturally also I was an understudy. So, when the occasion demanded it, when someone fell ill, I went on in quite important parts. One in particular which I took over, a character called Lord Burleigh in Maxwell Anderson's *Elizabeth the Queen*; that was with Doris Packer and Ian Keith starring. It proved quite an attention-grabber for me, probably because I was nineteen and the Lord Burleigh character was at least into his eighties! So it was very impressive to see a young man come out on the stage and play this old tottering fellow.

Your first film was Forty Thousand Horsemen *[1940].*

Yes, I was taken on by the director, Charles Chauvel, for a couple of weeks in a kind of a general capacity (which was typical of Australian films in those days), at about eight guineas a week. That was pretty well the standard top offering in those days to an established Australian actor in the theater; a guinea a performance for eight performances a week. Eight guineas a week was then the equivalent to about thirty-four, thirty-five United States dollars. I played four little bit parts in that film: I played a couple of Arabs (one was a carpet seller, the other was a customer), a blind beggar (I don't think he got into the film) and an Indian Sikh policeman. Shortly after that, I was called up into the Army; I was in the Army for about six years. After the war, Charlie Chauvel was casting for a film called *The Sons of Matthew*. When I went out to see him, he remembered that I had been in *Forty Thousand Horsemen* and he was very encouraging about me playing in *Sons of Matthew*. I finished up playing the lead in that film, which we primarily made up on the Lammington Plateau, in the southeast corner of Queensland. It proved to be one of the Australian classics of all time. It's a wonderful film about a pioneering family and it took a lot of very, *very* hard work by all of us. We started shooting it in the early part of March of forty-seven and we shot through to March of the next year. We had a lot of rain, a lot of very, very difficult circumstances; we had ancient equipment and film stock that was just terribly unreliable. We had to shoot some scenes over and over and over *again*, and it turned out that most of those scenes were the cyclone scenes in the film, and scenes which put a very great physical demand on myself and a couple of other players. But we persevered with that film; we *had* to! We shot it on and off quite spasmodically. As a matter of fact, during that year, there were a lot of periods of time when we didn't actually shoot: We were waiting to see if we could raise some more money, because we quickly ran out of the initial moneys that were raised. I finished my last shot for that film in January of 1949. The film was released in Australia around September of 1949 and it was a very good film for me — it attracted a lot of attention around the world, especially when it was previewed in the United States. It was released in the U.S. by Universal; they called it *The Rugged O'Riordans* [1949].

What was the Australian filmmaking scene like in the forties?

It was fairly lively; there were quite a few films made, as a matter of fact. It was very entrepreneurial; individual producers just had to get up their own money. In other words, there was no official government investment, no bank investments. It was private or distributor investment. Consequently, it *was* sporadic. Charlie Chauvel, who probably made only half

Michael Pate

a dozen feature films or so in a career that stretched from the late twenties until the late fifties, had great difficulty *always* as an independent producer raising money, but he somehow managed. It was always very, *very* difficult in the postwar years to get money together for the making of a film; and of course a film, once it got made, took a long, *long* time to recoup. *Sons of Matthew* took something like nine or ten years before it fully recouped; that's a long period of time to have *your* money — your personal film distribution company's money — invested. Certainly the investor/distributor made money in other ways: From having it in his theaters, and from charging the producer distribution fees and all of the expenses that go with that. But still it was a long period of time to have money locked up.

Today out here in Australia, it hasn't improved all that much, although there are areas of finance available to film producers. The recoup period has certainly shortened, but not all that very much. If you've got a reasonably successful film, you can probably get back your negative and marketing costs in maybe four to five years locally and worldwide.

How did you happen to end up in Hollywood?

In late 1950, after a successful theater season and tour of *Dark of the Moon*, I took an offer to do an interesting and very difficult but comparatively small part (the part of a retarded houseboy in a convent) in a play of Charlotte Hastings' called *Bonaventure*. With that particular company was an actress called Roberta Hunt, who said that I'd attracted quite a lot of interest in Hollywood with my performance in *Sons of Matthew*, and she suggested that I write to some of the bigger talent agencies and make a contact. Well, I felt that my letter would probably go straight into the nearest wastepaper basket, but she eventually persuaded me to write to a smaller agent called Maurine Oliver. Once she got this information, that I was in *Bonaventure*, Maurine spoke to Michel Kraike, who was producing the film version of *Bonaventure* over there; they were having quite some difficulty casting the part that I was playing on the stage. That's how I got to Hollywood to do the film, which was called *Thunder on the Hill* [1951].

Were you a movie fan during your early years?

I certainly was. I went to the movies regularly (every week) from around 1927, '28. My uncles and aunts were *mad* about the movies, and took me with them. My father also liked to go to "the flicks," as they were called then, and he'd often take me to matinees on Saturday afternoons — silent films then, of course — at a cinema that was really like a great big old barn, not really like a movie house at all. Alongside of it there was in another shed a nine-hole mini-golf course. Well, I paid my entrance fee only the *once* to

Frightened heroine Sally Forrest and glowering baddie Pate congregate outside *The Strange Door*.

that mini-golf course, because from then on, I used to go out and putt my way around that course and equal par and get *another* game free the following Friday night. Most importantly, each time I equaled the par of the course—I was very careful not to *lower* the par, just to equal it!—I got another free ticket to go to the movie matinee. So, I spent a couple of years (until I was about eleven years of age, I guess) never paying to go to those Saturday movies [*laughs*]! And I did see many very interesting films in those days: Some Lon Chaneys, like his *Phantom of the Opera*, and quite a lot of the Westerns — Hoot Gibson, Buck Jones, Tom Mix, all of those wonderful characters who probably influenced me later on in my career, to say the least.

Was it exciting to work in Hollywood?

It was one of the most exciting experiences professionally that I've ever had in my life, and I've been in the business since I was a youngster and done a lot of wonderfully exciting jobs. I just fell in love with Hollywood right off—as if I'd never been in love with it before, which of course I was. I always found the business totally exciting all my life, I never found it dull—never, never, never. Even when it's been hard slogging and you often work with people who are regular pains in the ass. It was never just a workplace to me. There were times when I went to work thinking, "Why in hell's name am I doing this piece of rubbish? Why didn't they get someone else?" And the obvious answer to *that* was, I didn't have enough in the bin; unless I went to work, I wouldn't be able to pay the mortgage and support my family! Beginning actor or star, sometimes we *all* go to work at stuff we're not particularly excited about, we often have to take a piece of shit and shine it like a diamond. This is part and parcel of being a professional actor. The lucky ones, I suppose, always make the films that they seem to want to make, but those of us in the rank and file, the ruck of professional workers in the film business, have to work at any number of parts or jobs which we sometimes might prefer not to. But as long as you think that it's exciting, or you can *make* it exciting for yourself, then I think it's always very worthwhile.

Your first horror film was a period chiller, The Strange Door *with Charles Laughton and Boris Karloff.*

Boy, that *was* a strange film, and a strange experience. Charles Laughton was an actor that I'd seen in any number of films, a person that was highly thought of. We'd all seen his Bligh and his Hunchback, and anyone that had played those two parts as superbly as he did *had* to have an awesome reputation. But by 1951, I would say that a *little* bit of the aura of Charles Laughton, "the star actor," had diminished. When I first went to Hollywood and met my present wife Felippa Rock, she told me that she had been associated with a theater company that did *Galileo* in Los Angeles with Laughton starring, and she told me quite a few things about his method of acting and his way of rehearsing (both himself and people that he was directing in the various plays). Laughton was a very, very curious man; in reading about him since in biographies, I realize that he was a man of great emotional complexity and of ... great personal *torment*, to say the very least. He most certainly did have his personal ... *desires*, let's say.

I never felt quite comfortable with Laughton, because you really couldn't be sure whether he was genuine when he said, "You were very good in a scene," or if he was "sending you up gutless" [pulling your leg].

Boris Karloff, Stephen McNally and Pate show slight concern for the anguish of wounded John Hoyt in a scene from Universal's *The Black Castle*.

It was very difficult to know — Laughton was a "cutie," and he liked to have his jollies by playing around with people mentally. He had quite a few shots at the juvenile lead, and a couple of other people in the cast. I don't remember him ever having a go at me; he wouldn't have lasted or got very far if he *had* [laughs]! I watched him have a very sarcastic dig at certain people, and cut other people off, and isolate himself. I thought it was very sad, it was a shame, because it could have been a rollicking kind of a fun picture and it turned out to be a little like treading on eggshells. But I certainly had great admiration if not *total* respect for him.

Laughton was certainly hammy in it.

Well, I don't know what you would call hammy. In *those* days, if these performances weren't considered hammy, then why should they be considered hammy now? Did *I* think that Laughton's performance was hammy then? Yes, to a degree — and, yet again, no, not necessarily. In those days, we were used to actors who chewed the scenery at times. His acting was certainly fulsome. Anyone would have seen that it was *big*; he pulled out all the buttons and stops, and tramped on the pedals the same way he did as Bligh, as the Hunchback. The same thing, for that matter, in *St. Martin's*

Lane [1938], when he does the Rudyard Kipling *If* poem as a busker outside the theater. Looking at the characters that he played, each one of them was a melodramatic character, one that couldn't be played in a close-to-the-vest style. Good or bad in the critical eye of today, that's up to the viewer himself, of course, but you have to look at performances for what they were at that particular time.

Did Joseph Pevney get to do much directing on The Strange Door?

Joe was a sweetheart, a very interesting person; I did a couple of other films with him, like *Congo Crossing* [1956], and also some television. Frankly, I don't remember much of his direction in *Strange Door* except that it was unobtrusive; probably a bit overshadowed by the *persona* of Laughton, who was inclined to be a little overbearing (to say the least!) in the scenes that he was involved in. Joe was a very workmanlike director, very quiet, unassuming — most of the time. On later productions, film *and* television, he was much more extroverted and we had a lot of fun. He was fond of a practical joke, and he pulled a few on me that were quite funny.

Did they shave your eyebrow for that scar effect?

No, it was parted and it was kept separate by waxing. Then I think maybe a thin strip of collodion painted onto that part, plus a little bit of "scar tissue" adhered to it. And it *did* look as though I'd been slashed across the eyebrow. So, no, my eyebrow wasn't shaved away; I wonder if I'd have wanted to do that. I suppose I would have ... if it was *really* important for the part!

Any other memories of the film?

I seem to remember that Richard Stapley, the young leading man, was given a really hard time; Laughton simply delighted in pouring that malmsey wine all over his head in the film. And [leading lady] Sally Forrest — a wonderful girl and a really hard-working young actress — sort of went through her paces wondering how in God's name she'd finished up in a picture like that! It *was* a rather curious kind of a picture to be in, for all of us! I did wear a beautiful pair of boots in it, they came up well above the knee to the middle of the thigh; I first slipped into them in the very pleasantly air-conditioned Universal wardrobe department, and for the five, ten minutes I had them on, they felt absolutely stunning. *But*, when we were doing the film and I had them on all day and it was hot and my feet started to swell, they were about a half-size too small for me. Particularly when I was running around. It was *very* heavy going! Ah, the things actors silently suffer for their craft...

You had a similar (but bigger and better) role in The Black Castle, *which many fans prefer to* The Strange Door.

That was a *much,* much more enjoyable film for me to do, because I had settled into Hollywood better then; certainly I rather enjoyed doing the film more than I had enjoyed the adventure with Charles Laughton. Plus, I knew Richard Greene and Stephen McNally, and of course Boris Karloff from *The Strange Door* already. Even the wife of the Maharajah of Cooch Behar [actress Nancy Valentine] played one of the parts in it! Yes, I think that *Black Castle* was an infinitely better picture than *Strange Door* all around; it had a more interesting story and it was a more vigorous type of film. There were a lot of good things in it. And I think that Nathan Juran's direction of it was very good; it was the first picture that he directed. I later did some television with him — *Time Tunnel* for Irwin Allen at Fox. Nathan was still trying to shoot television as he would shoot a feature, and of course Irwin came down on the set and rapidly changed *that* idea [*laughs*]! Nathan was a very highly talented man.

What memories of Karloff?

I thought Boris was one of the loveliest people that I'd ever come across. We had many a chat on the set over a cup of coffee, a cigarette or a pipe. I'd seen his work in any number of things, but I had no idea what kind of a *man* he was. He turned out to be such a charming, laid-back, relaxed Englishman, just a marvelous person. He was always considerate, always charming; he had a nice attitude toward "being Boris Karloff." I think, generally speaking, he was just a little tired of playing "the Boris Karloff part," but he never showed it all that very much. He just went about his work, did his business as it was expected of him, in the style that people had become accustomed to. Very contained, a little avuncular. That's a professional attitude. He was in a situation where you take the money and run, and I guess somewhere in the back of his mind he figured that that was the most secure way to do his work, and continue to live as comfortably as he'd always liked to.

Did you get the feeling that Karloff was giving condescending performances in Strange Door *and* Black Castle?

No, I just think that the parts weren't all that good. They were written so that Karloff could show off Karloff: "Here it is. Watch Frankenstein work!" That was all that was expected of him; he played all these later parts from maybe just a slight distance removed, but he was *never* condescending in *that* sense of the word. Someone said, "Here's another part, Boris, it's worth x-number of dollars," and so he went through the motions very professionally. And why not?

Any special memories of your Black Castle *co-stars?*

I thought Richard Greene was very good at what he did — that handsome, dashing young Englishman-type. I was never overly entranced with him as a *person*, but he and I got on well on that film. He was always very gracious. Stephen McNally I liked; he was a blunt, macho-type of fellow, wondering what in hell's name he was doing playing in a period film, but I thought he was terribly good in it with that patch over the eye. John Hoyt was a fine, solid character actor with a marvelous face and also a surprising physique — he was a physical fitness fanatic and worked out very strenuously. A very nice fellow; a little reserved at first, and with a terribly dry sense of humor. He was also in *Curse of the Undead*.

And Lon Chaney, Jr., who played the mute servant?

I've read all kinds of things about him being disadvantaged by a famous father, being a bit of a drunk (to say the least!), being occasionally obnoxious, etc., etc., but I found him to be a very warm, agreeable fellow. We talked about other films that he'd been in, especially *Of Mice and Men* [1939]; if all his films had been of that quality, he'd have probably been more highly thought of. He was very stereotyped at that time in the horror roles that he was doing, but he just simply went about his job; he wasn't really living in the shadow of his famous father, if ever he had. He was a very nice, gentle person and I particularly liked him. He was always very friendly to me, although as I've said I believe that he *could* be a handful when he was drinking.

You were convincing in your swordfight scene with Greene.

I got to be quite adept with a foil and also with the epee and even with a scimitar, so I did those dueling scenes myself. And people appreciated it if you *could* do those things. You had to learn the routines perfectly and *do* them immaculately; you couldn't flip around when you were using such weapons. The points were blunted just a little so that they wouldn't get into you if you got jabbed, but many a time you got nicked if you were careless. I remember Basil Rathbone having his whole wig cut right up the middle by Danny Kaye on *The Court Jester* [1956]; Danny did a couple of leaps forward unexpectedly and bounced the epee right off Basil's forehead, right through to the back of his head. It cut straight through his wig and into his pate, as a matter of fact! I don't remember whether there were stitches but there was quite a lot of blood where the epee grazed the top of his head.

How did filmmaking in Hollywood differ from filmmaking Down Under?

Down here in those years, we hadn't the greatest equipment — cameras,

Pate's sepulchral butler character contributed to the eerie atmosphere in the 3-D horror film *The Maze*. (Pictured: Veronica Hurst, Katherine Emery, Pate.)

lights, gear, they were all pretty ancient. The *people* down here were very skilled, they were very imaginative and very *ingenious*, to be able to do the things that they *did* on films. They'd studied and they'd been around the world, many of them, working in London, Hollywood, etc., and they managed to do some things in our films here with very, very minimal equipment. Some of their special effects work, models and matte work were absolutely extraordinary. But, as an example, we really didn't have even a proper looping system out here until about 1948 or so! So when I went to Hollywood and I saw the many film units that were working and the great technical skills that these units encompassed, when I saw the quality of the crews and the virtual stacks and stacks of equipment, it was just amazing to me. I was completely intoxicated with what I saw around me, it was like going to Disneyland. I was absolutely entranced with the incredible skill of all these wonderful technicians. It really was a revelation, and it was a great pleasure to suddenly find one's self in the midst of it all. Today, of course, we *do* have out here in Australia equipment as good as anywhere in the world.

Next came The Maze, *in 3-D for Allied Artists.*

I enjoyed being in *The Maze* very, very much. At one of the previews, a question that was directed at me was, "How did you devise that incredible walk?"—I had a sort of gliding walk, as though I were on an invisible moving pathway. It really was a very simple matter: During World War II service in the Southwest Pacific, I contracted a case of dysentery flexna. Over a long period of time, this causes a great deal of internal scarring of the intestines. And from time to time, this internal scarring can break away and you hemorrhage. I had it for thirteen years. As it built up over the war years, I treated it with sulfadiazine and refused surgical treatment for it after the war because no one knew how to clean it up.

It wasn't until 1952 or so that someone devised an operation where it was possible to cut away that scar tissue. So I went into the hospital and I had quite a long operation—it lasted five and a half hours or more. And they did an absolutely incredible operation and got rid of all that scar tissue. But of course, internally and externally, there was a huge amount of sutures and stitches. I came out of the hospital very weak, but almost right away I did a test for *The Robe* [1953] with Kathleen Crowley, and then I was asked to do *The Maze* by the Mirisch brothers. But I was feeling very tender around the backside; with all of those stitches inside and out, I was being very careful not to make any sudden movements! So, to protect myself, I devised this kind of locked-tight, grinding-my-buttocks-together walk for the part in *The Maze*. *That* accounted for the rather strange and wonderful type of gliding walk that I had in the film!

You weren't a bad guy in The Maze *but your sinister performance added to the atmosphere.*

The old butler wasn't a *bad* guy in the film, he just looked after the master of the manor—the enormous frog. My silver hairdo and the all-black outfit were [director] William Cameron Menzies' idea. I remember *The Maze* very well and all the people in it were so pleasant to work with. Of course, Richard Carlson was always an excellent actor. He had played in so many top films, and now he found himself in a B film like *The Maze*, but he was so relaxed and 100 percent charming. It was a very pleasant two and a half weeks making that film. And then the *next* two and a half weeks I spent doing *The Royal African Rifles* [1953] with Louis Hayward and the same girl as was in *The Maze*, Veronica Hurst. That was a fairly physical picture with a lot of running and diving in the river, all that kind of thing, but I felt a lot better by then and managed to handle all the physical stuff okay.

Any specific memories of Menzies? Richard Carlson said he "wasn't an ideal director."

I found him to be an erudite, marvelous, wonderful little pixie of a man, just great to be with. He may not have been an ideal director for Dick Carlson, but that's only his opinion. Bill directed a lot of films and had been around in the movies for a long time as an art director.

Was working in a 3-D film different than working in a conventional film?
I don't recall much about the 3-D aspects of that picture; I didn't notice anything particularly different with the camera or the set-ups or anything like that. I *did* later on in that same year [1953] when we shot *Hondo* in 3-D in Mexico, with *gigantic* cameras that looked very much like pantechnicons!

Do you recall the finale where the man-sized frog runs amok?
Who could forget it? It was pretty awful, as I recall, a bit outlandish — but, after all, they had to finish the picture. I don't know *what* they expected fans to swallow in those days; still, there were a lot worse pictures made than *The Maze*.

Do you remember who played the frog, by any chance?
No, but he was a very willing workhorse, going up and down those stairs in that awfully cumbersome suit and finally taking a flip off the parapet. The costume was made out of some rubberized material.

Were you a fan of horror, science fiction and suspense films?
I preferred a suspense film to a science fiction film. Horror films I think affect you in certain ways, depending on what age you are. The true horror films are the ones that you can still see as an adult and have your flesh creep. *Not* the violent ones — not the "chop off the heads and hands" kinds. Science fiction I was always interested in, but I never wanted to get involved with creatures crawling out of vents, those kind of things; I rather preferred the imaginative, rather intellectualized science fiction stories of, say, H.G. Wells, the kind that mixed social, economic, political elements, rather than just a run-of-the-mill horror film. I rather found some of the early horror films terribly funny — and later, when I saw them again, *hysterically* funny.

You've played more than your share of sinister types over the years. Do you enjoy playing villainous roles?
I think *everyone* enjoys playing a villainous role as an actor; it's always fun to do a really good villain, it's a chance to show another side of your "actor's personality." And it's challenging to think up ways of being *loved*

at the same time! I remember one critic who used to write for a magazine in New York who said that I played the most *likable* villains that he'd ever seen in the movies. Well, what may have accounted for it was the fact that I always played *my* villains as if I was the hero and all the *others* were the villains!

You got one of your biggest roles playing the vampire-gunslinger in Curse of the Undead, *with Eric Fleming and Kathleen Crowley.*

That film's been called a poor attempt to translate Transylvania to Wyoming, but I think they missed the point. Joe Gershenson was the producer and he was a very talented and perceptive man, though perhaps just a little bit bewildered or bemused by [director] Eddie Dein. Not that that was any surprise — Eddie was an *amazing* character. He lived up in the hills just above Laurel Canyon with his wife Mildred, who was a real sweetheart (the *two* of them were), in an old castle with a moat and a drawbridge that you drove over to get inside the entrance courtyard. He had loads of talent. He also used to make the greatest copies of Jackson Pollock paintings — you'd think they were originals. And he made some very imaginative movies. As a matter of fact, the original title of *Curse of the Undead* was *Eat Me Gently*, but Universal wasn't about to use *that* title, naturally! I got along tremendously well with Eddie, there was no bullshit about him, and we got through the filming of that picture pretty fast.

Did you enjoy your role in the film?

I enjoyed it very much; I thought the film went well, for what it was. It was stylized, it had good set design, very good lighting, it was photographed well. Eddie Dein was a dynamic if sometimes seemingly somewhat rough-mannered kind of man. Eric Fleming, on the other hand, had a few "questioning sessions" with him, but then, Eric had a tendency to do that at times. Eric was a very well-meaning actor/person and worked very hard, but he was inclined to be a little dour. Tragically, he lost his life in South America a few years after [his television series] *Rawhide* finished, when a stunt went wrong and he was washed over the falls in a canoe. And Kathleen Crowley was a lovely lady and a very hard worker.

And your opinion of the picture?

It didn't have a lot of money spent on it, and perhaps there were many things that could have been done with it. There *were* some scenes that were shockingly corny, no question about that, and one or two sets that looked as bare as a baby's bottom. But overall there were many very, very good

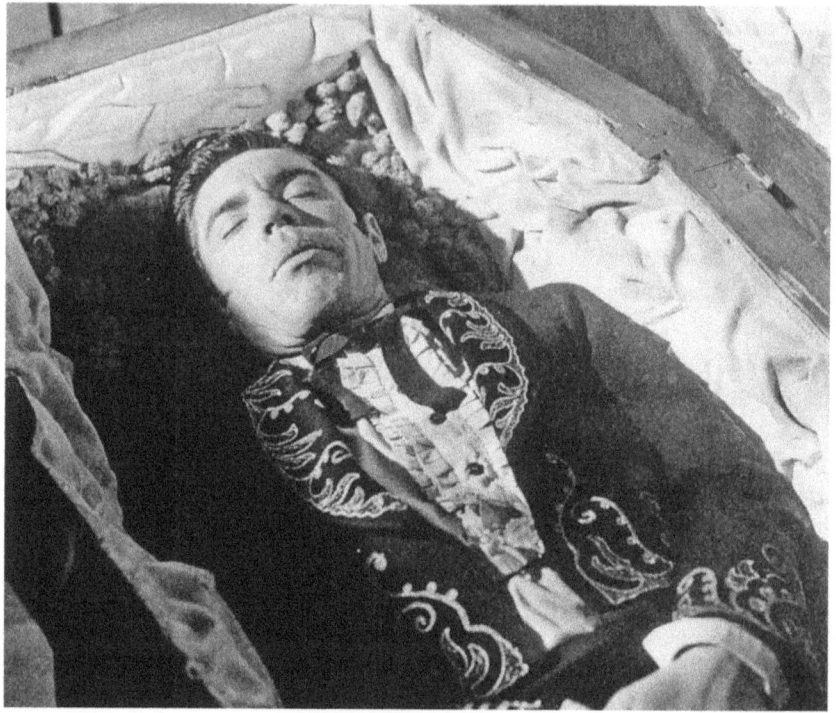

The screen's first six-shootin' vampire: Pate as Don Drago Robles in Universal's *Curse of the Undead* (shooting title: *Affairs of a Vampire*).

scenes in it. I loved my role and I just liked being in the picture. In 1959, going through Honolulu on my way to Australia, everyone was suddenly pointing at me and whispering, and I didn't realize what it was all about. Then, driving through the streets on my way to the airport, I saw *Curse of the Undead* advertised outside one of the theaters in Honolulu! The film *did* make quite an impression, I guess!

What are your favorites among your horror/SF films?
    Probably *Curse of the Undead* best of all, *The Maze* next, and *The Black Castle* after that.

You get a writing credit on Most Dangerous Man Alive.
    That was actually a story that Leo Gordon wrote; he came to me with it and I helped him rewrite it. At that time, it was called *The Atomic Man*. Leo eventually came *back* to me because he needed some quick money, so I bought out his interest in that story idea and I later turned it over to my

father-in-law [producer] Joe Rock and my brother-in-law [writer] Phillip Rock. The three of us optioned the treatment out in various ways, and Benedict Bogeaus took a final option on it. It was shot in Mexico with Ron Randell in the lead; I believe it was made in three half-hours as if it could be the beginning of a television series, but it was simply put out as a feature. We all made a little money on that from the options. But I never did see the finished film.

Did you enjoy playing the nefarious Sir Ratcliffe opposite Vincent Price in Roger Corman's Tower of London?

I loved doing it. It wasn't much of a script and everyone was very heavily "playing at the period," but amidst it all there was this marvelous Vincent Price who was able to "cod" the whole thing up ["send it up"] beautifully and yet make it hang together. No one really believed that it had anything to do with *Richard III* or the Tower of London or anything like that, it was just an excuse to do *that* kind of a horror film. Vincent Price and I had a lot of laughs; he's a great character and a tremendous actor, always has been.

How would you rate the performance he gives?

It doesn't rank with some of his other, incredibly wonderful performances, but I think any Price performance is always worth seeing. His style is totally unique. Roger Corman and his brother Gene were both extraordinarily clever producers who managed to make films on very small budgets and did very, very well with those films. We moved quickly on *Tower of London*, but I wouldn't say we rushed. We made it down at the old Producers Studio, just across Melrose from Paramount.

You also did more than your share of "fantastic television," including Thriller.

I enjoyed doing that *Thriller* episode ["Trio for Terror"], probably because of [director] Ida Lupino, who was a lovely person to work with. But I don't recall with any great pleasure the process of getting a plaster mask made for that show, because it was made under the old system of plaster-casting which was terribly uncomfortable and claustrophobic for the subject. Recently I did a *Mission: Impossible* out here, and I had to have another such mask made. It was made by a number of lady technicians, and it was a very simple process with a latex compound. It just went on and peeled off, no problems, no discomfort at all.

You had a small part as an evil nobleman in the fairy tale film Beauty and the Beast.

Pate and Vincent Price search for some hint of historical accuracy in Roger Corman's half-hearted *Tower of London*.

I haven't got much in the way of memories of the making of *Beauty and the Beast*, except that I had a few scenes with quite a lot to say. I don't think I saw the picture when it was released, but I did see it on television out here on a wintry Sunday afternoon a few years back and I was quite impressed with some of the scenes that I was in. I didn't think Mark Damon was right for the film; his performance left a lot to be desired. He looked as if he was pretty much lost in it. I also didn't think that his beast makeup was all that very good.

You moved back to Australia in the late sixties.

Well, first of all, I came out here and I helped produce *Age of Consent* for Columbia Pictures [in 1968]. I also did shoot second unit stuff ahead of the main unit. Then I got involved in doing quite a great deal of television production, live and taped. After that, I decided to do a television series called *Matlock Police* [Pate played the lead], and over four years I did about 192 hour episodes, which kept me occupied. Then, another short series (twenty-six episodes) called *The Power and the Glory*, in which I played Archbishop Malone, a magnificent character.

You've also done quite a bit of directing in Australia.

I was always very interested in directing. After all, there were many occasions, while I was acting professionally, that many actors really "directed" the scenes — especially in television with some of the ding-a-ling directors we had to contend with. When I decided to stay in Australia, I directed lots of stuff for television as well as second unit for the film *The Mango Tree*, which I wrote and produced in 1977. But it wasn't until *Tim* [1979] that I got to direct a full feature film. I wrote and produced that script and also directed it.

I have felt my career to be more gratifying in its diversity in Australia than what it might have been in the U.S. where most of my friends in the business are bored out of their gourds because old actors, *and* old directors, are seldom offered work these days. I also wrote a book in the United States called *The Film Actor* about 1967 — it's based upon classes I taught at the Screen Actors Studio in the early sixties. It's in a lot of libraries around the world. A few years back, I wrote another book about entertaining the troops in World War II, *An Entertaining War*.

Several of the more recent films in which you've appeared were directed by Philippe Mora.

In 1976, when I was long done with *Matlock Police*, I was about to go into feature production with *The Mango Tree*, but being familiar only with the personnel of small television units, I decided I should act in a film to have a look-see at a feature film crew. I asked my agent to see if there was a part in Mora's film *Mad Dog Morgan* [1976] which starred Dennis Hopper. (My son Christopher had already been cast.) It was pretty much a shambles of a film but I did learn a few things on location. Since *Mad Dog Morgan*, I have done several other films with Philippe, like *The Return of Captain Invincible*. I enjoyed doing the film even though it turned out pretty awful.

You even got to sing in there.

And the producer never asked me if I *could* sing! It was the first time I'd sung in a feature — I believe I once sang a song, an old Australian bush ballad, in a *Rawhide* episode. *Death of a Soldier* [1986] was another film of Philippe's; that was an enjoyable and stimulating experience for me since I had known, just in passing during the War years, the original of my character. Then I had a little bit in *Howling III*, which I simply did because Philippe asked me to. That really was a doozie of a film — it had some amazing effects in it — but I never did know what the whole thing was all about! I did my work one night at a posh new hotel here in Sydney, around the pool and in the gym — no strain. I think Mora's career is going along very well — he seems always to make the right connections. I also think he has more potential than his films show. I've also made films out here for [directors] Tim Burstall [*Duet for Four*, 1982] and Henri Safran [*The Wild Duck*, 1983].

I'm officially "retired" now but I keep busy handling the feature films we made, doing voice-overs and narrations, an occasional acting job if it appeals to me, writing a few film stories, playing golf regularly ... *talking to people who want to write articles about me* ... and so on. So basically I keep very busy.

Career-wise, have you attained most of the goals that you might have set for yourself?

In a way. But I don't think I set any real specific goals when I first got into acting. I thought, how nice it would be if I could simply continue to act, whether it be in the theater or in films or whatever. I wasn't able to go to university, I didn't come from a family that could provide me with a ready-made business to go into. I had to make a career for myself, and I was very fortunate to have had *enough* talent to do so — to become a professional actor. I wasn't deadset on being a "big star"; I saw too many unhappy people being "big stars." (You could see it all around you, and it's even worse today.) I just wanted to be well thought of in the profession, I wanted to be successful in the sense that I was in demand. But otherwise I was very happy just *being* in the profession.

Enjoy is the key word. If you don't, you shouldn't get into the business in the first place. Throughout over fifty years as a professional actor, I have *always* enjoyed working at my profession. So my advice to any aspiring actor is *enjoy*. Enjoy, and try to keep working!

MICHAEL PATE FILMOGRAPHY

Forty Thousand Horsemen (Universal/Goodwill, 1940)
The Rugged O'Riordans (Sons of Matthew) (Universal, 1949)
Bitter Springs (Savage Justice) (Rank/Ealing, 1950)
Thunder on the Hill (Universal, 1951)
The Strange Door (Universal, 1951)
Ten Tall Men (Columbia, 1951)
The Black Castle (Universal, 1952)
Five Fingers (20th Century–Fox, 1952)
Face to Face (RKO, 1952)
Target Hong Kong (Columbia, 1952)
Rogue's March (MGM, 1952)
The Maze (Allied Artists, 1953)

Julius Caesar (MGM, 1953)
Hondo (Warners, 1953)
Escape from Fort Bravo (MGM, 1953) Co-wrote original story
The Royal African Rifles (Allied Artists, 1953)
Houdini (Paramount, 1953)
Scandal at Scourie (MGM, 1953)
El Alamein (Columbia, 1953)
All the Brothers Were Valiant (MGM, 1953)
The Desert Rats (20th Century–Fox, 1953)
Secret of the Incas (Paramount, 1954)
King Richard and the Crusaders (Warners, 1954)
The Silver Chalice (Warners, 1954)
A Lawless Street (Columbia, 1955)
Skabenga (African Fury) (voice only; United Artists, 1955)
The Court Jester (Paramount, 1956)
Congo Crossing (Universal, 1956)
The Killer Is Loose (United Artists, 1956)
The Revolt of Mamie Stover (20th Century–Fox, 1956)
Reprisal! (Columbia, 1956)
7th Cavalry (Columbia, 1956)
Something of Value (MGM, 1957)
The Oklahoman (Allied Artists, 1957)
The Tall Stranger (Allied Artists, 1957)
Desert Hell (20th Century–Fox, 1958)
Hong Kong Confidential (United Artists, 1958)
Curse of the Undead (Universal, 1959)
Green Mansions (MGM, 1959)
Westbound (Warners, 1959)
Walk Like a Dragon (Paramount, 1960)
Most Dangerous Man Alive (Columbia, 1961) Co-wrote original story
The Canadians (20th Century–Fox, 1961)
Sergeants Three (United Artists, 1962)
Tower of London (United Artists, 1962)
PT 109 (Warners, 1963)
Beauty and the Beast (United Artists, 1963)
McLintock! (United Artists, 1963)
Drums of Africa (MGM, 1963)
California (AIP, 1963)
Advance to the Rear (Company of Cowards?) (MGM, 1964)
Brainstorm (Warners, 1965)
The Great Sioux Massacre (Columbia, 1965)
Major Dundee (Columbia, 1965)
The Singing Nun (MGM, 1966)
Hondo and the Apaches (MGM, 1967)
Age of Consent (Columbia, 1969) Associate Producer
Little Jungle Boy (Mass-Brown/Seven Television, 1970)
Mad Dog Morgan (Mad Dog) (B.E.F./Cinema Shares International, 1976)
Tim (Satori, 1981) Writer/Producer/Director
The Mango Tree (G.U.O./Pisces-Satori, 1982) Writer/Producer
Duet for Four (Partners) (Burstall, 1982)
The Return of Captain Invincible (Legend in Leotards) (7 Keys Films, 1983)

The Wild Duck (Orion/RKR Entertainment, 1983)
The Camel Boy (voice only; Yoram Gross, 1984)
Death of a Soldier (Scotti Bros. Pictures, 1986)
Howling III (Square Pictures, 1987)

As near as I can estimate, over the fifty years that I was active, I think I worked in around fifteen hundred features. And I probably worked in a couple of thousand television episodes.

Gil Perkins

A 1500-TITLE FILMOGRAPHY would be an impressive achievement for any actor — even a bit player — but for a stuntman, it borders on the phenomenal. Australian-born Gil Perkins racked up this imposing total (and did a few thousand television episodes on the side) in a 50-year stunt career which ran from the very beginning of the talking-picture era to the mid-1970s. Best known for stunt-doubling Western star William (Hopalong Cassidy) Boyd and comic Red Skelton, Perkins also stood in for countless other actors during that half-century stretch, working frequently in the horror and science fiction fields. He played a sailor in 1933's *King Kong* and doubled star Bruce Cabot throughout the picture, did Spencer Tracy's dirty work in MGM's *Dr. Jekyll and Mr. Hyde* (1941) and played Frankenstein in the battle scenes of the monster classic *Frankenstein Meets the Wolf Man* (1943). Gil Perkins remembers these experiences, serial skirmishes, *Teenage Monster* mashes and much *more* in this reminiscence of a career where the accent was on action.

How did you become involved on King Kong? *Because you were working a lot at RKO at that time?*

Well, yes, I was working at RKO, *and* various other studios. I started in this business as a young actor, and just a year or so before *King Kong*, by accident I became a double for a guy named Bill Boyd, who later became Hopalong Cassidy. I was his double beginning with a picture called *The Big Gamble* [1931]. Boyd's double in that broke his leg. I was working on the next stage, somebody said I looked like Bill Boyd and they hired me to take over. The next day I shot second unit out on Washington Boulevard, climbing up lamp posts and jumping out of windows. Boyd wasn't there, but the next morning he saw the rushes in a projection room and he said, "God, this kid looks more like me than *I* do. Let's grab him." I was so successful in that that people kept hiring me [as a stunt double] — RKO, Universal, Paramount, MGM. I used to work at RKO quite a bit, on Clark and McCullough two-reel comedies and other things like that, and some of them were directed by a guy named George Stevens, who later became one of the great directors in the business.

We started on *King Kong* around July of 1932 and worked through the Olympic Games — although I was able to see *some* of the Olympic Games because we worked nights sometimes on *Kong*. However, I had to miss some of 'em — I remember missing the 400 meters [swimming competition], which Buster Crabbe won from Gene Taris of France, because we made the switchover at that time, from nights back to days. I gave the tickets to the gal who

Previous page: "I had a pretty good education," says Gil Perkins, "and I always thought (even when I *was* a stuntman) that I wasn't particularly proud of it."

If Perkins (far right, foreground) could turn back the clock, he would think twice about a stunt career.

became my wife. (I also remember the Olympic Games tickets cost me three bucks apiece. It's a little different today!)

By the way, I worked in a picture called *Madison Sq. Garden* [1932] before I got on *King Kong* (I think I was one of the news reporters). They called me back for added scenes and retakes, and I said, "Jeez, I can't do it, I'm working at night [on *Kong*]." They said, "Well, we're gonna shoot in the daytime and we'll be down at the Olympic Auditorium, and you can sleep as much as you like in between scenes." Have you got any idea what it's like, trying to sleep in a fight stadium, *and* work all night? I got the worst dose of influenza I ever had, and I sweated worse than I ever had in my life. I'd get into bed and sweat up one side of the bed, I'd move to the other side, then I'd move to the other end of the bed and make the bed the other way. For two or three days, I was wringing wet all the time, and it took a hell of a lot out of me. But shortly after that, I went to Catalina with [director] Al Santell on a picture with Janet Gaynor and Charlie Farrell called *Tess of the Storm Country* [1932] and over there, in that ocean air and swimming in that water and eating good food and everything, I got back to normal again.

During those first weeks of production on Kong, *you played one of the sailors.*

Right. Then, in January of 1933, they started to do a lot of the action stuff that involved the lead, Bruce Cabot, and I doubled Cabot. But there was a break in between. We finished shooting *King Kong* [before the break] sometime in September [1932], then we picked up again in January. In October, during the hiatus, RKO wanted to make a picture with Bill Boyd called *Lucky Devils*, the first picture *all* about stuntmen, with Bill as the head stuntman. We were in the Depression and money was scarce as hell, and somebody said, "Where are we gonna get the money to make this?" Merian Cooper, who was the producer of *King Kong* and the head of the studio, said, "We've got [investor] Jock Whitney's money to finish *King Kong*— we've still got to do all the action and all the miniatures and everything, and we won't get to that for quite a while yet. We'll borrow some of this money from *King Kong*, make *Lucky Devils*, release it and get the money back before we even need it!"—which is just what they did. We made it in October and November, in about three or four weeks, they got it released around Christmas time, and they had all the money back by the next year. That was one of the offshoots of *King Kong* money!

Wasn't The Most Dangerous Game *also done around this time, on the* Kong *sets?*

Most Dangerous Game was shot during the middle of the year [1932]. I worked on that; I was in the ship's boiler room, playing a stoker, and Buster Crabbe was the other guy with me. The boat hit this reef and water came in the boiler room, and here we were being swirled around in the water, around the boilers. Anyway, when we got through with the job, which was several days, I said to Buster, "Are you going to try and stay in pictures, Buster?" And he said, "Gil, if I win in the Olympic Games, I'm gonna be a picture *star*." And then he *did* win the 400 meters in the Olympic Games. Right after that, Paramount cast him in a picture called *King of the Jungle* [1933], and he became a pretty big man in pictures!

Do you have any idea how many pictures you've been in?

As near as I can estimate, over the fifty years that I was active, I think I worked in around 1500 features. And I probably worked in a couple of thousand television episodes. I'd work at Universal in an episode of something in the morning, one at MGM in the afternoon and sometimes one at Paramount at night! That wasn't a run-of-the-mill thing, but that would happen sometimes. The same thing in pictures — sometimes I'd work on six different pictures in a week, because we worked Saturdays in those days, we didn't get a five-day week until 1956. One day in 1946 I was working on Burt Lancaster's first picture *The Killers*, doubling a guy named Jack Lambert. I had six jobs lined up for that *day,* if I could have taken them all! But sometimes, of course, I'd go on pictures like *The Sea Wolf* in 1930 or *Cavalcade* in 1932, where I'd be on it for weeks and weeks at a time; *Mutiny on the Bounty* in 1935, I was on it for five or six months; *Captains Courageous* in thirty-six, four or five months; [*The Adventures of*] *Robin Hood* in thirty-seven, almost six months; *Dodge City* [1939] and *Virginia City* [1940], both a couple of months.

Why was there a hiatus in the middle of shooting King Kong?

It was such a big job with miniatures, and the special effects people weren't ready for it. That was one of the reasons. And, of course, being in the Depression the way we were, and with money as scarce as it was, it just happened that they weren't ready to spend the money, I guess. Although, since they took $75,000 out to make *Lucky Devils* in October-November, I guess there *was* money available. But I didn't know any of the intricacies of that, or what went on there.

Why did King Kong *require two directors, Cooper and Ernest Schoedsack?*

Cooper didn't direct it, Schoedsack directed it. Cooper was the producer. And, of course, a guy named Willis O'Brien directed all of the miniatures. King Kong actually was about twenty inches high—it was amazing what they did with miniatures. For the inserts of Fay Wray in his hand, they made a huge hand with a cantilever elbow and a huge arm on a bar, and they could put her in this hand and operate it hydraulically—lift her up and down. Fay did that herself, because it was a big hand that they could sit or stand her in, and it was only a short distance above the floor.

Cooper does share a screen credit for directing Kong, *with Schoedsack.*

None of the time I was on *King Kong* [did Cooper direct], and I was there for three or four weeks in July, August, September of 1932 and I was there in January 1933. Cooper was the producer—he'd come around and talk to Schoedsack, so on and so forth, but he didn't actually physically direct any of the scenes. At least, *I* never saw him do that. Ernest Schoedsack was a nice guy—big, tall guy, around 6'4". Very easy to work with, and he knew exactly what he was doing, which is a big help. Well, *most* of the big guys in pictures then knew what they were doing; today, I think a lot of them *don't* quite know what they're doing. But *then,* most all of them did.

Bouncing up and down on King Kong's cliffside vine was no great shakes for an old hand like Perkins.

What were the stars of King Kong *like?*

Bruce Cabot [Jack Driscoll] was a very nice guy. He hadn't done much before that [in pictures], except he played a part in a thing called *Roadhouse Murder* [1932] that was produced by J. Walter Ruben. From that, they decided that he would make a good lead for *King Kong*, so they gave it to him.

As a stunt double, did you feel you looked enough like him?

No, I was a *lousy* double for him. But hanging off the side of a cliff, thirty feet from the camera, who the hell could tell? Hollywood audiences might have, but people out in Kalamazoo or Oshkosh, *they're* not lookin' for doubles [*laughs*]! Fay Wray [Ann Darrow] was a very nice gal; she was great to work with, too, we had a lot of fun with her. I worked with Robert Armstrong [Carl Denham] a lot; Bob was in *The Suicide Fleet* [1931] with Bill Boyd [and Perkins], and I worked with Bob subsequently, in other pictures. He was a nice guy, too. Most of the guys in the business were nice guys. There were a few guys that were really a pain, like George Sanders, the Englishman, he got to be a hell of a pain to work with. But the Cagneys and the Montgomerys, the Gables and the Gary Coopers and the Dick Arlens, they were all great people.

All the scenes aboard the ship, where you're playing a sailor — they were shot on a sound stage?

Yes, a sound stage at RKO. I don't remember ever going out on a real ship at all. We were on location near the ocean, down around Balboa a couple of times, but we didn't get out on a ship — not to my memory, anyway. I was also there for the big native ceremony — we watched them dancing in circles and hitting themselves on the chest and all that sort of thing. They hired a lot of black guys to play the natives in that scene; one of the guys, Everett Brown [the native in the ape costume], subsequently played the foreman of the slaves in *Gone with the Wind* [1939]. That was all shot on what we called the Forty Acres, which had been Pathé Studio. It was a big spread where we had sets and all kinds of things, and we shot those scenes down on the Forty Acres at night. Of course, that's where *Gone with the Wind* was made — where Tara was built — and the Atlanta station where they had all the wounded. We also did *Around the World in 80 Days* [1956] and a lot of other things over there.

Were you one of the sailors Kong shakes off the log into the chasm?

No, I wasn't one of those. And it wouldn't matter if you *did* fall off the log, because in the next scene you'd be back as a nondescript sailor and nobody would recognize you [*laughs*]!

Then you doubled Bruce Cabot in the scene where he and Fay Wray are climbing down a cliffside vine, escaping from Kong.

It was no great stunt: I was just hanging onto the liana (that's what *they* called the vine) and the ape was lifting it up and down and shaking it. Actually, it was being hoisted by special effects guys, off camera. Fay Wray had a stunt double there also, of course — her name was Cherie May. We had pads down below us, 'cause sometimes we were up as high as forty-five feet on this cliff set. She was not one of the best stunt gals that I knew. There *were* some great gals, but she was not one of 'em; she was a gal who didn't take very good care of herself—she smoked and all. She was trying her best, but at one point she couldn't hang onto me anymore and she fell about twenty feet onto the pads. She hit the wrong way and started to cough up blood, which scared the bejesus out of everybody, because she'd injured her lungs. That was shot on Stage Ten at RKO, up by the cemetery at the back end of the lot.

Is that you falling into the water in the high shot which follows?
  Yes. That we shot in the [studio] tank, on Stage Eleven, if I remember right. The stuntwoman was the same gal who was on the liana with me. I spent a couple of weeks doubling Bruce — mostly trying to escape from the monster, climbing rocks and all.

Do you ever think about writing your autobiography?
  I've had people tell me time and time again I should write a book, and there was one book called *The Real Tinsel* that I have a chapter in. But it's too much of an effort, really, and now at my age the only way I could do it would be to narrate it to some writer and let *him* do it. But, the Screen Actors Guild has four hours of me on audio tape, relating all the things from the time I started till the time I finished, and they shot four hours of me on videotape—the first two hours I did on my own, the last two hours I did with [stuntman] Tom Steele. They've edited that down to an hour and a half, and according to my wife and daughter it's wonderful—and *I* think it's pretty good, too. There've been a lot of books written about Hollywood, some good, some bad, some indifferent; I wonder if there's room for another one, anyway!

I wanted to ask you some more about Lucky Devils. *How much truth is there in its depiction of stuntmen?*
  I would say that it's pretty factual. The action—the stuff in the bank, the stuff out on Decker Canyon with the cars and the motorcycles, all the other stuff—that's pretty much the way stuntmen work. That, of course, was 1932, and the technique of stunt work *has* changed somewhat since then, because that's sixty-three *years* ago! But the action as you see it on the screen today, in the main, is pretty much done the way it was *always* done. The fights, for instance, are done the same way. The stuntmen today, I guess, do a hell of a job—maybe they're better than *we* were. But *my* experience was that, in the *first* ten years I retired, there were more stuntmen

badly hurt and killed than in the whole forty-five or fifty years I was in the business. I retired in seventy-two, so I'm talking about 1972 through eighty-two.

What about Lucky Devils' *depiction of stuntmen as extremely superstitious?*
  Well, *that* may apply to some of them, but it never applied to most of the guys *I* knew and it certainly didn't apply to me. The number thirteen, or walking under a ladder, or throwing your hat on a bed, or the many other superstitions — they never went with me. I would walk under ladders — unless, of course, there was a guy up there painting, *that's* a different thing [*laughs*]! But all those superstitions are a lot of crap, as far as I was concerned, just a lot of baloney. Now, I can't vouch for *everybody*, but the ones that I knew, like Bobby Rose, Billy Jones, Chick Collins, Paul Stader, Paul Baxley — the real *top* men among the stuntmen — I don't know any of 'em that were superstitious. By the way, Bobby Rose gave them a lot of the ideas for the stunts [in *Lucky Devils*] and he worked with the scriptwriters.

What did you do in the Fredric March Dr. Jekyll and Mr. Hyde?
  I did some of the fight stuff in the residential home, the place where Rose Hobart and her father [Halliwell Hobbes] lived. I didn't double Freddie March, Chick Collins did most of the doubling for him — breaking through the glass doors, for one thing. He said, "I'll go through so fast, it'll just shatter," and he went through real plate glass, not candy glass. But it all turned out fine. Where I was concerned, it was just general fight stuff in the house, and somewhere else out on the street, I think. It's so far back, I can't remember exactly now. The Spencer Tracy Jekyll and Hyde I remember better, because I doubled Spencer.

Did Chick Collins wear makeup as Mr. Hyde, or just some kind of mask?
  He was made-up as Mr. Hyde with a *part* mask. In the one with Tracy, I had a complete mask over my head and then a wig on top of it. It was one of those rubber-like masks, and then they made-up the mask with makeup. It was glued onto my neck and onto my head, with the wig over the top of it. When I ate with it, I had to eat through a straw, because the mouth would only open so much. I couldn't eat any solid foods, so my lunch every day was a malted milk or something like that!

How long were you on the Tracy Jekyll and Hyde?
  Oh, I would say probably three or four weeks in 1940. I doubled Tracy and I did all the fighting and stuff in that. Like the scene where Hyde has the fight with Donald Crisp, and Lana Turner, Crisp's daughter, gets

knocked down. They were shooting insert shots of my legs, just missing her breasts as I stepped on one side, in between her arm and her breast, and just missing her head with my boots. I had to avoid stepping on her boobs and all over her. I can't remember *all* the things I did in there; it was mainly fight stuff in different places. Vic Fleming directed it, and he was quite a perfectionist. I'd had quite a lot of experience with Vic on *Captains Courageous* and *Test Pilot* [1938] and other things like that that he made.

Who did your makeup?

Jack Dawn supervised it, but Bill Tuttle and Keester Sweeney, two of MGM's very good makeup men, did most of the work on me. Of course, Bill Tuttle succeeded Jack Dawn as the head [makeup] man at MGM, and he was the head man there for years, until MGM folded. When I first knew Bill Tuttle, he was a messenger boy at Fox in 1932 [*laughs*]! It just happened that he was very friendly with Jack Dawn, and Jack went to MGM to do a Norma Shearer picture. This was 1934. Jack did such a good job on Shearer, and Shearer liked him so well, that Irving Thalberg made him the head of the MGM makeup. And as soon as Jack was head of makeup, he called Bill Tuttle and said, "Look, you're not getting anywhere being a messenger boy at Fox. Come on over here and I'll make you an apprentice makeup man" — which he did. And Bill, of course, was quite artistic, and very good with everything he did. But, back to your question, Jack Dawn supervised and *sometimes* applied some of my [Mr. Hyde] makeup, but it was mainly the other two that did most of the work.

You must have known Spencer Tracy well from all the pictures you did with him, particularly Captains Courageous, *but can you specifically recall his attitude about* Dr. Jekyll and Mr. Hyde?

Yes, he was very gung-ho about it because he thought it was something that he could really get his teeth into and give a good performance. Which, of course, he did. But I always thought Spence could be a bit of an old woman, particularly around four o'clock in the afternoon when he got *tired.* I remember him screaming at Mickey Rooney one day — we were on the *Captains Courageous* set and Mickey was playing the piano. Spence was in his dressing room and he screamed, "Cut that god-damned piano! Shut up!" so on and so forth. Of course, had that been a few years later when Mickey was a big name, Mickey might have told him to go drop dead [*laughs*]! But this was 1936 and Mickey was sixteen years old. A very competent, great little actor, but he hadn't reached the importance he did later at MGM.

Both Lana Turner and Ingrid Bergman, in their autobiographies, wrote that on Dr. Jekyll and Mr. Hyde, *Victor Fleming roughed them up physically before emotional scenes.*

Well, what did they mean by that? Not hurt them, *physically.*

Ingrid Bergman said he slapped her around — hard — and Lana Turner said he hurt her arm.

I didn't witness any of that, and I was *there,* but *maybe* he did; I've known directors to do much worse than *that*! For instance, that German director, Erich von Stroheim. They were making a picture at Fox in 1932 called *Walking Down Broadway* [later retitled *Hello, Sister!*] and Boots Mallory had a scene in it where she was supposed to cry. And she couldn't get the emotion to cry and show any tears. So von Stroheim just slapped the bejesus out of her — one side of the face and then the other. It was one of the worst beatings — and she *cried*! She really cried *then*! And he shot the scene and got what he wanted. He was a pain in the ass to work for, he overshot many things, just like Josef von Sternberg. Von Sternberg was the worst. On *An American Tragedy* [1931] I saw him shoot a scene 106 times, and I couldn't see any difference between the second take and the hundred-and-sixth take [*laughs*]! I watched him shoot a scene fifty-eight times with Irving Pichel (who was a very good actor, and was playing the district attorney) and the man and the woman who were playing the girl's [Sylvia Sidney] parents. He shot that fifty-eight times, and they were *all* excellent actors. I couldn't see any difference between the first and the last take on that, either.

After the mid–1930s he was pretty much washed up.

That's right, Paramount finally got wise to him and just let him go. From then on, he never was much of a director. He did a picture called *Jet Pilot* with "Duke" Wayne and Janet Leigh in fifty-two, and RKO was very unhappy that they ever let him direct *that.* That was during the Howard Hughes regime.

What did you do as a stuntman in An American Tragedy?

I turned the canoe over up at Lake Arrowhead and "drowned" the gal who doubled Sylvia Sidney, a girl named Elsie Ware. Then I swam ashore. Then, after they found the body, the D.A. comes to talk to the father and mother of Sylvia Sidney, and that was the scene that von Sternberg shot fifty-eight times.

Do you recall what you did in She?

I think we did some high falls off rocks somewhere and we did some other things. That was about 1935, Helen Gahagan was the star, and it was one of Irving Pichel's first directorial jobs. I don't remember much more about it — that's one I never thought was much of a picture. I didn't like it.

That makes two of us!
    Bobby Rose was the stunt gaffer on *She*, if I remember right.

The stuntman who's most famous for playing monsters is Eddie Parker. How well did you know him?
    I knew Eddie very well. He doubled different guys [in monster movies] — he doubled Lon Chaney, for instance, in *Frankenstein Meets the Wolf Man*. Eddie sometimes doubled "Duke" Wayne, too. Eddie was good at fights and on the ground, but he wasn't any good up high. I remember we were doing *Seven Sinners* [1940] with Wayne, which was one of the great action pictures of our time in my opinion, and Eddie was supposed to do a big swing across a barroom and (when he came to the end of the swing) dive onto a group of guys fighting on the floor. But Dave Sharpe had to do it for him. (Of course, Dave wasn't really big enough to double Wayne, but swingin' on a line over a barroom, size didn't matter much because it goes so fast.) What Eddie did in the latter part of his life was, he and another guy went into the liquor business on Whitsett Boulevard and Riverside Drive, out in the Valley, and they did very well with their liquor store. But Eddie died [in 1960], and he wasn't very old.

From a stuntman's point of view, name one of the best directors you worked with and one of the worst.
    Well, I would say the outstanding director I worked with was Phil Karlson. He started as a second assistant at Universal about 1931 (that's when I first knew him), came up to be assistant director, and he was the assistant director on *Seven Sinners*. As a matter of fact, in those days, he was the stunt gaffer, too, because he'd learned all the things that go on and how to handle it. And then he became an associate producer and then a director. He knew how to direct action, if not *better*, than *as well* as any director I ever knew. I remember one time I saw a television interview with Sidney Lumet, a New York director who I think is a hell of a fine director, and the interviewer asked him, "Mr. Lumet, I know you watch other directors work all the time. Do you ever copy any of their work?" And Lumet's answer was, "Well, I suppose *unconsciously* you see things done by great men like Capra and Ford, and you may try to emulate 'em. But I'll tell you one director I *always* watch: I watch Phil Karlson's *action*. I think he's the greatest action guy I ever saw. When I shoot action, I try to remember how

Phil Karlson shot it." Now I, of course, am prejudiced in favor of Phil [*laughs*], 'cause I knew him so long, and I was the stunt gaffer on all his shows: I went to Canada with him, to Mexico, to Okinawa; down in Alabama on *The Phenix City Story* [1955]; I was on *Walking Tall* [1973] and *Framed* [1975], his two last pictures. *All* those things, I was the stunt gaffer. Early on, back in the fifties, he used to use two of us, Sol Gorss and myself, but Sol died at a very young age. So I just carried on and I was the guy from then on.

And how about a worst director?

In my experience, it could be a guy like Raoul Walsh: On *They Died with Their Boots On* [1941], five men were killed. They weren't exactly stuntmen, they were mainly Mexican riders trying to do stunts on horses. They were killed in chases — the horses just ran away with them, and they couldn't hold 'em back. That's how four guys were killed. Then there was another guy killed, a very nice, well-educated guy. His horse stumbled and fell and threw him, and he was riding with his sword out. He threw the sword ahead of him, and by some strange quirk of fate, the hilt hit the ground with the sword standing up and he fell on it and it went right through him. Eventually he died, a few days later, from that. I used to play tennis with him up at Jack Warner's home; his father was the vice president of Cadillac. He could have had any kind of job with General Motors, and here he was, trying to be an actor. And it killed him. I thought that Raoul Walsh should have been much more careful; some of these [directors] didn't care whether you hurt yourself or not.

The worst guy from that point of view, although he knew what he was doing, was a director named Ralph Ceder. Ceder used to direct a lot of stuff at the old Pathé studios, and then he directed things like all the second unit stuff on *The Fuller Brush Man* [1948] with Red Skelton and *The Good Humor Man* [1950]. He'd *kill* you if you didn't watch yourself, he really would. Back in 1931, when we were doing *Timber Beast* with Bill Boyd [released as *Carnival Boat*], we were in the High Sierras, and I was supposed to jump off a rock as a lumber train came by underneath (it was only doing about eighteen or twenty miles an hour). I was supposed to jump onto about the fifteenth car and then run, jumping from the tops of the logs, between the cars, all the way to the locomotive. We did it in cuts, coming down the mountain. We'd start at the top of the lumber camp and come down to a flat spot where the train would stop — they'd rest the train and let the brakes cool off before we came down the next session. Ceder [the second unit director] only had one camera and he had to shoot pan shots as we went by, he had to shoot from the logs forward and he had to shoot from the locomotive back, so we had to keep doing the thing over and over again. At one point, I thought the train was running away — it got to going so fast and rocking so much that I got down on the end of the log car and got ready to jump before the train left the tracks. However, before that happened, we hit one of the flat spots and the engineer was able to stop the train. That night, one of the forest rangers said to me, "Son, were you on that train down there today?" and I said yes. He said, "God, I thought it was running away!" and I said, "*I* thought it was, too!"

Anyway, some years later, we were on a picture (I think it was *The Fuller Brush Man*) and Chick Collins and Billy Jones and I were talking with one another about things that happened like this. Ceder was the [second unit] director on it and I was talking about this instance when I thought the train was gonna run away. Ceder overheard me and he said, "Gil, didn't you ever figure out why that happened?" and I said, "No, I didn't, Ralph."

Ceder said, "Well, the engineer wouldn't go over twenty-two miles and hour, that was company policy, and I wanted him to go faster. But the engineer said, 'No, I won't go over twenty-two miles an hour, I don't care if it's a movie company or *who* the hell it is.'" So, at the next flat spot where we stopped to cool the brakes, Ceder said to the engineer, "Look, take it easy for a while, I've gotta go to the bathroom. I'll be back in a little while." He walked down to the end of the train, which was a forty-one flat car train, and he took a leak, and on the way back he pulled all the compressed air out of the brakes on the last twenty cars. He just pulled the valves open and let the air out! He went back and said to the engineer, "Okay, let's go on," and when the engineer started up, he had brakes on the *first* 21 cars but not the *last* twenty, because the compressor had to pump the air back into the tanks. That's why the train ran away, and we could have gone off the tracks. But this is the kind of guy he was. I would say, from a stuntman's point of view, that he was the worst, although there were others that were not that great.

You were directed by James Whale in Journey's End *[1930].*

Yes, that was the first picture where I worked for him. I was an actor on that, I played Sergeant Cox. Whale was a competent English director (who could be very sarcastic at times). But he was very competent and he did several more pictures, and then in 1935, '36, much to my surprise, he made the first talking version of *Show Boat* with Irene Dunne. He did a very good job on it. I also worked for Whale on *The Invisible Man*, I was in some rabble-rousing scene. I can't remember exactly; it was something we did several different nights, nothing outstanding.

Was Whale sarcastic to the point where he was disliked by his cast?

Oh, no, he wasn't that bad. Colin Clive was the main lead in *Journey's End*; he was a very nice guy and a very capable actor, and he worked in other pictures in Hollywood after that. (Not a hell of a lot of them, because he died quite young.) At night, we shot out on what we called the back flats of MGM and Pathé, way back toward the oil field hills. While we were shooting at night, the last shots for *All Quiet on the Western Front* [1930] were being shot about a quarter of a mile away. So when their guns were going off, we had to quit shooting, and when *our* guns were going off, *they* had to quit shooting [*laughs*]!

You made serials at Columbia and Republic. Was there any difference between making a serial and making a cheap Columbia or Republic feature?

Not a hell of a lot. The same guys used to direct them, in the main, and all the Columbia serials were made by a producer named Sam Katzman. Jack English and Bill Witney, who had been editors, used to direct most of the serials at Republic; one would shoot one day and one would shoot the next day. I remember one day we worked on a hill, we started in the morning and worked over the flat surface and up over the hill and down, following the sun. We had 115 camera setups that day! Jack and Billy both knew exactly what they were doing. You'd finish doing a scene for Billy and he'd say, "*Cut-print-rightoverhere!*" and we'd start movin' for the next setup [*laughs*]!

How were the fight scenes done on a Republic serial?

We would do three or four (what we called) "fifty second" fights in a day. Now, fifty seconds doesn't sound like much of a fight, but on the screen it's a fairly long fight. The guys who did 'em mainly were Tom Steele and Dale Van Sickel and Duke Green and myself and Dave Sharpe. (This was before Dave went in the Air Force, of course.) We all knew how each other worked, so instead of the long, tedious rehearsals you have when you choreograph a fight today, we would just walk through and say, "I'll do *this*," "You do *that*," and we knew exactly what each other was going to do. And of course, with [directors] like Billy Witney, if there were some fluffs in 'em, if you made a mistake, they would just cut around it; they wouldn't go back and reshoot like a lot of directors (like Vic Fleming) would. These serials were made mainly for kids, for Saturday afternoon audiences, and they wouldn't notice if a punch missed — at least, I don't *think* they would, in the main. And, as I say, sometimes we would do as many as three or four big fights in one day. Then the actors would come in afterwards, the actors we were doubling, and do the close-ups.

And you'd do a whole fight in one fifty-second stretch.

Right, we wouldn't do it in cuts. If you were doing a big fight on a major picture, you'd do it in separate cuts. On a serial, *we'd* do the whole fight in a master shot, go right through. And then they'd cut in whatever they wanted with the actors.

How many cameras?

Generally one on the serials. Now, keep in mind, I didn't work on [the Republic serials] as much as Tom and Dale and Duke; *they* were on every one.*

And Sam Katzman?

I *liked* Sam, but he was a quickie producer. When *I* first ran into Sam, he was an assistant director at Fox — he was assistant to a director named Benny Stoloff in 1930. A few years later, he got to producing at a little studio on Santa Monica Boulevard, across from the Hollywood Cemetery. It was called Larry Darmour Studio, and Sam started making his serials there, *for* Columbia release. (And then later he went over onto the Columbia Sunset Studio, which before that had been Tiffany-Stahl, near the corner of where Sunset Boulevard runs into Hollywood Boulevard.) Later, he went to MGM as a producer and he did several of the Presley pictures! He used to make those in fifteen, sixteen, eighteen days.

Did you ever work with Elvis Presley?

The first fight that Elvis ever did in our business, I did with him in 1957 on a thing called *Jailhouse Rock*. I actually did it with *him*. MGM called me and said, "We want you to do a fight with Elvis Presley in the jail, and do it with Elvis, not his double." I said I didn't want to do it, and they asked why. "If I hit him on the chin, if I make a mistake (which *can* happen!), I'm in the doghouse!" "Aw," they said, "you won't do that. Come *on!*" So I went out and I did it with Elvis, and got to know him real well — we fought for a couple of days. I said to Elvis, years later, "You're a big man, Elvis. Why do you do these cheap pictures?" He said, "Gil, they pay me a million dollars to do 'em. I do 'em in fifteen days. I'm not an actor, I'm a singer. If they want to pay me a million dollars, I'll just take it and run." (Of course, in the sixties, a million dollars was a lot of money; today it's chicken feed, I guess, but *then* it was a lot of dough.) I'll always remember Elvis 'cause I worked on so many pictures with him, *Kid Galahad* [1962] and *Roustabout* [1964] and other things.

---

*Perkins is in the Republic serials *Spy Smasher* (1942), *G-Men vs. the Black Dragon* (1942), *Captain America* (1944), *Son of Zorro* (1947), *Jesse James Rides Again* (1947), *The Black Widow* (1947) and *G-Men Never Forget* (1947).

A lot of stuntmen, when they're interviewed, are asked to name the actors they liked to work with. I want to ask you— what actresses *did stuntmen like to work with?*

Barbara Stanwyck; Carole Lombard; Paulette Goddard; Jane Wyman ... there were a couple of others. Plus, there were some gals in the serial field, like Lorna Gray, that were very good. There must be more, but those are the ones I thought of right away. Stanwyck was one of *the* greatest, and so was Lombard. And — oh, how did I almost forget *this* one? — Jean Harlow. A *great* gal. I'll never forget, back in about 1934, doing a picture at MGM; at that time, we never had coffee on a set, or bagels, or Danish pastries, there was no such thing. Now coffee was starting to be brought in onto the sets, morning coffee and afternoon coffee and so on. The director, I think it was Jack Conway, said, "There's not going to be any coffee on *my* set. It's a lot of time wasted, guys going backwards and forwards and gettin' coffee!" And Jean Harlow looked at him and very calmly she said, "Jack ... if there isn't going to be any coffee on the set tomorrow morning, there's not going to be any Jean Harlow either. I don't know *how* you're going to make your picture." That took care of that [*laughs*]!

And she was the kind of "good gal" stuntmen liked to work with?

Great gal. I saw tears in Gable's eyes twice: Once when Harlow died, when we were on a picture called *Saratoga* at MGM in 1937, and the other time when we got the news that Carole Lombard had been killed (she was his wife) in 1942. As soon as he heard that Harlow had died, he said, "That's it. I'm going home." It was about midday at MGM when we got the news; he just walked out and got in his car and went home. More or less the same thing happened with Carole. Carole was killed at night, but for some reason he didn't seem to get the word till we were at a 7:15 [A.M.] call at MGM — he was making *Somewhere I'll Find You* with Lana Turner. He got the word and, again, he just went home. The two times I saw tears in his eyes were those two times.

How did you get involved with Jacques Marquette and Teenage Monster?

Jack Marquette was a camera operator who had worked at Fox and many other places; I knew him and had worked on shows with him. Jack got tied in with a writer and some other people like [property master] Dick Rubin and he decided to make a picture of his own and release it. He asked me if I wanted to come in on it. I think we all put up a couple of thousand bucks and we went ahead and made a picture which they called *Teenage Thunder* [1957]. We were just going to make the one picture and then *sell* it; we made it for 56,000 bucks and Allied Artists offered us 90,000 for it.

Gloria Castillo fends off the crude advances of *Teenage Monster* Perkins.

One of the grips and I wanted to sell *Teenage Thunder* to Allied Artists, because we said $34,000 was not a bad week's work. (It took us seven, eight days to make the damn thing.) But just about that time, a distributing company from New Orleans called Howco, which was run by a guy named Joy Houck and another guy, heard about *Teenage Thunder* and took a look at it and said, "You guys are doin' this all wrong. You should make two pictures back-to-back and release them together and get the whole rental." In those days, there were a lot of double features, and they said we should get the whole rental instead of just getting half of it. They said, "If you want to do this, *we'll* put up half the money, *you* put up half of it, and we'll make a *number* of pictures." Everybody thought this'd be a great way to make money and they let Joy Houck have the release of *Teenage Thunder*. He put up the money and the second picture we made was a thing called *The Brain from Planet Arous*, which was a science fiction picture. That cost us 72,000 bucks, if I remember right. And then they made *Teenage Monster*, which was made under the title *Monster on the Hill* and then changed. That cost us 54,000 bucks. We rented a little studio out on Cahuenga Boulevard, right across from Hanna-Barbera. We had a barn-like setup there for a stage and we had a cutting room and we had an editor under contract and we had another four or five stories lined up, one written by a well-known writer, Ray Bradbury. So, suddenly we were in the production business.

Then, we ran out of money and Howco said that things were tough and *they* couldn't get the money. They gave us a royal screwin'. None of us ever got our money out of it because these were high-binders, these guys. I had always been told, "When a picture doubles its original production cost, you're in the black." Well, the last time I saw the figures on *Teenage Thunder*, it had grossed three times what it cost and *Brain from Planet Arous* had grossed almost three times and *Teenage Monster* had grossed over twice. But none of us ever got a dime out of it. We would have had to take 'em to court in New Orleans and it would have cost us a lot of money to get the books audited, so we just let it go. A few years later I was down in Texas on a picture called *The Alamo* [1960] with "Duke" Wayne — we were shooting second unit there and we had a camera crew out of New Orleans. I said to the head cameraman, "Hey, do you know a guy named Joy Houck in New Orleans?" He said, "Do we? Everybody knows him! 'Cash-on-the-Barrelhead' Houck — you never work for him unless you get the money up front, 'cause if you don't, you'll never get paid."

So Howco strung you along by juggling the books, etc.?
Howco gave us a set of books where everything was doubled, or tripled. They showed us where they'd gotten 400 prints, and we knew they didn't, there were only 200 prints. They had made three airplane trips out to the Coast in their own little Cessna and we had agreed to pay 'em for one trip; they charged us for three, which was $8000 instead of $2000. There were *legal* costs and *exploitation* costs and all those "creative" costs — they had 'em *all*, so [according to the juggled books] there was never any money made off the pictures. And then later, I understand, they sold 'em each to television for $25,000 or $35,000 apiece. But that didn't make any difference, we never got any money out of 'em.

You're in the two Teenage *pictures. Were you in* Brain from Planet Arous?
No, I wasn't. There was really nothing for me to do in *Brain from Planet Arous*. So I was in the first one and the third one.

The Teenage Monster *does a lot of grunting and groaning throughout the movie. Is that you, or was that dubbed in later?*
That's me, *and* it was dubbed in later. As we made the picture, they let me speak in a fairly legible voice, without trying to muzzle it or slur it or do anything with it. Then, when they got a rough cut, Jack Marquette and the writer said, "Jeez, this guy is too intelligent. He's supposed to be a clod

and have a brain that doesn't work quite right, and yet he speaks in these intelligent sequences. We're going to have to wipe that all off the soundtrack, and you're going to have to just make sounds like *eek, aah, ooh, ahh!*" [*Laughs.*] So I spent a whole morning, or maybe most of a day in a sound recording room recording these sounds, which they dubbed in on the soundtrack.

I had a feeling that was the case. You'd come into a scene and go eek, aah, ooh and then people would respond to you as if you had *said something intelligible.*

Well, it was a quickie picture and we didn't have much money to spend on it, so it didn't get the treatment that a lot of the pictures got in those days [*laughs*].

You were about fifty then, and playing a "teenage" monster.

They didn't want me for it originally—they had a guy named Mike Ross, who was a big, tall actor, 6'5" or 6". But when they got him in the outfit and he had to run and do things, he had two left feet and two left hands. Jack Marquette said, "Gil, we're never gonna get it with *this* guy. What we're gonna have to do is build up some high boots for you, about six inches, to make *you* tall, and have *you* do it. Because you can do all the stuff we need, over the rocks and all that kind of stuff." So that's how I came to do it. But I was not the first choice, Mike Ross was, but Mike was such an *un-*handy guy that Jack and the others didn't think he would be able to handle the rough stuff.

How tall are you?

Well, I *was* six feet then.

Were you pleased in any way with the final results on Teenage Monster?

I felt it was something we just slapped together and that we could have done much better had we had more time and more money. And maybe the story wasn't that great. I was never particularly happy with it, or with what I did—I thought it could have been done better. Most of it was shot up at Iverson's Ranch, which is just above Chatsworth. We just picked locations at random and we didn't have any sets to speak of except in the studio—in our little studio, we had a few small, inexpensive sets. And I do remember that they made false teeth [for the Monster]—which I still have, as a matter of fact, I've got those teeth in a drawer here. They distorted my face.

You said Teenage Monster *was shot at Iverson's Ranch, but Jack Marquette remembers Melody Ranch.*

Melody Ranch was Gene Autry's — that's not far from Iverson's, it's just out in the Saugus area. We *did* have a day or two of location there, but it seems to me *most* of our location was Iverson's.

Jack Pierce, your makeup man on Teenage Monster, *had the reputation of being a very cantankerous and irascible individual.*

Those words you used describe him. I knew Jack Pierce from Universal: I had done several Frankenstein pictures in which I doubled Frankenstein, so I had to have the Frankenstein makeup on me. And in another picture, I doubled the Wolf Man and I had to have the Wolf Man makeup on me. So I'd been in the makeup chair with Jack Pierce making me up long before we got to *Teenage Monster*. On *Teenage Monster*, they decided (although Jack was expensive) that he was the best man to do it, so he was hired to do the job. I used to be in the chair for two to three hours in the morning to get the damn makeup on, and it took half an hour at night to get it off. Or even *more* than that. But he *was* a miserable old bastard. For those days, he *was* a genius; of course, today he'd be just one of a *number* of men who were great at that stuff. I see quite a lot of the [modern] makeups; for some reason or other, they think I *know* something about makeup, and I'm on the makeup committee that picks the nominees for the Oscar every year. We look at them at the Academy and vote on 'em. Of course, I've had a lot of experience with makeup; I did the *Jekyll and Hyde* show with Spencer Tracy, and on some of the *Red Skelton Shows*, I had a hell of a lot of makeup. And on a show [*House of Numbers*] with Jack Palance in fifty-seven, I did Jack Palance's bad brother, so I had to be made up like Jack Palance. So I had a lot of makeup on that.

Getting back to you playing Frankenstein and the Wolf Man — through the years, it's always been Eddie Parker who's gotten the credit for doing the stunt-doubling in those pictures.

Well, Eddie Parker did — Eddie did some of them *with* me. When I did one of the Frankensteins, he did the Wolf Man in the same picture. But I didn't do *all* the Frankensteins, just a couple of them. In one of the ones where Eddie played the Wolf Man [*Frankenstein Meets the Wolf Man*], the beautiful Hungarian actress Ilona Massey was the gal in it, and I had to carry her all around this basement with all this broken-down stuff in it. All she had on was a very pale blue, see-through negligee kind of thing and I think she had a pair of shorts, but she had no bra or anything like that. She was almost stark naked! I can remember somebody saying, "Jeez, I'd like to get this dame somewhere where I can *do* somethin' with her!" — I think that was a guy named Wes Hopper, a stuntman in those days. I had to carry her

Disguise the limit! Perkins, often made-up to resemble the stars he doubled, wore his most elaborate makeup in **Frankenstein Meets the Wolf Man** with Ilona Massey.

around in this cellar, with all the flood waters comin' down over all the crap that was in there.

Is that dangerous, to be on a set where that amount of water is crashing down on you?

No, not on *Frankenstein Meets the Wolf Man* it wasn't. But I'd been in other spots, like on the first talkie *Moby Dick* with John Barrymore in 1930. We were working at night and they had these 2000-gallon dump tanks above a spillway beside the ship. They had one on top of the other, so they'd have 4000 gallons, and maybe they'd dump the whole bunch all at once so it would hit the ship and break over the side. And if one hit you, it could take you overboard. We had that kind of experience on the first *Mutiny on the Bounty* in 1935, on the back lot of MGM, when they had the dump tanks dumping on the *Bounty* at night. Julie Bescos, who was one of the sailors/stuntmen, had been a top basketball player at USC and he was a hell of a guy. Well, the water just picked him up and washed him right over and down onto the concrete. Fortunately, it didn't hurt him badly, but I remember how upset Frank Lloyd the director was when it happened. I'd had some experience with that, so when I saw it coming, I turned sideways and grabbed on like grim death. Julie didn't know anything about it, so he got picked up and dumped over the side.

Did the Frankenstein Meets the Wolf Man *director Roy William Neill stage that climactic fight, or did you and Eddie Parker choreograph it yourselves, as you would on a serial?*

[Neill] just told Eddie and myself to work out a fight and let him *see* it. We worked out the thing, then we just walked through it [for Neill], went through the motions, and said, "This is what we'll do here," "This is what we'll do there." He told us what he wanted, where he wanted us to start and where he wanted us to finish and what kind of a fight he wanted it to be. Apart from that, he left us pretty well alone.

Any memories of working with Lon Chaney, Jr.?

Oh, sure, Lon Chaney was in *Lucky Devils*. He was also in *Bird of Paradise* with Joel McCrea and Dolores Del Rio in thirty-two and a number of other things there. *Of Mice and Men* [1939] catapulted him to stardom, and then he was under contract to Universal for several years after that. I got to know him the usual way of working around the studio with him; I don't know anything outstanding he did, except (unfortunately) when he got to Universal and got to stardom, he also got to drinking, and that didn't help his career. He got to be an alcoholic.

Dave Sharpe once said that, before you do a stunt, you'd better be 99 44/100 percent sure you won't hurt yourself. What's your number?

Well, I would agree with Dave on that statement. The only thing is, is your 99 44/100 percent sure exactly right percentage-wise? You might *think* it is [*laughs*], but it might not be! There was always the chance of a mistake, but most good stuntmen that knew what they were doing, like Dave and like Yak Canutt and the others, had it all pretty well figured out. But then, look at Yak Canutt, who was one of the great Western stuntmen (and he was good at other things, too). It was 1940 on *Boom Town* and *he* thought he had it all figured out: They had what was supposed to be a bucking mule, which was really a bucking horse with a mule's ears stuck on it, and Yak pulled this horse up into a high stance on its back legs, and it turned over on top of him. It fell right over backwards on top of him, and the horn of the saddle stuck in his gut. It damaged his insides and they had to take him to the hospital for some time, and that was the last stunt he ever did. So even though Yak thought he had it figured out, he pulled the horse right over on top of him, which he didn't expect to.

Dave Sharpe's number was 99 44/100, which you just agreed with. But what's the lowest you've ever gone? Have you ever been really shaky about doing a stunt?

Not really, although I *should* have been. Early on, on *Carnival Boat*, we had a scene where they were hauling logs up out of the forest on a high line with what they called a steel cable choker. They used to put the steel cable around one end of the log and hoist it up and drag it up through the dirt, but the director [Albert Rogell] thought that, to get Bill Boyd from the bottom where the lumber was, through the forest, up to the rail head, they would put *two* chokers on the log and haul it up sixty feet in the air, then take it through the forest at forty, fifty miles an hour. When I did the gag the first time, I ran up and jumped on the log, and all I had was just to hold onto the steel choker cable where it was strung up at the front of the log, and my cork shoes which I dug into the log. I had said to the special effects man running the machinery, "Now, when you take me up, don't take me up too fast. If you take me up too fast, the pulley block'll hit against the top and bounce the hell out of the log, and I may not be able to hang on." So he pulled me up at a reasonable pace but not very fast, and then he took me through the forest at fifty miles an hour with the log swinging from side to side. (Of course, they'd trimmed the trees on each side so you wouldn't hit them, or *hopefully* you wouldn't.) But, unbeknownst to me, the director went to this special effects man and said, "From the time Gil steps on the log, I want the log to go *as fast as you can* up and *as fast as you can* forward." I ran up for the next take and jumped on the log and, God, this guy took me up so fast, the pulley block hit the other block at the top and the log dived all over the place—fortunately, I was able to hold onto it. Then he whizzed me up through the forest. I got up to the top and he dropped me down, and I got off the log and ran out of the scene.

Bill Boyd had been watching from up on the top where I got off, and as I walked back, he said, "Whitey, come here." (He used to call me Whitey, I had a lot of blond hair in those days.) I went over and he said, "Sit down," so I sat down. And he didn't say anything. After about twenty or thirty seconds, I said, "Bill, what do you want?" He said, "I don't want anything, I just want you to sit there. Because nobody's ever been killed or badly hurt doubling me, and *you're* not gonna be the first guy. If Al Rogell hasn't got it now, he's not gonna get it, because you're not gonna do this again." So *that* [stunt] I was a little queasy about—*after* I started up, not *before*, because I didn't know what was going to happen.

In the sixties, when you started doing more acting than stuntwork, one of the pictures you did was Valley of the Dragons.

Oh, yes, that was at Columbia in 1961. I did quite a lot of work in that from an acting point of view. It was really one of Columbia's "quickie" pictures, but I think it came out all right. I was a caveman in that.

Any anecdotes about working on television in Batman?

I did a number of the episodes for television, and then we made the feature. We did some [falls] off the top of the submarine, falling about twelve feet into two or three feet of water, and I said to the director [Leslie Martinson], "Look, I can't give you a nice fall off this headfirst because I'll break my neck. I'll just hit the water as flat as a pancake" — which I did. And even *then*, my hands got the bottom.

What other stuntmen of your generation are still around today?

The only other one left is Wally Rose, who started in 1934, which was five or six years after *I* started. He didn't do much for some years, and he never was what I would call a top stuntman. He's still alive, he's eighty-three, but all the others that I worked with are gone. Of course, there were later guys who were good stuntmen, like George Robotham and Paul Baxley, and *those* guys are still alive. But they didn't come in till the mid–forties.

If you were young again, would you want to be a stuntman in today's Hollywood?

No, I wouldn't. I had a pretty good education, and I always thought, even when I *was* a stuntman, that I wasn't particularly proud of it. It was the Depression and *money* that made me a stuntman. If I were in Hollywood today, I'd go right to the camera department and try to get on as a film loader or as an assistant cameraman, and become a cameraman. That's a hell of a job — he's just as important as the director, he makes very big money, and he doesn't have to worry about the editing and all the other crap of a picture. I think that's what I would try to be. Some of the stuntmen had their sons follow them, like Joe Yrigoyen's son, young Joe — now he's walking with a permanent limp because he got badly hurt in a wagon turnover. And Yak's two sons are both out of the business, *they* both got hurt. Cliff Lyons, who was one of our great stuntmen, had two sons, and he told me, "They're not gonna *be* in the business, if *I* can help it." And they weren't — one's a lawyer and one's a doctor. And I always thought, "Well, there was one smart stuntman!"

And, if you could turn back the clock to the days that you entered the business, would you be a stuntman again?

I think I'd be a cameraman. I think I would have made a *good* cameraman.

[On a serial,] the director would say, "Okay, now drive down the street in this car." ... I'd drive away, drive quite a ways, then turn around and come back — and they'd be gone!... That's how fast they were shooting!

Walter Reed

HE'S THE SORT of actor that different sets of movie fans like to think of as "their own": Western fans remember Walter Reed best for his countless sagebrush roles, riding the range in frontier fare that went from low-budget television shows (*The Lone Ranger, Hopalong Cassidy*) to the latter-day John Ford Western classics (*How the West Was Won, Cheyenne Autumn*, etc.). But to science fiction buffs he's the hero who kayoed the *Flying Disc Man from Mars* in a 12-round Republic serial, and contended with mysterious creatures from "inner Earth" in *Superman and the Mole-Men* (opposite his good friend George "Superman" Reeves). No less heroically, he battled voodoo cultists and deadly snakes in the horror/adventure *Macumba Love*.

The son of an Army officer, Reed (real name: Walter Reed Smith) was born in Washington and grew up in Honolulu and Los Angeles, where he attended school with the children of the movie stars of that era. After his parents' divorce, and during the darkest days of the Great Depression, the 17-year-old Reed decided to try acting as a career and made a two-week trip to New York (via hitched rides on railroad freight cars, amidst hobos and tramps) to look for work on the stage. He worked in stock and on Broadway and, with an assist from actor Joel McCrea, broke into pictures in the early 1940s. A half-century and hundreds of roles later, Walter Reed (retired from acting since the late 1960s) is a frequent film festival guest with many reminiscences of movie adventures on, off and under the Earth.

Riding freight trains from Los Angeles to New York, during the Depression, when you were still a kid — what are some of your memories of that?

I got on a chain gang in Longview, Texas! A lot of us had gotten off the train and we were looking for something to eat, and this railroad cop named Texas Slim caught us. Every one of us that was underage, he just lined us up and kicked us in the butt and said, "Now, get out of here!" Well, the next day I tried to get out, but the train was going too fast — when I tried to grab on, it threw me. Texas Slim picked me up again and I got sentenced to thirty days [for vagrancy] on a work gang. They put chains on you at night, and in the daytime, you were out there breaking up rocks and stuff. I was only there three days: One day the guard said, "I'm going around the corner to go to the bathroom. Don't go anywhere." There were about 150 of us out there working on these rocks, the work farm was right next to the railroad tracks and the only thing in between was this two-foot fence. We saw a train going slowly up the hill, so we all jumped over this fence and got on it. The guard came back and saw all of us on the train, and we waved goodbye to us! Well, the state paid 'em fifty cents a day for each kid and we were all

Previous page: Movie and serial hero Walter Reed in a characteristic "ready-for-action" pose, this one from Republic's *Flying Disc Man from Mars.*

sentenced to thirty days, so they made $15 on each of us whether we were there or not [*laughs*]! It was all a big racket!

I also remember "nickeling up" on guys. The tramps would give me a nickel and I'd go to a bakery at five o'clock in the morning and say, "Could I have some yesterday's leavings?" (That's what they told me to say, "leavings"—I'd never heard that word.) The bakery guys would give me a big bag of the things they hadn't sold the day before, and they were fresh—cinnamon rolls and stuff. I'd hand the nickel over, acting like it was the last nickel I had, and they'd say, "Oh, that's all right, kid." So I kept the same nickel all the way across the country! And *that's* where I learned how to act, I think [*laughs*]—I'd have my lip quivering as I put the nickel out!

You were going to New York hoping to get work on the stage. But was your ultimate goal the movies?

Oh, I didn't know. But the stage did lead to me being in movies. By the way, I had already been in a picture, years before that, with just a couple of lines. It was a thing called *Redskin* [1929] with Richard Dix. I was thirteen years old. I've never seen the movie, and for all I know, my scene may not even be in it! (And I wouldn't recognize myself anyway!) But I kind of liked the "romance" of being an actor, and when I got to New York, why, I *loved* the stage and I did a *lot* of stock. I was in Kennebunkport, Maine, for two seasons, Ridgefield, Connecticut; Chattanooga, Tennessee—oh, a *lot* of places. And then I was brought out to California by a studio.

Once you did go under contract to RKO, was the life of a movie actor what you expected it to be?

Yeah. You got a seven-year deal with options, which means that every six months they could fire you. But your pay went *up* every six months if they *kept* you. I think I started for $150 a week but that was a *fortune* in those days for *me*—everybody else was makin' $25 a week, you know! The first picture I did at RKO was *The Mayor of 44th Street* [1942] with George Murphy; then I did shorts with Leon Errol and I also played opposite Leon Errol and Lupe Velez in the *Mexican Spitfire* series.

The first film you did that had a bit of a fantasy element was Angel on the Amazon.

I made that after I was out of contract from RKO. Vera Hruba Ralston was the star, playing this mysterious woman who, because of some terrible shock years and years before, *never aged*. George Brent played a pilot and I played his co-pilot. We were just *there*, me and Ross Elliott and Gus

Schilling. Our plane went down in the jungle, and when our guarantee was up, they just *left* our characters there, dropped 'em, and nobody ever explained what happened to us [*laughs*]! To bring us back for a couple of more scenes would have cost more money! That was at Republic, and they were *cheap* in those days! Vera couldn't act her way out of a paper bag, but she was a nice *person*. She was the girlfriend of Herbert Yates, the president of Republic, and somebody warned me, "Don't get *too* friendly with Vera, because Yates has the place bugged!" [*Laughs*.] I said hello to her every morning, and I'd talk to her when other people were around, but I never would sit down in the chair next to her if she was alone.

What do you remember best about working in Republic serials?
  Well, they were *fast*! The serials we would do in twenty-one days. For instance, the director would say, "Okay, now drive down the street in this car"—I drove all different kinds of old cars, because we had to match the old stock shots they were using [of car chases, crashes, etc.]. I'd drive away, drive quite a ways, then turn around and come back—and they'd be gone! [*Laughs*.] They would have already gone on to the next set-up, and I couldn't *find* 'em! *That's* how fast they were shooting! We did seventy-eight set-ups in one day—I hardly knew my leading ladies, all I had time to do was learn my lines. We did twenty-two pages a day, and on a feature, you're lucky if you do *two*! The thing that helped me there was my stock experience; you get used to doing a play *and* rehearsing another one for the *next* week.

Any idea what made Republic think of you as a serial star?
  I honestly forget how I happened to get in there; it might have been because they had a lot of stock shots of Ralph Byrd in older serials. I was kind of heavyset like Ralph was, and from about fifteen feet away, you couldn't tell whether it was me or Ralph [*laughs*]. I'm not sure that's why I got cast, but it sure *helped*! I'll tell you another funny thing: Franklin Adreon was the associate producer of *Flying Disc Man from Mars* and a very sweet guy, and he said, "Walter, how would you like to do the *next* one?" I said *sure*, so I did two serials right in a row. And the funny part about it is, I've always thought that the only reason that they gave me the part in the next one [*Government Agents vs Phantom Legion*, 1951] was because they'd made two suits for me and two for my double [*laughs*]. I've always been convinced that that's why I got to do the second one!

Any memories at all of your Flying Disc Man *leading lady, Lois Collier?*
  Yes, I do remember Lois. She was nice, and her husband made a fortune—he's the theatrical attorney who imported *Godzilla* from Japan, and he

A henchman of the *Flying Disc Man from Mars,* Richard Irving tries to polish off Reed in one of the serial's cliffhanger endings.

made a bundle on those. But I hardly remember the girl from the other one, Mary Ellen Kay. She lives in Scottsdale, Arizona, and runs an art gallery there now, I'm told. Somebody from one of the film festivals called me and said she'd like to talk to me again; to tell you the truth, I wouldn't know her if I saw her! The heavies in *Flying Disc Man* were Richard Irving and Harry Lauter, and Dick Irving turned into a very big producer. He didn't want me to ever tell anybody about that serial! And Harry Lauter was a good friend of mine.

My mother died about the eighteenth day of one of the serials, I've forgotten which one. Herbert Yates came down to the set and he said, "Look, we *can* stop [production] now, if you want us to. But, boy, I would sure like to have you finish this." This was on a Thursday and we worked Saturdays in those days, and I said, "Well, we'll have the service on Sunday." So we had the service then, and Yates always thanked me for it. He didn't pay me any more *money,* but he thanked me [*laughs*]! He was a nice guy.

Apart from Republic being cheap, was it a nice place to work?
    Yes. They did things cheaply but they were nice people and they made

money. And, hey, if you didn't wanna take the job, you didn't *have* to. I was the kind of guy that, no matter if it was a serial, no matter *what* it was, I did the best job I possibly could. And if I didn't want to do that, I shouldn't have accepted it.

Did you get to know the stuntmen, too?
   Oh, sure. My double was a guy named Dale Van Sickel, and *he* wasn't a bad actor. Tom Steele was another stuntman who worked the serials — he just died a few years ago — and also Davey Sharpe, who was probably one of the best stuntmen who ever lived. Those three did all the stuff at Republic.

Did you *have to be in good shape to do a serial?*
   Oh, boy, I'll say! You really had to get into condition, because you did stuff that you'd *never* do in any other sort of picture. For instance, the scenes where you'd jump out of a car just before it would crash. Davey Sharpe would be inside the car, out of sight, "blind-driving" it, and I'd be running alongside the car. Then I'd step onto an apple box and leap off of it and roll down a hill, and from where the camera was positioned, it'd look like I'd jumped out of the moving car. Well, the next day I had thirty ticks on my back, and they had to burn 'em all off! In one scene in *Flying Disc Man*, I'm hanging from one of the ties in a [sound stage] railroad trestle and I had to chin myself. Well, that's easier said than done — they asked me to do it about ten times and, God, I wasn't in the condition that an acrobat was in! After about the sixth, I couldn't do it anymore, and I said, "Dale, get in here and do a few chin-ups!"

Then also, at least once or twice a chapter, you were involved in fistfights.
   You'd occasionally get hit during the fights — I got hit very little, and the only people that ever hit *me* were the other actors, *not* the stuntmen. That can happen very easily. You work out a routine, but you can make mistakes. On a *77 Sunset Strip* Roger Smith tripped a little during a fight scene and I *cooled* him [*laughs*]! And *I've* been hit over the head with breakaway bottles that have knocked me out — things happen.

What else were you asked to do that was dangerous?
   I did something on *Flying Disc Man* that I didn't know was dangerous at the time. They saw a train coming down the track and the director said, "Gee, we can get a quick shot." I was in a parachute and harness, and he said, "Open it and lay down on the ground next to the track, as though you've just landed next to a passing train." After we did it, the special effects

man said, "You don't know how near you got to being killed." He told me that if the open parachute had gotten sucked under the train and got tangled around the wheels, I would have been dragged for *miles!*

The director was Fred Brannon. Was he any good?

He was *fast*. He used to be a prop man, and ... he couldn't direct. He was a nice guy, but very *macho*, you know. He thought he was a tough guy, and I had a little argument with him at the start of the picture. He said, "Oh, New York *ac-tor*, come here...!" and I finally got him behind the set and I said, "Look, don't start buggin' me or I'll ram your head in the ground." After that, we got along fine [*laughs*]!

Did you ever have to work with a director that you didn't get along with?

Yes, that was Sidney Lanfield. I was doing a television show opposite Jane Wyman and Lanfield always had to have a patsy to bug. He started giving me a hard time, saying, "No, *don't* do it *that* way, do it like Cary Grant, do it like Cary Grant!" I finally turned around and said, "Look, *I'm* not Cary Grant. I'm makin' about one-*tenth* of what *he* makes." Well, he kept doing it so I finally got him behind the process screen and I said, "I understand that Vic Mature threw you through one of these process screens." He said, "Well ... yeah." I said, "You wanna make it *two*?" Well, he started calling me *sweetheart* and *baby* and he came out with his arm around me, and we never had any trouble after that! But Gail Russell one time gave it to him. He used to keep a little riding crop with him and he *goosed* her. And, man, she grabbed that thing and hit him across the *face* with it!

Serials were a comedown for established actors, needless to say.

Oh, sure — anyway, as far as *I* was concerned, they were. One of my dear friends that lives up in San Francisco is Lyle Talbot and he and I both believe one thing: An actor's a *working* actor, and if you're not working, why, you're not an actor. We weren't people like Marlon Brando, who could hold out, *we* worked and worked — we were raising kids. I took almost anything that came along. And look at Lyle, he made the worst picture ever made, *Plan 9 from Outer Space* for Eddie Wood [*laughs*]! But, you want to know something funny? We both *liked* Eddie — I lent Eddie 150 bucks for his rent one time! He was a nice guy and if he'd had money, he could have made something pretty good, I think. (Lyle and I believe that — but nobody *else* does!)

How did you happen to know Ed Wood? Through Lyle Talbot?

No, I just happened to meet him one time and he wanted me to do a movie with Bela Lugosi. But he didn't have much money—"*much* money"?—he didn't have *any* money! He wanted to get some stationery that looked good and he needed to pay his rent, and I gave him the money to do it. And I guarantee you, knowing Eddie, he would have paid me back if he'd ever made it. But he just never made it.

I remember he went to Lyle's house one time — they'd been out drinking, and Lyle let him have the extra bedroom. And when they got up in the morning, Lyle and his wife and their kids, Eddie came out with Lyle's wife's bra on! So they kicked him out [*laughs*]! I remember watching Ed when he was filming at a motel complex where there was a pool; there were a couple of actors sitting there, a few reflectors and just a couple of guys helping him. All of a sudden the manager came out yelling, chasing Eddie out — but he had shot whatever he wanted by then [*laughs*]! He had *guts*, I'll say that for him!

Did you bother to see any part of either of your serials when they came out?
No.

Have you ever watched them on videotape?
Once! [*Laughs.*] I like the [*Flying Disc Man*] cliffhanger where I jump out of the plane, land in the bush, dust my suit off and I'm on my way! But, hey, the kids liked those things and those kids, when they see you, they know whether you're being phony or not. You have to respect the kids. And I used to love the serials myself—I used to go see those things every Saturday afternoon, with Joe Bonomo and people like that. And if the hero was doing it with tongue-in-cheek, he was wrong.

Between your two serials, you co-starred in Superman and the Mole-Men. *Any recollection of how you landed the part?*
I had done a Spic and Span commercial for Jessica Maxwell, the wife of [*Superman* producer] Bob Maxwell, so that's how I came to *his* attention. The director on that *Superman* thing was Lee Sholem — I call him Bud. We went to school together, he was my brother's best man and my brother was *his* best man! And the funny thing is, I saw him just *last week*, at a roast for Phyllis Diller, and that was the first time I've seen Bud in forty years. He wasn't the greatest director in the world but he knew his craft. He'd been a cutter and he was fast. And he did his homework, he'd have it all mapped out on the back of a [script] page, the movements he wanted to tell you about. He was a wonderful guy.

How well did you know George Reeves?
I had known George in the service, so we were old, dear friends and

Reed was friendly with "Man of Steel" George Reeves, and has his own theories about the actor's mysterious death. (Left to right: Ray Walker, Reed, Phyllis Coates and Reeves in *Superman and the Mole-Men*.)

we knew each other very well. He was one of the nicest guys who ever lived. I knew him when he was married and then also later [after his divorce], when he was going around with Toni Mannix. George and I used to get together a lot, maybe once every two weeks; we'd have dinner and a couple of drinks; talk about old times and sit around tellin' lies to each other [*laughs*]!

Did Toni Mannix ever come along?
   Yes, she used to come to our house on Sundays with George. While we were at church one time, she cut my daughter's hair into bangs and my wife was furious [*laughs*]! It took eight months to get it back to where we wanted it! Toni was a nice gal, though — she was an ex-showgirl, a Ziegfeld girl with

Paulette Goddard. She and her husband, [MGM executive] Eddie Mannix, had an understanding: He was hanky-pankying around with some nurse, and I'm sure Eddie knew about Toni and George.

Both Phyllis Coates [Lois Lane] and Jack Larson [Jimmy Olsen] have said that, as the Superman *series went on and on, George Reeves was drinking more and more.*

I didn't know that he *ever* drank when he was working. *Phyllis* would know, but Jack was a prissy little kid. They've interviewed him a lot of times about George and *he* didn't know much about George. So he worked with George, so what? *He* didn't know George's private life. Phyllis, he [Reeves] used to see a bit socially, but not Jack. Jack was always the juvenile — no matter *how* old he got, he still looked like a juvenile! — but he turned into a pretty good writer, I hear.

Was Reeves miffed that, after starting Superman, *he couldn't get too many other roles?*

He *knew* that going into it. When he took that [Superman] role, he talked to me and he said, "Well, if I'm gonna put a propeller on my nose, I've gotta make *money.*" He knew that it'd be the last thing he'd do, and it *was* — well, of course it was, because he *died.* But he'd have gone on and on and *on* in that thing, because *Superman* was always popular. Of course you know that George was in *Gone with the Wind* [1939], and he was a *very* good actor — he had very good training at Pasadena Community Playhouse. They put out some very good actors.

So, when you worked with him, he had a good attitude about playing Superman.

Oh, he joked about it, for crying out loud. He played it seriously when he was doing it, but when we were off-screen, he could kid about it. He used to stay in shape by digging cesspools for people on weekends, for a hundred bucks! With a shovel!

During his Superman *days?*

Yeah! That's the way he'd keep in shape!

Do you remember who doubled for Reeves in his takeoff "flying" scenes in Mole-Men? *It looks like it might be Dale Van Sickel again.*

I don't remember. But the first day we worked on *Superman and the Mole-Men* (which was the first Superman that they did), we were out in Culver City and George was on the top of this garage roof, and he was supposed to take off. They had him wired, and the thing broke. He fell on the ground from the top of the garage — it was a low garage, but he fell about ten feet. And he got up and he said [*firmly*], "That's the last time you ever fly me." And he never *did* fly again, he used a trampoline from then on. That's before the [special effects people] became experts, like on *Peter Pan* and stuff.

You didn't have scenes with them, but did you see the Mole-Men in action?
Oh, I knew one of them very well, Billy Curtis — he was the head Mole-Man. He kind of was the spokesman for *all* the midgets in pictures.

Do you believe that Reeves killed himself?
No, I *don't* believe he committed suicide; neither did his mother; neither did Damian O'Flynn, who was a very dear friend of ours. (Damian was in *Winged Victory* on stage with George and myself.) George wasn't the type to commit suicide. George was going around with Toni Mannix, but then George met this *other* girl; he loved her, but he didn't *like* her. I haven't the slightest idea who she was, I never met her, but George dropped Toni for this new gal. And I really was amazed, because George wasn't a deeply romantic guy. When he was going around with this girl, I don't think he wanted me to meet her, and so I didn't see him in the months just before he died. Somebody *killed* him, as far as *I'm* concerned; I don't know who.

You were interviewed by the police after he died.
Oh, yes, they talked to Damian and me. I told 'em that George had told *me* that he had $10,000 hidden in the house; I don't know if [his death] had anything to do with that. I understand that George was pretty looped — a little snockered — when he went to bed that night. But, knowing George, he wouldn't have put that Luger to his head and shot his brains out, even if he *was* drunk. And George wasn't a drunk — he wasn't an *alcoholic*. The difference is that a drunk doesn't have to go to AA. (That's a joke [*laughs*]!) Anyway, George never had a serious drinking problem; he drank pretty good *when he was off of work*, on a weekend or something. And when he worked, he was *serious* about his work. Now, this business that he was drinking "more and more" — well, maybe he was, I wasn't there, I didn't see him for six months after he started going around with this new girl. I saw him once during that time, when he had his new house up in Benedict Canyon. And, by the way, there was a theory that he committed suicide because he was busted [broke]. That was a lot of baloney, George had money, he knew what he was doing financially; the house that he had there would be worth $3,000,000 now.

Reed is even more annoyed with Ziva Rodann than he looks in this shot from *Macumba Love*.

What were some of your favorite roles?

I would say *Seven Men from Now* [1956] with Randolph Scott was my favorite. I played Gail Russell's husband, and Lee Marvin and Johnny Larch killed me in the last of it. Then I liked one I did in Mexico called *The Torch* [1950] with Paulette Goddard, and *Bombardier* [1943], which seems to be a very popular film still.

You were part of the Pine-Thomas stock company, you worked for Republic and on television — but you also worked regularly in big pictures with some great directors.

Well, I got into John Ford's stock company at the last. (I wish I'd gotten in earlier!) I was in four of the last pictures that he did and he liked me; I think if I'd come along earlier, I'd have gotten some big parts from him.

Do you remember working with Vincent Price in Dangerous Mission *[1954]?*

We shot that up in Glacier National Park; Vincent called it *She Lost It in the Crevasse*. Oh, we used to rib him! There were very staid, sedate people around in the Glacier Park Hotel, and during dinner one time, just as the dinner was served, we had two guys in white coats pick him up out of his chair and take him out — as though he was crazy, and they were carting him off to the nuthouse! And we didn't let him back to finish his dinner [*laughs*]! That hotel was on an Indian reservation, I think it was Blackfoot, and down the street about two miles, *off* of the reservation, was a gambling and drinking place. (You couldn't drink at the Hotel, because that was on Indian territory.) On the weekend, we'd get bored, so Vic Mature, Bill Bendix, Dennis Weaver, Vincent and myself used to hitchhike our way down there at night — people would pick us up, they hadn't the slightest idea who we were!

We shot the last shot of the picture at RKO. There was a special effects guy named "Dump" Landon — he was an expert with landslides and water and stuff like that — and after Vincent got finished that last day, "Dump" said to the director [Lewis King], "Are you sure that he's through now?" The director said, "Absolutely." "Dump" said, "Vincent, would you come over here in this telephone booth? We want to take a couple of stills of you in there." So he got in this fake telephone booth with no top on it, and Landon dumped sixty gallons of water on him [*laughs*]! Vincent was a heck of a good sport.

How did you end up starring in Macumba Love?

That's the one I did in Brazil. I had done *The High and the Mighty* [1954] — I did one scene with Mike Wellman, the director's [William Wellman] son. "Duke" Wayne came over to me: "Boy," he said, "old Wellman *really* likes you." Later, Doug Fowley, the actor [who was also in *The High and the Mighty*], was going to direct *Macumba Love* in Brazil, and he went to Wellman and asked, "Who should I get to star in this?" And Wellman said, "Get that Walter Reed, I like him." And so that's the way I got it, through Bill Wellman, Sr.! And Wellman's son Bill played my son-in-law in the picture. I remember we got to Brazil late one morning and Bill Wellman went to the bathroom, and when he came out, he said, "Gee, they have a foot bath in there." And it was the bidet! (When we all got back from Brazil I told his father about this, and he fell on the floor howling!) My daughter was played by a girl named June Wilkinson, who had these big boobs. She had an English accent, so in the picture, when she said [*in an English accent*], "Daddy dear," I said, "It's so good to hear your English accent, it reminds me so much of your mother." And we never mentioned it again [*laughs*]!

I enjoyed doing that picture, I got a trip out of it. Before we started, I went to Screen Actors Guild and they said, "We can't be responsible for what goes on down there" — I wasn't going to be protected by the Guild in any way, because it was going to be shot in Brazil. So I told [the moviemakers], "I want to be paid every Friday night in American Express traveler's checks." Which I was. Making that picture was a lot of fun; in fact, just the other day I talked to the black girl that was on the picture, Ruth De Souza — she played Mama Rataloy, the voodoo queen. She's about eighty-five now, maybe more than that, but she still does plays down there and is a very well-known actress in Brazil. At the time when I was there, there were only about fourteen actors in Brazil.

How did you like working with all those snakes?
The guy that was handling the snakes was named Jooveneel — I called him Juvenile [*laughs*]! One day a little tiny snake jumped out from a tree so I stepped on him, killed him — it was only about a foot long. And Jooveneel said, "If that snake had hit you, you would be dead within thirty seconds." It was one of the deadliest, most dangerous snakes down there! We worked with thirty-foot anacondas, so it was ... a little hairy! We'd be in the bushes and this Jooveneel would be in there with us — he didn't speak a word of English. And this snake that he was working with, this small anaconda, would bite him. He'd take a drink of whiskey and then he'd pour it on the bite. "Oh, he bites me all the time!" he said through the interpreter!

What were the girls like — June Wilkinson and Ziva Rodann?
June was a nice girl. She had the big body on her and all that kind of stuff [*laughs*], but she was a sweet young nineteen-year-old kid. She was an English girl, *not* a highly educated woman, but attractive. She used to call me Big Daddy, and she'd say, "Big Daddy, aren't you going to kiss me good night?" and I said, "How the hell can I *get* to you? I can't reach your face!" — because she had those big boobs sticking out there! Years later she invited me to her wedding down in Carmel — she married a very famous football player from Houston named Dan Pastorini, but that didn't work out.

And Ziva Rodann?
Well, Ziva was very self-centered: She was afraid her nose wasn't right and she'd have the makeup man do it a certain way, she'd be rubbing oil on herself all the time and all that kind of stuff. While we were shooting that first scene on the beach, she turned her head a certain way and upstaged me. I just turned to the director [Fowley] and I said, "Cut it!" And I said to her, "If you *ever* do that again, you'll be in blackface for the rest of the picture." I'd just get in her keylight, *that's* all I had to do [*laughs*], and she'd be in blackface for the *whole* rest of the picture. She said, "I don't know what you mean!" and I said, "Come on, honey, you know what you're doin'. Now knock it off." She got the message *real* fast and we got along fine after that, and I got so I *liked* her after a while. She was okay as an actress ... not *great*.

Nobody knew about it, but before we went down to Brazil, I rehearsed with these people, June and Ziva and Bill Wellman, Jr. We went to the Beverly Wilshire Hotel — we had a room there — and we rehearsed. You're not *really* allowed to do that [by the Screen Actors Guild], but these kids were young and I was the only one with experience, and we rehearsed the whole thing. Because film was *so* precious down [in Brazil] there we didn't want to make a lot of mistakes. So I did them a favor doing that.

Where did you stay?
I've forgotten the name of the hotel; they put us up in one of the best hotels in São Paulo.

How long were you down there?
I think about a month and a half — pretty long. They don't shoot very fast. Doug Fowley directed it, and he was wonderful. Of course, I knew Doug from way back; he's still alive. We had a Hungarian cameraman, a Russian makeup guy (who was also an actor), and the crew was Brazilian. And there were real voodoo people in the movie! One guy came up to me and gave me this little figure that he'd carved out of soapstone, and somebody said, "Oh, that's good luck." I said, "But it's *voodoo!*" And they said, "Look, there's good voodoo and bad voodoo. They *like* you!" I said, "Good! I'm gonna have them keep *on* liking me!"

Amidst all the dullness, there were a few decent "shock" moments in the movie, like that dead body that you unexpectedly pull up out of the ocean.
Oh, yeah! The guy that did that didn't know how to do it, and finally the director, Fowley, took his shirt off and his pants off and jumped in the water and said, "*This* is the way to do it!"
After the picture was over, they wanted me to stay 'cause they had to send the film back to Los Angeles to get it processed — until they heard from the lab, they didn't know whether it was good or not. After I finished my last scene, I said, "I'm through with the picture. Goodbye!" and they said, "Wait a minute! We have to keep you around." I said, "Well, if you keep me on salary, fine." So I went to Montevideo and to Argentina, and when they called me and said they didn't need me any longer, I flew back [to the States] from Argentina. But none of the kids wanted to go with me: Bill Wellman was homesick and June wanted to go back, and so did Ziva Rodann. But I figured, "As long as I'm *here*, I'm gonna look around!"

Did you think the picture would be any good?
No. But I'll tell you something, it made a lot of money. Early on, they

said I could have a salary or I could take five percent of the picture. I said, "You must be out of your mind! I don't want five percent of this thing!" And it made $3,000,000 in this country — that wasn't including the foreign rights. I would have made a *lot* of money on that show. A guy that I knew, a big shot in the publicity department of Universal, said to me, "You know, Walter, *we* almost bought the distributing rights to that thing, because we *knew* it would make money." Mike Ripps, who owned something like thirteen drive-in theaters in the South, was one of the producers, and he *knew* that he could make his nut back just off of his own theaters!

What did you think of it when you saw it?
It was corny, and also slow-paced. The first part of the picture, all that voodoo music and dancing — I thought they'd *never* get through with that! It went on and on and on! They got involved with the beauty of the dancing girls and things like that, they got carried away and forgot about the story sometimes. (Actually, what they probably were *really* doing, if you really want to know, was purposely dragging it out, because you can't sell a picture that's too short.)

In the sixties, you started to slow down work-wise quite a bit.
I had a massive heart attack [in the early sixties], when I was forty-seven. At that point I said to myself, "Hey, I'd better watch myself," so I moved to Ventura, California. I continued to act, but I didn't take my career that seriously after that. I'd made some money, I had money to tide me over. And, you know, it's a funny thing: If a guy's a good actor, he can make money on the outside real easy — 'cause he becomes a con man [*laughs*]! Richard Martin, who played Chito Rafferty in the Tim Holt Westerns, made a fortune selling insurance. Bob Clarke is the public relations man of a big bank. Russ Wade, a friend of mine who was at RKO, is the biggest real estate man in Palm Springs. The secret is personality — they know the right people, and they know how to deal with rich people and poor people. Believe me, a lot of 'em were very successful in business afterwards. I sold a little real estate for just a while.

My wife passed away about seven years ago. We were married for fifty-one years, and I miss the dickens out of her. I've been living alone since then. But I'm getting tired of cooking everything so I'm moving to a retirement community where you have your own apartment, but they cook for you and do your laundry and provide maid service and everything. It's not cheap, it's a class place. I looked around when I was first there and I said, "God, these people look *old*," but then it occurred to me that *I'm* old, too [*laughs*]! The average age over there is about seventy-five, and I'm going to be seventy-nine soon!

You dropped from acting in the late sixties.

I think the last thing I did was a picture in Arizona for [director] Budd Boetticher, I played the mayor of a town in *A Time for Dying* [released in 1971] with Audie Murphy. I'd been retired *then*, but Budd said to me, "Hey, come on down and do this thing." I did a lot of stuff for Budd—*Seven Men from Now, Red Ball Express* [1952], *Horizons West* [1952], oh, a *lot*. I was kind of Budd Boetticher's good luck charm. He still is going to do a picture in Spain (he's my age) and he wants me to come over. I said, "Budd, if you want me to say more than *hello*, you better have a teleprompter 'cause I can't remember lines anymore!" [*Laughs*.]

Could any*body lure you out of acting retirement at this point?*

Oh, no. I'm one of the few guys that, when I retired, I retired. A guy named Dick Benedict was an actor who became a pretty good director, and he said, "Walter, I have a job for you as a senator." I said, "Dick, no way." And Dick said, "You know, you're the first actor I ever knew who didn't say, 'Well, maybe just *one* more...'" I *retired*, I wanted to save my health—I've had *serious* heart trouble. But, you know, I've had a lot of sickness but I don't *hurt* anyplace and that's important. It's like my wife said: "At our age, if you wake up in the morning and you don't hurt a little somewhere, you're dead!" [*Laughs*.]

What's the key to being in demand as an actor, as you were in your day?

It's this simple: Just cut the mustard! I don't mean for that to sound conceited, I just mean that I had had sixty-eight weeks of stock and I knew how to hack it out! I was no Brando, but I was pretty good. In other words, I really worked at my craft. There was a group of us that worked a lot, like Harry Lauter and Myron Healey and Lane Bradford and Dick Curtis and myself. We worked a lot of Westerns—*Gene Autry*s, *Buffalo Bill Jr*s., *Annie Oakley*s and stuff—because they could *count* on us, *that* was the thing. It's like anything else: You have to do your apprenticeship if you want to be good.

WALTER REED FILMOGRAPHY

Redskin (Paramount, 1929)
The Mayor of 44th Street (RKO, 1942)
Framing Father (RKO short, 1942)

Seven Days' Leave (RKO, 1942)
My Favorite Spy (RKO, 1942)
Mexican Spitfire's Elephant (RKO, 1942)
Army Surgeon (RKO, 1942)
Bombardier (RKO, 1943)
Petticoat Larceny (RKO, 1943)
Mexican Spitfire's Blessed Event (RKO, 1943)
The Bamboo Blonde (RKO, 1946)
Child of Divorce (RKO, 1946)
Night Song (RKO, 1947)
Banjo (RKO, 1947)
Western Heritage (RKO, 1948)
Return of the Badmen (RKO, 1948)
Mystery in Mexico (RKO, 1948)
Fighter Squadron (Warners, 1948)
Angel on the Amazon (Republic, 1948)
Captain China (Paramount, 1949)
The Lawless (Paramount, 1950)
Young Man with a Horn (Warners, 1950)
The Eagle and the Hawk (Paramount, 1950)
The Torch (Eagle-Lion, 1950)
Tripoli (Paramount, 1950)
The Sun Sets at Dawn (Eagle-Lion, 1950)
The Racket (RKO, 1951)
Go for Broke! (MGM, 1951)
Submarine Command (Paramount, 1951)
Superman and the Mole-Men (Lippert, 1951)
Flying Disc Man from Mars (Republic serial, 1951)
Wells Fargo Gunmaster (Republic, 1951)
Government Agents vs Phantom Legion (Republic serial, 1951)
Bronco Buster (Universal, 1952)
Target (RKO, 1952)
Caribbean (Paramount, 1952)
Desert Passage (RKO, 1952)
The Blazing Forest (Paramount, 1952)
Horizons West (Universal, 1952)
Thunderbirds (Republic, 1952)
Red Ball Express (Universal, 1952)
The Man from the Alamo (Universal, 1953)
Gun Fury (Columbia, 1953)
The Clown (MGM, 1953)
Seminole (Universal, 1953)
War Paint (United Artists, 1953)
Forever Female (Paramount, 1953)
Those Redheads from Seattle (Paramount, 1953)
The High and the Mighty (Warners, 1954)
Dangerous Mission (RKO, 1954)
The Yellow Tomahawk (United Artists, 1954)
Return from the Sea (Allied Artists, 1954)
The Eternal Sea (Republic, 1955)
The Last Command (Republic, 1955)

Hell's Island (Paramount, 1955)
The Far Horizons (Paramount, 1955)
Bobby Ware Is Missing (Allied Artists, 1955)
Emergency Hospital (United Artists, 1956)
Seven Men from Now (Warners, 1956)
Rock, Pretty Baby (Universal, 1956)
Dance with Me, Henry (United Artists, 1956)
The Lawless Eighties (Republic, 1957)
Three Brave Men (20th Century–Fox, 1957)
The Helen Morgan Story (Warners, 1957)
Slim Carter (Universal, 1957)
Last of the Badmen (Allied Artists, 1957)
How to Make a Monster (AIP, 1958)
The Deep Six (Warners, 1958)
Summer Love (Universal, 1958)
The Horse Soldiers (United Artists, 1959)
Westbound (Warners, 1959)
Arson for Hire (Allied Artists, 1959)
Thirteen Fighting Men (20th Century–Fox, 1960)
Macumba Love (United Artists, 1960)
Sergeant Rutledge (Warners, 1960)
Posse from Hell (Universal, 1961)
How the West Was Won (MGM, 1962)
Advise and Consent (Columbia, 1962)
The Carpetbaggers (Paramount, 1964)
Where Love Has Gone (Paramount, 1964)
Cheyenne Autumn (Warners, 1964)
Convict Stage (20th Century–Fox, 1965)
Bus Riley's Back in Town (Universal, 1965)
Fort Courageous (20th Century–Fox, 1965)
The Money Trap (MGM, 1966)
The Sand Pebbles (20th Century–Fox, 1966)
Moment to Moment (Universal, 1966)
The Oscar (Embassy, 1966)
Panic in the City (Commonwealth United Entertainment, 1968)
The Destructors (Feature Film Corporation of America, 1968)
Tora! Tora! Tora! (20th Century–Fox, 1970)
A Time for Dying (Fipco/Etoile Distribution, 1971)

...I made two of the top ten turkeys ever made. That's a distinction! I mean, it means something! That means I did something!

Joseph F. Robertson

JOE ROBERTSON HAS BEEN active in the picture business for over 30 years, occasionally teaches cinema at Cal-State University, and is the author of two "how-to" cinema books. He's also quick (and proud) to point out that he produced *two* of the Ten Worst Films Ever Made. (Others may set that figure a bit higher.) Paradoxical? Not for a "big kid" like Robertson, whose happy-go-lucky adventures in picturemaking have included brushes with *The Slime People, The Crawling Hand* and, much more recently, *Auntie Lee's Meat Pies.*

Robertson was with the Marines during World War II and was later a major in International Banking and Finance at New York University. While working in Europe as a manufacturer's representative, he became interested in moviemaking, and upon his return to the States went to Hollywood and became a "show accountant" for George Burns' McCadden Productions (producers of television series like *Burns and Allen* and *The Bob Cummings Show*). Branching out into film production, he tackled the low-budget *Slime People* (directed by star Robert Hutton), *The Crawling Hand* and *Agent for H.A.R.M.*, worked in skin flicks and educational films, and has recently returned to horror with *Dr. Caligari* and *Auntie Lee's Meat Pies.* The self-described "kid from Queens" lists as his hobbies "sports, martial arts and girl-watching," and intends to continue making films "while I'm still young."

Where did you first learn some of the ins and outs of production?

At McCadden Productions. I was very fortunate, because they were very nice there. I *paid* everybody, so I had a certain "in," you know what I mean? And I could go anywhere I wanted, on the stages, on the sets, and talk to everybody. I could go into editing, learn a little about editing, learn a little about direction — *learning*, on the sets, all the time. And then I decided to do *The Slime People*, which was my first picture.

Where did the idea for Slime People *come from?*

We read a script called *The Slime People*, and we bought it. My then-wife Blair rewrote the script, we did the casting and made the film. Blair is a very successful producer now, she works for Spelling.

Robert Hutton told me that "Blair Robertson and Vance Skarstedt," who get screen credit for writing Slime People, *were made-up names.*

Oh, no, no. Vance Skarstedt was the original author and Blair did the rewriting. I raised the money; I was very good at that, because of my background. Things were different in those days. All the loopholes on tax writeoffs have now been closed — in those days, they were quite open

Previous page: Don't tell Joe Robertson that he made two of the worst movies ever made; that might tick him off. Tell him he made four or five of 'em.

[*laughs*]! Don Hansen was an investor and a friend of mine; he was very smart, very shrewd. Like a farmer with money—you know that type? I was very close to Don. He owned a propane company and he invented the propane carburetor, and he made a *lot* of money. He also owned a string of launderettes—as a hobby [*laughs*]. Ed Abrams was another investor, another good friend of mine.

How did you hook up with Robert Hutton?
Bob was in a play that we had seen, and we had a mutual friend who introduced us. We became very friendly, and when we decided to make *The Slime People*, I thought he'd be quite good for it.

It was also his first—and only—movie as director.
I backed him a lot, I was always on the set. And we had a second unit director, too, Bill Martin. He was an editor, I think, on the *Burns and Allen Show*, and he also did a series with his buddy Jackie Cooper called *Hennesey*; Bill was the associate producer on that.

Who cast the movie?
I did. One of the girls in *Slime People*, Susan Hart, she later married Jim Nicholson of AIP. (Susan made a *lllotta* money, boy.) We had Les Tremayne, Robert Burton—a number of good people. Burton had cancer, and I didn't realize it while we were making the film. He never said a word, never complained, and he passed away right after. (Originally we wanted to use Richard Arlen in that part but we couldn't, so I used him in *The Crawling Hand*.) William Boyce, who played the young marine, is quite rich now—he did not become an actor, didn't stay in the field, he went into real estate. That was that magic time when you bought houses and apartment houses to make a buck. He did that and became quite well off, and he's back in Oklahoma now.

For a low-budget picture, you had a lot of very good stuntmen in there.
Oh, yeah, they were all friends of mine. My friend is Bob Miles—Bob was married to Vera Miles—and we had the eight top stuntmen in the whole country in there. Most of 'em played Slime People. In fact, my brother, who was a lawyer, was visiting me from New York, and *he* was a Slime Man, too [*laughs*]!

How many costumes did you have?
We had eight, I think. I believe I paid $600 apiece for eight of 'em—it

Judee Morton shows a little skin as one of *The Slime People* shows a little interest.

was quite expensive, that was a lot of money in those days. Some company, whose name I forget, made 'em for me, a special effects company out here in the Valley. After the picture, I had 'em in my garage for a while and then I threw them out. But I understand that, a number of years ago, there was a big auction and somebody got one of those costumes — it went for $25,000.

Two of the Slime People stuntmen told me they were never paid.
   Oh, they were all paid. But, you know what it was, some of them were doing it as a favor to Bob Miles. We paid *some*, but some did it for nothing. They weren't paid, but it was because they did it as a favor.

Are you in any of these pictures?
   I'm in *Slime People*, I was one of the bums in the theater at KTTV — Ed Abrams was the other bum. (We had a lot of fun!) And Blair, who wrote it, played the woman who is interviewed by a television reporter. That

reporter's brother-in-law, by the way, was Clark Gable — his sister had married Gable. Dr. Tracy J. Putnam, who was one of the world's leading neurologists (and a friend of mine), was interviewed in that picture, too. He was a dean of neurology at Harvard, and he invented dilantin, the drug for epileptics. (His son Jock was the ambulance attendant in *The Crawling Hand*.) And Don Hansen was in *Slime People*, also, in one of the crowd scenes, running down the street. I'm lookin' at this guy, he's a multi-millionaire, you know, and he's running down the street like a little *boy*, with a stick in his hand! You had to laugh.

What kind of money were you working with?
  I would say maybe $80,000. Shooting was quite extensive, maybe twenty days. I could tell you stories that would make you pass out. Every night, I used to get people in to watch the dailies — we'd show 'em what we shot the day before, right out of the lab. And I'd raise money on the dailies for the *next day*— I'd get enough money to shoot again. (*The Crawling Hand* I had no problem, because Hansen put *all* the money up.) But on *Slime People* I had to raise the money on a day-to-day basis, every night — I remember my lawyer laughing over this. It was limited partnership agreement stuff— everybody takes a "piece," like "angels." We shot at KTTV, in Agoura, and at Whitman Field in Pacoima [the airport scenes]. The butcher shop belonged to Hutton's father-in-law. We also shot in Mandeville Canyon, a very expensive area in Bel-Air, after one of their big fires.

What was the matter with the "monster midgets" scenes you cut out?
  Oh, they were terrible. We had midgets playing voles, they were supposed to be an advance unit for the Slime People, but that was a fiasco. The people who did the Slime People's outfits did the voles, too, but they came out very bad, *terrible*, they just didn't work. So we just cut it out.

Robert Hutton described you as "completely crazy, like a little boy." Is that accurate?
  Basically, yes. I was very happy, I was very young, and I was amazed that I could get something on *film*! I'd see it on the screen and say, "My God, it's actually on film, it's being projected!"

How was the distribution handled?
  I did it. In those days, it was quite easy, because American International Pictures had set up various exchanges throughout the United States. All I had to do, really, was go through those exchanges. I went all around the country and I saw each person, gave 'em a print and made a deal, and then

they would distribute the film in their areas. So I used AIP's *modus operandi*. I had twenty-five, thirty, maybe forty prints. Later I distributed it as a double-bill with *The Crawling Hand*. It was quite simple because they had set it up very well, AIP.

So Slime People *was a moneymaker for you?*

Yeah, it was ... *all right*. It was *okay*, but it wasn't great. Those days were different than today — nobody made a lot of money in those days, because pictures like these had one-night showings. So there was really no *big* money in that. I made more *foreign* than I made domestic on *Slime People*, through British-Lion in London.

And were you happy at that time with the way the movie turned out?

At that *time*, yes. But, you gotta remember, that time was different. *The Slime People* is very *corny*—today, you lay on the floor laughing at it. But remember the *time*. Everything was a stereotype in a picture like that — for instance, there was always a *professor*, and the professor always had *daughters*. We put in all the stereotypes.

Who came up with The Crawling Hand?

Bill Idelson was one of the writers; he's a big writer, he did a number of series. And Herb Strock was the director on that; Herb was my mentor. Herb was a superb editor, and he kept *teaching* me, for twelve years. I learned and I learned and I learned from him. Herb was brilliant. He was a full professor at USC, in cinema. He directed *and* edited *The Crawling Hand*. We shot on actual locations, like USC, where we shot in the computer room. Another place we shot was an ice cream parlor in West Hollywood.

And you cast again, too.

Sure. The old lady was *great*, Arline Judge. I was playing the hand occasionally, and in one scene I was crawling up to her throat. As I'm doing this, I forget what I'm doing (I *do* get very intense), and I'm rubbing against her *boobs* with my hand. And she was so funny—she looked at everybody and she said, "I'm gettin' very fond of this boy!" [*Laughs.*] She was very funny, and very, *very* rich — she came there in a Rolls-Royce, diamonds, the works, down to this little place where we were shooting in South Central. It was funny. She was married at one time to Dan Topping, the guy who owned the Yankees.

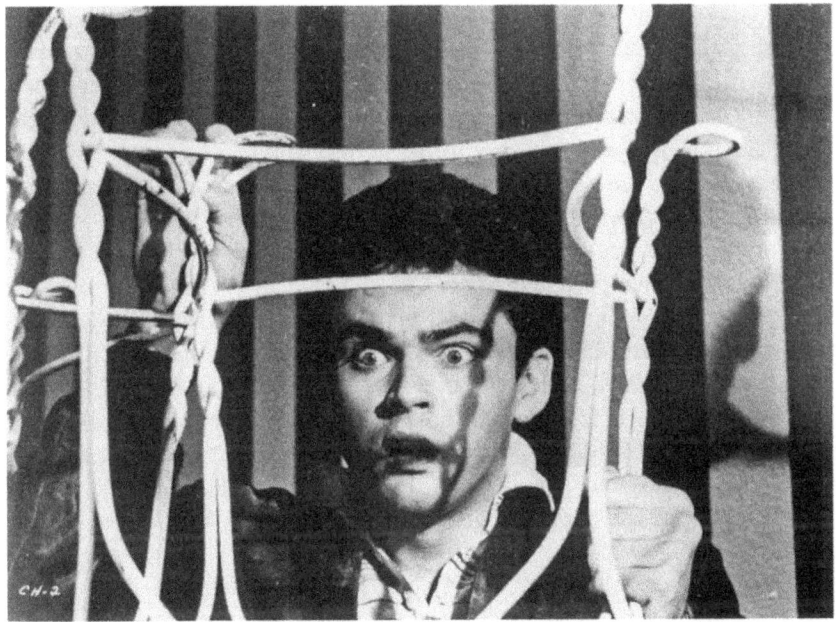

Teenager Rod Lauren is a victim of out-of-this-world influences in Robertson's senseless *The Crawling Hand.*

If she was so wealthy, what the heck was she doing acting in The Crawling Hand?

Just for a lark. Lonely, you know. She was famous at one time, but in 1962 ... it was like *Sunset Boulevard* [laughs]. And Alan Hale I loved, we got along very well. He played the sheriff, and one time when we were having a little trouble, he went out in the street and started directing traffic, keeping 'em away from the set. Nobody knew he was Alan Hale, they thought he *was* a sheriff. Also, one thing I'm a bug about is that I don't like anybody making a mess. I'm fanatical about that — you can't shoot in somebody's house and leave it a shambles. So I remember I was out on a lawn, picking up cigarette butts and little pieces of paper from somebody's lawn that we were shooting on, and I looked around and there was Alan doing the same thing. He said, "Joe, if *you're* gonna pick up, *I* can do it too." He was a very, very nice man.

What about the star, Peter Breck?

Peter's ... *not* a nice man. He was a wiseass. He got very mad at me. See, the original script was called *Requiem for an Astronaut*; and then, *we* decided to call it *The Crawling Hand,* for commercial reasons, to sell the damn picture. Well, he never forgave me for that, because he liked the other title. He just had an attitude. I had the same problem with a guy named Mark Richman on *Agent for H.A.R.M.*—the attitude. I don't understand that. One of my ex-partners was Stephen Boyd, and I got a partner right now, Pat Morita. These are very professional people, with no problems. With no egos. It's the people that are not quite "together" that give you this hard time. The bigger the star, the more a gentleman.

Richard Arlen—was he a gentleman?
 [*Gasps.*] Oh-h-h, *unbelievable*—a very classy guy. Kent Taylor was great, too. And Rod Lauren, who played the crazy kid—he was *all right*, but he was just a kid, and he never really "made it." You know, I turned down Burt Reynolds for the part that Rod Lauren played, 'cause I didn't think he could *act* [*laughs*]. Reynolds was very young at the time, he was only twenty-five, twenty-six. Then I turned down Raquel Welch on *Agent for H.A.R.M.* [for the part played by Barbara Bouchet]. Who knew?

Allison Hayes was also in Crawling Hand, *in a very small part.*
 There was a director named Bobby Gordon, and she was his girlfriend. I knew Bobby, and Bobby wanted me to use her, so I did. She was quite a competent actress. She was the *50 Foot Woman*, you know. By the way, my car is in *The Crawling Hand*—it was a Chrysler Town and Country convertible. I sold it for $15 because it needed brakes. Today, it's a *$200,000 collectors' item!*

You also had a mechanical crawling hand.
 There was a guy we called "Drunken Dunc" [*laughs*]—he was a very good special effects man, but he was always drunk! He made that with prosthetics and mechanics. I did the hand in close-up shots, but on the long shots we used the mechanical hand.

And you distributed this one, too?
 Yep. Again, the same technique as *Slime People*, through the AIP exchanges, and it worked very well. *In those days*, it worked. Today, it's so different, the whole *business* is so different. It's not the *same*, it's not *fun*. It's a *business*.

Which do you prefer, Crawling Hand *or* Slime People?
 Well, *Crawling Hand* is a much better-made film, but *Slime People* is much more *funny*. Kinky, and *flaky*, you know what I mean? I think it's more of a classic.

Even though it was a spy movie, you had a few good horror effects in Agent for H.A.R.M.

Blair wrote that script and we made it, and then we sold it outright to Universal. That was a little better-quality picture. You know how we did one of the scenes in there? You could do it yourself. You put a red [makeup] base on the actor's face — red like blood, right? Then you get Alka-Seltzer and you grind it down to a powder, and you put a little coloring in there, skin color. You put *that* on over the blood-red face and then the actor looks normal. Then you get an atomizer and you spray water on him, and what it does is, it activates the Alka-Seltzer. The whole face fizzes, and as that fizzes off, you see the red. It was so basic and simple, and yet *very* effective when you're going with a tight shot.

People poke fun at your movies. Does that bug you?

No, because I made two of the ten top turkeys ever made [*laughs*]. That's a distinction! I mean, it *means* something! That means I *did* something! (Am I right?) Even if you're a failure, it doesn't matter. You *tried*.

Speaking of failures, you worked a couple times with Ed Wood. Have you got a favorite anecdote about him?

Oh, I got so many, you'd lay on the floor. You could pass out with this guy! He was very masculine — even though he wore women's clothing, he liked women. I had a bar I ran for a hobby in North Hollywood, and he used to come in the bar. Mutual friends brought him in, and we became very close. He was brilliant, he could *write*— unbelievable! *Volumes* of writing!

It may not have been good, but it was fast, right?

And *terrible* films, they were the worst you've ever seen in your life. *Shocking*! And he was a drunk, he was always gettin' drunk. He used to wear this long, *horrible* silver lamé dress. And he was kind of *ugly*, you know? And then he's got these old woman's shoes, like from the forties, and stockings, rolled up to right below the knee. Then he had this horrible wig that didn't work, it was like a cheap wig and he put it on wrong. When he started off the evening, he'd put the makeup on *nicely*, around the wig. But as the evening progressed and he got half in the bag, the wig started to move away and you'd see the white skin. It was frightening, it'd scare the life out of you if you didn't know. I had to take him home a couple of times, and one time I couldn't find his house. I had a Jeep, top down, wind blowin', the wig was all over the place. And he had his leg up on the top of the Jeep, like a guy. Well, I forgot what kind of a guy I had with me and I saw these two nice little fourteen-year-old girls and I pulled up to 'em, I was going to ask 'em where such-and-such street was. And as I pulled up, they took one look at Ed and they started *screaming* and running down the street [*laughs*]!

Now, did he "get" something out of dressing like that, or did he just do it to shock people, to be a "character"?

The *psychological* thing that I understand is this: What he did is, he *loved* women so much that he wanted to emulate them ... but he was *not* gay. He wanted to emulate them, so that he'd become *part* of them. A very heavy, "trippy" thing. In the Marine Corps, he was at Tarawa. Four thousand boys went in, 300 came out. He went into battle with his battle fatigues; underneath that, he had a red bra and red panties. He told me he hoped to hell he got killed at Tarawa, because he could never explain if he was *wounded*! He was a classic guy! And he died *terribly* broke, drinking, just totally wiped out. He worked [wrote and acted] for me in a [softcore] picture called *The Photographer* [1969].

So even though you knew what a flake he was — you don't mind me calling your dead friend a flake, do you?

[*Laughs.*] That's all right.

— you still let him get involved with one of your movies?

Well, I was *there* [*laughs*]! And it worked out okay. And then I used him [as an actor] in another one I did, *Mrs. Stone's Thing* [1970]. He had a tremendous personality, he was always jolly and laughing. He made you *happy*.

How long were you involved with making that kind of softcore movie?

I wasn't in it too long; it didn't *last* that long, because it went right into hardcore. Right now, they're "in" again. *Playboy*, they're selling some of their videos up to a hundred thousand pieces. It's unbelievable! And it's not hardcore, it's soft, it's like it was in the sixties [*laughs*]!

When did you write those two books of yours?

I wrote those about ten years ago. I've got two more being published pretty soon; they reflect what's happening *today* [in the movie industry]. I have an editing company, too, Pacific Beach Productions, and we do a lot of editing. We have the Toaster, the whole schtick. I write terribly technical books; in fact, one book, *The Magic of Film Editing* [1984], is part of the curriculum at USC.

And recently you've been producing again: Dr. Caligari *and* Auntie Lee's Meat Pies.

Caligari was with a fellow named Steve Sayadian. I had cut his movie *Cafe Flesh* [1982], and then we became friends. Technically he's a still man, an art director, and everything moves in *front* of the camera. It's called "bio-mechanical directing."

There's such a thing, or that's what he calls what he does?
No, that's it! It's almost *artificial* in the way you move in front of the camera, and you back it up with these *great* art layouts, vivid colors. We won a lot of acclaim with the picture, it's unique.

And you had confidence, going into this with him, that this would be a salable movie?
Oh, yes, but *not* a big one, it never makes a *lot* of money. It's an *art* film. And we played all the art circuits. The NuArt on Santa Monica Boulevard, we were down there for six months. If you've seen the original *Cabinet of Dr. Caligari*, you remember the abstract sets and the crooked doors and the elongated drawings. It was very arty in its day, and *we* brought it up into the nineties. It was very effective. And it was a very serious shoot — everything was terribly serious. Steve directed it, and he's kind of a dark, melancholy type of guy. Very intense ... nervous ... but he did some great stuff.

Would you use him again?
[*Pause.*] Only for certain films. See, that's the big problem with Steve, he's not a run-of-the-mill guy, you couldn't ask him to do certain things. He could do *Batman*, for example, he's sort of Tim Burton–ish, but he couldn't do comedy, he couldn't do...

He couldn't do Auntie Lee's Meat Pies.
No! I wrote that script, and then I went to a fellow named Gerry Steiner and Gerry financed it. Gerry was *very* active in this thing. Gerry cut it, too, and he was one of those cutters who "can't let go." A very "German" type of cutter. The rule of thumb is, if you can cut it out and it doesn't interfere with the picture, then it should never have been *in*. I'd want to cut away from a scene in a room but, no, Gerry says, the characters have to *leave* the room. What the hell do they have to leave the room for, why not just *cut* to something else? Some cutters can't understand that, the people have to *come into* every goddamn room and they've got to *leave* every room! Old-fashioned, "I-have-to-do-it-*this*-way" bullshit.

And he directed it, too.

No, he didn't, *I* did, but he's *saying* he did. But I don't mind him thinking that. You could put down "co-director" if you want, make him feel good.

Any on-set anecdotes you'd care to mention?
Not too much. I became very, very close with Pat Morita, and Pat was great; the girls were great; Karen Black was superb, and she was *sick* all through the whole picture. Terrible fever. But when she was up there, you wouldn't even know it. She's a pro, and funny, too, *very* funny. We also had Huntz Hall and Pat Paulsen in there, they're personal friends of mine and they were great.

And did you like the finished picture?
No, not really. It's too long. It's 110 minutes, it should have been 85 minutes. That would have made a big difference, the cutting. Otherwise, it was fine. The *production* was superb.

Profitable?
So-so. A little too much money went into the production. When you make the kind of things we're talking about, you've got to do it for like $800,000. This was a million and a half. Art films like this have to be *very* well-done for like 800,000, and *then* you'll get a profit. You put a million and a half into one and you're getting yourself into trouble. I mean, a real good art film means that nobody *likes* it [*laughs*]! Five percent of the people who watch it, like it, right? But that's okay *as long as you've got* a low enough budget so you can recoup on that five percent.

You're calling Auntie Lee's Meat Pies *an art film?*
Semi. It's a black comedy. The girls are great.

What are you most proud of in your career?
I think the most proud that I was, believe it or not, was of my *books*. When something's printed, you can begin to say, "Well, hey, people really *believe* in me." When the book publishers say, "Okay, Joe, we're gonna give you a thousand dollar retainer, we're gonna print your book," *then* I say to myself, "Gee, maybe the kid from Queens is okay."

What's the key to being in the industry as many years as you have, and always maintaining your sort of "happy," "crazy kid" attitude?
[*Laughs.*] The key is to be broke! I was a millionaire three times; making money is easy. But *having* money is not good for me. I don't like to have

money, I like to be broke. It's a psychological disorder! I don't watch sunsets when I have money, I get *involved*. In-bred, way deep inside, I'm an accountant, so if I follow the stock market, I get so involved that I'm not *happy* anymore. I don't run up to Carmel or drive along Highway One or daydream or kick back. When I have no money, I *do* those things. For me, *that's* the key.

*You know, when you do horror pictures,
you have to have someone who really believes in this
stuff. I don't think we were equipped to do real horror
pictures for some reason.*

Aubrey Schenck

THIS ENTERPRISING LITTLE independent movie company was instrumental in resuscitating the dormant Gothic horror genre in the mid-1950s, bringing back the tried-and-true horror characters (the Frankenstein Monster, the mad scientist, the mummy, etc.) in well-mounted low-budget productions. They punctuated their plots with ground-breakingly gruesome and violent touches that prompted one reviewer to predict that viewers with weak stomachs might be "nauseated." England's *Kinematograph Weekly* wrote of their initial chiller, "Seldom, if ever, has the X certificate been so richly earned." The company is, of course, Aubrey Schenck's Bel-Air Productions, which — long before Hammer — started to combine classic horror plots with up-to-date scare tactics (gory surgical scenes, disembodied limbs, etc.), while at the same time filling their casts with the all-time horror greats.

Schenck and his partner Howard W. Koch formed the production company in the early 1950s and began to supply a steady stream of Westerns, cop movies and other action dramas for United Artists release. In 1956, the company veered off in the profitable new direction of horror, starting with the enormously successful *The Black Sleep*, and following with *Voodoo Island*, *Pharaoh's Curse* and (for Allied Artists) *Frankenstein 1970*. While Koch went on to work for Frank Sinatra Enterprises (and later headed up production at Paramount), Schenck stayed true to his adventure-picture roots, and added to his filmography the popular *Robinson Crusoe on Mars* and the Philippine-made *Daughters of Satan* and *Superbeast*. Long retired from the business, Aubrey Schenck provides the "inside story" on his illustrious career in action, horror and exploitation features.

How did you first get into picturemaking?

I practiced law for seven years [1932-39] in New York City, connected with the legal department of 20th Century–Fox. I was also an assistant to [Fox president] Spyros Skouras, who was based in New York. I had written a story called *Shock* which I submitted to the studio, and they offered me a specified sum of money for it. I told Mr. Skouras I would rather go out and produce the picture than take the money. He said, "Well, you have no experience in that," and I said, "I'll take my chances." They gave me that chance; I went out to Fox and worked under Brynie Foy, who was the head of the B department. They put this picture in the B category; it was called *Shock* with Vincent Price, directed by Alfred Werker. Well [*laughs*], the picture became an instantaneous hit, and they elevated it to an A picture — it opened on Wilshire Boulevard at an A theater!

Initially Shock *was going to have a top director, Henry Hathaway.*

[Fox production chief Darryl] Zanuck thought the script was so good,

Schenck (seen here in a 1939 pose) looks back with pride on his prolific career as an exploitation movie expert.

he gave it to Hathaway and [Louis] de Rochemont, the producer. I cried a little, I guess [*laughs*], and somehow or other it came back to *me*, they let me produce the picture. Vincent Price was perfect for the picture, he happened to be great. (*Any*thing Vincent did was great.) I think the budget on *Shock* was $375,000.

You didn't take screen credit for writing the story.

[*Emphatically.*] No. I came up with a lot of the original stories but I *never* did that to the screenwriters, I let them have the full screen credit. I could have taken *fifty* credits for inventing stories, if I'd wanted to. But I would present the stories to the screenwriters, and if they did the screenplays, I was satisfied. I thought *Shock* was a good picture, right from the preview on — that was when Fox decided to put it in the A theaters as a top picture, rather than a second feature.

After that it was easy going, because when Brynie went over to Eagle-Lion, he took me with him and I became executive producer over there. That was the beginning of my career. When I was at Eagle-Lion, we were in the old PRC studios, right abutting Goldwyn Studio. It was small, about eight or nine stages. A big financier named Robert Young was the owner. He was the head of the Baltimore and Ohio [B&O] Railroad; when he bought the B&O Railroad, for some reason, PRC was one of the companies included in the purchase [*laughs*]! So when he bought PRC, he tried to make it into a grade-A studio called Eagle-Lion. They had their own distribution — that's where Arthur Krim started, he was our first president. Later on, Eagle-Lion was sold out to United Artists.

In general, are you an on-the-set, hands-on producer?

I'm an entrepreneur from the beginning of the story to the editing, which by the way is my forte. I *love* the editing room and I am, I would say, a seasoned cutter. But I wouldn't say that I was on-the-set — once my director took over, I let him have it. If he wasn't up to snuff, he wasn't hired again. But I left 'em alone, I gave the directors full rein.

You must have liked Alfred Werker, then — he did a number of your movies.

Oh, I made three or four pictures with Al. We also did a picture at Eagle-Lion that I *didn't* get [screen] credit for — I was like executive producer on *He Walked by Night* [1948], which Al directed. Then he also did *Repeat Performance* for me, and *Rebel in Town* [1956]. By the way, do you know who our casting director was at Eagle-Lion? "Swifty" Lazar! That's where he started, with *us*! Oh, I could tell you stories about him, he was a character!

Out of all the movies you've done which I've seen, my favorite is Repeat Performance *the fantasy where a girl re-lives one year of her life.*

That was a strange thing. I found that story in *Redbook* magazine and bought it, and in that original story, the heavy was the *girl*. The problem then was to find the right actress — remember, Eagle-Lion didn't have access to too many stars. We said, " 'Swifty,' we have to get a girl," but there was nobody that we could get that was tough enough [to play the part]. We were after Bette Davis, but of course that was impossible. So we switched the story around so that the heavy became the *man* [Louis Hayward] instead of the girl. We had Joan Leslie as the girl, and *she* couldn't play a heavy. I think the way the original story read was better, the story was *much* better with the girl being the heavy. But it *was* a good picture in the end, it turned out very well.

Repeat Performance *was Eagle-Lion's first big-budgeted picture.*

The whole picture cost something like $600,000. I was a *little* disappointed with it — I thought the writer did a good job, *everybody* did a good job, but I couldn't get out of my mind how much better it would have been if the *woman* was the tantalizing villainess. It would have been *stronger*. Not that Louis Hayward didn't do the heavy part right, but you *expected* a man to be that way. What threw you when you read the original story was that the *woman* was so diabolical.

Contrast working at Fox and at Eagle-Lion.

Oh, it was entirely different, my *job* was different. Brynie gave me full rein, even though I had only made three pictures with him at Fox. Brynie was the kind of a head producer who gave anybody that worked under him full authority to do what he thought was right. In those days, star value was the big thing, and it was a little tough to get stars to come work at Eagle-Lion, 'cause they were under contract to big studios. But on the whole we did pretty good, we had some big hits like *T-Men* [1947] — that was a thing I made for Eddie Small, which was released under the Eagle-Lion banner. It grossed $3,000,000, which in those days was a terrific thing, and it was the start of a great director, Tony Mann.

I particularly like his Westerns.

After a while, [James] Stewart wouldn't *do* a Western without him! Oh, Tony was great. But when I hired Tony [*laughs*], Small was in Europe, he didn't know I had hired him. And when Small found out, he got mad as hell, because in the strike in forty-three or forty-four, Tony had gone out on strike on Small! (Small wasn't the kind of guy who'd forget a thing like that.) But when Small saw *T-Men*, he relented, he said, "You did a good thing."

At Eagle-Lion you also worked with William Castle.

[*Laughs.*] Oh, Billy, one of my best friends! Billy and I used to work together, coming up with crazy ideas. While I was at Eagle-Lion, he came over and he had an idea: "Let's do a picture called *Destination Moon*." We went in to see Krim, and Krim thought we were crazy guys! He thought it was a preposterous idea, he just didn't believe in it. Then later on he *did* take the thing on, he let George Pal make it. But Billy and I had the idea to do it first, we had the [Robert Heinlein] novel — we even had the title registered. Bill was a fascinating guy, the greatest idea guy I ever met.

Howard Koch said you were the greatest story and idea man he ever met.

I *had* to be, because with the money Howard and I had to spend on the movies we made, I *couldn't* go out and buy stories or plays or anything like that. By the way, Howard was a remarkable guy. He was on *Shock* as a second assistant director — that's where I spotted him. Then when we went to Eagle-Lion, I said, "Listen, how would you like to be a *first* assistant?" Well, he nearly fell off the chair [*laughs*]! Because, in those days, it was unheard-of; in a studio, you went fifteen, twenty years before you "graduated." But I didn't believe in that. If I spotted talent, we gave him a chance.

Which of your movies are you proudest of?

I can name 'em: *T-Men*; *Beachhead* [1954], a World War II thing; *Robinson Crusoe on Mars* (regardless of what it grossed, it was a great idea); *Ambush Bay* [1966], a damn good war picture, honest as heck; *Up Periscope* [1959], which I made at Warners with Jimmy Garner; and *Shield for Murder* [1954], a little picture that I let Howard and Eddie O'Brien co-direct. That movie grossed a *lot* of money, you wouldn't believe how much; on television, it's made a fortune. And I made a picture at Universal that I thought was a great picture but they didn't do anything with it, *Target Unknown* [1951]. It was a great idea, it was about aviators who were captured by the Germans — it was a hell of a well-done picture. Sometimes pictures were well-done but they got swallowed up, because distribution in those days was entirely different — back then, they had the star system. If some of these pictures were made *today*, now that people don't care *who's* in it, some of 'em would be terrific grossers. Plus, nowadays they spend $10,000,000 on advertising. I don't think we ever had a budget over $50,000 for advertising.

You made your first horror movies for your own production company, Bel-Air. How did that come into existence?

I was at Universal and I got a call from Eddie Small; he said, "I'm forming a company with Sol Lesser and Sam Briskin. Would you like to be our executive producer?" I said, "Sure!" I had two years to run on my Universal contract, but I told [Universal executives] Leo Spitz and Bill Goetz I wanted to leave. They said, "Boy, you're makin' a mistake. You're goin' with the three toughest guys in the business." I said, "Well, I'll take my chance"—but they were *right*. The first script I submitted to 'em, the three guys disagreed on it. One guy said he liked it, another said he *dis*liked it—they couldn't get together. So I knew right then that this wasn't for me.

I was sitting in a bar and I had a story right in my hands called *War Paint*. Sitting next to me was the head of distribution for United Artists, Bill Hinemann. He said, "Is that a picture?" I said, "It *could* be a picture—it's a treatment," and I told him about it. He said, "I'm gonna call Krim tonight, I want you to make that picture for us." Well, I submitted a budget, we got Robert Stack to star, and that was the beginning of Bel-Air.

And Howard Koch was in it with you right from the beginning.

He was made producer, because [*laughs*] at that time I had another deal with Howard Hughes at RKO. I couldn't use my name on *War Paint* [1953], because the contract was still running at RKO, so I just presented the picture and let Howard Koch be the producer. But with Hughes, you *never* made a picture—that was a *joke*! You never even *saw* the man! (By the way, a couple of years later, my uncle Joe Schenck heard about this and he said, "Why didn't you tell *me*? I can do *any*thing with that crazy Howard, I would have got you a million dollars for the breaking-up of the contract!") The *sweetest* thing that an actor ever did for me was done by Robert Stack. The first week of *War Paint*, we were supposed to pay everybody on a Thursday, and our money hadn't been placed in the bank. Stack could see I was worried as hell and he came to me, and I told him what was happening; I said, "I may miss the payroll." He said, "*You* won't miss the payroll. How much will you need for this week?" I think it came to something like 36 or 40,000 dollars. He said, "*You'll* have it." Fortunately, just before the time that *he* was going to put up the money, the money came through the bank and we were able to go through with the payroll. Of course, he was a very rich man, but isn't that something? You won't find that from too many actors.

What was Koch like as a partner?

He was a remarkable guy, I'm tellin' you. He had *some* personality! He would go to locations and people would bend over backwards for him—we got things that no other companies could get because of his way of dealing with people. That's his great forte, his personality and his ability to convince people to do things his way.

I've yet to interview anybody that worked with him that didn't talk about how much they liked him.

That's why I made him a first assistant! You'd say to him, "Howard, we're a little behind schedule," and he'd put you back on schedule the next day!

Throughout your career, you've specialized in action and exploitation-type movies.

I did 'em for two reasons. *One*, they're cheaper to make, and we were always limited in our budgets; and, *two*, you didn't have to have top names, you could start with young directors and people like that. You *gravitate* into that kind of a picture, whereas if you had big stars at your disposal, you would look for a big book, a best seller, a play or something like that. It's easier to do it *that* way; I think *we* had a tougher time of it.

In the mid-fifties, when the old-time, Gothic-type horror movies were out of vogue, you made one which became a big hit, The Black Sleep.

I don't remember right off where we got the idea, whether I came up with it myself or somebody presented it to us. Gerald Adams, who wrote the story, did a few Westerns for me, he was a good writer, and the screenplay was written by John C. Higgins, who was one of the goddamnedest best writers in that town, *brilliant* writer. All I can remember is that I said, "We'll get every goon in the business for this that we can lay our hands on!" [*Laughs.*] Bela Lugosi, he was so far gone, he didn't know that he was in the *picture* even! Then later, we sent Lugosi up to San Francisco for an opening of the picture, and he tried to jump out of the hotel window!

What about some of your other "goons"?

Lon Chaney — well, he drank too much, and I think it killed him in the end. On *Big House, U.S.A.* [1955], you know how many drinkers I had there? There was Brod Crawford, who was always soused but never missed a line; there was Bill Talman, who drank; Lon Chaney; and Ralph Meeker, who kept up with the rest of 'em. Chaney was a sweet guy, provided he knew where he was at the moment. And John Carradine, I'll give you the greatest anecdote you ever heard about him. We were doing a picture called *Desert Sands* [1955] in Yuma, Arizona. Now, Carradine had a pretty big part, and the assistant director said to me, "I can't keep track of this guy and get him to bed at night" — Carradine was coming in bleary-eyed every morning. So I said, "Let me find out where he goes at night." I traced him to San Luis, which is a little town over the border from Yuma, in *Mexico*. He was in a cafe doing Shakespeare for his dinner and his drinks, in this little cantina! And there wasn't a person there that understood *one word* he said, they were all Mexicans [*laughs*]! This is all true, so help me! And Basil Rathbone was a very fine fellow, a gentleman, very nice. Same as Karloff, who was in *Voodoo Island* and *Frankenstein 1970*. Karloff I had no trouble with — except he was the *stingiest* guy that ever lived [*laughs*]!

For instance?

Well, when you'd go out to dinner, or to *any*thing, he always liked to be treated. But he was a fine gentleman and he had a good *mind*, very erudite — exactly the opposite of what he was in pictures.

You originally approached Peter Lorre to play the Akim Tamiroff part in Black Sleep.

I told you, we approached *every*one, and we got what we could get, that's all. We had a limited budget. Probably Lorre was just asking too much money.

Were you on the set of Black Sleep *much?*

[*Laughs.*] Well, I played a part in it — right when the picture starts off. I was in the scene in Newgate Prison, I had a mustache. I may have had one word to say.

What part did Edwin Zabel play in Bel-Air Productions?

Zabel played no part in the creative end at all. He was then the head buyer for Fox West Coast theaters, and I thought it'd be a good idea if he got involved with me. He became a partner; if I was not making a picture and needed the money, he would pay my salary; and when the pictures came out, he was a great help, booking the pictures in the top theaters of the Fox chain. So he was very instrumental in the monetary end, not in the creative.

Black Sleep *has some very gruesome horror scenes for a fifties movie, like the brain surgery and the murder of the housekeeper.*

For the scene where Rathbone operated on the brain, we had a brain surgeon right on the set with Reggie LeBorg, and we were using his hands as the surgeon. And the housekeeper was set on fire by the monsters after they got out of the dungeon. I think that was a stunt*man*.

Did you feel you were sticking your necks out a little with the excessive gruesomeness?
No.

What kind of money were the horror stars paid?
The highest-paid one got 10 or 15,000, that was Basil Rathbone. Chaney would get about five bills a week, Carradine the same, maybe 750. Bela — well [*laughs*], what was the minimum then? — 350 or 400 a week.

Why was Lugosi paid the least?
Oh, my God, we had to carry him from place to place, he didn't even know he was *gettin'* paid [*laughs*]. He was so drugged, he didn't know where he was. Tor Johnson, the giant Swedish wrestler, carried him — literally *carried* him in his arms — to the set each day.

Would you say Lugosi was more trouble than he was worth?
No, he wasn't trouble — he was *numb*! That's the best word to describe him!

What do you recall about LeBorg?
Reggie was the kind of director who, if he'd had any guts, if he'd had a Tony Mann ego, could have been one of the best directors out here. He had great taste and he was a very sensitive guy, but he was *scared* of the schedule, he was *scared* of *every*thing. Tony Mann, who didn't give a damn, became a big director because that's what directors *have* to be. They have to say, "Damn the producer. Damn *every*thing."

You respect directors who say, "Damn the producer"?
Sure I do! My resentment is that I didn't go into directing myself, I might have been very good at it. But I didn't have the *time*. I was makin' more pictures as an independent than some of the *studios* [*laughs*]!

And Black Sleep *ended up doing very well money-wise for UA.*
Oh, sure. I don't think UA ever lost a nickel on us; every damn picture we made for them sooner or later turned a profit. I can't think of a loser.

Did you have anything to do with the publicity push that UA put behind Black Sleep? *The horror stars who went on tour, and the wax figures they sent around?*
We never had the time to get into the publicity of our pictures or the handling of 'em, 'cause we were making one picture after another. UA put

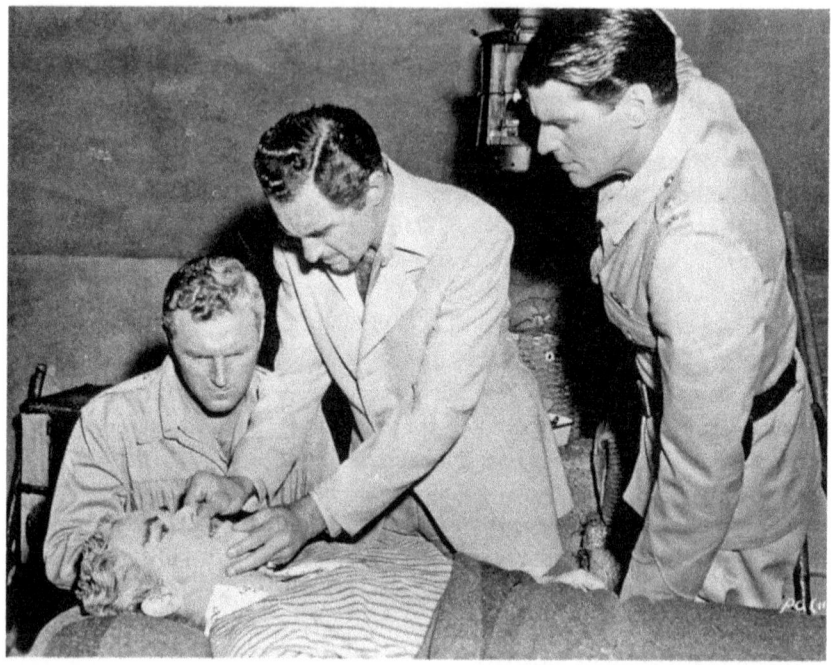

George Neise, Guy Prescott and Mark Dana hope that dry skin and gingivitis are the worst parts of the *Pharaoh's Curse*.

Black Sleep out on a double-bill with *The Creeping Unknown*, an English picture.

Your next horror films were Pharaoh's Curse *and* Voodoo Island, *a twin-bill for UA.*

Pharaoh's Curse was a little B picture — we spent $90,000 on it, for God's sake. Lee Sholem was the kind of director who, if you gave him a six-day schedule, he brought it in in *five*. In fact, Howard gave him a nickname, "Roll 'Em" Sholem [*laughs*] — Howard was the first to call him that, and then he was known all over the industry as that! I like Death Valley so I went along with 'em when Sholem made *Pharaoh's Curse*, just 'cause I like being there; I didn't interfere with the shooting, though. Where we got the star [Ziva Rodann], I don't know. We probably gave her $350 a week, something like that. The idea *of Pharaoh's Curse* came to me when I thought back about the guys who opened King Tut's tomb — each one of those guys died because they were instrumental in the unveiling of the tomb.

And Voodoo Island?

Oh, *that* picture didn't come through. You see, you can't put Karloff doing a *good* part — he has to be the heavy or it's *wrong*. That was a lost cause. Making those man-eating plants the heavy, that didn't make any sense. But, hell, you take a chance. With Karloff's name, we thought we had a good chance, but it didn't work out. I'm not proud of that picture at all.

Why did it have to be shot in Hawaii?
Well, because we had done *Beachhead* there and Howard knew his way around. We made two pictures at the same time [*Voodoo Island* and *Jungle Heat*, 1957] and it was a little cheaper, that's all. On *Beachhead* I was there for the whole picture, I watched that one very carefully, but on *Voodoo Island* I wasn't there. I was home doing five or six *other* stories!

Any other memories of Voodoo Island?
No. I only have memories of *good* pictures [*laughs*]!

What did you do for William Castle on Macabre? *I know you were involved without credit on that one.*
Howard did his "production work" for him, because this was Bill's first picture as an independent and he didn't know the ropes. So he gave us ten or twelve percent of the picture just to take care of his production needs, that's all. We had nothing to do with the making of it from a standpoint of shooting or anything like that.

Horror-wise Frankenstein 1970 *came next, with Koch directing.*
We made that because we had a three-picture deal with Karloff; we had to pay him $30,000 whether we used him in a picture or not. So we went to the guys at Allied Artists — they wanted pictures — and we made it quickly for them. It was like a pick-up deal. I think we made it for $110,000, they paid us $250,000 for it — an outright buy.

That's one movie where you did *take a story credit.*
Yeah, with the publicity guy, Chuck Moses, we get the story credit. (I wonder why I did that [*laughs*]?) The story *was* my idea. The screenplay was by Dick Landau, who just died recently. He was a good writer. We shot it at Warner Bros., because we were doing pictures there at the time — two Mamie Van Dorens, *Violent Road* [1958] and so on. So we rented space.

What do you think of Frankenstein 1970?
[*Hems and haws.*] Well, that wasn't Howard's metier. Howard, he

Director Reginald LeBorg demonstrates the approved method of fighting a carnivorous plant in Schenck's *Voodoo Island*. (Pictured: Beverly Tyler, LeBorg, Rhodes Reason.)

himself didn't like doing these horrible things, with eyes poppin' out and things like that. That wasn't his bag. You know, when you do horror pictures, you have to have someone who *really* believes in this stuff. I don't think we were equipped to do real horror pictures for some reason.

Black Sleep *is generally considered the best of that bunch.*

Yeah, *Black Sleep* we were lucky with, because the people that were *in* it were believable.

The cast of Frankenstein 1970 *was a screwy bunch.*
   [*Laughs.*] Yeah! "Red" Barry was in it, and also [L.A. television personality Tom] Duggan. He committed suicide later on, but he was always drunk anyway, what the hell.

The papers said he died in a car crash.
   He did not. The papers may have said that, but he fell out of the window at his beach apartment, I *know* that. The producer of Duggan's show, Irwin Berke, was also in *Frankenstein 1970*, playing the police inspector. I cast *him*, too [*laughs*] — what can I tell you? Listen, I did the craziest thing a man *ever* did: When Sinatra got his Oscar for *From Here to Eternity* [1953], I said, "Gee, if you put these singers in a different medium, they become big stars." So we had a *hell* of a Western [script] called *Quincannon, Frontier Scout* [1956] and I said, "Let's turn Tony Martin into a Western star!" That was my biggest mistake! He was the *sweetest* guy in the world, but he was no Westerner — when he got up on that horse, it was a wonder he didn't fall off the other side [*laughs*]! And he was even embarrassed playing the part — *he* shouldn't have taken it, *I* shouldn't have given it to him! So that was one of my big flops of all time, spoiling a goddamn good Western story by putting Tony in it.

So would you say that that's true of Frankenstein 1970, *too — that it was a mistake having "Red" Barry and Tom Duggan in there?*
   No, that didn't make any difference. When you have Karloff in something like that, people either look at Karloff or they don't look at the picture. And that "monster" of Karloff's, that didn't scare you at all, either [*laughs*].

Ib Melchior first announced Robinson Crusoe on Mars *around 1960, when he was going to make it for a nothing company called Herts-Lion.*
   Well, that didn't happen, and then *I* heard about it. The title intrigued me, so I paid him a certain amount of money — took an option on it for a year or so. I peddled it around and I got the Paramount people interested. I was in Europe at the time when the head of distribution, Barney Balaban, called me into the Savoy Hotel in London and said, "That thing that you submitted to us, *Robinson Crusoe* — how soon can you make it?"
   Later on, after it was finished, we had quite a controversy on that picture. I didn't like the title — I wanted to call it *Mars Project One*. I told 'em, "With *Robinson Crusoe* in the title, people will think we're making a satire or something!" Still, they stuck with *Robinson Crusoe on Mars*. But I think that I was right, 'cause the picture didn't do as well as it might have — it

Director Howard W. Koch and Mr. and Mrs. Boris Karloff share a laugh behind-the-scenes on *Frankenstein 1970*.

grossed all right, but nothing terrific. And it was a matter of *how* they released it, too. In those days, you didn't release a picture in early June, when the kids were still in school. Today that's a *good* release, but in the old days you waited till the Fourth of July and thereafter. Now, Paramount had a Jerry Lewis picture ready to go so they put the Lewis picture [*The Patsy*] and *Robinson Crusoe on Mars* together and released 'em as a double-bill, in early June. I think that was a bad release date. Do you know the reviewer for the [*New York*] *Daily News*, Kate Cameron? She gave it four stars, which was unusual. I gave her a private screening up at the Paramount building, and she thought it was the best thing in science fiction she ever saw. And, of course, since then, a *lot* of people who do critiques on science fiction *have* put that picture way, way up, 'cause we were so honest in just following the Defoe story. A lot of people thought we'd put in monsters and things like that, which we didn't.

There were *monsters in the original script.*

[*Contemptuously.*] Yeah — oh, *yeah*! I really bought just the title and the idea of this man being stranded on Mars. The rest of it [writer] John

Higgins wrote; and, of course, the director contributed a lot. Byron Haskin was a great guy on science fiction. Haskin did a lot of work, and he was a delight to work *with*, very easy.

Did Ib Melchior have any input once you got involved?
 Oh, absolutely not.

Would you have let him direct the picture?
 Oh, no, *no-o-o*! Paramount wouldn't 've accepted him — in those days, a budget of $1,200,000 was a big budget and a picture like that required [a well-established director]. Byron Haskin had done *War of the Worlds* and other top pictures. I think *Robinson Crusoe* came in at $1,150,000.

Was it your idea to cast unknowns?
 Yes. We thought that was the only way to make it believable. As a matter of fact, Robert Culp was up for the picture at one time, but he was too well-known, it wouldn't look authentic to have him up there as an astronaut. So we found this young fellow Paul Mantee, who I thought was excellent. All the outdoor stuff was shot in Death Valley and everything else was in the studio *except* one part we shot at the Union Ice Factory — that's where we had the sequence where the ice caves in.

Did you yourself scout out the Death Valley locations?
 Yes, Haskin and I spent about three weeks doing that. We were nearly caught in one of those flash floods, in one of the canyons. We were on foot, and we ended up running along the ledge of a canyon. It's a very tricky thing when you look for locations there, especially if you're flying — there are downdrafts, and your little plane can get caught in one of those drafts. When we made the picture, the whole company (eighty people) stayed at the Death Valley Ranch, in bungalows.

Were you happy with the special effects?
 [Lawrence] Butler was terrific; he did the miniatures on his own ranch in Fallbrook. He was a disciple of William Cameron Menzies, who was a wizard at this stuff.

You talked about doing a sequel around that same time, Robinson Crusoe in the Invisible Galaxy.
 Well, I might have *talked* about it, but I don't think we really ever had any plans to do a sequel. Maybe if *Robinson Crusoe on Mars* had been a tremendous box office success, we would have thought about a sequel.

When Vic Lundin ("Friday") was interviewed by Starlog, *he called you a "very strange and distant man" who lost interest midway through* Robinson Crusoe on Mars *and wrote the picture off.*

Here's a guy I picked up off the street, 'cause I wanted a face that was unknown. I gave him his first chance, and he ought to be happy. He was unheard of before and *after* that. Put no faith in what he has to say. I dispute it on every possible grounds.

You worked with Vincent Price again in a Western, More Dead Than Alive *[1969].*

I had a real good rapport with the man, even though there were many years between my first and second picture with him. I used to enjoy his *cooking,* even! There's a scene in *More Dead Than Alive* where [actor] Paul Hampton kills Price, and the special effects guys put wires on Price, under his clothes, to jerk him backward, as if the forty-five was so close to him, it sent him hurtling through the air. And I remember [*laughs*], Price asked me, "Isn't it kind of dangerous?" And I said, "No—if it was, we wouldn't do it." We were sort-of friends, he was a delightful personality. The man was *brilliant,* his knowledge of paintings and art and all.

How did you start making movies in the Philippines?

I had a friend, George Montgomery, who broke the ice making a few independent pictures there. George told me about a cameraman working down there who was as great as any cameraman that we have here; and he also said, "As for technicians, you can take four or five key people. The rest of the people you can hire there, and they'll be just as satisfactory as anybody you could get in Hollywood." I found the story *Ambush Bay* which was *supposed* to be laid in the Philippines, so I went over, looked over the place, and decided to do it there. Then after *Ambush Bay* I made *Impasse* [1970] with Burt Reynolds, then *Daughters of Satan* and *Superbeast.*

How did Daughters of Satan *come about?*

Right then, about seventy-one or seventy-two, some of the cheap little horror pictures were doing terrific business. Arthur Krim called me one day and said, "Listen, you're an expert on makin' cheap pictures. Give me a horror double-feature." So we thought up *Superbeast* and *Daughters of Satan* and I think we made the combination for $550,000, the *two* pictures.

And you were on hand throughout?

Oh, yeah. When I went there, I was really my own unit manager *besides* producer, because I knew the Philippines so well and I knew how to work

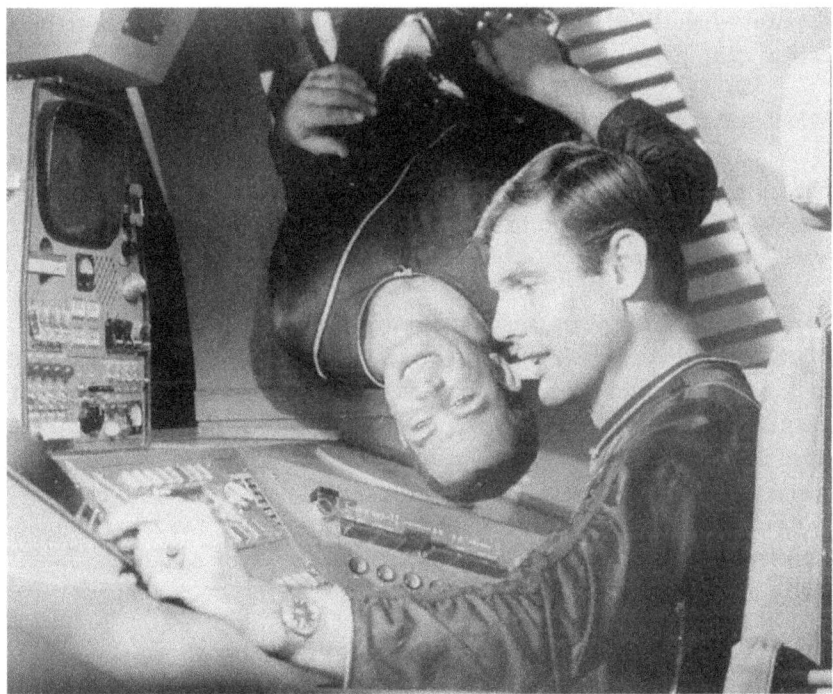

In Schenck's opinion, casting unknowns was the only way to make *Robinson Crusoe on Mars* believable. (Pictured: Paul Mantee and Adam West.)

with these guys. *Daughters of Satan* was with Tom Selleck and, let me tell you, he wasn't the ladies' man that he is today! He was *scared* of the girls [*laughs*]! He was very modest, a very nice kid. And [director] Holly Morse was a good man. I was happy with *Daughters of Satan*, I thought it was an unusual picture. We didn't hoke it up, which you *could* have done with witchcraft; I thought John Higgins wrote a good story.

And Superbeast?

I remember at the beginning I had a director on it [Allen Miner] who I had to throw off, and I put in my son George to finish the direction. (I think he did a good job.) But the guy who was originally directing didn't want to work Saturdays. Well, on location, you *gotta* work Saturdays or you lose a whole day — you pay the crew and all. But he was a rich kid and he thought he didn't *have* to do it, so I let him out, that's all. We shot that in the jungle, about forty miles south of Manila. Those people in the Philippines are the greatest. As a matter of fact, Bob Aldrich wanted to do a picture there and I spent two weeks with him, tipping him off to people and all. And when the picture [*Too Late the Hero*, 1970] was over, he sent me a case of champagne, he said, "Boy, you saved me."

Which was better, Superbeast *or* Daughters of Satan?

Oh, *Daughters*. On *Superbeast*, we didn't have the kind of artists you need when you're making a story about a man transforming into an animal; we tried to bite off more than we could chew. What the story really was, was *Most Dangerous Game*.

Why did you finally retire from the picture business?

I wasn't that old [at the time], I was sixty-seven years old, but they were looking for younger people. Also, I didn't want to go back to working for a studio on a salary basis (I was an independent too long), but when you want to make new deals, you always have to cross-collateralize your other pictures. Well, with interest up to fourteen and fifteen percent in the seventies, I'd be risking the profits I was already making if I cross-collateralized *those* pictures to get new money. It was not to my advantage, financially. So I gave up the idea, that's all.

What else would you like people to know about your overall career?

[*Laughs.*] Well, I think I was as *prolific* as any independent producer, looking back on all the pictures that I made or supervised or was executive producer on. From a point of view of *prestige*, I don't think I had *that* kind of a reputation; my thing was *quantity*, I wanted to keep busy. There was one year when I made *fifteen* pictures and delivered 'em to United Artists, which for an independent was unheard of. And a lot of the things I *did*, I did myself; I didn't go out and buy a lot of stories or plays or books, most of my pictures came out of my fertile imagination. (Howard Koch *still* calls me, *still* asks for stories—"You thought 'em all up back in the fifties, the sixties, why can't you do it now?" I told him, "I don't know—maybe the facility dried up or something!") So I'm satisfied, looking back. I'm not an egotist by nature so I can't brag about it, but I made a number of pictures that I can look back on with great pride.

The name of the game was to come up with a good marketing approach and try to have the elements that we market within the film. Promise something and try to deliver it. That was what we tried to do, within our limitations of available money.

—Sam Sherman

IT'S THE SORT OF Cinderella story that ought to warm the hearts of B movie maniacs: A film fan from his early youth, New York–born Sam Sherman has parlayed his love *for* and knowledge *of* motion pictures into a lifelong career, beginning as a contributor to Warren Publications (*Famous Monsters of Filmland, Wildest Westerns*) and then moving into the more adventurous areas of film distribution and production. Admittedly, the drive-in style movies made by his Independent-International Pictures Corp. (Based in East Brunswick, New Jersey) aren't exactly the kind that are talked about much on Oscar night. But — importantly for Sherman — they've been consistently popular and profitable, and — importantly for us — they've furnished some memorable last (or nearly last) looks at fan favorites like Lon Chaney, J. Carrol Naish, Robert Livingston, Kent Taylor, Reed Hadley, Donald Barry, the Ritz Brothers and other movie greats of yore. The friendly and eminently knowledgeable Sherman shoots from the hip (automatically pausing to spell out all tricky proper names — an interviewer's dream!) as he talks about the only film company that one part hard-nosed aggressiveness, one part wistful Hollywood nostalgia and one part gore-oriented marketing ever combined to build.

How early in your life did you know that you wanted to become part of the motion picture industry?

Like a lot of young people, I was a hobbyist in still photography and in movies. I used to make my own little eight millimeter movies; collect eight millimeters films; watch things on early television; record snippets of old background music off television; etc., etc., etc. I liked all that sort of thing, and I wanted to get into the film industry. At the time, circa 1956, there were three colleges that offered major concentrations in film techniques: UCLA, USC and the City College of New York. Going to California would obviously be very expensive; also, I graduated high school at the age of sixteen, an immature sixteen. It was just not in the cards that I was going to be set loose on my own at sixteen and go out to the West Coast. Of course, I always felt that had that happened, I probably would have ended up in one of the big studios, because they always "shopped" those schools.

So you ended up attending CCNY.

I read about the City College Film Institute in an issue of *Popular Photography*, and it motivated me to want to try to go there. Basically, the City College Film Institute was created during the Second World War to make training documentaries for the Office of War Information; they were tied

Previous page: Samuel M. Sherman, still behind the camera in 1992.

in with government and documentary and more artistic films, and I was thrust into this kind of setting as a fan of B pictures — horror pictures, serials, Westerns, things like that.

Not the kind of budding filmmaker they expected.

Right. One semester I had to make a short film and, unable to get an idea that would work, I kept delaying it. I got down to the last week or two of the term, and the professor teaching the course — who was also the head of the Film Institute — threatened to fail me if I didn't make a film. Most of the other students were making films that went with the Film Institute: an old man in a park feeding pigeons, a ballerina dancing in a very fancy atrium while a man does a clay sculpture of her; that kind of thing. The professor said to me, "Why don't you make a movie about a vampire that raids a blood bank?" Now, the reason he said this to me was because I was part of the Student Government Cultural Agency that showed rented films: Harold Lloyd in *Grandma's Boy* [1922], *East of Eden* [1955], *Love Me or Leave Me* [1955], etc. Well, when we ran out of money, I went ahead and brought in films that I owned, or that I had borrowed from friends. I ended up running *The Mask of Fu Manchu* with Boris Karloff, *Flash Gordon* serials, whatever. It's hard to think that in those years people were so far removed from this, but the school came out against me when I ran things like that. The school paper wrote me up and it was like I was really trashing the school's reputation, like I was showing hard-core pornography [*laughs*]! But we're talking about another era.

So you were branded "the horror man."

And since that had happened, I decided to go ahead and challenge the professor, and make a film that was like the vampire film he had suggested. I came up with an idea to do something called *The Weird Stranger*, and I got my friend Norman Michaels [later the co-author of *The Films of Sherlock Holmes*] to star in this. He was a great fan of Lon Chaney, Sr.'s, and fancied himself a makeup artist, and he played a character in black, a Phantom of the Opera type. This was my introduction to quickie moviemaking: I shot this less-than-one-reel, sixteen millimeter film in one day. Everybody else was shooting for months and months, went on and on; what *I* did was make a very detailed script/shot breakdown. We started in a basement on 47th Street near 9th Avenue in Manhattan; we shot up at Biograph Studios in the Bronx; and we ended up at my house in the Bronx and my screening room in the basement, where we shot the end of it! We cut it together rather quickly; I dubbed lip-synched dialogue in; I had snippets from old background scores from thirties and forties horror films; you can guess what the thing was like. In short, I ended up with the most advanced film that was made that term, but done very, very quickly. The professor didn't like the idea that I was sort of putting him down, my having made the film as a reaction to his comment, but he had to give me an "A" because it was technically head and shoulders above anything else that was done that term.

Years later, I went back to the Film Institute when they went into a retrospective of past years; they had made much more sophisticated things after I was there. Then they made an announcement: "And now we're going to show our favorite film in the history of the whole City College Film Institute." And up comes *The Weird Stranger*—and no one even knew I was there [*laughs*]!

You later wound up working for Warren Publications on a variety of their magazines.

When the first issue of *Famous Monsters of Filmland* came out, I was impressed by it and I wrote to Jim Warren out of the blue. Norman Michaels had a big collection of stills and other material, so Norman and I started out doing some research and supplying stills to *FM*. That very rapidly got me involved in working for *Favorite Westerns of Filmland*, and from doing research, I ended up doing articles for *Famous Monsters, Favorite Westerns* and quickly became the editor of *Favorite Westerns*, which became *Wildest Westerns*. Along with doing that, I brought in my friend Bob Price, who also was a historian/collector/researcher. He and I edited *Wildest Westerns*, and when that got to the point where we felt that it was not going to be continued by Jim Warren, we came up with an idea to do a catch-all magazine [*Screen Thrills Illustrated*] that covered the things that the other magazines didn't: all the comic book characters that had been adapted into serials or films, the Bowery Boys, Laurel and Hardy, the Marx Brothers, right down the line. This was before Andy Warhol, before the nostalgia explosion. We invented the first such thing of its type, a nostalgia publication that was nationally sold. And we found that, by writing about things that *we* found interesting, it became a rallying point for fans who liked similar things. We quickly rose from nothing to having more subscriptions than *Famous Monsters*. But it just was premature, ahead of its era. I'm pleased that there are people I've met through the years who enjoyed it.

Warren gets bad press thanks to the continuing efforts of Forry Ackerman. What's your lowdown on Warren?

Jim Warren was terrific because he let us do what we wanted. He let us loose with printer's ink and publisher's cost, let us do anything crazy we wanted to do. Jim was everything I wasn't when I met him: worldly, a businessman, clever, a good promoter. He always said to me, "I am your mentor!" [*laughs*] — really! And I guess I learned from Jim Warren about entrepreneurialism and having to live by your wits and run a company without financing. I can't speak to any problems that anyone *else* has had with him; I *can* tell you that Jim is very mysterious and difficult to figure out. But I respect him; He's very brilliant, a great innovator in the fields he's been in, and probably one of the most clever people I've known in my life. I'm proud to say that I still have him as a friend after all these years.

I came up with the idea of having the Screen Thrills Film Festival at the New Yorker Theater and I pitched this to [theater head] Dan Talbot. I came to Dan with the idea of putting on a festival of old serials; people hadn't seen them in theaters for umpteen years, except maybe at some scratch-house in god-knows-where. I told Dan, "*Screen Thrills Illustrated* is willing to co-finance this with you," and he challenged me: "It's a great idea and I'd like to do it with you, but nobody has these prints." A dumb kid and an enthusiast rather than a businessman, I told him who the distributors were. We talked and talked, and I put a lot of effort into this. This was one of my early lessons in what it's like to get a good screwing and not enjoy it: Dan — certainly a man of very low morality — then went out on his own and he followed up on every lead I gave him. He started out by getting *Flash Gordon* and *Buck Rogers* features, put them on one show, and it went through the roof. Nobody had ever done that in an art theater before, and it absolutely crocked them. I think he must have done over $10,000 on the weekend alone, it was unbelievable — I went there and it was packed. Then he went and, based on what I wanted to do (which was run a whole serial at once), he got the *Batman* serial from Columbia and ran it in one sitting.

Through the roof again.

You betcha. And this was all my idea. Now let me tell you where this went: The Playboy Theater in Chicago found out about this through Columbia, and they went ahead and put on the *Batman* serial. The same thing, tremendous business. Columbia continued to do this in other markets. Meanwhile, this all came to the attention of [producer] Bill Dozier at Fox, and they said, "We'll revive *Batman* as a television series." Now, I'm not saying that without Sam Sherman, this wouldn't have happened, 'cause I didn't invent Batman, but that *is* the chain of events. So the idea of having people take your ideas and run with them has always bothered me.

Another such thing happened at Republic Pictures; I had a very good relationship with Dave Bloom, who was the head of Republic Pictures' television division. I showed him *Screen Thrills*, showed him the articles about the Republic serials — he didn't even have a list of the serials Republic had made, he had no idea! Well, I liked the guy; unlike Dan Talbot, who was just another user, I liked Dave Bloom. I gave him a list and I had an idea for him: Remarket the old serials. I got them to print up a lot of serials, and they remarketed them to television. And I also suggested, why not make feature versions out of them and put *them* on television? (A lot of stations wouldn't play serials; [the chapters] were an awkward length, fifteen minutes or less. Where are you gonna put that?) I explained the whole idea to him and I even gave him a quote as to what it was going to cost him to have me cut these serials. I gave them the idea and they did it themselves.

The Century 66 package of 100-minute serials, you're talking about.
Believe me, I'm not the only one who liked Republic serials, but I was the one who started what these people did. I *was* responsible directly for those *Batman* prints creating that Batman trend, and then that other situation where Republic made these Century 66 features, twenty-four or twenty-six of 'em. And these were not the only things that happened. I went through a few of these incidents where I came up with good ideas, other people ran with them, and I got nothing out of it. At that point I decided I couldn't ally myself with other companies, I had to have my own company so that I could work autonomously. If I was successful, I would benefit; if I failed, at least I tried. That was my idea.

So what were your first steps in getting your company going?
I had a friend named Ed Finney, who was the discoverer of Tex Ritter; Ed made thirty-two Westerns with Tex, making him one of the top Western stars. Ed was a producer, but also a lover and collector of old movies. Along the line, I said to him. "Whatever happened to Denver Dixon?" who made the 1928 silent Western *The Old Oregon Trail*, which is like a mini–*Covered Wagon*—a really nice independent film, shot in Oregon. Ed said, "He and his son just made a new film." So through Ed Finney, I met Denver Dixon, whose real name was Victor Adamson. He had worked in the early silent movies, on the East Coast, on the West Coast, began to produce his own films, at one time owned studios — he was a very successful small independent. His son was Al Adamson. [In 1995, police found the murdered body of 66-year-old Al Adamson beneath his Indio, California, home.]

And you became friendly with Dixon?
Not only that, but I helped him with some foreign distribution on some of his product; that was how I got involved with distribution. And Al wanted to start to direct. I saw in this situation a nucleus that maybe could be pulled together, our disparate elements moved together and a company

formed. I should point out that, in that era, New York was invaluable because all of the distribution was done out of here; the major circuits were here, the major networks were here, the major companies all did their distribution out of New York, and having someone in New York was important. I decided that the best way to learn about distribution was by thrusting myself into it. So I bought the original negative to the 1934 Majestic picture *The Scarlet Letter*.

In 1964, I was in the Army and I was in an accident, and Denver Dixon, who was then rather old, drove cross-country to see me in the hospital. He said to me, "We've got to get you out of here, you've got to become a distributor." There's this moment in your life where all of a sudden the light flashes through the clouds, everything clears up, you look ahead and you see that well-defined path. For me, that moment came when Denver Dixon said to me, "The major studios are not interested in what *you* want to do and what my *son* wants to do. If you want to be in this business, you better get your own distribution."

And he taught you to be a distributor?

While I was still in the Army, we started releasing *The Scarlet Letter* throughout the South theatrically — a 1934 picture, in 1964 [*laughs*]! I had bought *The Scarlet Letter* from Irwin Pizor; Irwin's dad William Pizor was one of the real pioneers in the industry, one of the greats. Irwin was always interested in what I was doing, and we became friendly. He and his partner Dan Q. Kennis had a company at that time called Teledynamics Corp. Irwin was affluence personified: tailored to the nines, nice mustache, gold watch chain. He was the epitome of a film mogul on a high level, and a very educated man in addition. He's just a beautiful person and I was bowled over by getting to know him.

Another fellow he had working with him had a small desk in the corner of Irwin's big, elegant office. He was a nice informal guy and he loved the enthusiasm I had for *The Scarlet Letter*. He said, "By the way, my wife's uncle Robert Vignola was the director of *The Scarlet Letter*!" This man's name was Kane W. Lynn, and Kane Lynn had been a much-decorated World War II hero in the Philippines. Kane liked movies, had formed a partnership with [Philippine-based producer/director] Eddie Romero and made several pictures, including *Lost Battalion* [1961]; a very nice horror picture called *Terror Is a Man*; and a picture called *The Scavengers* [1959], also known as *City of Sin*, with Vince Edwards. Kane formed a partnership with Irwin Pizor and Eddie Romero (Eddie in the Philippines, Kane and Irwin in New York) called Hemisphere Pictures, and they had just made a picture called *The Raiders of Leyte Gulf* [1963]. It was a very good film, shot in

English, with a mostly Philippine cast. (They were attempting to distribute this and they were getting $35 playdates in the South when Denver Dixon was getting $100!)

But what Hemisphere was coming up with was basically a lot of Filipino war movies.

Yes. In fact, Kane went to the Philippines and produced two Jock Mahoney pictures back to back, *The Walls of Hell* [1964] and *Amok*. *Amok* was made for Bob Lippert at 20th Century–Fox and released as *Moro Witch Doctor* [1965]. I've never seen it but it's not supposed to be good. Fox was upset because, of the two pictures, they didn't get the better one, which was *Walls of Hell*. *Walls of Hell* was sensational, a great movie. I'm not saying good, I'm saying *great*. It has not survived basically because it's in black and white. I saw the first screening—the Department of the Navy was there, important people, and they applauded. It played the RKO circuit in New York as the co-feature with *Darling* [1965] from Embassy. Believe me, it was a good movie.

Was it you who steered Hemisphere in the direction of horror films?

Who else [*laughs*]? I told these fellows, "You're really going in the wrong direction with these war films." They said, "We make 'em for x-amount of dollars, we sell the foreigh, we make a tremendous profit. Anything we get in the U.S. is gravy." I said, "Why don't you work it backwards? Make something that makes a profit in the United States and the foreign'll be gravy, 'cause you're here." Based on *Famous Monsters* and explaining it to them and talking to them about AIP, I convinced them to go into horror pictures. They did this by taking *Terror Is a Man* and retitling it *Blood Creature*, and putting with it *Walls of Hell*. Where they used to make $35 flat rental on the war pictures, with *Blood Creature* and *Walls of Hell* they were ending up with two, three, four thousand dollars a booking in some situations. I had an opportunity to participate in this and observe it as it happened. I got to the point where I did the campaigns for them: I did the writing of pressbooks, the designing of ads, I produced the trailers and the radio and television spots. That's where I learned to do all that type of thing, learning on the job. It was a test lab for me, but also I was getting some money out of it.

Where's Al Adamson while all this is going on?

At this time, Al was beginning to get involved with wanting to make pictures. He came into New York and I tried to tie Al in with Hemisphere, because I was already involved with them. It didn't take, like a vaccination that doesn't take; everybody got along, everybody liked one another, but Kane was really running the show and Kane was devoted to the Philippine situation. He felt he could do more in the Philippines for less than Al could do in Hollywood. That was basically it, and he was not wrong about that because the Philippine pictures had unbelievable production value, they looked very expensive. The Philippines had a cottage film industry going back to the silent era, but they were strictly shot in the local language called Tagalog and they were never dubbed, never seen out of their market. What Kane did led to the emergence of Cirio Santiago, led to Roger Corman going over there, New World and Dimension Pictures being involved, and *all* those Philippine pictures like *The Big Doll House* [1971] — *you* know all of them. It all was a result of Kane and Eddie Romero. Kane Lynn was the first person to make Philippine productions worldwide product.

In 1968, Kane said to me a famous line that everybody now quotes back to me: "Sherman, we're going to send you to Manila!" [*Laughs.*] Since I had a technical background in film production and other areas, he wanted me there to polish up some of these productions. In the sixties, while the pictures made in the Philippines had good production value, they still were recording sound on optical track, believe it or not — I was stunned! I'll never forget the first time we screened *Brides of Blood*, which was originally called *Brides of Blood Island*. It was in New York and Eddie Romero was at the screening, and there was a scene in which Kent Taylor and John Ashley were out on this beach. I heard some noise on the track and I said, "What does that mean, Eddie?" He said, "That's a whistle." I said, "Can't that be *eliminated*?" and he said, "No. The Philippines is a noisy place to make movies." And it was really true, there *were* a lot of problems. Kane had me fix some of these pictures up here — I redid the music, changed the effects, remixing the whole thing, changing the titles. I did a lot of post-production patch-up work on these films — *Brides of Blood*, *Mad Doctor of Blood Island*, pictures like that. And then it got to the point where Kane wanted me to be the head of production for Hemisphere in the Philippines.

Well, I must say it didn't appeal to me, there was nothing exotic-sounding about it. I felt it was a third-world, depressed area with bad hygiene. People carry sidearms and nightsticks, they get annoyed and all of a sudden you're dead — it just didn't seem like I wanted to go there [*laughs*]! So I said, "Kane, I think I want to get involved with Al and stay here, go to Hollywood. I don't wanna go to the Philippines." Al and I had been trying to start our own distribution company for many years, unsuccessfully. Along the way, I had made a lot of friends, and one of these friends was Dan Kennis, who by then had left Teledynamics.

And that's when Kennis got involved with you and Adamson.

Right. Danny and Al and I formed Independent-International Pictures Corp. towards the end of 1968. Al was staying in a small room at the Edison Hotel, Broadway and 46th Street — not exactly glamorous [*laughs*] — working on things that *we* were trying to do. He had a film that we couldn't market for various reasons and I came up with a list of titles out of my head. That list of titles included *Satan's Sadists*, which I liked. The next morning, Al said, "I've written a story for a movie to be called *Satan's Sadists*." My first attitude was, "Hey, why'd you take my title that I wanted to use for that other picture?" And [*laughs*], I'll never forget what Al said: "Don't worry about that, I know you, you'll think of another title! I need this *now*!" With that, he was able to call the gang in his picture the Satans — it all started with that title! Al read his story to everybody and everybody liked it, and Al went back to Hollywood with the idea it was going to be made.

I was concerned that the picture would be devoid of names because it was such a violent story. We had seen a film that Ray Dorn had made called *Free Grass* [1969] — as a matter of fact, *Free Grass* had been given to *me* to try to sell. The stars of the picture were Richard Beymer, Russ Tamblyn and Lana Wood. Eventually, Ray Dorn himself released the film. He was not a distributor, but he owned Hollywood Stages at 6650 Santa Monica Boulevard in Los Angeles where Al had his office.

Lots of schlocky films were made there, including Boris Karloff's last four pictures.

Hollywood Stages was an interesting little place. It was the home of *The Incredible Two-Headed Transplant* and *Dracula vs. Frankenstein*, *Brain of Blood* and *Horror of the Blood Monsters*, all these crazy pictures — this was the Poverty Row of the sixties and the early seventies, it really was. But it was a nice atmosphere because you didn't feel a sense of competition with the other people; everybody helped each other, we all borrowed from one another. We'd have actors and production people who'd all hang out in different offices. It was really a very nice place and we met a lot of nice people there. I don't know if Al would feel as nostalgic as I do, because it was just four walls, his office there, but I enjoyed it when I used to come out. And Ray Dorn was an exceptionally nice person — he would give you the shirt off his back. If he felt you needed help, he'd give you money, he'd give you whatever you wanted. Just a nice person, really first-rate.

Anyway, we had this picture *Free Grass* that we were trying to sell back here and we just couldn't *give* it away, *nobody* wanted it. It was neither fish nor fowl — it wasn't a motorcycle film, it wasn't a youth rebellion film, it just didn't make any sense. It was well-made — directed by Bill Brame, a good director — but it just did not lend itself to marketing. (The only release I know of that *Free Grass* got was at a multiple in the Michigan area, and I remember somewhere there was a campaign, "The stars of *West Side Story* together again — Beymer, Tamblyn, Wood!" It was *Lana* Wood [Natalie's sister], which made that very funny!) But we knew through seeing it that Russ Tamblyn was now working in independent pictures, which he had never done before with the exception of a picture or two he made for AIP in Japan. Tamblyn was a big star and had a lot of respect. So through Ray Dorn and that picture, Al got Russ Tamblyn, who wore the same outfit (or at least the same hat) he had worn in *Free Grass*.

Were you out there on the Coast when Satan's Sadists *[1969] was made?*
   No, I was not, but I gathered (because there were a lot of girls on the picture) that there were people chasing them, and the resultant activities going on [*laughs*]! Al hired a cameraman who'd never shot a feature, who'd been an assistant and done documentaries — name of Gary Graver — who's had terrific success since then. He's directed, he's produced, he's a really nice guy. Gary started on *Satan's Sadists*. And Greydon Clark was an assistant to Al on that picture, helped him with everything; he learned a lot about production on that film and played a very nice role [Acid]. Greydon Clark, too, has since gone on to make a lot of films, and he met his wife on that picture [leading lady Jackie Taylor]; her total involvement in show business at that time was that she was Chuck Connors' secretary [*laughs*]! And Al met [his actress-wife] Regina Carrol when he went out to have lunch at a coffee shop down the block from Hollywood Stages, a shop that was owned by Regina's father Barney. Regina was a dancer who'd had a specialty act in Las Vegas; she had worked in some films, but she was basically in between Vegas gigs and she came back to help her father out, waiting on tables. Al ordered something and she came over and spilled coffee on him [*laughs*], and that's how the relationship began! (And there's been a lot of coffee spilled *since* then!) They became friendly and he felt that she could play that part, and the part was named for her — her name is Regina, she played the part of Gina in the film.

What was Russ Tamblyn like?
   He was just looking to work. Al gave him a certain amount of free rein, to work on and create his own character, to improvise in some spots. I think Russ added a lot to the quirky nature of the film. That great closeup — "Yeah, I guess I am a rotten bastard" — I used in the trailer.

I'm gonna tell you something: When you set a schedule and you shoot the film, and everything works out and there are no problems (you don't have to go back and have major retakes or changes), those pictures always tend to be successful, in my opinion. And *Satan's Sadists* was one of those things where everything worked out. We screened *Satan's Sadists* here and it was very good; for the type that we were trying to do, it really worked out well. Mike Curb, who was very popular in the music business (later in politics) — his organization agreed to score the movie, do a soundtrack album, and he had a composer by the name of Harley Hatcher come up with a really great score and nice songs. We polished this all off with nice animated titles by my friend Bob LeBar. We all liked *Satan's Sadists* and it was decided that we would consider making a deal with AIP and Sam Arkoff. But *my* great scheme was to start a distribution company; I said, "We could go to AIP with it and they would most likely do a better job than we would do. But if *we* release it, it's a great leader to start a company off with. It would be better that we distribute that picture than give it to somebody else." As it turned out, for a first release for a new company, *we* did a better job than AIP would have done, because we didn't have anything else that was important. Our whole *life* was that picture [*laughs*]!

I went to L.A. in May of sixty-nine when the first corrected print was ready at the lab, picked it up and took it with me. I put the thirty-five millimeter print in one carton — pretty heavy, with a nice piece of rope around it [*laughs*] — and I flew from L.A. to Dallas, to Kansas City, to the South, up to Cincinnati, up and down, here and there. I leapfrogged the country. Now, you've got to remember, in those years, these drive-in type pictures were booked to get as good playing time as you could in the summertime, and that time was eaten up months in advance. Everybody said to me, "You're too late, you won't get any dates." But I'm a perpetual optimist, so I said, "I think it's a good film and I think I can sell it." Well, let me tell you, *I* didn't have to sell it, the film sold itself. The film screened *incredibly* well. And I gave luncheons — the luncheons helped — and I talked to exhibitors about what the company was going to be and other films we were going to make. I came back to New York with approximately 500 playdates in the summertime, which was unprecedented, unheard of! The first world premiere of this movie was held in two cities: The initial one was Birmingham, Alabama, with the Cobb Theater, and to pizzazz it up, we had Regina Carrol fly in from Hollywood to appear with it. And I was her chaperone, because she was Al's girlfriend. I chaperoned her around from newspaper interview to radio interview to television station interview, and we were given the red-carpet treatment; she was the guest star at the Shriners' big circus. It was a terrific, terrific time, believe me, really wonderful. We also went to the Jet Drive-In in Montgomery; we drove there in a car without air-conditioning on the famous road that had the Selma-to-Montgomery march. A one hundred degree day, no air-conditioning!

Your publicity sought to somehow tie the Manson murders to the picture.
    We're talking about something that happened over twenty years ago, so I don't remember exactly now what the connection was. Manson had *been* somewhere where this was shot or they had *known* him, or Manson had worked on the engine of a car — there *was* some real connection. I think I remember being on the phone with Regina and she said, "God, they arrested this guy Manson. He was working on our car when we were shooting!" — something like that, some weird connection that triggered this thing. I figured, "Let's milk this picture as much as we can," and I came up with a loose tie-in with this. If you want to call that tasteless, go ahead — talk about going to extremes! — but in those years I didn't care, I was very aggressive with this sort of thing. Today I wouldn't do it, but I came up with something on the heels of that horrible tragedy that tied the movie into it.

Marketing can be everything when you're trying to make a go of it with low-budget pictures.
    The name of the game was to come up with a good marketing approach and try to have the elements that we market within the film. Now, we can't promise that it's going to be a Hammer picture, which is made for a budget of ten times what we were spending; we can't compete with those people. But we *can* put some oldtimers in it, some gimmick, some something. Promise something and try to deliver it. That was what we tried to do, within our limitations of available money.

With a tag line like "The Most Vicious and Violent Film of the Decade" on Satan's Sadists, *what was your target audience?*
    Drive-ins; people who were looking for titillation and exploitation. In Boston, *Satan's Sadists* we played in December and there was a blizzard and the roads were closed. And at one drive-in, people went out in that deep snow and came to that drive-in and watched that movie! I've never heard of anything like that. I've heard of places in the South where it was so hot that people couldn't stay in their cars at the drive-ins, but this was unprecedented.

So Satan's Sadists *was a big success for you.*
    The film was extremely successful. We then inherited other pictures

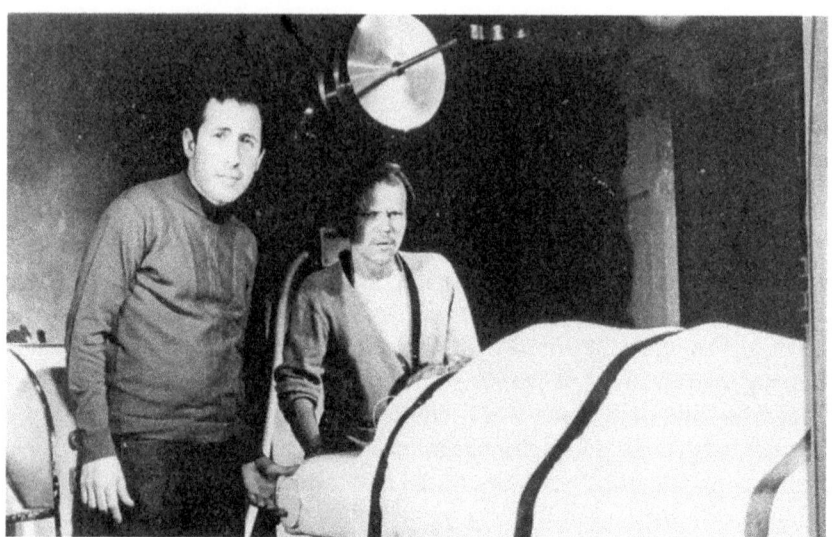

Sherman and Lee James prepare the Monster (John Bloom) for a scene in *Dracula vs. Frankenstein*.

that Al had made prior to that, and those pictures we went ahead and did things with. That includes *Five Bloody Graves* [1969], the Western — we added a little nudity in an opening tag scene to the film. Then we had what became *Blood of Ghastly Horror* [1971], *Hell's Bloody Devils* [1967], *Horror of the Blood Monsters*. These are long, complex stories and maybe we cannot get into them; I was involved with Al on some of these pictures (some on the set, some from a distance) prior to Independent-International. I just want to mention the five pictures that we started with, those four and *Satan's Sadists*.

What memories of working with John Carradine in a lot of these films?
He was just a very professional kind of guy; the only thing he really liked talking about was *Stagecoach* [1939].

What's the full story on the genesis of Dracula vs. Frankenstein?
It went through a long process and it was what I called "a difficult picture." The pictures that go easily, like *Satan's Sadists*, are very nice and you feel good about them; the pictures that are long and drawn-out and redone and changed and a pain in the neck, they're pictures that you can't warm up to very well. (At least *I* cannot.) The original production was to be called *Blood Freaks* (*The Blood Seekers* was our production title), and the original script was pretty gory. We wanted to get Paul Lukas to play the role that

J. Carrol Naish wound up taking. Lukas had the same Hungarian voice as Lugosi, and I felt he would have been very good. Lukas agreed to do it, but then reconsidered — it was so bloody, he decided not to. Also scheduled to be in the picture was Broderick Crawford in the part Jim Davis eventually took, the police detective.

Unfortunately, the picture had to go into production on a certain date because it was the only day certain actors were available, the studio was available, etc. There were elements that weren't fully ready to go but, to make a long story short, the picture *had* to be shot that way. We ran a rough cut of what had been shot up to a certain point, and it just didn't seem to have enough bite. Admittedly, Al was going to add some other things to it, but I still felt it wasn't strong enough and we needed something more exploitable. So we kept editing and trying to figure out a way to make it more exploitable, and eventually I came up with this business of adding Dracula and Frankenstein, neither of whom were in it originally. We went back and reshot a substantial portion of the film, eliminating a lot of the confusing elements, like a motorcycle gang. You have vestiges of that left in the film, but a great deal of that has been dropped. (At one time we wanted to play that up based on the success of *Satan's Sadists*, but that was really an extraneous element in a horror film.) We put these other elements in the film and it went through a prolonged series of reedits with different editors, etc., etc. I now wanted to call it *Blood of Frankenstein* but it *still* wasn't strong enough, so I came up with the idea of Dracula *vs.* Frankenstein — a fight between the vampire and the monster. We shot that on the East Coast, those last twenty minutes, which were added last. It went through three separate filmings — this was the *Heaven's Gate* of Independent-International [*laughs*]! The fact that the picture ended up finished at all is one of life's miracles, and the fact that it's had as wide a release as it's had in all media is just fantastic.

Anthony Eisley says it's the worst movie he ever did.
   My opinion is that *his* opinion stems not from being in the movie. He must have seen it on television or at a screening, and he must have really been upset that we killed him off at the end of the picture.

Which he didn't know you were going to do.
   Of course he didn't know! But there was no way we could see clear to pay him to come to the East Coast and film new scenes — when we got down to the end, *everything* was being done on pennies. And so the only thing we could do was to kill him off. And yet, as much as he may dislike that, that's one of the highlights that a lot of people *love* in the film. You've

never seen a movie where the nominal hero is just killed off like that. It's definitely unusual, it comes out of left field, and yet it *does* work.

Look, don't get me wrong; I'm one of the biggest critics of the movie. There are a lot of things wrong with it, we *know* that [*laughs*] — we had nothing but problems from the word go, disaster after disaster. Naish and Lon Chaney were very sick throughout the picture.

Was Naish really confined to a wheelchair by that time?

He was not, although legend has made that the case. Naish, as a matter of fact, did not even know how to *use* the wheelchair, and in the lab scenes we had a lot of trouble keeping him away from the side where the high-voltage things were rigged, for fear that he'd electrocute himself. He was a very spunky guy, a tough old codger. I was talking to him — I thought he'd have a sense of humor — and I said, "Well, Mr. Naish, I know this is not exactly PRC..." And he snapped, "You bet your ass it isn't!" [*Laughs.*] But all his stuff was filmed at Hollywood Stages, which is a nice big commercial studio; he had a nice place to sit; he had food when he wanted it; people were attentive to him; he was courted with probably more respect than he got from big companies; and yet he was not well and he was sort of like *grumpy*, where you couldn't kid around with him. I never felt that moment of informality with him, he was pretty much on the stiff side. But if he didn't need the money at all, maybe he shouldn't have done the picture. My opinion is that, when people are so ill that they look as bad as Naish and Chaney did, they shouldn't work. When I saw the stills of Naish, before I even saw the dailies or anything, I couldn't believe that was him, he'd changed so completely.

But you wanted Naish and Chaney for the picture regardless?

Al was the one who was taken in. Jerry Rosen, the agent who represented them, gave Al a good deal, and when Al heard Naish and Chaney, it sounded fantastic. Al made the deal, and he hadn't even seen them. Then he saw them and it was too late! Chaney couldn't talk, he had cancer of the throat; he was big and bloated from chemotherapy or from drinking or cirrhosis of the liver, some health problem. Naish had false teeth that clicked, he looked like he was dying. Should *we* be blamed for that? I feel that the wool was pulled over our eyes on that. Unfortunately, because they look so bad, they set the tone for the whole picture and there's nothing that can undo that. Yet even *with* that, there were a few places where they had their moments. And the film has some appeal to the Universal fans, having Dracula and Frankenstein in it, Chaney and Naish...

All that fifties music...
Well, *that* turned out to be by accident. My friend William Lava had written the original music for the picture, and he died while we were still editing the film. So when we reshot the picture, padding out the ending, we just couldn't repeat his music any more — it was just too much! The bulk of the music in the picture was an original score, and those Universal cues — from *Creature from the Black Lagoon*, some of the Paul Sawtell cues, music from *Kronos*— we just got from libraries to pad it out with something different. As it turned out, the fact that that music had the identity with the older films gave *Dracula vs. Frankenstein* a further little bit of *some*thing that people pick up on.

How did you get on with Chaney?
I wasn't there for that but I *can* pass on to you some of the things that happened, because I know it from Denver Dixon. He had known Lon Chaney since the thirties and had worked in pictures with him. Denver told me that Chaney was dying from cancer of the throat and that he was constantly tired, he had to lie down between takes. And Chaney kept saying, "Denver, you and I are the only two left ... they're all gone ... I wanna die now. ...There's nothing left for me, I just wanna die." He kept saying that throughout the shooting of the movie. So you got a man here who had been a heavy drinker; he's got cancer; he's very ill, *was* dying, *knew* that he was dying, *wanted* to die. Certainly not the elements that make up great acting in a movie! And yet, you'll have to admit that even in that non-speaking role, he *did* bring some pathos to the character. Originally there was a voiceover that he did, that was supposed to be like narration; you'd see him and hear his thoughts. But his voice was just so raspy and so impossible to understand, we had to drop it.

Still, there's something very pathetic and tragic about seeing Naish and Chaney in the movie; me, I don't like it, because I liked both of them.

Any anecdote about Angelo Rossitto or John Bloom?
For the part of Grazbo the dwarf, the only person I could think of was Angelo Rossitto, because I thought so much of him from the Monogram Lugosi pictures. Jerry Rosen, the agent, also had a dwarf as a client. But I said to Al, "No, I want Angelo Rossitto, there's nobody else you can use in the picture." Al said, "Where can I get in touch with him?" and I said, "I don't think he's acted in years, but he has a newsstand on Hollywood Boulevard." Al said, "How am I gonna *find* him?" I said, "Please."

Al went out on Hollywood Boulevard, walking up and down for two weeks, looking for Angelo Rossitto. No Angelo Rossitto. Finally he said to me, "I can't find him! I refuse to spend another day wandering around like an idiot on Hollywood Boulevard, looking for your man! We've got to go with Jerry Rosen's dwarf"—and at that point, I had to agree. Who's Rosen's dwarf? Angelo Rossitto [*laughs*]!

And on the other end of the spectrum, how about 7'4" John Bloom?
I'll never forget one day when John Bloom was being made up as the Frankenstein Monster, and he's moaning with his eyes closed and his hands clasped over his stomach: "I hope we're gonna get this done on time! I don't have *time* for this! I hope we're gonna be finished!" He's muttering, muttering, muttering, so finally I say, "John, what's the matter?" He says, "This is tax season. I've got to be working tomorrow on income taxes!" He was a tax accountant, and in films as a monster only because he was 7'4" [*laughs*]! Isn't that what you call "theater of the absurd"?

One other anecdote. I wanted to have the original lab equipment from the 1931 *Frankenstein* in *Dracula vs. Frankenstein*, so Forry Ackerman (who was helping us make the picture) said, "I'll take you to [their designer] Ken Strickfaden's house." And so Forry took me to see Strickfaden—a nice man. Strickfaden took us out into his workshop, it may have been in a garage or someplace—there was all kinds of wild stuff there. And then he excused himself—he said, "Wait here for a minute. I've gotta do something. I'll be right back." Where he had to go was to throw a switch, because he had me standing on a steel plate. A bolt of lightning went through the air, and stopped *right at my right toe.* You should have seen me jump a couple of feet off the ground—we knew who was in control from that point on [*laughs*]!

Ken Strickfaden was very proud to be a member of the International Brotherhood of Electrical Workers, which at the time my uncle was the head attorney for. Strickfaden said, "Oh, if I could *only* get written up in their journal." I called my uncle, I sent him the material, and they did a big, big spread on Kenneth Strickfaden. More than the money I paid him, more than anything, that was what I did for Ken Strickfaden, and he loved it.

What do you say to people who dismiss low-budgeteers like yourself and Al Adamson, and the kinds of movies you made?
When you're doing pictures like these, unless you're an independent multi-zillionaire, you're doing 'em to be able to support yourself. Which is hard to do if you're not allied with a major company and on a salary. So in the independent film, if you don't have access to a rich uncle and you've got to scrape to put the money together, you've got to control the budget carefully, control the schedule carefully, you've got to try to make as good

Behind-the-scenes on *Dracula vs. Frankenstein* with John Bloom (Frankenstein), Sherman, Zandor Vorkov (Dracula) and Al Adamson.

a picture as you can make within those limitations and you have to market it well and hopefully be successful. That's what we have done: We've come up with genre product to make a profit for the company. Sure, people can look at something and say, "Al Adamson is the world's worst director" — but it's not true! Al is very serious, a good director, very good at dealing with many situations in making films. He's very competent and he has a lot of good ideas. He's taken a lot of blame on a lot of these pictures, but *I'm* responsible, because *I* forced him into it. *He* didn't want to do these films, but I said, "Al, this is what we have to do to be successful with certain limited resources." The films *he* wanted to do, had he done them, would have been better pictures than what I wanted to do. *But*— they wouldn't have been commercial. Couldn't have been marketed. Wouldn't have had the gimmicks or the exploitation.

So I-I did what it did in order just to survive on the "low end" of the industry.

Well, we didn't have the resources of AIP or companies like that, we had to really, *really* use our wits and let necessity be the mother of invention. We succeeded at it, succeeded where a lot of others failed. Someone once said to me, "Any low-budget independent picture *has* to make a lot of money." It's not true! And many of the people — I won't name names —

who are considered cult directors of these genre movies have never made any money in the industry. I don't know how they've supported themselves, I really don't. Al took the money that he made making small pictures, invested it in real estate and other properties and he is very well-off today because he has done that.

You say his reputation as a director would be better today if he'd been allowed to do pictures nearer his heart?

Yes, his reputation would be different, *but*— no one would want to know about him. He could have gone into directing episodic television, but Al was truly the product of his own father. Universal, in the mid-twenties, wanted to buy Denver Dixon's production unit and Denver said, "No, I want to work for myself." Al has had opportunities to work on television and he's turned 'em down. He had a friend by the name of Leonard Freeman, who produced *Hawaii Five-O*; unfortunately, he died on an operating table during open heart surgery at a comparatively young age. Had Freeman lived, Al might have gone in a different direction. But Al is fiercely independent, I am in a way, too, and I guess Denver was — I think we both got that from Denver. Al didn't like working with or for people who didn't truly understand the medium. And there are a *lot* of people in this industry who get thrust into positions of power, and they truly don't know what they're talking about. And they take people like Al and drive 'em up a wall. Maybe *I* have a little more patience, maybe I can work with those types — Al can't, he just doesn't like that.

Lenny Freeman was going to do a Movie of the Week for CBS and he came to Al and said, "Al, I want you to produce a movie for me and I want you to do it in such a way that it'll be very cost-controlled," etc., etc. Al did not direct *Cry Rape* [1972] but he produced it — a top-rated movie, and it won an Emmy. Okay? And Al went on to do *Hammer* [1972] with Fred Williamson for United Artists; again, he did not direct it, it had a director who, believe me, was not as good as Al. And yet Al was able to *direct* the *director* and make a pretty good film out of it. And there are other projects that he's been involved with for major studios, which you're not aware of.

The point I'm trying to make is that Al is a consummate professional and has a lot of ability. All the sleazy things were done, generally, at my direction. He's done what he wants and he's been successful, made a lot of money, and so obviously what Al has done has been right for himself. And he has confounded his critics. [Al Adamson was murdered in 1995.]

Talk about Brain of Blood.

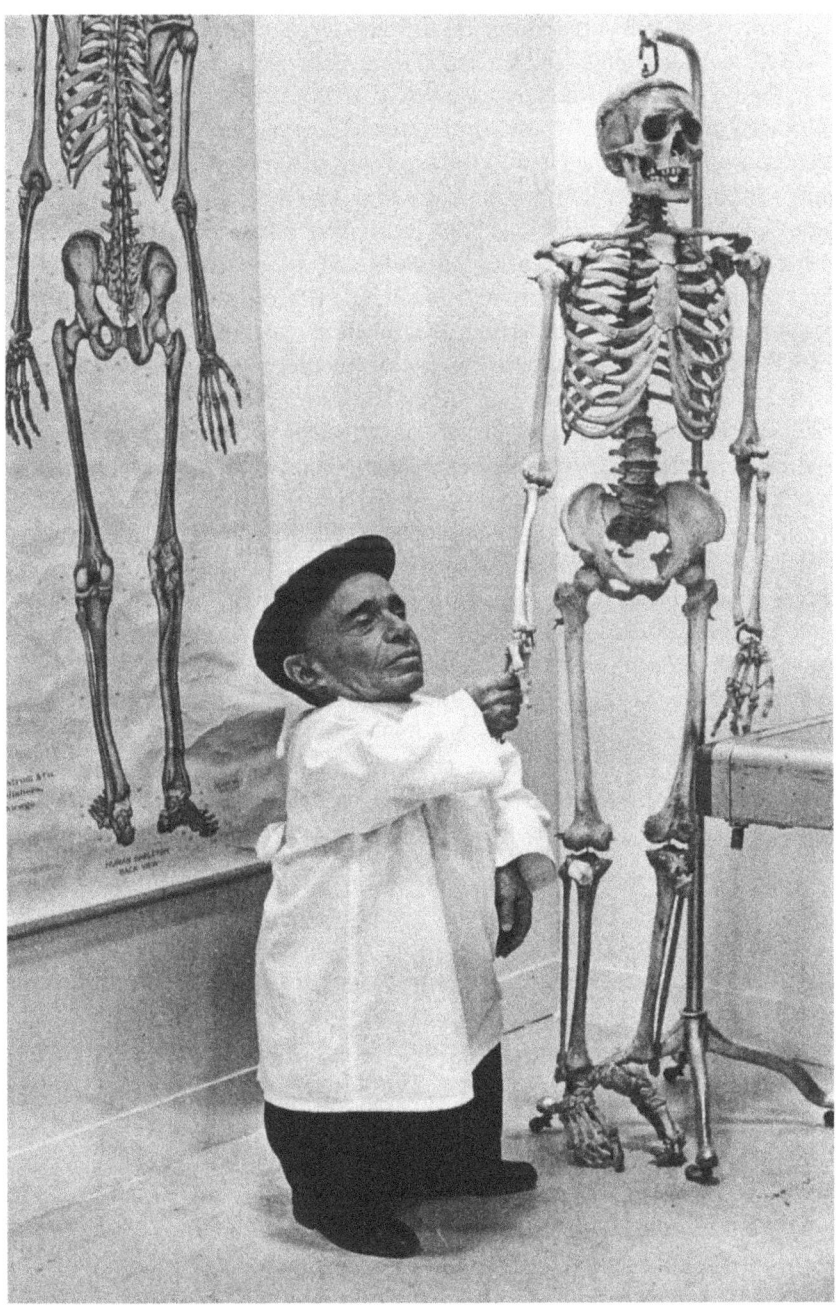

Angelo Rossitto (the one on the left) gets acquainted with one of his *Brain of Blood* co-stars.

Brain of Blood is interesting. Eddie Romero gave me a script called *The Beast of the Yellow Night* and I didn't like it. Eddie is very, very intellectual in many ways and maybe he's on a level I'm not on, but this had a Faust story with cannibalism — ooh, I just *hated* it! Anyway, he made it and gave it to Larry Woolner for New World to distribute. Hemisphere was originally supposed to get it and didn't, and this left Kane Lynn without a picture. So I said, "Why don't you have Al and myself make a picture for you?" President Nasser had died in Egypt, and that gave me an idea: A Middle Eastern ruler has died, and scientists take his brain out, put it in another body, give it plastic surgery so he looks like the original character, and then restore him to power. That was the idea of the picture, a takeoff on Nasser dying. So I went ahead and called Reed Hadley, who I'd become friendly with; he agreed to be in that picture and play the ruler. That was the last film he did. And Al got very lucky in getting Grant Williams, the Incredible Shrinking Man, who was just great in that picture. And Roger Engel, a.k.a. Zandor Vorkov — Forry Ackerman and his wife Wendy came up with that name — played Mohammed and Roger was *excellent* in that! He was reaching beyond what he could do in *Dracula vs. Frankenstein* — he was not good in that [as Dracula] — but in *Brain of Blood* he was *very* good. We knocked that thing out in seven days for next to nothing. The only thing bad about it was the egghead on John Bloom. That was the problem of having no money, and having amateurs do the makeup. But I felt everybody was happy with the film. Kane used one of his reissue pictures as the second feature and *Brain of Blood* has done very well over the years.

This business of constantly retitling the pictures, umpteen times — isn't that dirty pool, to try to pull in the same audience twice?

No, no — and I'll tell you why. Let's begin with the fact that I didn't invent that, that was historical exploitation tactics going back to the silent era. There was usually a passage of several years [between release and re-release], and in the drive-in market, the next generation was now there. It was basically a sixteen-, seventeen-, eighteen-year-old audience; let five years pass and you've got people who were eleven, twelve, thirteen, and couldn't *go* to those drive-ins, now coming to see whatever it is.

What kind of money, on the average, went into an Independent-International picture?

Under $150,000 — whereas the competitors were making these pictures for $350,000 to 500,000. Just think about that. And not necessarily making better films than ours. The *real* better films tended to be in the $700,000

Sherman (center) with cameraman Gary Graver and director Al Adamson on the set of *Horror of the Blood Monsters*—"probably the worst picture that I was ever involved with."

to 800,000 area, not down in our area.

Around this time, too, another biker film, Angels' Wild Women *[1972].*
 That one was originally called *Screaming Angels,* and it was an attempt to do a motorcycle film that had the motorcyclists be good and had a Manson-type cult that was bad. *Easy Rider* [1969] had come, and after that point there was a trend *away* from showing the motorcycle gang to be the bad group; in *Easy Rider* you got an idea of these people being outcasts from society who were good, who were misunderstood. So I felt that we should make another motorcycle picture, but bring back the Manson idea; shoot it at the Spahn Ranch where the Manson gang had been. We had some members of the Manson gang in it, people who had been hanging around; I don't know if they were killers or not [*laughs*]!

Was New World cutting into your pie with their half-alike pictures?
 New World used the same branches that we used around the country, and gave them an investment opportunity. Where the branches used to get twenty-five percent, they gave them forty percent. And all the guys were not booking my pictures; once New World came along, they said, "Well, we've got this deal with Roger Corman and Larry Woolner, we're making

forty percent," etc., etc. I was very, very depressed; what was I going to do? I remember walking uptown with Danny Kennis feeling like we were out of the whole business, like it was all over for us. We'd just started the company and along comes New World, monopolizes all the branches with their forty percent deal and we're out of the picture! And as we were walking up 8th Avenue, seeing the Gulf and Western Tower looming up large in front of us, I said, "Danny, I've got it. These people are greedy; we'll offer them forty-five percent commission, five percent more than Roger Corman's offering. And we'll charge them less money. They'll pay less and they'll get more." I went ahead and came up with this plan for *Angels' Wild Women*. The picture opened in Rochester and did $17,000 gross the first week.

Let's finish up with this motorcycle stuff. You asked me not to ask, but can you talk a little about Hell's Bloody Devils?

Hell's Bloody Devils was a picture that Al had done before the formation of I-I, originally called *The Fakers*. The producer of the picture was a writer/producer named Rex Carlton, who had made *The Brain That Wouldn't Die*. Rex borrowed money from all kinds of unsavory types to make two films, *Nightmare in Wax* and *Blood of Dracula's Castle*. And through a—let me use the right word here—a *contrivance*, somebody managed to foreclose on the two pictures. This wiped everybody out ... nobody was ever paid ... the negatives went elsewhere. Al and I worked on *Blood of Dracula's Castle* and we were both wiped out. The whole thing was highly illegal, but it happened. We first found out about it when we were at a New York lab, discussing with one of the executives there what they were doing—we were looking to buy things. He said, "Oh, we just foreclosed on two negatives." It was *Nightmare in Wax* and *Blood of Dracula's Castle*.

That night, we saw Rex Carlton and told him this—and he turned white. Because he had apparently borrowed money [to make] these films from some tough characters. That was a Thursday night. Sunday he was back in L.A. ... sat down in a bathtub ... put a gun to his head ... and killed himself. This left this picture *The Fakers*—which was a good crime/action picture—for Al to try to sort out. It was a nightmare as far as the implications of everything concerned with that film, which involved threats on our lives and everything. All kinds of unsavory people came out of the woodwork, guys Carlton was involved with. Eventually we straightened this out, but the picture had no marketing hook for the United States. So we added motorcycle scenes to it, calling it *Hell's Bloody Devils*.

Another thing I remember is that there was a real-life motorcycle gang in the film, and during production they were busted for carrying weapons by the California Highway Patrol. But according to Al they were nice people, so what can I tell you [*laughs*]?

Independent-International veered off its usual course with movies like Naughty Stewardesses *[1973] and* Blazing Stewardesses *[1975].*
  Kane Lynn had been very successful with a picture called *Swingin' Stewardesses* [circa 1972] and Hemisphere made a lot of money on it. They were going to go public, but they made so much money on that film, they said, "No, we don't need that deal now." Also, I should tell you that by this time Kane and Irwin Pizor had gone their separate ways, and Irwin joined our company. We had a good portion of Hemisphere at Independent-International [*laughs*] — Dan Kennis, Irwin Pizor and myself. Irwin felt, watching what Hemisphere was doing, "Gee, they're making a bundle on a stewardess picture," and Danny said the same thing. And they felt *we* should have a picture like that. But you couldn't buy a picture like that ready-made, we had to do it ourselves. Al didn't want to do it at all; he said, "I draw the line here. I've done all these sleazy things, but this sounds like a porno film. I want no part of it."
  I said, "Al, it won't be that way. I want to make a good film and I want to make a film that I can feel proud of even though it's a sex film" — which I personally didn't want to make myself. "Let's make this comparable with what Ross Hunter was doing at the majors. A slick film of its nature. It'll be the Ross Hunter production of stewardess films." I wrote this thing, I produced it, I was involved with it intimately, and it was a hard process, very difficult. The thing that encouraged me was my idea to have in the story an older, wealthy man that gets involved with some of these young girls. I went to a friend of mine, Bob Livingston, who was my alltime favorite from Republic Studios and a friend of mine since 1959. I thought the world of him and I knew him very, very well. I said, "Bob, I've talked to you so much about coming out of retirement to do a film. How 'bout this?" He said, "Oh, that's great. Dirty old man with young girls? That's me!" [*Laughs.*] In fact, he was a writer and he knew dialogue, and he helped me with the script and the dialogue. Everybody worked on this picture to make it a good film, and (you don't mind if I take some justifiable pride) *Naughty Stewardesses* was outstanding of its type in that era. It was a sensation, it just went through the roof, a very successful movie.

The average moviegoer, walking out of a theater after seeing an average I-I picture — did he get his money's worth?
  I felt so. People keep writing to us, so they must have liked 'em. I had somebody telling me his child was conceived at a drive-in during one of

these things [*laughs*]! *Horror of the Blood Monsters* was probably the worst picture that I was ever involved with, and yet it has more fans than anything I've ever done. Diane Keaton was at our office when she was doing her film *Heaven* [1987], looking to buy stock footage, but all she wanted to do was see *Horror of the Blood Monsters*—don't ask me where she heard of it! She was lying on the carpet in our screening room watching this thing, laughing hysterically and having the time of her life!

What's different about Independent-International in recent years?

What we were not prepared for was the closing of almost every drive-in in the United States. There were approximately 5000 and we based our prime business on making and distributing films to that market. Along with that, the approximately 125 regional sub-distributors went out of business, dropping down to about five. So most of the companies like ours that distributed to that market have all gone out of business. I detected this trend early on, but I never trusted any one area of the market, so I attempted to buy and distribute/make and distribute pictures that would go to other markets which included television, foreign, eventually home video. We've called our company "a major studio in a teacup," because we've done everything the majors have done, but on a small scale. And we've survived by appealing to the other markets. We've *made* pictures in the last 15 years—*Nurse Sherri* [1979], *Midnight* [1981], *Raiders of the Living Dead* [1986], things of that nature—but we've also been able to put television packages together, sell to cable, sell to home video, so on and so forth.

And the future?

Hopefully, we'll continue onward, attempting to do some bigger things. At the moment, the company is involved with a European base, and co-productions, and representing companies from Europe in the United States as they represent us over there. And we have potentially some better things on the horizon than we've had to this point. The end, believe me, is not yet.

None of the other directors that I worked with had the taste that James Whale had, or the command.

Gloria Stuart

IT CAN'T BE what she set out to do when she began her acting career, but Gloria Stuart, along with Fay Wray, holds the title of the movies' first "scream queen." Other leading ladies had shrieked their way through shockers in the pre-talkie era, but in silents, no one can hear you scream; Stuart's appearances in Universal's *The Old Dark House*, *The Invisible Man* (both directed by James Whale) and *Secret of the Blue Room* made her one of the first actresses to become associated with horror during the genre's early heyday. Dramatic and stage roles would have been more to her liking, but Stuart accepts her status as Universal's first First Lady of Horror staunchly, talks about the experience of working with Whale at film seminars, and recently captivated an audience of her fans at the 1993 Famous Monsters convention.

Stuart was born in Santa Monica, did some acting while in college at the University of California at Berkeley and later worked on stage in little theater productions. Universal enticed the glamorous blond actress with the assurance of "big plans," but outside of her Whale films — *The Old Dark House* (1932) with Boris Karloff, *The Invisible Man* (1933) and the dramatic *The Kiss Before the Mirror* (1933) — their promise went unkept as the studio stuck her in a long series of unmemorable program pictures. After her stint at 20th Century-Fox turned out much the same way, Stuart went back to the stage and then, in the mid-1940s, retired from acting. Since then, the wife and mother has taken up painting and has had one-woman shows in New York, Austria and Italy ("I'm a primitive"), and in the 1970s returned to acting, on television (*The Waltons*, the television movie *The Legend of Lizzie Borden*) and on the screen. Widowed since 1978 and now a great-grandmother (nine times over), she still recalls her brushes with the Universal monsters as some of the brightest moments of her movie acting career.

How did you make the move from stage to screen actress?

I was playing at the Theatre of the Golden Bough in 1930 and '31 in Carmel by the Sea. A director named Morris Ankrum came up from the Pasadena Playhouse to direct a play I was in, *Carl and Anna* by the German playwright Frank. After he went back, he wrote and asked me if I would be interested in doing Chekhov's *The Sea Gull*. The man who was the head of Pasadena Playhouse, Gilmor Brown, had a private theater called the Bank Box, and Morris wrote and said, "Would you like to do *The Sea Gull* in the Bank Box?" I said sure, and at that point I said to myself, "Pasadena is very close to Hollywood." So I called my parents and they got hold of a man who thought I should be in pictures, and *he* called the casting director at Paramount. And the man that I was playing opposite in *The Sea Gull*, Onslow Stevens, had the Universal casting director over. So opening night of *The*

Previous page: Gloria Stuart co-starred in two of Universal's greatest horror films, but she felt that the "whole studio was ... from hunger!"

Sea Gull (which Morrie directed), the two casting directors were in the audience and they *both* asked me to make tests. I didn't have an agent, and I was really not interested in film — I wanted to go to New York and go on the stage.

What were your screen tests?
I did a scene from *The Sea Gull* for both Universal and Paramount, and they both offered me contracts. It went to arbitration with the Motion Picture Producers Association, and whoever was arbitrating said, "Why don't you toss a coin?" so they did, and Universal won.

What was Universal like in the early thirties?
Of course, I had no frame of reference when I signed in 1932. If I had, I would never have signed there, I would have signed with Paramount. I had the option [of which studio to choose], but I was not advised by my agent, or by *any*body, that I *did* have the option. The money that Universal offered was almost twice as much as Paramount had offered, and Universal offered voice lessons and all that sort of thing that Paramount didn't. But Universal was then a B studio, which I didn't know. I was very … snobbish about movies. My goal was the New York stage, and I thought that it would be easier to come from Hollywood with some kind of a reputation, to work in New York, than it would be going cold. That's why I signed. Universal was very — there's a Yiddish word — *patchke*. The office buildings for the directors and producers, and the little cottages for the "stars" — not that there were very many, just Margaret Sullavan and Boris Karloff! — were *shanties*. The makeup room, the wardrobe — all very primitive, all probably put up in the twenties, or the *teens*! They were *nothing*. The publicity director, Johnny Johnson (who was a doll) had one office the size of an anteroom [*laughs*]! The whole studio was … from hunger!

And yet they offered you more money than Paramount did?
Yes, they did, and I have no idea why. And I was so innocent and so inexperienced, and very anxious to work, that the money made the difference. I didn't know about the stature of Universal as opposed to Paramount. Paramount had Chevalier and Claudette Colbert and Miriam Hopkins, it was a first-class studio, but *I* didn't know that. My agent should have given me some information about that, but she didn't. Fortunately, the first couple of years that I was at Universal, James Whale used me three times and John Ford used me, and Universal loaned me out to Warner Bros. and RKO, where I made good pictures. The pictures I made at Universal, with the exception of the James Whale films, were terrible — really

B, B, B stuff. I remember one day Junior Laemmle called me into his office, he had a great big *pronunciamento* for me: He was going to cast me in a Tarzan picture. I knew Olivia de Havilland and Bette Davis, they were beginning to make noises at Warner Bros., and I said, "No way!" That was the end of that! Ugh!!

What kinds of movies would you like to have starred in?
Bette Davis' and Olivia de Havilland's and Norma Shearer's [*laughs*]!

What was the feeling that the rest of Universal's actors had about the B-type movies?
All I know is that we all considered it *slumming*.

Do you remember how you got your part in The Old Dark House?
James Whale asked for me. My first picture was [*Street of Women*, 1932] at Warner Bros. — they ran my test and they borrowed me for that Kay Francis picture. The second picture, I think, was the John Ford picture *Air Mail* [1932] at Universal. James may have seen me in *Air Mail* — he wanted me and I went into it.

What movie directors did you work with who were better *than James Whale?*
None. He was a very talented director, he knew exactly what he wanted, he knew the camera (he had all the camera layouts on his script every morning), he knew lighting — he'd come from the enormous international success of [the play and movie] *Journey's End*. Very particular and very explicit; he had enormous taste. He really knew what he was doing. I would say that none of the other directors that I worked with had the taste that James had, *or* the command. I think John Ford worked into it later, because he certainly made some great pictures, and so did George Stevens...

But not *at the time you worked for them?*
No.

And Whale as a person? You socialized with him?
[*Laughs.*] Yes, he used to take me down to the theater, the Biltmore, and I saw Katharine Cornell in *The Green Hat* with him — I went to several plays with him. (I was not giving dinner parties in those days, that came later, so I never had him at home.) Also, Universal let me play at the Pasadena Playhouse, in *Romeo and Juliet* and *Twelfth Night* and *Peer Gynt*, and James came over to see me and we had dinner and so forth.

Stuart in the clutches of mad butler Morgan (Boris Karloff) in James Whale's black-comic masterpiece *The Old Dark House*.

What do you remember about your Old Dark House *co-stars, like Charles Laughton and Melvyn Douglas?*

Laughton was wonderful — *The Old Dark House* was his first [American] movie. I remember, in the scene when he arrived at the house, he was supposed to be out of breath and so forth, so he ran up and down the stage. I said to him, "What are you doing?" and he said, "Well, I'm supposed to be out of breath when I get here." I said, "Can't you *fake* it?" and he said, "Oh, no, that's not the way I work at all!" [*Laughs.*] Method actors! But I was very impressed with Laughton, and of course Melvyn Douglas was a beautiful actor and a beautiful man. He and I — and a few dozen others! — were co-founders of the Screen Actors Guild. He was a great liberal, and I worked for his wife [Helen Gahagan] when she was running for office. Raymond Massey was great, too — it was a beautiful cast. The only problem was, Melvyn and I were the only two Americans, the rest were all English. They quit at eleven o'clock and at four o'clock for the tea routine — and never asked us to join them. Which I always found rather ... primitive. I don't think it ever occurred to them [to invite the Americans] — it wasn't 'cause they didn't like us, because it was a beautifully integrated cast. It just didn't *occur* to them *not* to be rude!

And Karloff — did you enjoy working with him?
 Very much. He was a brilliant man — erudite, beautifully educated. He came in at three or four in the morning so they could do his makeup, which was heavy and cumbersome. So naturally you're not given to a lot of horsing around or light conversation during the day [*laughs*]. But he was a lovely man. These were all brilliant, professional actors, all friends of James' — you know, he only went first-class.

Did you get to know Jack P. Pierce, the makeup artist?
 Oh, he was a *darling*. *Very* temperamental, up to a point, and then he was a pussycat. Being made-up by Jack meant that I had to come in very early, so very early on, I said to Jack, "Are you doing any corrective things?" He said, "No — why?" I said, "Can I put my own makeup on?" In the pictures I was in, Jack was doing heavy makeup like Karloff's, so forth and so on. So he was very happy to get *rid* of me. There weren't any extra makeup men or women at Universal at that time, you either had Jack or you did it yourself. So I did it myself! I made-up myself the whole time I was at Universal. But the hair dressing and the makeup, as I remember, were in the same *shack*, and so we *did* see each other. He was darling and enormously talented.

One of the best scenes in Old Dark House *is when Eva Moore taunts you as you're changing clothes for dinner.*
 Eva Moore was Laurence Olivier's first wife's [Jill Esmond] mother. The story went that she was one of Edward VII's ... *favorites*, let's put it that way! At least, that's what I was told. She was a very accomplished character actress, and you would never have guessed that she was once a great beauty, but then, look at *anybody* old, old, old. Another famous scene is when James put me in that pale pink satin, bias-cut, Jean Harlow dress and I said, "*Why*? Nobody else changed for dinner. I don't understand." He said, "When Karloff chases you through the halls, I want you to be like a *flame*, like a *dancer*, going through, and I want that light down the dark halls." Well, you know, you didn't argue with Whale, but — it *was* pretty ridiculous. Anyway, that's what he wanted and that's what he got. I was making use of all this ... nonsense that James had whipped up!

The old woman [Elspeth Dudgeon] who plays an old man in Old Dark House *— were you aware of her true sex?*
 No. This was part of James' style, he kept it to himself. Well, maybe Ernest Thesiger and Eva Moore knew about it, maybe the *English*

Stuart and James Whale both saw through *Invisible Man* Claude Rains when he began trying to upstage the actress.

character actors did, but none of the rest of us did. It was a very delightful surprise!

Were you aware as you were shooting that there was a lot of humor in Old Dark House?

You know, I don't think so. I think I was too young and too inexperienced to know that. At that age, and making eleven films in one year, I was only involved with myself [*laughs*] — I really wasn't working on anything else! I was *sleeping* a lot, too!

Was all of Old Dark House *shot at Universal?*
Yes. The rainstorm sequence was done at night, on the back lot, with a tremendous line of hoses and wind machines. I thought *The Old Dark House* was a wonderful film.

Do you remember where you saw it for the first time?
No, I don't remember where I saw it, but I saw it. I went to all my previews — and I went to all my rushes! My whole career, I never missed rushes. I wanted to see how I was being lit, how I did the scene; several times, I asked if I could do it over, which was never granted me. But I went religiously.

Did you ever read the book Old Dark House *was based on — or* The Invisible Man?
[*Laughs.*] No!

Carl Laemmle, Jr., the head of production at Universal, announced that he had great plans for you, but pictures like Old Dark House *were the exception rather than the norm.*
He didn't have great plans for me because that studio was not making great films regularly. Once in a while they came up with an *Old Dark House* or a *Back Street* [1932] or something, but most of them were made by independent producers using Universal facilities. Junior Laemmle was very nice — I can't fault him — but Irving Thalberg he wasn't.

Did you have much to do with Carl Laemmle, Sr.?
No, no — I don't think I ever even met him.

You next appeared for Whale in a very small part, as the wife who is murdered at the beginning of The Kiss Before the Mirror.
Paul Lukas was the star of that, and he said to me one night, "I am quitting at six o'clock." I said, "What do you mean?" He said, "I am through working at six o'clock. I have had eight hours work, and that is enough for an actor." Well, it was a great idea for *me* because, you know, women, with the makeup and the hair and so forth. I said, "Do you think you're going to get away with it?" He said, "I will get away with it. It is time for actors to only work [a certain number of] hours a day." These were the days of

fourteen-, sixteen-, eighteen-hour days for actors! So he quit that night at six o'clock and everybody went into shock and the front office got involved and somebody came over to the set...! (Whale was not crazy about it, either.) I thought, "Gee, that's a wonderful idea. If *he* can do it, *I* can do it!"

Two or three nights later, after thinking about it very carefully, I said to James, "I'd like to go home at six o'clock." He looked at me and he said, "*You, too?*" *Et tu, Brute?* He said, "Gloria, don't try it. We're on a very tight schedule" and so forth. I said, "But Paul is *right*," and he said, "Well ... don't try it." *So-o-o* ... I didn't try it. But, anyway, eventually the Screen Actors Guild was formed, and Paul was one of the movers and so was Melvyn and so was I. That's what I remember about *Kiss Before the Mirror*.

How much were you getting paid by Universal?

I think I started at $125 a week. (Paramount had offered me $75.) After six months or a year, it went to $250 and then [over a period of years] $500, then $750, then $900. I think $1200 was the top. I started at Fox at $750 and went to $1000, then $1500. (That was a *lot* of money in those days!)

How did you enjoy working with Claude Rains in The Invisible Man*?*

Not at *all*. He was *molto difficile*, he was an an "actor's actor" and he didn't really *give*. One day he [tried to steal a scene] and I said to James, "James, look what he's doing." And James said, "Now, Claude — don't get *naughty*." [*Laughs.*] James said, "We can take it over and over and *over*, because we'd like half of Gloria!" But that's the kind of actor he was.

And as a person, between takes?

We were not social. This was an enormously tough role for him. My only scenes with him were when he was in the full costume of the Invisible Man, and it was very difficult for him. So [between takes] he was either resting or studying or whatever, I don't know, but there was no socializing.

There was a lot of high-spirited acting by some of the actors in Invisible Man. *What was the atmosphere on the set during the time you worked on it?*

On James' sets, there was no horseplay or fussing around. On John Ford's sets, there were always a bunch of Irishmen — you know [*laughs*], Cagney, O'Brien, McHugh and so forth — and there were a lot of fun and games. But on James' sets, no.

Was Whale's homosexuality an open secret?

Plying Lionel Atwill with liquor won't get him to disclose the *Secret of the Blue Room*. (Pictured: Atwill, Stuart, Paul Lukas.)

Well, I was not aware or conscious of it, or even gave it a thought. It may have been an open secret, but I didn't know about it; he took me to the theater quite often and he was a friend. I don't know — I must have been very innocent, or inobservant, or whatever you want to call it, but as far as I was concerned, he was just a dear man. I did a seminar at Filmex on James Whale and someone said to me, "How did it feel, Miss Stuart, making *classics*?" and [*laughs*] I said, "We didn't know we were making classics, we just were hoping we were making a good movie." But *all* of James' films are classics.

You were also in a horror mystery called Secret of the Blue Room, *with Lionel Atwill.*

You know what Universal used to do? They had some kind of tie-up with Ufa, the great German company, and Ufa would send over a German film and Universal would use all the exteriors and long shots and whatnot from Ufa. Then they would fill in, at Universal, with the close shots. I always understood that that was the case with *Secret of the Blue Room*. Lionel Atwill was what we call an "actor's actor," very much involved with one's self. He had been a fantastic matinee idol, but of course by the time he got to Universal he had a little pot, and he seemed old to me at that time — but probably was only in his late forties or early fifties. He was a brilliant actor.

Do you like horror or suspense films like the ones you made?
No, no, no — I never listened to murder mysteries on the radio and I don't watch them on television or in the theaters. They *scare* me!

One of your Universal loanouts was to Sam Goldwyn for the fantasy Roman Scandals. *Is there an anecdote that goes with that film?*
[*Laughs.*] Well, I met my second husband there — the father of my daughter! I was lying on a sofa in my slave outfit and reading a Chinese newspaper, and this man came up and said, "Do you read Chinese?" I said, "Fluently." I didn't even look up, because [this sort of thing] happened so often; I knew there was a man standing there, that's all. And I went on reading. He said, "My name is Arthur Sheekman, and I'm one of the writers on the picture." I said, "Why didn't you write me a better part?" [*Laughs.*] I *still* didn't look up. He said, "May I introduce myself?" I said, "You already *have*!" and I went on reading! So he came around in front and put the paper down and he said, "Would you like to have dinner with me?" And that man became my husband — that's my *Roman Scandals* anecdote! Also, I played the Princess Sylvia in the movie, so our daughter, born two years later, is named Sylvia.

That was when I left Universal. I got pregnant and had my child, my beautiful daughter, and I said to my husband, "I don't want to go back to that studio." It said in my contract that I had to come back in two months (or so) after the birth of a child, so I didn't lose any weight *on purpose* because I didn't want to go back. My husband negotiated with one of his best friends and I had an offer from 20th Century–Fox — they bought my contract. Universal sold me to Fox with the proviso that I would do (I think) two pictures a year for Universal. My daughter was born in thirty-five so that must have been the year all this happened, and I stayed at Fox until thirty-nine.

Around the time you left Universal, they announced that you were going to co-star in The Invisible Ray *with Karloff.*
That's the first I ever heard of it!

You returned to the stage in 1939. That's where your heart was all along?
Yes. I did summer theater all up and down the East Coast — it was

wonderful. I dropped out of pictures because I was very disappointed with my career. Even at Fox, [Darryl] Zanuck only used me in Shirley Temple pictures, or with the Ritz Brothers, or I was making a B picture there for [producer] Sol Wurtzel. This was not my idea of what I wanted to do! So my last picture there was 1939. My first husband had gone around the world—he stayed at Angkor Wat in French Indochina!—and he told me all about it. One day I said to Arthur, "My contract is finishing and your contract at Metro is finishing. Let's go around the world." He said, "Okay!" So we left ten days later, we went around the world. This was thirty-nine. We were in Europe when the war broke out.

Then you came back, and made a few more pictures at the same time you lived at the Garden of Allah.

Yes, I did. Living [at the Garden of Allah] was a divine experience. I was there three and a half years and there was a great parade of people through there—Dorothy Parker, Robert Benchley, Charlie Butterworth, Artie Shaw, Natalie Schafer (who later became one of my best friends), John Carradine (he lived right next door), Louis Calhern, Dorothy Gish, oh, so many. And I worked at the Actors Lab and I went out with Dana Andrews during the war doing *Mr. and Mrs. North*, and I went with Sam Levene doing *Three Men on a Horse*. I was very busy during those years at the Garden.

And one of the movies you did at that time was The Whistler *[1944] for director William Castle.*

That was purely freelance. I did *The Whistler* because Bill Castle asked me to do it, and I thought maybe I might want to go back to film acting. (I decided I didn't.) Bill was very young and very gung-ho, and very talented, I thought. It was a very pleasant engagement.

Did you ever see Castle's remake of The Old Dark House?

No.

And in the last fifteen years or so, you've been back in movies occasionally.

And I must say, the films that I have made since I came back, with Goldie Hawn [*Wildcats*, 1986] and Peter O'Toole [*My Favorite Year*, 1982] and Jack Lemmon [*Mass Appeal*, 1984]—those have been fun. The reason I did it: It's a discipline, and I guess, being an actress, you *need* a discipline. It keeps you taking care of yourself, and also, it's very nice to be stroked by young men who come up and say, "My father photographed you in such-

and-such, and he wants me to say hello," or, "My mother worked with you, and she remembers you"—it's very nice!

In 1983, the man who was supposed to have been the best man at my first wedding (I married his best friend) walked back into my life, and now we're together. He [Ward Ritchie] is one of the world's most prestigious graphic artists and book publishers and printers, and so I bought a private press in 1983 and I've been printing what is known in the trade as "artists' books" since then, along with the acting. I wear a lot of hats [*laughs*]! So I'm very busy as an artists' printer at this point.

Have there been any acting challenges in your recent set of movies?
No.

Do you plan to be acting again in the near future?
It depends. I've had several offers, especially in television, but I don't want to commit to a series because I like to travel, and [*laughs*] I've already proven what I can do. If I can get an interesting part, I'd like to do it. But there aren't very many parts for eighty-three-year-old ladies!

GLORIA STUART FILMOGRAPHY

Street of Women (Warners, 1932)
Air Mail (Universal, 1932)
The Old Dark House (Universal, 1932)
The All-American (Universal, 1932)
Laughter in Hell (Universal, 1932)
The Cohens and Kellys in Hollywood (cameo appearance; Universal, 1932)
Roman Scandals (United Artists, 1933)
The Kiss Before the Mirror (Universal, 1933)
Private Jones (Universal, 1933)
The Girl in 419 (Paramount, 1933)
It's Great to Be Alive (Fox, 1933)
The Invisible Man (Universal, 1933)
Secret of the Blue Room (Universal, 1933)
Sweepings (RKO, 1933)
Beloved (Universal, 1934)
I Like It That Way (Universal, 1934)
I'll Tell the World (Universal, 1934)
Here Comes the Navy (Warners, 1934)
The Love Captive (Universal, 1934)
Gift of Gab (Universal, 1934)
Maybe It's Love (Warners, 1935)
Gold Diggers of 1935 (Warners, 1935)
Laddie (RKO, 1935)
Professional Soldier (20th Century–Fox, 1935)
The Prisoner of Shark Island (20th Century–Fox, 1936)

36 Hours to Kill (20th Century–Fox, 1936)
The Girl on the Front Page (Universal, 1936)
Wanted! Jane Turner (RKO, 1936)
The Crime of Dr. Forbes (20th Century–Fox, 1936)
The Lady Escapes (20th Century–Fox, 1937)
Girl Overboard (Universal, 1937)
Life Begins in College (20th Century–Fox, 1937)
Rebecca of Sunnybrook Farm (20th Century–Fox, 1938)
Change of Heart (20th Century–Fox, 1938)
Island in the Sky (20th Century–Fox, 1938)
Keep Smiling (20th Century–Fox, 1938)
Time Out for Murder (20th Century–Fox, 1938)
The Lady Objects (Columbia, 1938)
The Three Musketeers (20th Century–Fox, 1939)
It Could Happen to You (20th Century–Fox, 1939)
Winner Take All (20th Century–Fox, 1939)
Here Comes Elmer (Republic, 1943)
The Whistler (Columbia, 1944)
Enemy of Women (*Mad Lover*; *The Secret Life of Paul Joseph Goebbels*) (Monogram, 1944)
She Wrote the Book (Universal, 1946)
My Favorite Year (MGM/United Artists, 1982)
Mass Appeal (Universal, 1984)
Wildcats (Warners, 1986)

Stuart also cameoed in one of Paramount's *Hollywood on Parade* shorts in 1933.

[Ed] Wood cast a lot of his friends; I call 'em his "menagerie" of people. Just a lot of odd sorts. All pleasant and nice, but they were just kind of... strange individuals, you know?

Gregory Walcott

WHERE IN THE WORLD is there less justice than there is in the fact that Edward D. Wood, Jr.—infamous as Hollywood's worst director—is currently on the receiving end of more attention than most of the industry's *great* directors from years past? One place to look might be in the plight of character actor Gregory Walcott, who appeared in many major films before *and* after he was the (very) hesitant star of Wood's "little gem" *Plan 9 from Outer Space* (1959). To many, he is best remembered for this one notorious false step in an otherwise respectable acting career—an experience, and an irony, which he regards with characteristic frankness and humor.

Walcott was born (1/13/28) in Wendell, North Carolina, grew up in that area and went into the Army just after the end of World War II. After leaving the service he grew restless on the East Coast and, with $100 in his pocket, thumbed his way west to pursue an acting career. An agent who spotted him in a little theater play helped Walcott land his debut movie role in *Red Skies of Montana* (1952), and two years later, on the strength of his performance as a drill instructor in the Marine Corps movie *Battle Cry*, he was placed under contract to Warner Bros. ("I had a fairly decent career going prior to the episode of *Plan 9*—a lot of folks don't know that!") He co-starred (as a drill instructor again) in another Marine Corps classic, *The Outsider* (1961), which earned him a Universal contract and his own television series, *87th Precinct* (1961-62) with Robert Lansing. Walcott still acts today—most recently (and pertinently here), in Tim Burton's new biopic *Ed Wood*.

Talk about how you first became involved on Plan 9.

My wife and I had been married about a year and we lived in a lovely little cottage across the street from the First Baptist Church of Beverly Hills, which we attended occasionally. A man named Ed Reynolds was a member there. Ed had come out from Alabama and he was a great movie fan—he was from a religious background and was terribly impressed with C.B. DeMille's *The Ten Commandments*. He came to Hollywood to make Biblical epics. He realized that I was right across the street from the church (he'd seen me in *Battle Cry* and *Mister Roberts*) and he would talk with me—he talked with me about films and asked questions, and shared with me his desire to make Biblical films. You try to be patient and understanding with people like that, but I didn't *encourage* him too much because, knowing he had no background at all in film production, I didn't *want* to encourage him too much—you can really get taken in this town. He'd talk to me, and I just kind of smiled and nodded and said, "That's good, that's good."

But, by crack, he came to me one day and he said he was going to

Previous page: Gregory Walcott's career survived the terrors of *Plan 9 from Outer Space*.

produce a film starring Bela Lugosi, and he wanted me to play the young romantic lead. I said to him, "But, Ed — Bela Lugosi's *dead!*" He said, "Well, there's a very ingenious writer-director named Ed Wood who has this footage of Lugosi that he is writing a screenplay around. It's going to be very clever." I had never heard of Ed Wood, *never*, but I said, "Let me read the screenplay." I read the screenplay and it was the most gosh-awful thing I ever read in my life. A *child* could have written better dialogue! It made no sense, it rambled and it went in and out of situations. I said to Reynolds, "This is a terrible script, and I just hate to see you get involved in it." He said, "No, no! I want you to meet this director." So he arranged for a luncheon with Ed Wood and me in a restaurant in Los Angeles called Tail o' the Cock. We went to lunch that day and there was Ed Wood waiting, smiling, telling me how great I'd be in the film. I was told that the special effects would be sensational, etc., etc. I had a *lot* of reservations about participating in this film, but Ed Reynolds was such a sweet, naive guy that I gave in; having built up a *l-i-t-t-l-e* bit of a name in Hollywood, I thought, "Well, maybe it'll lend to the success of the film." So I *very* reluctantly did the film — without even telling my agent! I did it surreptitiously, over a period of four days.

Was Reynolds also Ed Wood's landlord?

Here's the real story on that: Ed Reynolds worked as an electronics salesperson. He and his wife Pauline lived in an apartment house in the Hollywood area, and I think *probably* what happened was that they got their apartment free if they would manage the others. Wood was one of the tenants. So Ed Reynolds was not the owner or the manager of the apartment house as his *profession*, but was in charge of the apartments and he had to deal with Ed Wood as a tenant.

On the first day of shooting, November 30, 1956, Reynolds was quoted in The Hollywood Reporter *as saying that he would be producing a series of horror pictures, "the most horrifying since the Frankenstein era."*

Ed Reynolds came out to the West Coast to do religious epics, and Wood saw a piece of bait here. Wood convinced Reynolds that religious pictures were very expensive because of the costumes and the sets, and told him that he should start out making smaller films and build his bankroll. The thing that was hot at that time was science fiction films, and Wood *just happened* to have a science fiction script ready to go! (*Grave Robbers from Outer Space* was the original title of *Plan 9*.) Wood had written it around the footage of Bela Lugosi, and he convinced Reynolds that he could make his money quickly from science fiction films, *then* get into his costume-epic, Biblical films. That was how that began.

How quickly did you realize that you had made a mistake, getting roped into Plan 9?

[*Laughs.*] The very first day! I came onto this little tiny set, and I could see that it was amateurish — it looked like a play that a class of sixth graders had put together! I could tell right away that everything had an amateurish look. And none of the people on the show, *except* some of the crew, were mainline Hollywood-type people. Most of the rest of the actors were what is referred to as *fringe* actors — none of 'em had ever done any real, major films, or any mainline films. The set had a "carnival" feeling about it, it was not like any movie set *I* had been on. I had just gotten through working with John Ford and Mervyn LeRoy, and those sets had a feeling of professionalism. This set of Ed Wood's!

Wood cast a lot of his friends, I call 'em his "menagerie" of people. Just a lot of *odd sorts*. All pleasant and nice, but they were just kind of ... strange individuals, you know? They wandered around the set, and, for example, the guy that stood in for Lugosi [Tom Mason] was a chiropractor, and he was goin' around the set offering to adjust people's necks [*laughs*]! Odd things like that! It just didn't have the feeling of a *real*, professional Hollywood movie set. After watching Ed Wood direct that day, I came home and I said to my wife (*prophetically!*), "Honey, this has got to be the worst film of all time!" I actually *said* that. And, unfortunately, it came to pass! It was just a totally undisciplined set, and I had a bad feeling right from the very beginning.

When you were first introduced to Wood, did you get the feeling he knew your work?

Well, Ed Reynolds had already told him about me. And at that point, of course, Wood was anxious to please Reynolds because Reynolds had money with which to do the film. Reynolds wanted me to do the leading man role and, of course, Wood was agreeable to that.

The question of "talent" aside, did you like Wood?

You *had* to like Ed Wood, he was a very likable, personable guy. Pleasant and friendly and outgoing — he *did* have a certain charm. I had looked into his background a *little* bit beforehand and what I found was that he was a fringe director, he did not make mainline Hollywood films or what we call union films. His were small, very, very low-budget films. I could give an illustration of what his films were like: If you would take a Russ Meyer film, Wood's film would be about ten rungs lower than *that*! People refer to Wood's films as B films. But they *weren't*; many B films were very good, you know. Ed Wood films were not even union, they were way, *way* down the scale from a Russ Meyer film! They were sleazy, thrown-together, cheap, *cheap* films. That was what I had discovered and I was very reluctant to go into this thing. But I did it as a favor for Ed Reynolds.

Wood showed interest, or maybe just pretended *to show interest, in the church in order to get Reynolds "hooked."*

Yes. In fact, Wood began to attend the church, and so did some of his "entourage," his "devotees," his "menagerie"—they began to follow him over to the church. The minister was a man who had just come out from San Antonio, Texas, and he got excited about this chance to lead some "movie people" into the faith [*laughs*]! He started working on that conversion [with Wood] and then, lo and behold, there was any number of them—Wood's entourage—making their professions of faith. And they were *baptized*. I didn't like to be judgmental, but I couldn't help but sense that this was a superficial interest in the faith. I was there the night that Ed Wood was baptized—he was in a white robe and duly immersed. Later on, Tor Johnson and some of the others were, too. Of course, Tor was too big to be baptized in the church baptistry, so he was baptized in one member's swimming pool on a Sunday afternoon—there were four, five, six that were baptized the same day that Tor was, in the swimming pool. So, yes, they did get very, very interested in religion for a while, because the word was around that Ed Reynolds was a bankroller.

The minister you mentioned—was he the one who's in Plan 9?

No. The reverend that was in the movie was named [Lyn] Lemon; he was a friend of Ed Reynolds and he was the pastor of *another* church. Lemon put a little money in the film and subsequently played the role. The pastor of the Beverly Hills church was Dr. John Daniel Brown.

And Dr. Brown had nothing to do with Plan 9, *other than accepting Wood and his cronies into his "flock."*

Dr. Brown was a very ambitious-type man who was eager to make a name for himself in the Southern Baptist convention. He had come from San Antonio, and it was quite a thing to announce that he had come to the West Coast to "preach to the stars"—he said he was "called to preach to the movie stars." When Ed Wood and his entourage of friends began to come around, Brown started to salivate, and he announced in the Southern Baptist paper that he was baptizing movie stars [*laughs*]. The truth of the matter

A quarter-century before *Plan 9 from Outer Space*'s "Golden Turkey" pantheonization, Walcott watched Ed Wood direct and realized it would be "the worst film of all time." (Pictured: Tom Keene, Paul Marco, Duke Moore, Mona McKinnon, Walcott.)

is, not a single one of them had ever worked a day on a mainline film!

Any memories of the other investors, like Hugh Thomas?

Hugh Thomas was also a member of the church. He came from down South and was managing the Carlton Theatre on Western Avenue, where the film had its eventual premiere. He and his wife were a very nice couple. The other associate producer, along with Hugh, was Charles Burg — he was one of the deacons of the church.

At the end of the movie, Dudley Manlove, who played the spaceman, talks about God. Was this Wood's attempt at keeping his churchgoing investors happy?

Now that you mention it, I have never thought of that. You know [*laughs*], that could very well be! But all *I* remember from that scene is the line, "Your stupid minds! Stupid! Stupid!" *That* stands out so much, that's all I can remember!

Was there any such thing as rehearsal on Plan 9?

[*Laughs.*] No. Ed Wood was not so much concerned about *quality* as he was *content*. We might run through things one time, and then we'd shoot it. Most directors will rehearse with the actors, discuss the motivation, what he wants, what he has in mind. Ed Wood didn't. He would just *start!* And if you got the lines in — whether they made sense or not — that was the way he printed it. I don't think I *ever* saw him do another take. And *if* an actor made a *very* bad flub, Wood would say, "Keep going," and then he'd come in and cover it with a closer shot.

Did you ever offer to change any of your own dialogue, to make it less incomprehensible?

I don't recall. In that time, my attitude as a young actor was to try to take the lines *as written* and do the best I could. I think I did change some lines *arbitrarily*, which he never questioned.

You said you were on the picture for four days.

There were four actual production days, and then there were any number of days that Wood spent doing those — ugh! — those so-called special effects shots. Also, there were other exterior shots where Wood held the camera himself and shot, like people riding down the freeway pointing at the flying saucers. Or the scene where a woman runs into a telephone booth — those were m.o.s., silent shots. (That particular woman was Ed Reynolds' wife Pauline.) Those were not "production shots," they were just "on-the-street" shots that Wood actually filmed himself.

Does working in a movie so small-time affect a good actor's performance?

It *does*. If you're not getting much from another actor, or from the director, then it drains *you*, it limits *your* creativity. You have to put out *more* energy and more thought to try to make it convincing.

The closest you came to having a "professional" actor opposite you in Plan 9 *was Tom Keene.*

Tom had worked a lot as a Western actor in days gone by. Tom did seem to know what was going on on this set, *but* he did a very strange thing one day that Ed Wood corrected (and I kind of admired Wood for). Wood's script was full of long, flowing, crazy lines — they were technical things, hard for Tom to memorize. (Hard for *any*body to memorize!) Tom Keene came to the set one day and he just couldn't remember his lines. Ed Wood did something that was very clever and interesting: He was off-camera and he said Tom Keene's lines, and Tom would say 'em back. In other words, they put the camera kind of close-up on Tom, then Wood would say the lines *to* him and Tom would repeat the lines exactly as Ed had said them. Then in the editing process, Wood snipped his voice out. That's how they got through that scene, and I thought that was kind of interesting.

What about some of the other people in the cast, like Tor Johnson?
　　Tor began to come around to the church quite regularly, and he was a very sweet, pleasant man — like a big teddy bear. And I will say this about Tor: Of all the people that made an indication of being converted to the faith, I think Tor was the only one that was really serious about it. You couldn't help but like Tor, and I *did*—very much. The only time I saw Tor get angry was the day on the set when he came up out of the grave. He had to get his suit really dusted down, to look like he was coming out of dirt, and of course Tor was so huge that all of his clothes had to be tailored — they were expensive. Tor got very angry, he was demanding that they buy him a new suit or something like that. I forget exactly what it was, but I do know that he was angry that day because his suit was so messed up. And "Bunny" [John Breckinridge] was a very affected looking and sounding chap! He, too, was typical of the *unusual* individuals that Ed Wood drew to himself.

Wood is infamous for his cross-dressing — and his boozing — but you saw none of that during Plan 9?
　　On that set, he wore regular clothes and he pretty well kept a moderate decorum. And [drinking-wise], not at all. Maybe at home, at nighttime, alone, or with his chums, he drank, but all the time he was around the Baptist people, he kept his nose clean.

How much were you paid to star in Plan 9?
　　It was understood that it was such a low budget that it was going to be S.A.G. scale. That was, what, close to forty years ago so I don't remember exactly how much it was, but it was around $200 a day. I agreed to work for scale, because I wanted to see Ed Reynolds get his film done. At the end of the four days, Reynolds himself walked up to me and handed me a check. And I was to learn *years* later that it was not a union film, and I could have been in a lot of trouble [for working in it].

Where did you see the movie for the first time — and did it confirm all your fears?

You said it! When the film was completed, they had a screening at the Carlton Theatre. (I guess this was probably three months later.) We were all invited to go down there, and I was curious to see what they were going to do with it; they only shot four days on the set, and how much can you get in four days? My wife and I went down to see it — it was *kind* of in a black neighborhood, and a lot of kids came into the show. My wife and I sat in the balcony, and from the *moment* that the thing started with Criswell, I began to slink down in my seat. And at the moments that the film was supposed to be frightening, the kids would *laugh* — and I would slink deeper and deeper and *deeper* as it got worse. The cars would go from day to night, night to day, and I thought it was awful.

When the thing was finally over, I tried to sneak downstairs and get out of there *fast*. But poor, sweet, dear Ed Reynolds was already waiting by the popcorn machine, waiting for *congratulations*. He was like a proud papa, having given birth to a beautiful blond-haired, blue-eyed child! I walked past him and he said, "What do you think, Greg?" And I said, "Well, Ed ... it's an *interesting* film." Then, as I walked down the sidewalk, Charles Burg ran and grabbed me and said, "Greg, what do you think?" I remember distinctly what I said to him: I said, "Charles, it's kind of like a Dagwood sandwich — it's got everything in it!" Wood had taken pieces from here, from there, from this, from that — stock footage, things that made no sense, just threw 'em in there, and I referred to it as "like a Dagwood sandwich."

When *Plan 9 from Outer Space* fell apart, Ed Reynolds was out of money, his investors were screaming for their money, and he hit upon hard times — that *Plan 9* thing wiped him out. Apparently Hugh Thomas went back down South, and Reynolds and his wife took over managing the Carlton Theatre.

Just to make some extra money.

Just to *survive*, yes! Ed Reynolds passed away about two years later — he was maybe fifty-four, fifty-five, not too old. And I think that the stress and the disappointment of *Plan 9*, that whole debacle, that fiasco, the failure of *Plan 9* — I think it shortened his life.

You said that you never worked under conditions that primitive before. Did you ever work under 'em after?

[*Laughs.*] It has been said (I don't think it's necessarily true) that *Plan 9* didn't do my career any good, and I did go through a dry period there for about three or four years. I worked on one film that was considered a very bad film, *Jet Attack* [1958], about two years later; that was with John Agar. That was a modest-budget film for American International. Then I

Walcott and star/director Clint Eastwood between takes on *The Eiger Sanction*, shot on location in the Swiss Alps.

worked on a Western at about the same time, *Badman's Country* [1958] with George Montgomery [and Walcott as Bat Masterson]. But they were B-type films, they weren't the real *low*-low-low budget like Ed Wood films were.

If you could turn the clock back and not be in Plan 9, would you do it?
 I have never had anybody ask me that [*laughs*]! Well, my altruism; my response would probably be to try to help out Ed Reynolds. Career-wise, I would not do it.

In the sixties, you traveled 250,000 miles, in the U.S. and abroad, to speak at youth rallies, colleges, civic clubs and churches, and were presented with a honorary Doctor of Laws degree at Georgetown College [Kentucky].
 In those days, I did quite a bit of public speaking — it was during the era of my early life, and it seemed the right thing to do. I spoke about family relationships — motivational-type speaking. I chose to do it, although it took me away from my family quite a bit, and in some ways I regret [the traveling], because had I given more attention to my film career, I think I would have probably gotten further ahead.

How busy have you been acting-wise in the last several years?
   I took a retirement at sixty, which was five years ago. Oh, they still call me back to work — I guest-star on *Murder, She Wrote* about every two years, and now I just worked for Tim Burton on this *Ed Wood* film. To be honest with you, I don't know whether it's because I became disenchanted with "the new Hollywood" or because my creative interests went in another direction, but I just kind of lost interest in show business. The last few years I've devoted to writing. I've written screenplays through the years, some short stories and essays — writing has been kind of a mistress that has been wooing me. So I decided to retire from show business, and now that all of my children are graduated from college and married, my wife and I can live a quieter, more reflective life. We're enjoying life, collecting a bit of art, and I'm doing some writing, which I'm thoroughly enjoying. But, as I said, they still call me back to work, and I'm kind of like a firehouse dog — if I hear the bell go off, I begin to salivate.

What was the first you heard of the Tim Burton Ed Wood movie?
   I got a phone call, I think it was from Harry Medved, saying, "Have you heard? Tim Burton is going to do a picture about Ed Wood." I said [*laughs*], "Good Lord, what *for*?" Harry said, "He's fascinated with Wood's life." I said, "Well, there's no doubt about it, he was a very strange, unusual, bizarre, off-the-wall fellow!" That was the first time I heard.

How did you get involved in the movie?
   About two months ago, July [1993] I guess, Burton's associate called me and asked me if I would come in and talk to Burton. I didn't really have any desire to be connected with [*Plan 9*] — people had been saying, "Why don't you call up [Burton], go over there, maybe get on the film?" I wanted to *distance* myself, actually, from *Plan 9*. But then Burton's associate called and said Burton would like me to come in and *chat*, he wanted to get some information from me. So I went over to his office on Sunset Boulevard. Burton said to me that he had seen a lot of tape and read a lot of interviews about Ed Wood and the making of *Plan 9*, and he felt that what I had to say was more credible than the other stories. I have always tried to be accurate — a lot of the stories I've read *have* been greatly embellished. (The guy's life was so *bizarre*, you don't have to embellish it to make it interesting!) Burton asked me a few questions about Wood, *plus* he had heard that I had my original screenplay from *Plan 9* and he wanted to just see it out of curiosity. So I brought it over and we had a nice chat for about forty-five minutes. And he was very gracious — just like an ebullient kid, he was *bouncing* and *laughing*, slapping his knee. Of course, he's got the

Walcott, Juliet Landau (as Loretta King) and Johnny Depp (as *Ed Wood*).

reputation around town of being the "boy genius" and I had no idea what to expect — I was thinking that maybe he'd be eccentric and temperamental. But I found him to be quite charming, even child-like! He was very pleasant to talk to.

And then you did end up with a little part in the picture.

I was told that the writers had written the part of Ed Reynolds for *me* to do. Of course, Ed Reynolds was a short, stubby guy — chunky. (You can see him in *Plan 9*, playing the grave digger.) I'm 6'4" and I don't look at *all* like Ed Reynolds. So we all agreed that I would not be right for that part. Anyway, Tim Burton asked me if I would consider doing, for the *fun* of it, just as an inside joke, a cameo role. I said, "Why not? Might be kind of fun." By that time I had read the script and gotten to know Tim Burton, and I felt it would be quite an interesting film. I play one of the investors who puts money into one of Wood's earlier films, I think it was *Bride of the Monster* or something like that. It was just a day's work, a *fun* day, working with Martin Landau, who I've worked with before. By the way, he looks *exactly* like Bela Lugosi, and he has perfected the imitation and he is going to be sensational.

You've worked with Mervyn LeRoy, Don Siegel, Otto Preminger, any number of great directors— many of whom will never get the amount of attention Ed Wood has gotten. What's the lesson to be learned?

[*Laughs.*] Sometimes we all think that the world is not fair. And maybe life, in the ultimate realm of things, *is* not fair. Maybe it *is* a crapshoot. That's the only way I can think to explain that.

A lot of people put down Ed Wood's films, how trashy and cheap they were — I'm one *of* those people! But I must say this about him: He was diligent and fervent and energetic about his work. Though it turned out to be trashy stuff, perhaps in the case of Ed Wood, *effort* needs to be acknowledged as well as *art*.

GREGORY WALCOTT FILMOGRAPHY

Red Skies of Montana (20th Century–Fox, 1952)
Above and Beyond (MGM, 1952)
Fearless Fagan (MGM, 1952)
Ruby Gentry (20th Century–Fox, 1952)
Battle Cry (Warners, 1955)
Mister Roberts (Warners, 1955)
The Court-Martial of Billy Mitchell (Warners, 1955)
The McConnell Story (Warners, 1955)
Strange Lady in Town (Warners, 1955)
Texas Lady (RKO, 1955)
The Steel Jungle (Warners, 1956)
Thunder Over Arizona (Republic, 1956)
The Lieutenant Wore Skirts (20th Century–Fox, 1956)
The Persuader (Allied Artists, 1957)
Jet Attack (AIP, 1958)
Badman's Country (Warners, 1958)
Plan 9 from Outer Space (DCA, 1959)
On the Double (Paramount, 1961)
The Outsider (Universal, 1961)
Captain Newman, M.D. (Universal, 1963)
Bill Wallace of China (Logos Productions, 1967) Also co-producer
Prime Cut (National General, 1972)
Joe Kidd (Universal, 1972)
Who Stole the Shah's Jewels (Italian, 1972)
The Last American Hero (Hard Driver) (20th Century–Fox, 1973)
Thunderbolt and Lightfoot (United Artists, 1974)
The Sugarland Express (Universal, 1974)
A Man from the East (Eastman; E Poi lo Chiamarono il Magnifico; Magnifico, l'Uomo dell'Est) (United Artists, 1974)
The Eiger Sanction (Universal, 1975)
Midway (The Battle of Midway) (Universal, 1976)
Every Which Way But Loose (Warners, 1978)
Norma Rae (20th Century–Fox, 1979)

Tilt (Warners, 1979)
House II: The Second Story (New World, 1987)
Ed Wood (Touchstone Pictures, 1994)

    Walcott is seen in the *Plan 9 from Outer Space* clips included in *It Came from Hollywood* (Paramount, 1982).

Very often, each new project is a different ... genre than the picture you had just done previously, so you have to get in there and research that new subject matter.... Which is what I did [on The Day the Earth Stood Still*]— to the limited degree one could do it on the subject of flying saucers!*

———————Robert Wise———————

IN 1951, DIRECTOR Robert Wise brought to the screen one of the best and most famous movies in the then-new Hollywood trend toward science fiction films: *The Day the Earth Stood Still*. And now, almost half a century later, he answers some new and offbeat questions about his classic film — and speculates about what the world would really be like had we been forced to live with Klaatu's (Michael Rennie) well-meaning but deadly threat from space.

Born in Indiana, Wise was forced to drop out of college during the Depression, and entered films (via RKO) as an assistant cutter in 1933. After years in the cutting room, he made a name for himself with his editing of the Orson Welles classics *Citizen Kane* (1941) and *The Magnificent Ambersons* (1942), and later went on to become a director for RKO's B unit (working at first under producer Val Lewton). His subsequent directing credits have straddled most every genre and included such financial and critical hits as *Somebody Up There Likes Me* (1956), *I Want to Live!* (1958), *West Side Story* (1961) and *The Sound of Music* (1965) — the latter pair earning him Best Director Oscars. Now in his eighties, Wise still works in film and attends festivals with energy and enthusiasm of a far younger man, and looks back here on the time when he was one of the prime movers and shakers who made *the Earth stand still*.

Who first approached you about doing The Day the Earth Stood Still*?*

I was under non-exclusive contract to 20th Century–Fox, and one day I got a call from Darryl Zanuck, who was running the studio. He said, "Go over and see Julian Blaustein, the producer. He's got a script I think you might be interested in." I was between assignments because I had just finished some film [*The House on Telegraph Hill*, 1951]. I went over to see Julian, and that was it: There was a first-draft screenplay [of *Day the Earth Stood Still*] already done by Edmund North for Blaustein. Blaustein gave me the script and I went off and read it and loved it. Immediately I came back and said, "Let's make it." Julian Blaustein was very good, one of the best producers I ever worked with. He was very creative, had very good ideas. He was a very bright, intelligent man who contributed a lot, I'm sure, to the screenplay. I don't know where the idea of doing the movie came from; it was based on a story by Harry Bates [*Farewell to the Master*] and I don't know whether it was Julian's idea or if Eddie North came to him or how it came about.

Any guess as to why Day the Earth Stood Still *appealed to Zanuck in the first place? Science fiction was not an established genre then.*

I really don't know, I never discussed it with Darryl. This was a smaller

Previous page: Robert Wise says he has 10 or 12 favorite films — and that ***The Day the Earth Stood Still*** is "one close to the top."

budget picture and he usually concerned himself more one-on-one with larger budgets. He had a program of pictures to make and Blaustein was one of his top producers of the more modest budget pictures. *The Day The Earth Stood Still* wasn't exactly a B picture, but it was not a big, big, *big* budget for those days. I don't even know whether Zanuck had read the script or if he just knew about it from Blaustein, who had told him about it and thought it would be something I'd be interested in. However, Zanuck had a very big role to play in one important factor later on, and that was the casting of Michael Rennie.

Was Day the Earth Stood Still *then your biggest budget to date?*
No, I'd had a big Western at Fox called *Two Flags West* [1950] which was a larger budget. I can't remember all the budgets from those days, but I know that *Two Flags West* was a big location picture, very expensive. The budget on *Day the Earth Stood Still* I'd imagine was around $900,000 or $1,000,000, something like that.

And that still wouldn't qualify as an A picture in 1951?
No, it was sort of a middle-ground picture.

Even if it wasn't 100 percent A-caliber, it was still the first "big" American science fiction picture.
There was no question that we'd have all the facilities and all the ability to do it there at 20th Century–Fox, we'd have fine crews and fine technicians and all of that. And the special effects people, of course, were very good there. Very often, each new project is a different subject matter, a different *genre* than the picture you had just done previously, so you have to get in there and research that new subject matter, that new *genre*, and find out as much as you can about it. Which is what I did—to the limited degree one could do it on the subject of flying saucers [*laughs*]! So on *Day the Earth Stood Still*, I talked to some science fiction people. I'd never been a big science fiction buff, although as a kid I had read a number of the out-of-this-world science fiction magazines. But I wasn't a buff of science fiction reading as I became an adult.

What initially "grabbed" you about Day the Earth Stood Still*?*
Two or three things. Number one, it was (for once) an alien from outer space who was not an *evil* alien. Also, it was a science fiction film set on Earth here, and I thought that was marvelous. I liked the setting, the fact that it was in Washington, the heart of our country; I thought that made it very real, very believable, very mundane. I tried to heighten that with my

Patricia Neal is propped up into Gort's arms in this *Day the Earth Stood Still* publicity photo.

casting, too. I wanted to make it just as credible and believable as it could possibly be, and I think that's one of its strengths.

You believed in UFOs at the time.

Yes, I did, I've *always* believed in the possibility of UFOs. If we on Earth here can think that *we* are the only possible intelligences in the whole big universe out there, that's got to be the biggest ego trip in the *world*. I've never *seen* any UFOs, but I've talked to people who feel they have and I *sure believe* in the possibility.

Did you provide any screenplay input?

Oh, just the usual things; I can't tell you this, that and the other. Usually a director comes in and says, "Well, I don't like this transition," or, "This bothers me," or maybe he objects to a few lines of dialogue. I didn't do any *major* changes on it at all, no, I just maybe sharpened it up a bit.

In pre-production, you went to Washington, D.C., to pick some locations for the second unit team.

I picked the locations with the second unit director [Bert Leeds]. We decided that the only way we could possibly make it for the kind of money Fox wanted to spend was to have the Washington shooting done by a second unit using doubles for Klaatu and the little boy. I lined up pretty much *all* the shots, I went over *ev-er-y-thing* with the second unit director and how I wanted it shot and where the angles should be from, so he had a pretty good map of what I wanted laid out for him when he shot the stuff.

When Darryl Zanuck first started talking about the project, he reportedly thought of Spencer Tracy as Klaatu.

I don't think I ever heard of Spencer Tracy being mentioned for it — this is the first I've *ever* heard of *that*. When I came on it, all three of us (Blaustein, Eddie North and I) had Claude Rains in mind. He was a fine English character actor and we thought he had the right quality. As it turned out, *fortunately* for us, he was in a play in New York [*Darkness at Noon*] and couldn't get out of it. We were starting to think of other people when we got this memo from Darryl Zanuck, who said in the memo, "I have just come back from England, and while I was there I saw a young man on the stage. He's a very good actor, I think, and he has a very interesting look. I think he's screen material and I've signed him to a contract with Fox and I think you should take a look at him for the lead in our film." That was Michael Rennie. Now, that was a big plus for us because here was a man who'd never been seen on the [American] screen before. That brought much more credibility to it than, for instance, if we'd *had* Claude Rains.

What was Rennie like to work with?

Oh, he was fine, he was very professional. He liked the script very much, liked what it had to say. (We *all* believed very much in its message, the warning about the dangers of nuclear warfare.) He believed very much in that, and he was very good to work with, a warm, easygoing guy. I can't tell you any *anecdotes* particularly, I don't remember any, it's been too long, but he fit right in and he suited the part all the way through. He later did a number of [American] pictures and went into a television series [*The Third Man*] — he had quite a career after that, before he died.

Did you ever use him again in anything?

No, I had no opportunity to use him again.

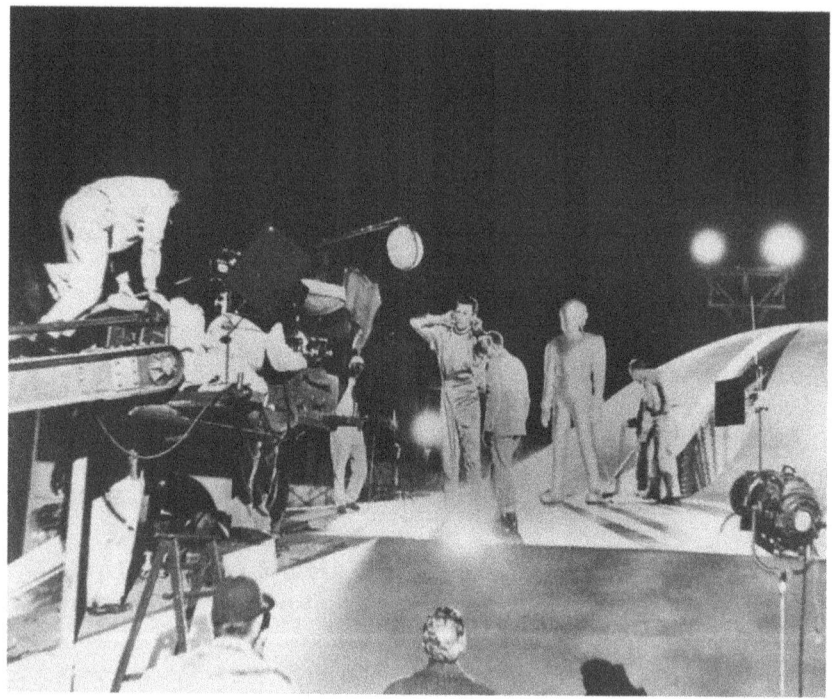

One of the things Wise likes best about *The Day the Earth Stood Still* is the fact that Michael Rennie (hands on ears) "was not an *evil* alien."

You've said that you didn't realize, as you were making Day the Earth Stood Still, *that it was a Christ allegory. And yet when Zanuck offered the picture to Claude Rains, he told Rains he'd be playing "a modern Christ"— so Zanuck knew!*

Isn't that interesting! Speaking of that, I think one of the things that helped the [allegorical element] was the fact that we had Michael Rennie playing it. He was tall and thin and kind of ascetic; had you put the beard on him, he could have been the Christ figure. But, honest to God, none of us working on the picture knew it [was an allegory]; it was only later, after the picture came out, that people started noticing. Once it was *pointed out* to us, we felt like, "Of course!" and we didn't know why we hadn't seen it! That came as a real surprise to me. I had the book too close to my face, I think!

Is it true that the censors had an objection to Klaatu's being brought back to life in the movie?

I've had that question put to me before, but I don't recall *any*thing like that. I don't remember there being any objection; it would seem to me that would be kind of a crazy, phony objection.

Would you say that the people who made Day the Earth Stood Still *were taking a career risk, making a movie with such a liberal message during such a conservative era?*

No, there didn't appear to be any problem. I've been told many times, "It seems kind of strange that Darryl Zanuck would go for something like this, him being a big Army man and very much a conservative," but I think Darryl always looked at projects as entertainment and as possibilities for profit, and put aside any political considerations. The only time we ran into any sort of problem was when we thought we could probably get all the Jeeps and tanks and the equipment we needed in Washington from the Army. But when you want anything from the Army, you have to give them the script to read before they'll let you have the materiel, they have to approve the script. Well, they turned us down, they didn't like what the movie had to say. (Don't you think that's interesting?) But Fox had an office in Washington, a lobbyist, I guess, and *he* got a bright idea: He went over to see the National Guard in Washington, or just outside of Washington. And *they* had no problems with the script. So all the people, equipment, and soldiers and all that you see in those night scenes, chasing around in Washington, are actually the National Guard, not the Army.

Any comments on some of the other people in your cast — Patricia Neal and Sam Jaffe?

I'd done a film with Pat before [*Three Secrets*, 1950] and she was just marvelous to work with, very warm and really very effective; she could accomplish a lot without *doing* very much. I thought she had just the right quality and I think she was lovely as the mother of the little boy. (Who was one of the best kid actors I've ever worked with, Billy Gray.) And of course Sam Jaffe was a *dream* to work with. I got to know Sam on the picture and we remained good friends almost up to his death — I'd see him every so often and have a fine evening with him. He was brilliant, and I thought his casting was just right on the nose for playing Einstein. It was perfect. That was the only time I worked with him.

Whose idea was it to get those real-life radio and television commentators to be part of the movie?

I can't remember, but I think very likely it was in the script. (It was not *my* idea.) Once again, we were making every attempt to make it as real and as believable and as credible and as "everyday" as we possibly could.

What would you have done differently with more money?

Michael Rennie brought the needed Christ-like quality to Klaatu while Patricia Neal was "very warm and really very effective" as his Earth liaison.

Very little. Today, I suppose, those special effects we had might be a little more sophisticated, work a little better, although they seemed to do the job for us at the time. It seemed to me we got pretty much everything we wanted; we would probably shoot it in color today, I suppose, there wouldn't be anything wrong with that with *that* film. (Although I *love* black and white. *The Haunting*'s the last black and white film I made, and I suppose I'll never make another one.)

How about, with more money, shooting the scenes in Washington yourself?

Oh, yeah—*any* director loves to do *all* of his shooting. I was reluctant to [turn it over to the second unit] but I agreed to it because I *had* to, for budget reasons. But I agreed to it *only* with the proviso that I could go to Washington with the second unit director and really sort of lay it out for him, and just have him follow through with the shots.

Is there anything you did in Day the Earth Stood Still *that you regret?*

Oh, I don't really think so. That sounds smug, I know [*laughs*], but I don't mean it to be that way. If I *really* looked at it and examined it, I'm *sure* I'd find a few things that maybe could be a little better, a little sharper; some dialogue that could be better from today's perspective. But I think by and large it holds up damn well after all these years.

Now the opposite *of that last question: Name the touches in which you take the most pride.*

Yes, I can name one in particular; it's a *stunt*, one I'm proud we got away with. We had a man named Lock Martin inside the rubber suit of Gort, Klaatu's robot, and he could no more lift up Patricia Neal than he could lift up—the White House [*laughs*]! And yet I had to have him pick her up in his arms and carry her into the spaceship. So we had to find *some* way to do this. This is what we did: When she fell, she fell down out of sight, behind a wall or a door or something. I had the camera pan Gort as he walked over to Pat, and the camera "lost" him when *he* went behind the door. I held my camera on the door—*stopped* the camera, didn't move it, left it right there. Then we brought in a derrick and put the rig on Pat, the harness around her, and the wire on the derrick. We lifted Pat up; turned Gort around; and put her in his arms, with all her weight on the wire. Then I called *action* and started the camera again, panned as Gort came out, and there was the actual Pat Neal being "carried" in his arms. We had to establish that that was Pat, and *then* we had a shot of Gort's back where he's walking away with her; he's carrying a lightweight dummy there, which we got away with.

Do you recall when you saw the full picture for the first time?

That would have been when I saw the first cut, in the studio, in a projection room. The feeling [amongst us] was very good, very strong. But there was one *very* important element that wasn't there: the music. Bernie Herrmann, of course, later supplied the music, and I don't know if I've had any picture in which the underscoring contributed so much as in that picture. I thought Bernie and his use of the synthesizer and the theremin was *so* effective, it added a little bit of an "out of this world" edge to it. It made a marvelous contribution to the picture. Of course, I'd worked with him previously on *Citizen Kane* and *The Magnificent Ambersons*, he was Orson Welles' composer and conductor on those films. Also, I did another film with him called *All That Money Can Buy* [1941]; he won the Academy Award for that score. So I knew Bernie very well.

What do you think about all the talk, down through the years, of a sequel?

My agent was called, *many* years ago now; they wanted to know if I'd be interested in doing a sequel. I told him, "Hell, no"—I'd done my piece, I didn't want to do that, I don't believe in those things. My understanding is that Ray Bradbury worked on the story for a sequel for some time over there; he turned it in and they didn't like it, and it was just put on the shelf. I've heard that there's talk of *remaking* the picture, which of course I don't like at all. There's talk of remaking *The Haunting*, too.

What do you think the real-life reaction would have been if the events depicted in Day the Earth Stood Still *had actually occurred?*

I think there would (obviously!) be a hell of a lot more acceptance of the fact that there are other intelligences out there; there'd probably be much more research into it, and attempts to invite more aliens to our planet. The whole attitude that *we* are the only intelligent life in the universe would have been blown up! If all these things had really gone on, the world would not have any nuclear silos—all that would be gone, finished up. All that stuff would be behind us, and we wouldn't be having the problem we're having now with Korea and *their* threat of nuclear arms. I think it would be a much more peaceful world. I don't know that it would do much about Bosnia and *those* areas, but certainly I think the world would be free of the nuclear threat.

Would you say that The Day the Earth Stood Still *had a positive effect on your career?*

Oh, I think so, yeah. It was *very* well received. *West Side Story* [1961] and *The Sound of Music* [1965] are my most popular, widely known films but, interestingly enough, I think next to those are *Day the Earth Stood Still*. It comes up whenever I go out to film festivals; I was just abroad to two film festivals, one in Deauville, one in San Sebastián, Spain, and they talked about that picture and told me they liked that picture. So I think it probably *is* the best known of the balance of my films—that and *maybe Star Trek*, which *I* don't put in the same league.

Where do you rate Day the Earth Stood Still *on the list of your own personal favorites?*

I've done thirty-nine films and I've been asked many times, "Do you have a favorite?" I *don't* have; I don't know whether many directors have a single, *one* favorite. I have about ten or twelve favorites out of that thirty-nine and *The Day the Earth Stood Still* certainly is one of them — one close to the top.

A Salute to Edward D. Wood, Jr.

"IN THE GAME OF LIFE, it is not the critic who counts — not the man who points out how the strong man stumbled or how the doer of a deed could have done better. It is the man in the arena who matters. Far better it is to dare mighty things ... than to take rank with those poor spirits who neither enjoy much or suffer much."

Theodore Roosevelt penned those words in 1899, a quarter-century before the birth of Ed Wood, so it seems unlikely that it was Wood and his many detractors to whom our 26th president referred. Teddy R. may be one of the few people *not* to weigh in on the subject: Snatching defeat from the jaws of victory, Wood won the not-so-coveted title of Worst Director of All Time in 1980, voted in by the readers of Harry Medved and Randy Dreyfuss' *The Fifty Worst Films of All Time*. Since that milestone event in junk-film history, the late writer/producer/director has been the subject of much attention: The back-handed accolades have included film festivals, television, magazine and newspaper coverage, a 1992 biography and now an $18 million film bio from Tim Burton (who has himself left few fingerprints in the annals of orthodox filmmaking!). Wood has also become the recipient of more public bashing — sometimes affectionate, more often mocking and "superior" — than any other bad filmmaker who ever lived.

Needless to say, the SF/horror film "cognoscenti" were fully aware of Wood and his amateurish/charming/aberrant movies for years before his "Golden Turkey" glorification, but they never imagined that this offbeat auteur who worked on the fringes of the outskirts of the periphery of the motion picture industry would achieve any more mainstream attention *after* his miserable death (1978) than he had in his life; even *Variety* failed to run an obituary. But amidst the on-screen debris of cheapjack Wood movies like *Bride of the Monster* and *Plan 9 from Outer Space*, there's also a mesmerizing quality — elusive, tough to define and perhaps a bit embarrassing to acknowledge — which the "simpatico" Ed-heads and bad-film junkies have spent recent years examining under their microscopes.

"A filmmaker's style emerges through *all* the individual choices he makes over the course of a shoot; you can't *will* a style in advance too much. Wood was probably *the* most off-the-cuff director in the world," says *Plan 9*'s foremost authority, screenwriter Mark Carducci. "Wood's style emerged from that quality, and in the end, we're *haunted* by his films. So

Previous page: The Man You Love to Hate (or Hate to Love, or Hate to Hate, or Love to Love; pick one): Edward D. Wood, Jr. (All art by Drew Friedman and courtesy of Kitchen Sink Press.)

there *is* a kind of talent there. Lots of people can shoot off-the-cuff and have a tin ear for dialogue and that kind of thing — but *their* films are totally forgettable. So, with Wood, there *is* some alchemy that went on. Despite all of Wood's shortcomings, his films are haunting — maybe not haunting *all* the way through *every* film, but haunting enough that they've gotten under the skin of many people. So there *was* a unique talent at work."

"It's interesting that Tim Burton is the one who's making *Ed Wood*; they're both unconventional filmmakers," says AIP honcho Sam Arkoff. "*However*, there *is* a difference. Tim Burton is an exceptionally talented man, and I don't really think that Ed Wood was."

Had Bela Lugosi known that Ed Wood was a transvestite, "it would have been hands off, Lugosi wouldn't have touched him with a mile-long pole," says Alex Gordon.

Already the experts are disagreeing, which fits the pattern: No one ever had to *make up* stories about Ed Wood (war hero, angora fetishist, crossdresser, maverick moviemaker, boozehound) but apparently many people have, because too many of the tales are contradictory, others not borne out by what is on screen in his movies. Naturally, discrepancies must be expected when various people talk about events of 30 and 40 years ago — especially when the people attached no special importance to them at the time. But can it be that some of the stories told about Ed Wood were fabricated by his self-interested cohorts, or that some tales were just figments of their fevered imaginations? Or figments of *Wood's*? (There was no abundance of teetotalers or rocket scientists in Wood's band of merry men — and women.) Rudolph Grey apparently couldn't sort out all the conflicting stories and presented *Nightmare of Ecstasy: The Life and Art of Edward D. Wood, Jr.* as an oral history rather than a straight biography. Burton's movie, which used Grey's book as a basis, doesn't separate the fact from the fiction, either. Could our hearts stand the shocking truth anyway?

> "Now I tell you a tale of the Threshold People, so astounding that some of you may faint!" — Criswell, **Night of the Ghouls**

One of the first things done right by Edward Davis Wood, Jr., after arriving in Hollywood was to link up with Alex Gordon, a British movie fan seeking work in the picture business. Prior to his encounter with Gordon, the Poughkeepsie, New York–born ex–Marine had eked out a perilously precarious living in the film capital, working occasionally (on both sides of the camera as well as on stage) and getting nowhere. Gordon, like Wood, had moviemaking in his blood; *unlike* Wood, he had the diligence to work toward that goal, something the flighty, elbow-bending Wood too-often lacked.

The pair were introduced in 1952 (the year Gordon arrived in Hollywood) by cowboy star John Carpenter, whom Wood was helping to write a cut-rate Western, *The Lawless Rider*. "Eddie seemed like a very personable, very nice young fellow to me," Gordon recalls. "Needless to say, I didn't guess at the time that he had a drinking problem, and all the other things he had been involved with. And I didn't know, also, that he actually knew very *little* about script breakdowns and things like that. He was supposed to make up a production board for the picture and act as assistant director, but he knew nothing whatsoever about that, because when Yakima Canutt came on as director, he said, 'Who did this breakdown?' It was impossible to work with, and Canutt had to redo the whole thing!"

Due in large part to Carpenter and Wood, the movie went nightmarishly over budget; Gordon calls the experience (which dragged on into 1954, when the film was finally released by United Artists) "a bloodbath." Gordon continued to associate with Wood, however, "because I needed somebody to write on spec, and he was the only one I could get at the time. (I don't know why at that time I didn't think *I* could actually write a screenplay, because I certainly wrote some *after* that.) So, I was desperately trying to persuade Eddie, in between drinks, to write a few pages."

Gordon was responsible for the "turning point" in Wood's career, introducing him to horror star Bela Lugosi. Gordon and his New York-based brother Richard had known Lugosi for several years and had begun "agent-ing" for the actor, lining up jobs on television and setting up a revival tour of *Dracula* for him in England. Alex Gordon had written a story called *The Atomic Monster*, discussed it with Lugosi and approached Wood about helping him turn it into a script. "So, we did, over many drinks; *that* was when I found out he would rather sit in a bar than work. When it was all finished, we went to see Lugosi at his apartment on Carlton Way and I introduced him to Wood. Lugosi was at the point where he would do virtually *anything* to get a picture."

An aficionado of the old-time horror films and Westerns, Wood had been a Lugosi "worshipper" who, says Gordon, "especially liked Lugosi's

Universal films, particularly *Son of Frankenstein* and *Dracula* — all of the ones where Lugosi was the lead. He liked *The Phantom Creeps* serial, but he was mainly into features where Lugosi had something meaty to do. Virtually anything with Lugosi from the thirties, Eddie was very keen on."

Early on, what did Lugosi think of eager-beaver Wood? According to Gordon, "Lugosi liked him very much, he thought he was a very nice guy, very capable. Lugosi was particularly enthusiastic about the fact that Wood wanted to write scripts *for him* which hopefully would be set up. Lugosi did *not* like gays — anything to do with gays, he would abhor — and he never *dreamed* for a moment that Eddie was a transvestite. (Not that transvestite is necessarily gay, of course.) But had he known that Eddie had those kind of tastes, it would have been hands off, Lugosi wouldn't have touched him with a mile-long pole, because Lugosi was very much of a womanizer and very straightforward and old-fashioned in his beliefs."

"In my opinion," adds Sam Arkoff, "Wood was quite normally sexed. (I had, of course, no *personal* indication, you know [*laughs*].) But Wood generally had a girl. In fact, he almost *always* had a girl, and it struck me that *she* generally had a car. I don't think he had a car. So if he wanted to get around, he needed a girl!"

When the *Atomic Monster* project suffered several setbacks, Wood went ahead instead with *Glen or Glenda* (1953), a twin-pack of delirious deviancy, partly inspired by the then-current Christine Jorgensen publicity. In the Wood-written, produced and directed feature (Wood was in his twenties), two stories are related by a psychiatrist (Timothy Farrell) to a hard-nosed police inspector (Lyle Talbot). The first stars Wood (acting as "Daniel Davis") as Glen, who can't bring himself to tell his fiancée (Dolores Fuller) about his cross-dressed alter ego "Glenda"; the second features "Tommy" Haynes as Alan/Ann, a hermaphrodite (or was it a *pseudo*-hermaphrodite?) who springs for a sex-change operation *á là* Jorgensen. There was no mistaking Wood's earnestness in trying to get his transvestites-are-people-too message across, and also no way to take any of it seriously; an expressionistic dream sequence (complete with a leering Devil and finger-wiggling harpies) is no weirder than the "legitimate" dramatics it interrupts. This "picture of stark realism" presents the invention of the automobile as grounds for Wood to squeeze into women's satin undies; stock footage of a native dance, a steel mill and stampeding buffaloes contribute to the validity of other unexplicit points; and Bela Lugosi, playing a mystical, god-like "scientist," rants and rambles, reads a nursery rhyme and exhorts mortals to "Pull the string!" Purportedly, Lugosi *did* know what the film was about but you wouldn't know it from his dialogue, which gives every indication of having been written with the sole objective of preventing Lugosi from even guessing.

Alex Gordon, who persuaded Lugosi to do the movie, insists, "I didn't tell Lugosi anything about the story or anything like that, all I told him was that if he wanted to work for one day for $1,000, Ed Wood had something that he could do. And Lugosi said fine, because he needed the money for rent. He *never* read the script, he *never* knew anything about the picture, he never *saw* it and he had no idea what it was all about. All he did was sit there and do what he did, and that was completely separate from anything else."

According to makeup artist Harry Thomas, one of the behind-the-scenes Wood regulars, "This picture was about Wood's lifestyle, it was symbolic of what *he* went through. Although a transvestite, he loved *women*. He was a heterosexual who liked feminine clothes. What that picture was, was Wood's hidden life." In the semi-autobiographical film, Glen's frilly fetish is rationalized via events from Wood's real life: Wood's mother used to dress him in girls' clothes as a child. ("Glenda," according to head-shrinker Farrell, was "invented as a love object to take the place of the love he never received in his early youth, through lack of it from his parents.") But even the poignancy of this presumed cry for help gets lost amidst the dysfunctional drama, atrocious acting, senseless dialogue, a celestial, church-like musical score and enigmatic closeups on ears and a radiator. And the one movie to give us a *good* look at Wood — who somewhat resembled Errol Flynn — is the one where, without his trademark mustache, he's a dead ringer for *Mr. Ed*'s Alan Young!*

There's no denying *Glen or Glenda* its freakish fascination, and if what Wood was doing was setting out to be the world's worst director, *Glen or Glenda* was a good wind to have at his back, propelling him on his course.

> "My mind's in a muddle — like in a thick fog. I can't make sense to myself sometimes!" — Ed Wood, ***Glen or Glenda***

Wood had his fickle finger in several other projects throughout this same period (mostly cowboy-related), many in association with Gordon, with whom he briefly shared an apartment — and where Gordon saw Wood in women's clothes for the first time. "Sam Arkoff happened to be up at the apartment — Eddie wasn't there — and I was having a meeting with Arkoff

---

*At least Wood was in interesting company in tackling the ticklish topic: The other "artist" to explore these twin themes in the 1950s was calypso singer "Charmer," who sang "Is She Is, or Is She Ain't," about a man undergoing a sex change operation. On the flip side of the record, he croons about his friend Johnny, who wears his girlfriend's nylons. "Charmer" calls himself Louis Farrakhan today.

about something. There was a knock and I opened the door and it was this gorgeous blonde, in the angora outfit and everything. We didn't realize it *was* Eddie but, anyway, it was. Arkoff was more amused than anything else, but he also thought that it wasn't a good idea for me to live with somebody like that."

Arkoff remembers it differently. "Some time after I first met Wood, which was in my office in the lawyers' building on Selma and Hollywood, I got a call to come *right* into the office because there was a new client asking for me. So, I came in and there was this nice-looking woman, dressed to the gills — a hat with a big brim, the works, really very attractive. I talked with this person, but there was something [odd] about her, I really *couldn't* put my finger on it. We were discussing some project and she wanted to finance it. At the end of an hour, I realized it was *Ed*," Arkoff laughs. "In person, in the ordinary course of activities, that was the first time I had ever seen a transvestite. And that was the only time I ever saw him in women's clothes. *Why* he came in those clothes on that particular occasion, I haven't the slightest idea. Ed was a rather interesting guy, I must say."

Jail Bait (1954), about a fugitive killer (Timothy Farrell) forcing a plastic surgeon (Herbert Rawlinson) to give him a new face, was one of Wood's better films, although it was the basic idea ("lifted," screenwriter Gordon freely admits, from a 1930s movie), not Wood's handling, that provided most of its points of interest. Interesting, too, was the quirky, typically "Woodsian" cast, in which oldtimers (Rawlinson, Lyle Talbot, Bud Osborne) rubbed elbows with a rising star (Steve Reeves) and assorted members of the Wood "menagerie" (Farrell, Dolores Fuller, Conrad Brooks, etc.). Fuller, Wood's girlfriend in real as well as *reel* life (*Glen or Glenda*), "was a complete disaster as an actress in anything she did," remembers Gordon, who objected to her presence in their movies. "That she would have the absolute *gall* to consider herself an actress or step in front of a camera when she was the most wooden thing since Charlie McCarthy was really just incredible. Because of Eddie's adulation, she figured she was going to be the next big star. And she knew *I* did not see that at all, so she was certainly *cool* towards me. Not nasty or anything — just a tremendous ego!" *Variety*'s "Neal" caught *Jail Bait* at the Monterey Theatre in Monterey Park (the very theater where part of the film was shot), gave it a bad writeup but added that, considering the budget, ($21,600), it was bound to turn a handsome profit for Wood. But Wood entrusted *Jail Bait* to a crooked distributor and, characteristically, came away without a nickel.

Arkoff: "Wood had what a great many producers and would-be producers have, a desire to make pictures, but one of his problems was that he

Drew Friedman

A face worthy of horror fandom's Mount Rushmore: Tor Johnson, the lumbering Swedish actor/wrestler elevated to Z-grade stardom by Ed Wood.

was a terrible businessman — you couldn't hardly *call* him a businessman, he was generally 'in problems.' In our time, we [at AIP] found a great many first-time directors — Francis Ford Coppola, Woody Allen, Martin Scorsese, *many* of them, and somehow you can sort of [see their potential]. There's something about them, it's very hard to define — sometimes it's a curious energy or a curious mental bent. Ed didn't have that. All Ed had was the desire, and he did what he could, but almost everything he ever did had a habit of turning sour, particularly on the money end."

"But you had to admire the man because *he made movies*, on almost no money at all," notes Wood's actor-friend David Ward. "And there were so many people back then, before his time, and to this day, who try to make movies and *fail* — something always seems to go wrong. But *he* got 'em made."

By far Wood's best movie was *Bride of the Monster* (1956), which is what the much-delayed *Atomic Monster* ended up being called when it finally began lighting up theater screens. Lugosi had his final speaking role as the mad Dr. Vornoff, hiding out in "the old Willows place" near Lake Marsh, creating torrential rainstorms, unleashing a giant octopus, kidnapping hapless passers-by and attempting to transform them into "atomic superbeings." Lugosi's lair looked more like a 1950s kitchen than any self-respecting mad scientist's hi-tech laboratory — just one of the movie's *many* liabilities — but the aging, ailing horror star rose to the challenge, giving one of the most entertaining performances of his later years, backed up by a fun cast which also included Tor Johnson as Lugosi's monstrous mute servant Lobo. (Alex Gordon discovered Lobo *not* "in the wilds of Tibet," as Vornoff did, but in some old movie, possibly a Cecil B. DeMille. Gordon and Wood tracked down the mountainous wrestler Johnson and found that he was "delighted" at the prospect of working in *Bride*. "We didn't even talk money; he didn't seem to have an agent, he was going to handle it himself," says Gordon.)

Bride of the Monster has the delightfully hokey, fleabag ambiance of Lugosi's old Monogram melodramas — Gordon purposefully wrote a Monogram-type story in hopes that it would appeal to the folks at Allied Artists, Monogram's 1950s incarnation. Wood later claimed that the screenplay was his alone, giving Gordon credit only for the basic idea of a swamp and an octopus, but Gordon insists — convincingly — that the storyline was all his; what Wood did was contribute "about 50 percent of the dialogue." (Lugosi's famous speech — "I have no home!" — was Gordon's.) Production was the usual comedy of errors, well documented elsewhere; the best known story about *Bride* centers on the broken-down octopus prop which, legend has it, Wood broke into Republic and stole. (Gordon, who was on tour with cowboy star Gene Autry while *Bride* was being made, casts doubt on *that* apocryphal-sounding story as well, categorizing it as "a complete and utter lie! A deal was made with Republic to rent that.") Contrary to another oft-repeated lie, Lugosi doesn't flub and refer to Tor Johnson as "gentle as a *kitchen*" (kitten) in the movie. And stories of Lugosi working all night in Griffith Park aren't confirmable by watching the movie, in which stunt man Eddie Parker takes his place; Lugosi's few seconds on camera in the park scene (a couple of closeups) look to have been shot on a dark *indoor* set. (Could even *Wood* have been so inept a filmmaker — and so inconsiderate a human being — as to keep frail, sick Lugosi out in a cold park all night, and not use him in a single shot?)

In April 1955, Lugosi committed himself to the L.A. General Hospital's mental health and hygiene department for treatment of his drug addiction, and a premiere of *Bride of the Monster* (at that point titled *Bride of the Atom*) was held at the Hollywood Paramount to raise money for the destitute actor. (The screening followed a showing of *The End of the Affair* starring Deborah Kerr, Van Johnson and Peter Cushing — putting past Dracula Lugosi on the same twin bill with future Van Helsing Cushing!) Ticket sales were poor, according to Paul Marco (Kelton the Cop in Wood's three horror movies), even Lugosi's old "home studio" Universal balked at buying a block of tickets. Lugosi was released from the hospital in August, married for the umpteenth time, played a mute servant in *The Black Sleep* and died in August 1956. ("Legend" says that Wood's script *The Final Curtain* was clutched in Bela's hands when his body was discovered, but Lugosi's final bride Hope — the "discoverer" — puts the pin in that mythical bubble: "Oh, that's a lot of feathers! Nonsense. He was stretched out on the bed. He wasn't reading any script.")

Obviously it was a time of upheaval for Wood: Not only was his only "star" gone, but Gordon also went his own way, joining with Arkoff and James H. Nicholson to build up a company that would eventually be called

American International Pictures. Having an "in" (Gordon) at an up-and-coming movie company seems like an opportunity Wood could have tried to exploit, but, "He never thought that, because of our 'friendship,' I should try to get him into AIP," says Gordon. "And Arkoff didn't think that Wood was really somebody that he wanted to bring into the company. He didn't think Eddie would fit in."

Was it the transvestite tendencies, perhaps, that had Arkoff shutting AIP's door on Wood? "I don't think that's true, we dealt with a lot of —*characters!*" Arkoff laughs. "But I didn't like dealing with people whose word I couldn't depend on. So if somebody who had a reputation for dishonesty or unreliability came to me with a project, I probably wouldn't be interested. It wouldn't have been worth it [to rely on a Wood type] — *one person* running wild can damn you forever with other people. So, fundamentally, Alex is not wrong, I *wouldn't* have had enough faith in Ed to ever put him in charge of a picture — not because I had anything against Ed, but simply because he just couldn't operate [properly]. It's one thing to have somebody who has tremendous talent and maybe you have to cater to that talent occasionally. But we really didn't cater to idiosyncrasies, particularly from beginners."

If Ed Wood had been honest, reliable *and* a transvestite, would Arkoff have put him in charge of a movie? "Oh, yeah. The transvestite thing wouldn't have bothered me — as long as he didn't embarrass anyone with it. Frankly, it didn't embarrass *me*. After all, this town [Hollywood] is *filled* with all kinds of types, all kinds of sexes, all kinds of religions. That's one of the things that makes it interesting! But we were making twenty, twenty-five pictures a year, and you can't have too many 'loose cannons' around!"

Bela Lugosi was dead, but Ed Wood wasn't about to let that stop him from making another Lugosi movie. Wood had on hand some miscellaneous footage of Lugosi romping in a graveyard and around a house (Tor Johnson's), and the idea of building a movie around these scraps occurred to him. The problem, of course, was money. Would it be possible to find a backer for a movie whose star had already *died*?

"Barnum sure was right!"— Kenne Duncan, *Night of the Ghouls*

J. Edward Reynolds was a member of the First Baptist Church of Beverly Hills, a big movie fan and a would-be producer of Biblical epics. Ed Wood, Jr., cash-strapped young producer whose future plans hinged on convincing Reynolds to make a horror movie instead, argued that Biblical movies were a pricey proposition, and that the thing to do was to make *smaller* pictures first. The fish, a big one, bit: Reynolds not only lined up other investors for the project but also a star, actor Gregory Walcott, who attended the same church — a church that Wood and his flunkies, anxious to please Reynolds and the other Baptist bankrollers, began frequenting as well.

The resulting film was Ed Wood's favorite, *Plan 9 from Outer Space*— hailed by many as "The Worst Film Ever Made," and standing tall almost 40 years later as Wood's main claim to disrespectability. A wild pastiche of mismatched shots, ludicrous special effects, inept writing and acting and all of the other key "Woodsian" elements, it tells of silver-suited invaders raising the dead in order to conquer the world. On Wood's budget, of course, the "conquering horde" was restricted to Lugosi (seen in the old footage), a Lugosi double (Tom Mason), a "ghoul woman" (television horror movie hostess Vampira) and a murdered cop (Tor Johnson). Most of the movie was shot in just four days on poor sound stage sets at the misnamed Quality Studios. (In one of the movie's few exteriors, Wood donned a woman's nightgown and doubled for leading lady Mona McKinnon.)

Contrary to rumor, there was no Ed Wood script in Bela Lugosi's hands when he died in bed in August, 1956.

Plan 9's endearing ineptness, its lineup of kitsch stars (Lugosi, Vampira, Tor, "host" Criswell), a memorable musical score, the occasional crude/spooky image — and the way that the entire enterprise reeked of Wood's earnest, naive desire to "do good" as a director — combined to place *Plan 9* on a rickety pedestal in the annals of bargain-basement moviemaking. It was also "the epitome of what Wood did as a filmmaker," says Mark Carducci, who put 18 months of his life into the exhaustive *Flying Saucers Over Hollywood*, a 111-minute video documentary on the making of *Plan 9*. "It was a ludicrous *and* haunting film at the same time. And when I began to look into Ed Wood's life in detail, it turned out that his life was ludicrous and haunting as well — in the *extreme*. And the haunting aspects of Wood's life, the aspects that have a certain amount of pathos, really were what compelled me to make this documentary, because if it had just been this inept man who wanted to make a fast buck in filmmaking, *that* wouldn't have been a story worth telling.

"The closer I got to shooting interviews, the more complex the documentary became — the more I learned, the more I *wanted* to know. It was so fascinating that the project got bigger, more complicated and more encyclopedic, and the desire to do a very complete job instead of a kind of hop-skip-jump over Ed Wood's life and *Plan 9*'s production history — *that* impulse emerged instead." Among the 30 interviews which partially make up the video tribute, Carducci also debunks the much-told tale that *Plan 9*'s flying saucers were actually hubcaps or paper plates; Wood used a flying saucer model then available in toy stores. (In Tim Burton's *Ed Wood*, they're hubcaps again. When the legend becomes truth, print the legend.)

Wood considered *Plan 9* his "little gem," its stars went on to iconographic immortality, worst-film fans dote on it and everybody was happy — everyone except, perhaps, poor, bamboozled J. Edward Reynolds, who took Wood's financial bath *for* him when *Plan 9* did its expected belly-up on the balance sheets. "Reynolds was out of money, his investors were screaming for their money, and he hit upon hard times — that *Plan 9* thing wiped him out," says Gregory Walcott. "[He] passed away about two years later — he was maybe fifty-four, fifty-five, not too old. And I think that the stress and the disappointment of *Plan 9*, that whole debacle, that fiasco, the failure of *Plan 9* — I think it shortened his life."

> "We only have one life to live. If we throw *that* one away, what is there left?" — Lyle Talbot, *Glen or Glenda*

Tim Burton's *Ed Wood* wraps up with a scene set at the *Plan 9* "world premiere," shutting out of the director's film bio his third and final horror movie, *Night of the Ghouls*. *Ghouls* received equally short shrift in real life, collecting dust in storage for 25 years because, after making the film, Wood was never able to scratch up the money to pay the lab bill. Much misinformation about the movie cropped up between May 1958 (when production wrapped), and 1983, when it premiered on home video via Nostalgia Merchant. Wood himself was partially responsible, announcing (during pre-production) that his cast would include Dudley Manlove, Mona McKinnon, Tom Keene, Tom Duggan and Roy Barcroft, none of whom appear; somehow Vampira and even Lon Chaney, Jr., were erroneously added to the cast list in some movie reference books. Kenne Duncan, a B Western and serial heavy, actually fronted the cast of Wood regulars in a movie which, to the surprise of many, turned out to be a sequel-of-sorts to *Bride of the Monster*.

While *Bride of the Monster* dimly resembled the old Lugosi/Monogram horror movies in story and atmosphere, *Ghouls* has a number of touches reminiscent of Lugosi's *Mark of the Vampire* (1935): "The old Willows place" (from *Bride*) is shunned and feared by locals the way Lugosi's castle was in *Mark*; ghostly figures drift in and out of shadows and fog in scenes too much like *Mark* to chalk up to coincidence; and at the end, the whole spook business turns out to be bogus. Duncan is the fake fakir Dr. Acula, a turbaned scam artist staging phony séances in the Willows place (none the worse for wear after burning and exploding at the end of *Bride*); Duke Moore, the LAPD's resident "ghost chaser" (previously featured in *Plan 9*), is assigned to investigate mysterious events near the house. Paul Marco turns up a third time as Patrolman Paul Kelton and makes reference not only to *Bride of the Monster* action but also to the "space people" of *Plan 9*—an indication that Wood thought of the three movies (*Bride*, *Plan 9*, *Ghouls*) as a continuing series. (It's surprising to find that the swamps, quicksand and alligators of *Bride* are in the vicinity of the East Lost Angeles police station!)

Perhaps the 25-year wait to see *Night of the Ghouls* was just too long a buildup, or perhaps it *is* necessary to see Wood's films for the first time during childhood to find them attractively atrocious as an adult: *Ghouls*, murky and unimaginative, lacks the charismatic weirdness of its predecessors—neither good enough to produce the intended effect nor bad-funny enough to compensate. Duncan, looking old (and sleep-deprived), lacks the required "villainous vibes," and Moore, the "hero," cuts an unattractively ridiculous figure tackling the case in a full dress suit. Nearly all of the claustrophobic movie takes place on the ultra-cheap police station or "haunted house" sets; characters wander around slowly, as though underwater, through darkness, while annoying narration *tells* us what Wood is *showing* us. The incomparable Tor Johnson has too little screen time, the unbearable Paul Marco too much. Among the movie's few "highpoints," Wood indulges in his favorite fetish again, dressing up as a female phantom ("The Black Ghost"), and we get a good look at Tom Mason (Lugosi's *Plan 9* stand-in), here playing one of Duncan's henchmen; he's an exact double for Ross Perot, right down to the over-barbering and big ears.

According to Mark Carducci, there's a segment of fandom which embraces Wood's movies, even the least of them (like *Night of the Ghouls*), strictly on the basis of the ambiance that results from their poverty of resources. "There's an area of filmmaking that I call 'the universe of the unintentionally surreal,'" says Carducci. "It's defined by things like hollow post-production sound; very little dialogue in sync sound; stiff acting; a lack of exteriors (maybe just stock shots); dark camerawork, etc. Some people are more attracted to this 'cinematic netherworld' than others. If you like *avant garde* cinema, I think you'll be able to easily make the switch into Ed Wood's universe, 'cause I think he's unintentionally a bit closer to

Drew Friedman

"That [Dolores Fuller] would have the absolute *gall* to consider herself an actress or step in front of a camera when she was the most wooden thing since Charlie McCarthy was really just incredible." — Alex Gordon

an *avant garde* filmmaker than he is to a narrative storyteller in any kind of a commercial mode. In fact, I think he was the king of the universe of unintentionally surreal filmmaking, and that was always an attraction for me."

Deep down, did Ed Wood even *care* how his movies turned out? Is it conceivable that he didn't know that the pictures he was producing were something less than masterpieces? "No, he thought they *were* masterpieces!" Alex Gordon replies. "He was very earnest about it; he didn't do anything trashy deliberately. He thought everything that he was doing was a masterpiece, and he worked very, very hard. He would be up all night, typing and working. He thought everything he did was just great, and if there was anything that wasn't up to par, that was all due to the budget, due to the fact that he had to work so cheaply. He thought *his* stuff was just great." Nostalgia Merchant apparently disagreed; cashing in on the Wood vogue, their tongue-in-cheek *Night of the Ghouls* packaging "warned" potential buyers, "Do Not Watch This Film!" (See Rudolph Grey's *Nightmare of Ecstasy* for the full rundown on the rest of Wood's film work.)

There was more nightmare than ecstasy in Wood's final years, with Wood and second wife Kathy a-slosh on the shallows of the river of life; Wood dashed off political campaign literature, drank, dashed off dirty books, drank, dashed off dirty movies and drank some more. Evicted from their rat-hole apartment, the Woods moved in with actor Peter Coe, in whose bed the 54-year old Wood quietly and unexpectedly died on December 10, 1978. The groundswell of interest in the man and his films began a few years later, perhaps primarily because of Harry Medved and Randy Dreyfuss' "worst-films" books — which Bill (*Keep Watching the Skies!*) Warren told Harry Medved should include *Plan 9*. (Harry had never heard of it.) *It Came from Hollywood* (1982), Paramount's pandering paean to Grade-Z cinema, featured a Wood segment hosted by John Candy. Bad-movie buffs organized festivals and celebrated Wood's achievements in print. Paramount

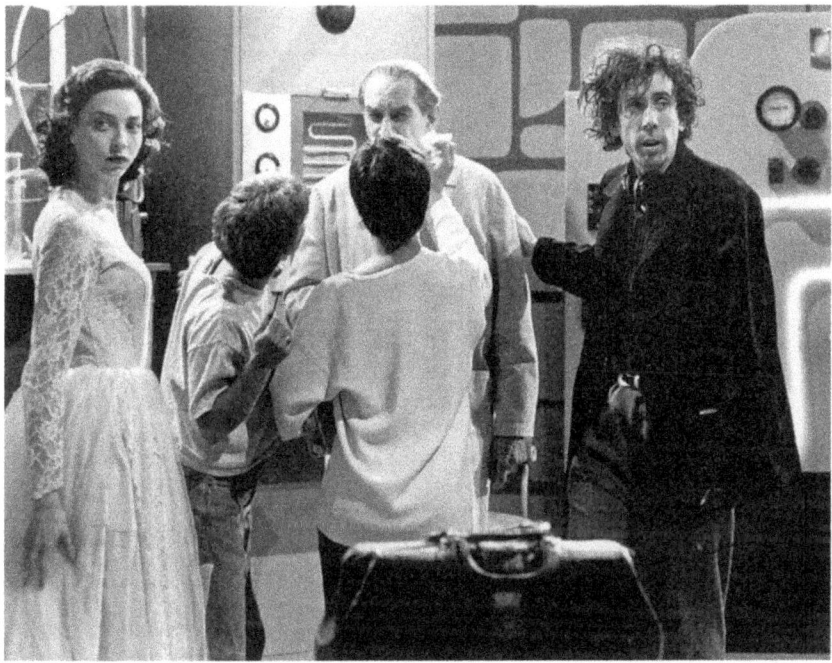

Martin Landau gets his Oscar-winning Lugosi makeup touched up in this behind-the-scenes glimpse at the making of *Ed Wood*. (Left-right, Juliet Landau, Martin Landau, director Tim Burton.)

reissued *Glen or Glenda,* reportedly at the prompting of Warren Beatty, who had recently been spotted (along with Diane Keaton) amidst the cheering crowd at a Wood triple-bill.

Rudolph Grey's Ed Wood biography, the result of 10 years of research and hundreds of interviews, gave the freaky Wood phenomenon further impetus, culminating now in the Tim Burton biopic, which Carducci calls "a humanistic comedy of errors of the life of this man." (The movie features, in small parts, Gregory Walcott and Conrad Brooks.) Alex Gordon wonders how the Burton film can be even halfway accurate if key people in Wood's life, like himself and Arkoff, aren't depicted, fictionally or otherwise. Arkoff chimes in, "I'll tell you one thing about Burton: He is a unique director. I don't know what he's gonna come out with, but I think he's capable of making unique, 'bigger-than-life' pictures. And I have a feeling that Tim has a surprise in store for us with *Ed Wood.*"

Is it fair that Ed Wood, whose whole life was movies, has gone down in the record books as the world's worst director? (Then again, is it fair that Wood should go down in the record books *at all,* when so many other, better directors have been forgotten?) And, watching all of this from the Great Beyond, what does Wood think of the devastatingly derisive reaction to his life's work? A roundup of reactions and final comments:

Alex Gordon: "I think that [in the Great Beyond] he's probably thinking about two things. One is that it's kind of a shame and it's not fair that he had to live hand-to-mouth, he never had any money and he had to scrape and he couldn't give his wife a little bit of a better life — and now that he's dead, everybody's cashing in on him and people are *making* a lot of money on his name. But on the other hand, I think he probably thinks, 'Well, maybe I'm getting a little bit of recognition, and people are at least talking about me and seeing some of my stuff.' It's an ambiguous situation there, on one hand, sadness, on the other, a measure of contentment."

Gregory Walcott: "He was diligent and fervent and energetic about his work. Though it turned out to be trashy stuff, perhaps in the case of Ed Wood, *effort* needs to be acknowledged as well as *art*."

Sam Arkoff: "I remember that he had a sense of humor when he wasn't being harassed. Unfortunately, this is a game where, if you're underfinanced, you're *always* being harassed."

David Ward: "He gave some good actors — *older* actors that were *good* actors, who were on their way down — he gave them *work*. People like Kenne Duncan, Bud Osborne, Lyle Talbot, Bela Lugosi, Tom Tyler, Tom Keene. Ed had his faults — a *lot* of 'em! — but for doing things like that, you had to admire the man."

Paul Marco: "Through these *Worst Films* people, Ed has finally become a name: He'll live a long, long time in the books, and I hope there'll eventually be many good things said about him, not just the bad."

Dolores Fuller: "He had creativity and the ability to make something out of nothing. If he'd had decent budgets *and been dependable*, I think he might have contributed a great deal to our industry. But once he started drinking, people wouldn't give him a chance."

Harry Thomas: "Working with Wood was one of the most interesting experiences I've had in the motion picture business, and I'd do it all over again. And I will say that, through the history of picturemaking, these films of Wood's will stand out ... like a sore thumb!"

Mark Carducci: "If you're a humanistic person, you can't help but feel for Ed Wood — *and* be haunted by the bizarre life that he led and the bizarre person he was."

> "I'm afraid the end of study is only the beginning of reality!" — Dolores Fuller, *Glen or Glenda*

Index

*Page numbers in **boldface** refer to photographs.*

The A-Team (TV) 2
Abbott, Bud 151, 176
Abrams, Edward Finch 257, 259
Ackerman, Forrest J 290, 304, 308
Ackerman, Wendayne 308
Adam at 6 A.M. (1970) 159
Adams, Gerald Drayson 275
Adams, Julie 22, 75
Adamson, Al 292, 293, 294 95, 296, 297, 298, 300, 301, 302, 303–04, 305, **305**, 306, 308, **309**, 310, 311
Adler, Stella 134, 137
Adreon, Franklin 238
Adventures in Paradise (TV) 83
Adventures of Captain Marvel (1941 serial) 49, 50, 51–58, **51**, **53**, **56**, 59–60
The Adventures of Robin Hood (1938) 213
Adventures of Superman (TV) 116, 117, 140, 244
Affair in Trinidad (1952) 18
Agar, John 75, 76, **179**, 179, 180, 181, 182, 336
Age of Consent (1969) 204
Agent for H.A.R.M. (1966) 256, 262, 263
The Agony and the Ecstasy (1965) 163
Air Mail (1932) 316
Airport 1975 (1974) 169, 172
The Alamo (1960) 184, 227
Albers, Hans 108
Aldrich, Robert 109, 118, 285–86
Alexander, Ross 149
Alexander, Scott 139, 141
All Quiet on the Western Front (1930) 223
All That Money Can Buy see *The Devil and Daniel Webster*

Alland, William 76–77, **176–77**
Allen, Irwin 4, 196
Allen, Woody 360
Alyn, Kirk 60, 103, 105
Ambush Bay (1966) 273, 284
An American Tragedy (1931) 219
Anders, Merry 6, 9, 10
Anderson, Maxwell 189
Anderson, Richard 3
Andrews, Dana 324
Andrews, Julie 99
Angel on the Amazon (1948) 237–38
Angels' Wild Women (1972) 309, 310
Anka, Paul 176
Ankers, Evelyn 79, 148, 154, 155–56, 158
Ankrum, Morris 314, 315
Annie Oakley (TV) 251
Ansky, S. 102
Antosiewicz, John 6
Arkoff, Samuel Z. 3, 35, 192, 355, 357, 358, 359–60, 361, 362, 367, 368
Arlen, Richard 257, 262
Armstrong, Robert 215
Arnold, Jack 73, 82, 177, 181, 182, 184
Around the World in 80 Days (1956) 81, 215
Arquette, Patricia 140
Arsenic and Old Lace (stage) 156
Ashley, John 2, 295
Astaire, Fred 19
Attack of the 50 Foot Woman (1958) 262
Atwill, Lionel 322–23, **322**
Auntie Lee's Meat Pies (1992) 256, 264, 265–66
Austin, Charlotte 7–24, **7**, **10**, **12**, **17**, **21**
Austin, Gene 8, 18
Autry, Gene 229, 361

Baby Peggy 58–59
Bacall, Lauren 9
Back Street (1932) 320
Badman's Country (1958) 336
Baer, Buddy 176
Bailey, Jack 125
Balaban, Barney 281
Ball, Lucille 85
Ball, Suzan 85
Bancroft, Anne 9, 10, 11, 16
Bandit 6
Baragrey, John 90
Barcroft, Roy 364
Barker, Lex 71, 72, 106
Barnett, Buddy 6
Barrows, George 10, 16
Barry, Don "Red" 20, 21, 281, 288
Barrymore, John 230
Bartók, Béla 27
Bates, Harry 342
Batman (1943 serial) 291, 292
Batman (1966) 233
Batman (TV) 99, 163, 233, 291
Batman and Robin (1949 serial) 60
Battle Cry (1955) 328
Baxley, Paul 217, 233
Baxter, Les 3, 5, 25–37, **25**
Beachhead (1954) 273, 279
The Beast from 20,000 Fathoms (1953) 102, 115–16
The Beast of Budapest (1958) 18
The Beast of the Yellow Night (1971) 308
The Beast Within (1982) 36–37
Beatty, Warren 134, 367
Beauty and the Beast (1963) 188, 203
Bee, Molly 176
Beery, Noah, Jr. 156
Benchley, Robert 324
Bendix, William 247
Beneath the Planet of the Apes (1970) 162, 168–69, **172**
Benedict, Billy 50, 54, 55, 58
Benedict, Richard 251
Bennet, Spencer Gordon 104, 105, 106, 107
Bennett, Charles 3, 4
Bennett, Constance 152
Benny, Jack 67
Berger, Sidney 43
Bergman, Ingmar 35
Bergman, Ingrid 218–19

Berke, Irwin 281
Berle, Milton 40
Bernds, Edward L. 2
Bernhard, Harvey 36
Bescos, Julie 230, 231
Bettger, Lyle 71
Beware! The Blob (1972) 153
Beymer, Richard 296, 297
Beyond the Valley of the Dolls (1970) 171
Bienstock, Freddy 137
The Big Doll House (1971) 295
The Big Gamble (1931) 210
Big House, U.S.A. (1955) 275
Big Jake (1971) 184
The Big Valley (TV) 66, 85
Bird of Paradise (1932) 231
Bisset, Jacqueline 163
Black, Karen 266
The Black Castle (1952) 188, **194**, 196–97, 202
The Black Cat (1941) 148, 149–52
Black Friday (1940) 148–49
Black, Karen 266
Black Sabbath (1964) 34
The Black Scorpion (1957) 66, 78, 79–81
The Black Sleep (1956) 26, 270, 275–78, 280, 361
Black Sunday (1961) 31, 34
Blackhawk (1952 serial) 103–04, 105–06
Blackmail (1929) 4
Blanchard, Mari 71, 72
Blaustein, Julian 342, 343, 345
Blazing Stewardesses (1975) 311
Blood Alley (1955) 176
Blood Creature see *Terror Is a Man*
Blood of Dracula's Castle (1969) 310
Blood of Ghastly Horror (1971) 300
The Blood Seekers see *Dracula vs. Frankenstein*
Bloody Mama (1970) 118
Bloom, John **300**, 303, 304, **305**, 308
Blue Hawaii (1961) 137
The Bob Cummings Show (TV) 256
Boetticher, Budd 251
Bogeaus, Benedict 202
The Bold and the Beautiful (TV) 102, 120
Bombardier (1943) 246
Bonanza (TV) 5
Bonaventure (stage) 191
Bonomo, Joe 242
Boom Town (1940) 231

Boone, Richard 96–97
Booth, Adrian 225
Booth, John Wilkes 102–03
Bouchet, Barbara 262
Boulle, Pierre 167
Boyce, William 257
Boyd, Stephen 262
Boyd, William 59, 60, 210, 212, 215, 221, 232
Bracken's World (TV) 169
Bradbury, Ray 227, 350
Bradford, Lane 251
The Brain from Planet Arous (1958) 226, 227
Brain of Blood (1971) 296, 306–08, **307**
The Brain That Wouldn't Die (1962) 310
Brannon, Fred 241
Breck, Peter 261–62
Breckinridge, John 334
Brent, George 237
The Bride and the Beast (1958) 7, 8, 11, 13–18, **17**, 26
Bride of the Monster (1956) 124, 131, 134–36, 142, 143, 145, 339, 354, 360–61, 364, 365
Brides of Blood (1968) 295
Bridges, Lloyd 84
Briskin, Sam 274
Broadway (1942) 150–51
Broderick, Helen 150
Brolin, James 163, 164
Bromfield, John 179, 180
Brooke, Walter 117
Brooks, Conrad 359, 367
Brooks, Mel 119
Brown, David 170, 171, 172
Brown, Everett 215
Brown, Gilmor 314
Brown, Helen Gurley 170, 171
Brown, Hiram, Jr. 51
Brown, John Daniel 331–32
Brown, Johnny Mack 159
Brown, Robert **93**, 95
Browning, Ricou 176, 177, 178, 179, 181
Brunas, John 4, 6
Brunas, Mike 4, 5, 6
Brunas, Ruth 6
Buck Rogers (1939 serial) 291
Buffalo Bill Jr. (TV) 251
Burg, Charles 332, 335
Burns, George 98, 256

Burr, Raymond 11
Burstall, Tim 205
Burton, Robert 257
Burton, Tim 124, 127, 134, 139, 141, 328, 337–38, 354, 355, 364, 367, **367**
Butler, Lawrence 283
Butterworth, Charlie 324
Byrd, Ralph 238

The Cabinet of Dr. Caligari (1919) 265
Cabot, Bruce 210, 212, 214–15, 216
Cabot, Susan 71, 72
Cafe Flesh (1982) 265
Café of Seven Sinners see *Seven Sinners*
Cagney, James 321
Cahn, Sammy 137
Caidin, Eric 6
Calhern, Louis 324
Calhoun, Rory 90
Calvert, Steve 16, **17**, 91, 92
Cameron, Kate 282
Cameron, Rod 159, 184
Candy, John 366
Canutt, Yakima 231, 233, 356
Capra, Frank 124, 220
Captains Courageous (1937) 213, 218
Carducci, Mark 6, 354–55, 363–64, 365–66, 367, 368
Carl and Anna (stage) 314
Carlson, Richard 110, 111, 199, 200
Carlton, Rex 310
Carnival Boat (1932) 221-2, 232
Carnival of Souls (1962) 40, 41–47, **44**
Carol, Sue 151–52
Carpenter, John (actor) 356
Carradine, John 93–94, 148, 156, 157, 275–76, 277, 300, 324
Carrol, Regina 297, 298–99
Carroll, Earl 66, 67, 68
Carroll, Leo G. 76
Carson, Johnny 140
Case, Tom 177
Castillo, Gloria 159, **226**
Castle, William 273, 279, 324
"Castle of Frankenstein" 1–2
Cat on a Hot Tin Roof (1958) 22
Cavalcade (1933) 213
Ceder, Ralph 221, 222
Chamberlin, Philip 6, 139, 143, 144

Chandler, Jeff 184
Chaney, Lon 192, 197, 289
Chaney, Lon, Jr. 154, **155**, 156, 197, 220, 231, 275, 277, 288, 302, 303, 364
Chapin, Lauren 176
Chapman, Ben 176, 180, 185
Chauvel, Charles 190–91
Chekhov, Anton 314
Chester, Hal E. 115, 116
Chevalier, Maurice 315
Cheyenne Autumn (1964) 236
CHiPs (TV) 153
Christian, Linda 71
Citizen Kane (1941) 53, 76, 342, 350
The City of Sin see *The Scavengers*
Clark, Bobby 210
Clark, Greydon 297
Clarke, Robert 250
Clifford, John 39–47, **39**
Cline, William C. 52
Clive, Colin 223
Coates, Phyllis 243, 244
Cobb, Lee J. 11, 102
Cocchi, John 6
Cocoon (1985) 162, 173
Cocoon: The Return (1988) 162, 173
Coe, Peter 156, 366
Coghlan, Frank, Jr. 49–63, **49, 51, 53, 56**
Cohen, Herman 6, 89, 91–92
Colbert, Claudette 124, 315
Cole, Dennis 163
Cole, Nat "King" 137
Collier, Lois 150, 154, 238
Collins, Andrew "Ace" 5
Collins, Chick 217, 222
The Colossus of New York (1958) 2
The Comancheros (1961) 184
The Comedy of Terrors (1964) 28, 33, 34
Conan Doyle, Arthur 4
Congo Crossing (1956) 195
Connors, Chuck 297
Conquest of Space (1955) 102, 117–18
Considine, Tim 176
Conway, Jack 225
Coogan, Jackie 12
Cook, Carole 84
Cooley, Spade 83
Cooper, Gladys 151
Cooper, Jackie 58, 59, 257

Cooper, Merian C. 212, 213
Coppola, Francis Ford 360
Corday, Mara 65–85, **65, 68, 74**
Corman, Gene 203
Corman, Roger 26, 32–33, 118, 203, 295, 309, 310
Cornell, Katharine 316
Corrigan, Ray 153
Cortés, Hernán 80
Cosmopolitan (magazine) 170
Costello, Lou 151, 176
The Court Jester (1956) 197
The Covered Wagon (1923) 60, 292
Crabbe, Buster 148, 211, 212
Craig, James 156
Craig Kennedy, Criminologist (TV) 69
Crawford, Broderick 149, 150, 152, 154, 275, 301
Crawford, John 105
Crawford, Lester 150
The Crawling Hand (1963) 256, 257, 259, 260–62, **261**
Creature from the Black Lagoon (1954) 176, 177, 303
The Creature Walks Among Us (1956) 184, 185
Creatures of the Red Planet see *Horror of the Blood Monsters*
The Creature's Revenge see *Brain of Blood*
The Creeping Unknown (1956) 278
Crisp, Donald 217
Criswell 335, 363
Crosby, Floyd 26
Crossroads at Laredo (1948) 144
Crowley, Kathleen 87–100, **87, 89, 91, 93, 97, 199, 201**
Cry of the Banshee (1970) 27, 36
Cry Rape (1972 TV movie) 306
Cukor, George 112
Culp, Robert 283
Cunha, Richard E. 2
Curb, Mike 298
Currie, Louise 50, 53, 54, 57
Curse of the Demon (1958) 4
Curse of the Undead (1959) 87, 88, 94, 96–98, **97**, 188, 197, 201, 202, **202**,
Curtis, Billy 114–15, 245
Curtis, Dick 251
Curtis, Tony 72, 78
Cushing, Peter 361

Daddy Long Legs (1955) 8
Damato, Glenn 6
Damon, Mark 203
Dana, Mark 278
Dangerous Mission (1954) 246–47
Daniel and the Devil see *The Devil and Daniel Webster*
Dante, Joe 6
Dark of the Moon (stage) 191
Darkness at Noon (stage) 345
Darling (1965) 294
Darro, Frankie 54
Daughters of Satan (1972) 270, 284–85, 286
Davidson, John 53, 54
Davis, Bette 73, 272, 316
Davis, Daniel see Wood, Edward D., Jr.
Davis, Jim 301
Dawn, Jack 218
A Day of Fury (1956) 73, 77
The Day the Earth Stood Still (1951) 342–51, **344, 346,** 348
The Deadly Mantis (1957) 78
Death of a Soldier (1986) 205
De Brulier, Nigel 54
Defoe, Daniel 282
de Havilland, Olivia 316
Dein, Edward 98, 201
Dein, Mildred 98, 201
De Jarnette, Bill 46
de Lacy, Robert 54
Del Rio, Dolores 231
DeMille, Cecil B. 328, 360
Denning, Richard 79, 80, 91, **91,** 92–93
Depp, Johnny 139, **338**
de Rochemont, Louis 271
Desert Sands (1955) 275–76
Desiree (1954) 8
De Souza, Ruth 247–48
Destination Moon (1950) 273
Destination Tokyo (1943) 4
The Devil and Daniel Webster (1941) 350
The Diary of Anne Frank (1959) 96
Dick Tracy Meets Gruesome (1947) 158
Dietrich, Marlene 152
Dietz, Jack 81, 115
Diller, Phyllis 242
Dix, Richard 237
Dixon, Denver 292, 293, 303, 306
Dr. Cadman's Secret see *The Black Sleep*

Dr. Caligari (1990) 256, 264–65
Dr. Jekyll and Mr. Hyde (1931) 217
Dr. Jekyll and Mr. Hyde (1941) 210, 217–19, 229
Dodd, Claire 152
Dodge City (1939) 213
"Donovan's Brain" 117
Doran, Ann 12
Dorn, Ray 296, 297
A Double Life (1947) 5
Douglas, Melvyn 317
Douglas, Michael 159
Dowling, Constance 108
Dowling, Doris 108
Dozier, William 291
Dracula (1931) 357
Dracula (stage) 356
Dracula vs. Frankenstein (1971) 296, 300–04, **300, 305,** 308
Dreyfuss, Randy 354
Drums Along the Amazon see *Angel on the Amazon*
Drums Across the River (1954) 71
Dudgeon, Elspeth 319
Duet for Four (1982) 205
Duggan, Tom 20–21, 281, 364
Dukesbery, Jack 6
Duncan, Johnny 60
Duncan, Kenne 364, 365, 368
Dunne, Irene 222
The Dunwich Horror (1970) 35, 102
Dupont, E. A. 70
The Dybbuk (stage) 102

Eason, B. Reeves 57
East of Eden (1955) 289
Eastwood, Clint 66, 75, 77, 84, 96, 182–83, 185, **336**
Easy Rider (1969) 309
Ed Wood (1994) 124, 127–28, 139–42, 143–44, 145, 328, 337–39, **338,** 354, 355, 364, **367,** 367
Edward VII 318
Edwards, Vince 293
Egan, Richard 114
The Eiger Sanction (1975) **336**
87th Precinct (TV) 328
Einstein, Albert 111
Eisley, Anthony 301–02

374 Index

Elizabeth the Queen (stage) 189
Elliott, Ross 237
Elliott, Sam 163
Ellison, Art 45
Ellison, James 158
Ely, Ron 163
Emery, Katherine 198
Empire (TV) 114
Empire of the Ants (1977) 153
The End of the Affair (1955) 361
Engel, Roger *see* Vorkov, Zandor
English, John 51, 223
"An Entertaining War" 205
Entertainment Tonight (TV) 47, 53
Errol, Leon 237
Esmond, Jill 318
Evans, Linda 85
Evans, Maurice 165
An Evening of Edgar Allan Poe (TV) 30
Everson, William K. 6

Fade to Black (1980) 153
Fain, Sammy 137
Fairbanks, Douglas 54
The Fakers see *Hell's Bloody Devils*
The Fall of the House of Usher see *House of Usher*
"Famous Monsters of Filmland" 2, 288, 290, 294
"Fangoria" 2, 5, 6
The Far Horizons (1955) 18
"Farewell to the Master" 342
The Farmer Takes a Wife (1953) 9, 10, 90
Farrakhan, Louis 358
Farrell, Charles 211
Farrell, Timothy 357, 358, 359
"Favorite Westerns" see "Wildest Westerns"
Fear (1946) 158
The Felony Squad (TV) 163
Female Jungle (1956) 93, 94
Ferrare, Cristina 163
"The Fifty Worst Films of All Time" 354
"The Film Actor" 205
"The Films of Sherlock Holmes" 289
Finney, Ed 292
Fitzgerald, Michael 6

Five Bloody Graves (1969) 300
The Flame Barrier (1958) 88, **93**, 94–95
Flash Gordon (1936 serial) 291
Flash Gordon Conquers the Universe (1940 serial) 148
Fleming, Eric 96, 201
Fleming, Victor 218, 219, 223
Flying Disc Man from Mars (1951 serial) 235, 236, 238–39, **239**, 240–41, 242
Flying Saucers Over Hollywood (documentary) 363–64
Fonda, Jane 132
Foran, Dick 159
Ford, John 60, 109, 110, 176, 184, 220, 236, 246, 315, 316, 321, 330
Forrest, Sally **192**, 195
Forty Thousand Horsemen (1940) 190
Foster, John 6
Foster, Preston 91
Foster, Susanna 152, 156
Fowler, Gene, Jr. 2
Fowley, Douglas 247, 248, 249
Fox, Michael 101–21, **101**, **113**, **117**, **119**
Foxfire (1955) 71
Foy, Bryan 270, 271, 272
Framed (1975) 221
Francis Joins the Wacs (1954) 71
Francis, Kay 316
Francis, Robert 184
Franciscus, James 169, **172**
Frank, Leonhard 314
Frankenstein (1931) 304
Frankenstein Island (1982) 3
Frankenstein Meets the Wolf Man (1943) 210, 220, 229–31, **230**
Frankenstein 1970 (1958) 8, 18–21, **21**, 270, 276, 279–81, **282**
Franz, Arthur **93**, 94, 95, 98
Free Grass (1969) 296–97
Freed, Arthur 8
Freed, Clarence 8
Freeman, Leonard 306
Fresco, Erin Ray 6
Friedman, Drew 6
Frogs (1972) 35
From Here to Eternity (1953) 281
Frontier Badmen (1943) 154
Fuller, Dolores 123–45, **123**, **126**, **131**, **133**, **144**, 357, 359, **366**, 368
Fuller, Lance 15, 16, 17
Fuller, Robert 82

The Fuller Brush Man (1948) 221, 222
Funicello, Annette 176

Gable, Clark 124, 225, 259
Gabor, Zsa Zsa 106
Gahagan, Helen 219, 317
Galileo (stage) 193
Gam, Rita 134
Garland, Judy 59
Garner, James 273
Gassman, Vittorio 108
The Gauntlet (1976) 84
Gaynor, Janet 211
The Gene Autry Show (TV) 251
Gentle, Lili 163
George, Jack 105
The George Burns and Gracie Allen Show (TV) 256, 257
The George Sanders Mystery Theater (TV) 119
Germonprez, Louis 52
Gershenson, Joseph 201
The Ghost Goes Wild (1947) 158
The Ghoul Goes West (unmade) 134
The Giant Claw (1957) 66, 73, 74, 81–82
Gibson, Hoot 192
Gilda (1946) 69
Gilford, Gwynne 153
Gingold, Mike 6
The Girl in the Kremlin (1957) 106
Girls on the Loose (1958) 73
Gish, Dorothy 102, 103, 324
Gittens, Wyndham 57
The Glass Wall (1953) 108
Glasser, Albert 2
Glen or Glenda (1953) 124, 127, 128–29, 130, 132, **133**, 134, 135, 140, 142, 143, 145, 357–58, 359, 367
Goddard, Paulette 225, 244, 246
Godzilla, King of the Monsters! (1956) 238
Goetz, William 274
Gog (1954) 102, 108, 110, 111, 112, **113**, 114–15
Gold (1934) 108
"The Golden Turkey Awards" 366
Goldwyn, Sam 323
Goliath and the Barbarians (1960) 30–31
Gone with the Wind (1939) 59, 215, 244

The Good Humor Man (1950) 221
Gordon, Alex 132, 136, 356–57, 358–59, 360, 361, 362, 366, 367, 368
Gordon, Gloria 9
Gordon, Leo 202
Gordon, Richard 356
Gordon, Robert 262
Gorilla at Large (1954) 10, 11, 16
Gorss, Sol 221
Government Agents vs. Phantom Legion (1951 serial) 238, 242
Grable, Betty 9, 90
Grandma's Boy (1922) 289
Graver, Gary 297, 309
Gray, Billy 9, 347
Gray, Lorna *see* Booth, Adrian
Grayeagle (1978) 30–31
The Great Circus Mystery (1925 serial) 58
Green, Duke 223, 224
Green, Howard 139
The Green Hat (stage) 316
Greene, Richard 196, 197
Greer, Jo Ann 18
Grey, Rudolph 138, 142, 143, 355, 366, 367
Grey, Virginia 91
Griffin, Merv 90
Grunfeld, Svea 18
A Guide for the Married Man (1967) 164
Gun Riders see Five Bloody Graves
Gwynne, Anne 6, 147–60, **147**, **153**, **155**, **157**

Hadley, Reed 288, 308
Hale, Alan, Jr. 261
Hall, Huntz 266
Hall, Jon 154, 159
Haller, Dan 26
Halsey, Brett **183**, 184
Hammer (1972) 306
Hampton, Paul 284
Hansen, Donald J. 257, 259
Harlow, Jean 225
"Harper's Bazaar" 189
Harrison, Linda 161–74, **161**, **167**, **170**, **172**
Harryhausen, Ray 115–16
Hart, Susan 5, 257
Harvey, Herk 6, 40, 41, 42, 43, 45, 46
Haskin, Byron 117, 283

Hastings, Charlotte 191
Hatcher, Harley 298
Hathaway, Henry 271
The Haunted World of Edward D. Wood, Jr. (documentary) 143, 144
The Haunting (1963) 22, 349
Hawaii Five-O (TV) 306
Hawn, Goldie 324
Hayes, Allison 71–72, 75, 262
Haynes, "Tommy" 132, 357
Hayward, Louis 199, 272
Hayworth, Rita 18, 69
Hazel (TV) 98
He or She see *Glen or Glenda*
He Walked by Night (1948) 271
Healey, Myron 251
Heaven (1987) 312
Heinlein, Robert A. 273
Hello, Sister! (1933) 219
Hell's Bloody Devils (1967) 300, 310
Hennesey (TV) 257
Hennesy, Tom 175–85, **175**, **179**, **183**
Henreid, Paul 73
Herold, David 102–03
Herrmann, Bernard 349–50
Heston, Charlton 163, 166, 169, 184
Hickman, Bo 177
The Hidden Face see *Jail Bait*
Higgins, John C. 275, 282–83, 285
The High and the Mighty (1954) 247
Hilligoss, Candace 40, 41, 42, 43–44, **44**
Hitchcock, Alfred 4
Hobart, Rose 217
Hobbes, Halliwell 217
Holdren, Judd 105
Holt, Tim 250
Home of the Brave (stage) 102, 103, 108, 109
Hondo (1953) 200
Hopalong Cassidy (TV) 236
Hope, Bob 40, 140
Hopkins, Miriam 315
Hopper, Dennis 205
Hopper, Wesley 229
Horizons West (1952) 251
Horror of the Blood Monsters (1970) 296, 300, **309**, 311–12
Horton, Edward Everett 158
Houck, Joy 226, 227
The Hounds of Zaroff see *The Most Dangerous Game*

House of Frankenstein (1944) 147, 148, 156–57, **157**
House of Numbers (1957) 229
House of Usher (1960) 26, 27, 28, **29**, 36
The House on Telegraph Hill (1951) 342
How the West Was Won (1962) 236
How to Marry a Millionaire (1953) 89
Howard, Eva 4
Howard, John 3, 4, 117
Howard, Ron 173
Howling III (1987) 205
Hoy, Robert 183, **183**, 184
Hoyt, John **194**, 197
Hudson, Rock 78, 184
Hudson, William 13
Hughes, Carol 148
Hughes, Howard 219, 274
Hunt, Roberta 191
Hunter, Kim 164, 165
Hurst, Veronica **198**, 199
Huston, Walter 107, 120
Hutton, Robert 3, 4–5, 256, 257, 259

I Changed My Sex see *Glen or Glenda*
I Led 2 Lives see *Glen or Glenda*
I Want to Live! (1958) 342
Idelson, William 260
Impasse (1970) 284
The Incredible Shrinking Man (1957) 77–78, 308
The Incredible Two-Headed Transplant (1971) 296
Indusi, Jeff 6
Indusi, Joe 6
The Innocents (1961) 22
Invasion of the Animal People (1962) 5
The Invisible Boy (1957) 26
The Invisible Man (1933) 222, 314, **319**, 320, 321
The Invisible Ray (1936) 323
Irving, Richard 239, **239**
It Came from Hollywood (1982) 366
It Happened One Night (1934) 124

Jack and the Beanstalk (1952) 176
Jacobs, Arthur A. 2
Jacobs, Arthur P. 164, 167
Jaffe, Sam 347

Jagger, Dean 112
Jail Bait (1954) 124, 129, 135, 143, **144**, 145, 359
Jailhouse Rock (1957) 296
James, Lee **300**
Janssen, David 75, 78
Jeffrey Jones, Private Eye (TV) 69
Jet Attack (1958) 336
Jet Pilot (1957) 219
Joe Forrester (TV) 84
Johnson, Ken 30
Johnson, Tom 6
Johnson, Tor 136, 277, 331, 334, 360, **360**, 361, 362, 363, 365
Johnson, Van 184, 361
Jones, Billy 217, 222
Jones, Buck 192
Jorgensen, Christine 128, 357
Journey's End (stage) 316
Journey's End (1930) 222–23, 316
Judge, Arline 260–61
Jungle Heat (1957) 279
Juran, Nathan 196

Kane, Joe 6
Karaszewski, Larry 139, 141
Kardos, Leslie 13
Karloff, Boris 19, 20, 21, 33, 34, 148–49, 150, 154, 156, 158, 188, 193, 194, 196, 276, 279, 281, 282, 289, 296, 314, 315, 317, 318, 323
Karloff, Evelyn **282**
Karlson, Phil 220
Katzman, Leonard 81–82
Katzman, Sam 12, 81, 82, 102, 103, 106, 107, 108, 223, 224
Kay, Mary Ellen 239
Kaye, Danny 67, 197
Kazan, Elia 22
Keaton, Diane 311–12, 367
Keene, Tom 332, 333–34, 364, 368
Keep Watching the Skies! (book) 366
Keith, Ian 189
Kellaway, Cecil 115, 116
Kelly, Dan 150
Kelly, Grace 14
Kennis, Dan Q. 293, 295, 296, 309–10, 311
Kerr, Deborah 22, 361
Kevan, Jack 177

Kid Galahad (1962) 224
Killer Ape (1953) 106
The Killers (1946) 213
King, Lewis 247
King, Loretta 134–35, 136, 143
King Kong (1933) 210–12, **211**, 213–16, 214
King of the Jungle (1933) 212
The Kiss Before the Mirror (1933) 314, 320–21
Kit Carson (TV) 69
Klamt, Frances 9
Knowles, Patrick 152
Koch, Howard W. 6, 18–19, 270, 273, 274–75, 278, 279–80, 282, 286
Kohner, Paul 69
Kohner, Walter 69
Koster, Henry 151
Kraft Television Theatre (TV) 90
Kraike, Michel 191
Kramer, Stanley 136
Krim, Arthur 271, 273, 274, 284
Kronos (1957) 303

Ladd, Alan 151, 152
Laemmle, Carl 320
Laemmle, Carl, Jr. 316, 320
Laine, Frankie 18
Lamb, John 177, 178–79
Lambert, Jack 213
Lamparski, Richard 152
Lancaster, Burt 213
The Land Unknown (1957) 5
Landau, Juliet **338**, 367
Landau, Martin 139, 141, 142, **339**, 367
Landau, Richard 279
Landres, Paul 95
Lanfield, Sidney 241
Lansing, Robert 328
Laramie (TV) 82
Larch, John 246
Larson, Jack 244
Lassie (TV) 5
The Last Frontier (1927) 60
The Last of the Mohicans (1932 serial) 57, 58
Laughton, Charles 193–95, 196, 317
Lauren, Rod 261, 262
Lauter, Harry 239, 251

Lava, William 303
The Lawless Rider (1954) 356
The Lawyer (1970) 99
Lazar, "Swifty" 271
LeBar, Bob 298
LeBorg, Reginald 276, 277, 280
Ledebur, Friedrich 12, 13
Lee, Peggy 137
Lee, Pinky 67
Leeds, Bert 345
Legend in Leotards see *The Return of Captain Invincible*
The Legend of Lizzie Borden (1975 TV movie) 314
The Legend of Lylah Clare (1968) 118
Leigh, Janet 219
Lemmon, Jack 324
Lemon, Lyn 331
LeRoy, Mervyn 330, 339
Leslie, Joan 272
Lesser, Sol 274
Let's Make Love (1960) 112
Levene, Sam 324
Levitt, Stan 43
Lewis, Jerry 69, 164, 282
Lewton, Val 342
Lincoln, Abraham 102
Lindon, Lionel 81
Lippert, Robert L. 294
Livingston, Robert 288, 311
Lloyd, Frank 230
Lloyd, Harold 289
Lombard, Carole 225
The Lone Ranger (TV) 236
Lonely Man see *Five Bloody Graves*
Long, Richard 66, 72, 75, 79, 81, 82, 83–84, 85
The Long Gray Line (1955) 184
The Longest Yard (1974) 118
Lorre, Peter 33, 34, 276
Lost Battalion (1961) 293
Lost Horizon (1937) 4
The Lost Planet (1953 serial) 102, 104–05
Lost Women see *Mesa of Lost Women*
The Lost World (1960) 4
Lourie, Eugene 116
Love Me or Leave Me (1955) 289
Lubin, Arthur 148, 149, 151
Luce, Greg 6
Lucky Devils (1932) 212, 213, 216–17, 231
Ludwig, Edward 80

Lugones, Alex 6
Lugosi, Bela 130–31, **131**, 132, 141, 142, 149, 150, 154, 156, 242, 275, 277, 301, 303, 329, 330, 339, 356–57, 358, 360, 361, 362, 363, **363**, 368
Lugosi, Hope 361
Lukas, Paul 301, 320, 321, **322**
Lumet, Sidney 220
Lund, Jana 20
Lundigan, William 112–14
Lundin, Vic 284
Lupino, Ida 203
Lydecker, Howard 55
Lydecker, Theodore 55
Lydon, Jimmy 158
Lynn, George 53
Lynn, Kane W. 293, 294, 295, 308, 311
Lyons, Cliff 233
Lytess, Natasha 9

M Squad (TV) 5
Macabre (1958) 26, 279
McCrea, Joel 231, 236
McCullough, Paul 210
McDonnell, Dave 6
McDowall, Roddy 76, 77, 165
McHugh, Frank 321
McKinnon, Mona 126–27, **126**, 130, 138, 332, 363, 364
MacMurray, Fred 140
McNally, Stephen **194**, 196, 197
McQueen, Steve 82
Macumba Love (1960) 236, **246**, 247–50
Mad Doctor of Blood Island (1969) 295
Mad Dog see *Mad Dog Morgan*
Mad Dog Morgan (1976) 205
Madison Sq. Garden (1932) 211
"The Magic of Film Editing" 264
The Magnetic Monster (1953) 102, 108–10
The Magnificent Ambersons (1942) 342, 350
Magnificent Obsession (1954) 75
Mahoney, Jock 294
Majors, Lee 85
Mallory, Boots 219
Maltin, Leonard 53, 54
A Man Alone see *The Killers*
Man-Eater of Kumaon (1948) 14

The Man from Bitter Ridge (1955) 66, 71, 72, 73
Man from Blackhawk (TV) 82–83
The Man Who Knew Too Much (1934) 4
The Man Who Shot Liberty Valance (1962) 184
The Man Who Turned to Stone (1957) 8, 12–13, **12**, 20
The Mango Tree (1982) 204, 205
Manlove, Dudley 133, 332, 364
Mann, Anthony 272–73, 277
Mannix, Eddie 244, 245
Mannix, Toni 243–44
Mansfield, Jayne 94
Manson, Charles 299, 309
Mantee, Paul **283**, 285
March, Fredric 217
Marco, Paul 143, 332, 361, 365, 368
Marie, Lisa 140
Mark of the Vampire (1935) 364–65
Marquette, Jacques 225, 227, 228
Marshall, Herbert 110, 112
Martin, Lock 349
Martin, Richard 250
Martin, Tony 281
Martin, William 257
Martinson, Leslie 233
Martucci, Mark 6
Marvin, Lee 11, 246
The Mask of Fu Manchu (1932) 289
Mason, Tom 330, 363, 365
Mass Appeal (1984) 324
Massey, Ilona 229–30, **230**
Massey, Raymond 317
Master of the World (1961) 28, 32, 36
Matheson, Richard 26
Matlock Police (TV) 204, 205
Matthau, Walter 184
Mature, Victor 241, 247
Maxwell, Jessica 242
Maxwell, Robert 242
May, Cherie 215–16
The Mayor of 44th Street (1942) 237
Mayor of the Town (TV) 118
The Maze (1953) 188, 198, 199–200, 202
The Mean Machine see *The Longest Yard*
Medavoy, Mike 162
Medved, Harry 337, 354, 366
Medved, Michael 366
Meeker, Ralph 275
Melchior, Ib J. 281, 283

Melford, Frank 81
Men of Boys Town (1941) 51, 52
Men of Texas (1942) 149
Menuhin, Yehudi 189
Menzies, William Cameron 199, 200, 283
Meredith, Burgess 99
Mesa of Lost Women (1953) 126
Meteor Monster see *Teenage Monster*
Meyer, Russ 331
Miami Rhapsody (1995) 145
Michaels, Norman 289, 290
Middleton, Charles 148
Midnight (1981) 312
Miles, Bob 257, 258
Miles, Vera 257
Milland, Ray 80
Miller, Arthur 112
Miller, Dick 118
Mineo, Sal 176
Miner, Allen 285
Mission: Impossible (TV) 5, 203
Mr. and Mrs. North (stage) 324
Mr. Ed (TV) 98
Mister Roberts (1955) 328
Mr. Terrific (TV) 50
Mitchell, Cameron 3, 11
Mitchell, Thomas 118
Mix, Tom 192
Moby Dick (1930) 230
Mogambo (1953) 14
The Mole People (1956) 5
Money from Home (1953) 69
Monroe, Marilyn 9, 10, 100, 112
Montez, Maria 154
Montgomery, George 284, 336
Montgomery, Robert 89
The Moonlighter (1953) 140
Moore, Dickie 59
Moore, Duke 332, 365
Moore, Eva 318, 319
Moorhead, Jean 9
Mora, Philippe 205
More Dead Than Alive (1969) 284
Morita, Pat 262, 266
Moro Witch Doctor (1965) 294
Morrow, Jeff 74, 81, 82
Morrow, Susan 71
Morse, Hollingsworth 285
Morton, Judee **258**
Moses, Chuck 279
"The Most Dangerous Game" 286

380　　　　　　　　　　　　　　　　　　Index

The Most Dangerous Game (1932) 212
Most Dangerous Man Alive (1961) 202
Mrs. Stone's Thing (1970) 264
Mulhall, Jack 54
Muni, Paul 107, 120
Munster, Go Home! (1966) 153
Murder in the Blue Room (1944) 153–54
Murder, She Wrote (TV) 337
Murphy, Audie 71, 78, 251
Murphy, George 237
Murray, Ken 40
Music Out of the Moon (album) 26
Mutiny on the Bounty (1935) 213, 230–31
My Favorite Year (1982) 324
Myerson, Bess 88
Myra Breckinridge (1970) 171

Nader, George 78
Nagel, Anne 149
Naish, J. Carrol 288, 301, 302, 303
The Naked Gun (1956) 78–79
Nasser, Gamal Abdel 308
Naughty Stewardesses (1973) 311
Neal, Patricia 344, 347, 348, 349
Neill, Roy William 231
Neise, George 278
Nelson, Lori 178, 179, **179**, 180, 181, **183**, 184
Nelson, Ricky 138
Newman, Alfred 8
Nicholson, James H. 5, 26–27, 31, 35, 257, 361
Nielsen, Ray 6
Nigh, William 152
Night of the Demon see *Curse of the Demon*
Night of the Ghouls (1958) 364–65, 366
Nightmare in Wax (1969) 310
"Nightmare of Ecstasy: The Life and Art of Edward D. Wood, Jr." 132, 142–43, 355, 366, 367
Norris, Richard 116
North, Edmund 342, 345
Novak, Kim 118
Now, Voyager (1942) 73
Nurmi, Maila see Vampira
Nurse Sherri (1979) 312

O'Brien, Edmond 273
O'Brien, Pat 321
O'Brien, Willis H. 213
"An Occurrence at Owl Creek Bridge" 42
O'Connor, Donald 156
Of Mice and Men (1939) 197, 231
O'Flynn, Damian 245
O'Herlihy, Dan 83
O'Herlihy, Michael 83
The Old Dark House (1932) 314, 316–20, 317, 324
The Old Dark House (1963) 324
The Old Oregon Trail (1928) 292
Oliver, Maurine 191
Olivier, Laurence 120, 318
One Million Years B.C. (1966) 165
Osborne, Bud **144**, 359, 368
O'Toole, Peter 324
The Outlaw Josey Wales (1976) 84
The Outsider (1961) 328

Packer, Doris 189
Paget, Debra 9, 80
Paige, Robert 154
Pal, George 117, 273
Palance, Jack 229
Palmquist, Dan 46
Panic in Year Zero! (1962) 34
Parker, Dorothy 324
Parker, Eddie 220, 229, 231, 361
Parker, Sarah Jessica 124, 134, 140, 145
Parla, Paul 6
Partners see *Duet for Four*
Pastorini, Dan 248
Pate, Christopher 205
Pate, Michael 96, 97, **97**, 187–207, **187**, **192**, **194**, **198**, **202**, **204**
Patrick, John 102, 103
The Patsy (1964) 262
Patterson, Lee 82
Paulsen, Pat 266
Payne, John 82
Peer Gynt (stage) 317
Peerce, Jan 67
Pembroke, George 53
Perkins, Gil 209–33, **209**, **211**, **214**, **226**, **230**
Perkins, Millie 96
Perrin, Nat 132

Perry Mason (TV) 11
Peter Gunn (TV) 82
Pevney, Joseph 71, 195
The Phantom Creeps (1939 serial) 357
The Phantom of the Opera (1925) 192
Phantom of the Opera (1943) 156
Pharaoh's Curse (1957) 270, 278, **278**
The Phenix City Story (1955) 221
The Philadelphia Story (1940) 4
The Photographer (1969) 264
Pichel, Irving 219, 220
Pierce, Jack P. 229, 318
Pine, Robert 153
Pink Cadillac (1989) 84
Pit and the Pendulum (1961) 26, 36
Pizor, Irwin 293, 311
Pizor, William 293
Plan 9 from Outer Space (1959) 127, 142, 143, 241, 328–36, **332**, 337, 338, 354, 363–64, **365**, **366**
Planet of the Apes (book) 164, 167
Planet of the Apes (1968) 76, **161**, 162, 164–68, 167, 169
"Plus" 5
Plympton, George H. 104
Pollock, Jackson 201
Post, Ted 169
Power, Tyrone 114
The Power and the Glory (TV) 204
Preminger, Otto 339
Prescott, Guy 278
Presley, Elvis 137, 224
Presley, Elvis, Jr. 144
Price, Bob 290
Price, Stanley 51
Price, Vincent 27, 28, 29, 30, 32, 34, 203, 204, 246–47, 270, 271, 284
Problem Girls (1953) 70, 71
Putnam, Jock 259
Putnam, Tracy J. 259

Quantum Leap (TV) 5
The Quatermass Xperiment see *The Creeping Unknown*
Queen for a Day (TV) 125, 140
Queen of Outer Space (1958) 2
Quincannon, Frontier Scout (1956) 281
Quinn, Anthony 80

The Raiders of Leyte Gulf (1963) 293–94
Raiders of the Living Dead (1986) 312
Rainbow 'Round My Shoulder (1952) 8, 18
Rains, Claude **319**, 321, 345, 346
Ralston, Vera Hruba 237, 238
Randell, Ron 202
Rathbone, Basil 30, 33, 34, 197, 276, 277
The Raven (1963) 26, 28–29, 33, 34
Raw Edge (1956) 66
Rawhide (TV) 96, 189, 201, 205
Rawlinson, Herbert 359
Ray, Fred Olen 6
Ray, Nicholas 35
Reagan, Ronald 92
"The Real Tinsel" 216
Reason, Rhodes 280
Rebel in Town (1956) 271
Red Ball Express (1952) 251
"The Red Skelton Show" (TV) 229
Red Skies of Montana (1952) 328
"Redbook" 272
Redskin (1929) 237
Reed, Donna 18
Reed, Walter 235–53, **235**, **239**, **243**, 246
Reeves, George 117, 236, 242–45, **243**
Reeves, Steve 359
Rennie, Michael 343, 345–46, **346**, 348
Repeat Performance (1947) 271, 272
The Restless Gun (TV) 82
Rettig, Tommy 176
The Return of Captain Invincible (1983) 205
Return of Captain Marvel see *Adventures of Captain Marvel*
Revenge of the Creature (1955) 175–85, **175**, **179**, **183**
Revenge of the Dead see *Night of the Ghouls*
Reynolds, Burt 169, 262, 284
Reynolds, J. Edward 328–29, 330, 331, 333, 334, 335, 336, 338, 362–63, 364
Reynolds, Pauline 329, 333
Richman, Mark 262
Ride 'Em Cowboy (1942) 149, 151
Riders to the Stars (1954) 102, 108, 110, 111–14
Ridges, Stanley 148
Riding with Buffalo Bill (1954 serial) 105
Ripps, Mike 250
Ritchie, Ward 325

Ritter, Tex 292
The Ritz Brothers 288, 324
Rivers, Johnny 138
The River's Edge (1957) 80
Roadhouse Murder (1932) 214
The Robe (1953) 199
Robert Montgomery Presents (TV) 89–90
Robertson, Blair 256–57, 259, 263
Robertson, Dale 82, 90
Robertson, Joseph F. 255–67, 255
Robinson Crusoe in the Invisible Galaxy (unmade) 283
Robinson Crusoe on Mars (1964) 270, 273, 281–84, 285
Robotham, George 233
Rock, Felippa 193
Rock, Joe 202
Rock, Phillip 189, 202
Rodann, Ziva 246, 248, 249, 278
Rogell, Albert S. 149, 152, 232
Roman Scandals (1933) 323
Romeo and Juliet (stage) 317
Romero, Eddie 293, 295, 306–08
The Rookie (1990) 84
Rooney, Mickey 50, 59, 218
Rose, Bobby 217, 220, 233
Rosen, Jerry 302, 303
Ross, Mike 228
Rossitto, Angelo 303–04, 307
Roustabout (1964) 224
Rowan, Don 148
The Royal African Rifles (1953) 199
Ruben, J. Walter 214
Rubin, Richard M. 225
The Rugged O'Riordans (1949) 190, 191
Rush, Barbara 75
Russell, Gail 241, 246

Sabu 14
The Sacred Idol (1959) 33
Safran, Henri 205
St. Martin's Lane see *Sidewalks of London*
Sanders, George 119, 215
Santell, Alfred 211
Santiago, Cirio 295
Saratoga (1937) 225
Sargent, Malcolm 189
Saroyan, William 69
Satan's Sadists (1969) 296–300, 301

Sauber, Harry 102, 103, 107–08
Sawtell, Paul 303
Sayadian, Stephen 264–65
Scapperotti, Dan 6
The Scarlet Letter (1934) 293
The Scavengers (1959) 293
Schafer, Natalie 324
Schaffner, Franklin J. 164, 165, 166, 169
Schenck, Aubrey 269–86, **269**
Schenck, George 285
Schenck, Joseph M. 274
Schiller, Norbert 20
Schilling, Gus 237–38
Schnitzler, Arthur 46
Schnitzler, Peter 46
Schoedsack, Ernest B. 213
Science Fiction Theatre (TV) 108, 116–17
Scorsese, Martin 360
Scott, Randolph 184, 246
Scouts to the Rescue (1938 serial) 58
"Screen Thrills Illustrated" 290, 291
Scrivani, Rich 6
The Sea Gull (stage) 314, 315
The Sea Wolf (1930) 213
Searl, Jackie 59
Sears, Fred F. 82, 104
Secret of the Blue Room (1933) 314, 322–23, **322**
Seiter, William A. 151
Selleck, Tom 163, 285
Serling, Rod 117, 167
Serpent of the Nile (1953) 112–13, 118
Seven Men from Now (1956) 246, 251
Seven Sinners (1940) 220
77 Sunset Strip (TV) 66, 240
Shamroy, Leon 165
Shapir, Ziva *see* Rodann, Ziva
Sharpe, Dave 55–56, 58, 103, 220, 223, 231, 232, 240
Shaw, Artie 324
She (1935) 219–20
Shearer, Norma 218
Sheekman, Arthur 323, 324
Sheen, Charlie 84
Sheena, Queen of the Jungle (TV) 70
Sherman, Sam 287–312, **287**, 300, 305, 309
Sherrill, Billy 138
Shield for Murder (1954) 273
Shock (1946) 270–71, 273
Sholem, Lee 242, 278

Shore, Dinah 125–26, 129
Show Boat (1936) 222
Sidewalks of London (1938) 195
Sidney, Sylvia 219
Siegel, Don 339
Silent Death see *Voodoo Island*
The Silver Whip (1953) 90
Simms, Al 33
Simpson, O. J. 83
Sin Town (1942) 150, 152
Sinatra, Frank 67, 281
Siodmak, Curt 108, 109, 111
Siodmak, Robert 109
The Six Million Dollar Man (TV) 5
Skarstedt, Vance 256
Skelton, Red 67, 210, 221
Skouras, Spyros 270
Slack, Freddie 31
Slave Girl (1947) 150
Slide, Kelly, Slide (1927) 59
The Slime People (1963) 256–60, 258, 262
Small, Edward 272–73, 274
Smashing the Crime Syndicate see *Hell's Bloody Devils*
Smith, George Ivan 188
Smith, John 82
Smith, Kent 102
Smith, Maxwell 115
Smith, Roger 240
So This Is Paris (1954) 66, 72
Somebody Up There Likes Me (1956) 342
Somewhere I'll Find You (1942) 225
Son of Blob see *Beware! The Blob*
Son of Frankenstein (1939) 357
Sondergaard, Gale 151, 152
The Sons of Matthew see *The Rugged O'Riordans*
Sorel, Sonia 94
The Sound of Music (1965) 99, 342, 350
Space Master X-7 (1958) 2
Space Mission to the Lost Planet see *Horror of the Blood Monsters*
Spencer, Douglas 117
Spenser: For Hire (TV) 5
Spitz, Leo 274
Spring Parade (1940) 151
SSSSSSSS (1973) 171
Stack, Robert 274
Stader, Paul 217
Stagecoach (1939) 300
Stanley, Ginger 178, 181

Stanwyck, Barbara 140, 225
Stapley, Richard 195
Star Trek—The Motion Picture (1979) 351
"Starlog" 6, 79, 284
Steele, Tom 216, 223, 224, 240
Steiner, Gerald M. 265–66
Stevens, George 96, 210, 316
Stevens, Inger 42, 100
Stevens, Onslow 315
Stewart, James 272
Stewart, Larry 103
The Sting (1973) 172
Stoloff, Ben 224
Stone, Cliffie 144
Stone, Jeffrey 106
Stone, Oliver 173
Storm Over Africa see *The Royal African Rifles*
The Story of Mary Surratt (stage) 102 03
Strange, Robert 53
The Strange Case of Doctor Rx (1942) 148, 152, 153
The Strange Door (1951) 188, 192, 193–95, 196
Strasberg, Lee 90
Street of Women (1932) 316
The Streets of Laredo see *Crossroads at Laredo*
Strickfaden, Kenneth 304
Striepeke, Dan 171
Striking Distance (1993) 145
Strock, Herbert L. 108, 109, 111, 260
Stuart, Gloria 313–26, 313, 317, 319, 322
Stuart, Randy 78
Sudden Impact (1983) 84
The Suicide Fleet (1931) 215
Sullavan, Margaret 315
Summerland, Augusta see Harrison, Linda
Superbeast (1972) 270, 284, 285–86
Superman and the Mole-Men (1951) 236, 242–45, **243**
SurfSide 6 (TV) 82, 83
Sweeney, Keester 218
Swires, Steve 6

T-Men (1947) 272, 273
Talbot, Dan 291–92

Talbot, Lyle 132–33, **144**, 241, 242, 357, 359, 368
Talbot, Nita 84
Tales of Terror (1962) 33–34
Tales of Wells Fargo (TV) 82
Talman, William 275
Tamblyn, Russ 296, 297
Tamiroff, Akim 276
Tap Roots (1948) 75
Tarantula (1955) 66, **68**, 73–77, 78, 81
Target Earth (1954) 88, **89**, 90–93, **91**, 94
Target Unknown (1951) 273
Tartikoff, Brandon 85
Tarzan and the She-Devil (1953) 70–71
Taylor, Elizabeth 22
Taylor, Jackie 297
Taylor, Kent 262, 288, 295
Teenage Monster (1958) 148, 158–59, 210, 225–29, **226**
Teenage Thunder (1957) 225–26, 227
Temple, Shirley 9, 180, 324
The Ten Commandments (1956) 328
Terenzio, Maurice 6
Terror in the Midnight Sun see *Invasion of the Animal People*
Terror Is a Man (1959) 293, 294
Tess of the Storm Country (1932) 211
Test Pilot (1938) 218
Texas to Tokyo see *We've Never Been Licked*
Thalberg, Irving G. 218
Them! (1954) 75
That Mad Mr. Jones see *The Fuller Brush Man*
Thesiger, Ernest 319
They Died with Their Boots On (1941) 221
They Still Call Me Junior (book) 50
The Third Man (TV) 345
The 39 Steps (1935) 4
This Island Earth (1955) 5
Thomas, C. J. 144
Thomas, Danny 99, 140
Thomas, Frankie 60
Thomas, Harry 124, 358, 368
Thomas, Hugh 332, 335
Thomas, Marlo 99
Thompson, Brett 143, 144
Three Men on a Horse (stage) 324
Three Secrets (1950) 347
The Three Stooges 2, 3

Thriller (TV) 98–99, 176, 203
Thunder on the Hill (1951) 191
Tigger 6
Tight Shoes (1941) 150
Tilton, Martha 154
Tim (1979) 204
Tim Tyler's Luck (1937 serial) 60
A Time for Dying (1971) 251
The Time of Your Life (stage) 69
The Time Tunnel (TV) 196
Timpone, Tony 6
Tom Corbett, Space Cadet (TV) 60
Tomb of the Living Dead see *Mad Doctor of Blood Island*
Too Late the Hero (1970) 286
The Toolbox Murders (1978) 3
Top Man (1943) 156
Topping, Dan 260
The Torch (1950) 246
Tors, Ivan 102, 108, 109, 110, 111, 112, 114, 116, 118
Toscanini, Arturo 90
Touch of Evil (1958) 5
Tourneur, Jacques 4
Tower of London (1962) 188, 203, **204**
Tracy, Spencer 210, 217, 218, 229, 345
Tremayne, Les 257
Tucker, Tanya 138
Turner, Lana 71, 106, 217, 218–19, 225
Tuttle, William 218
Twelfth Night (stage) 317
The Twilight Zone (TV) 42, 116, 117, **117**, 167
Two Flags West (1950) 343
Tyler, Beverly **280**
Tyler, Tom 50, 54, 55, 58, 368

The Uninvited (1944) 22
Up Periscope (1959) 273
Usher, Marge 143

Valentine, Nancy 196
Valle, Gil 151
Valley of the Dragons (1962) 232–33
Vampira 140, 363, 364
Van Doren, Mamie 77, 279
Van Heusen, James ("Jimmy") 137
Van Sickel, Dale 223, 224, 240, 244

Variety (1925) 70
Vaughn, Kerry 156
Vaughn, Robert 98–99
Velez, Lupe 237
Vignola, Robert 293
Violent Road (1958) 279
Virginia City (1940) 213
Vogel, Virgil W. 3, 5
von Sternberg, Josef 219
von Stroheim, Erich 219
Voodoo Island (1957) 270, 276, 278, 279, 280
Voodoo Tiger (1952) 106, 107
Vorkov, Zandor 305, 308
Voyage to the Bottom of the Sea (1961) 4

Wade, Russell 250
Wade, Stuart 159
Wagner, Robert 90
Wagon Train (TV) 5
Walcott, Gregory 327–40, 327, 332, 336, 338, 362–63, 364, 367, 368
Walker, Clint 184
Walker, Helen 70
Walker, Ray 243
Walking Down Broadway see *Hello, Sister!*
Walking Tall (1973) 221
Wallach, Eli 9
Wallis, Hal B. 69, 137
Walls of Hell (1964) 294
Walsh, Raoul 221
The Waltons (TV) 314
Wanted: Dead or Alive (TV) 82
War of the Satellites (1958) 118
The War of the Worlds (1953) 283
War Paint (1953) 274
Ward, David 360, 368
Ware, Elsie 219
Warhol, Andy 290
Warner, Jack L. 116, 221
Warren, Bill 366
Warren, James 290–91
Warren, Jerry 2–3
Washburn, Bryant 54
Waterfront (TV) 91
Way...Way Out (1966) 164
Wayne, David 9
Wayne, John 176, 184, 219, 220, 227, 247

Wayne, Michael 176, 184
Weaver, Dennis 247
Weaver, Jon 6
Weaver, Julie 6
Weird Woman (1944) 148, 154–56, 155
Weisman, Ben 137
Weiss, Adolph 15
Weiss, Adrian 13, 15, 16
Weiss, George 128, 132, 141
Weiss, Louis 13, 15, 17
Weiss, Samuel 15
Weissmuller, Johnny 106–07
Welch, Raquel 65, 262
Weldon, Michael 6
Welles, Orson 342, 350
Wellman, William Jr. 247, 248, 249
Wellman, Michael 247
Wellman, William A. 247
Wells, H. G. 189, 200
Werker, Alfred L. 270, 271
West, Adam 285
West Side Story (1961) 297, 342, 350
Westmore, Bud 177
Westmore, Wally 177
We've Never Been Licked (1943) 149
Whale, James 222–23, 314, 315, 316, 318, 319, 320, 321, 322
What Ever Happened to Baby Jane? (1962) 118
The Whistler (1944) 324
Whitney, Jock 212
The Wild Duck (1983) 205
Wildcats (1986) 324
"Wildest Westerns" 288
Wilkinson, June 247, 248, 249
Willes, Jean 13
William, Warren 158
Williams, Grant 77, 308
Williams, John 28
Williams, Lucy Chase 6
Williamson, Fred 306
Willis, Bruce 145
Winged Victory (stage) 245
Winters, Shelley 118
Wise, Robert 341–51, 341
Withers, Jane 158
Witney, William 51, 54, 57, 223
The Wolf Man (1941) 158
Women's Penitentiary I see *The Big Doll House*
Wood, Edward D., Jr. 6, 8, 15, 124, 125,

126, 127, 128, 129, 130, 132, 133, 133, 134, 135, 136, 138–39, 140, 141, 142, 143, 144, **144**, 145, 241–42, 263–64, 328, 329, 330–31, 332, 333–34, 335, 336, 337–38, 339, 353–68, **353**, 355
Wood, Kathy 140, 366
Wood, Lana 296, 297
Wood, Natalie 176, 297
Woods, Donald 69
Woolner, Larry 308, 309
Worth, Harry 53, 54–55
Wray, Fay 213, 215, 314
Wurtzel, Sol 324
Wyman, Jane 75, 225, 241

X— The Man with the X-Ray Eyes (1963) 34

A Yank in Indo-China (1952) 102, 103
The Yankee Clipper (1927) 59, 60
Yankee Pasha (1954) 66, 71
Yates, Herbert J. 238, 239
Young, Carleton 54
Young, Robert (financier) 271
Young Frankenstein (1974) 102, 119
Yrigoyen, Joe 233

Zabel, Edwin 276
Zanuck, Darryl F. 163, 171, 271, 324, 342, 343, 345, 346, 347
Zanuck, Lili Fini 163, 173
Zanuck, Richard 162–63, 164, 165, 166, 167, 168, 169, 170, 171, 172, 173, 174
Zeisler, Alfred 158
Zugsmith, Albert 77, 106

www.ingramcontent.com/pod-product-compliance
Ingram Content Group UK Ltd.
Pitfield, Milton Keynes, MK11 3LW, UK
UKHW041921140426
5217IPUK00014B/259